The Soldiers

AN ANATOMY OF THE BRITISH ARMY

The Soldiers

An Anatomy of the British Army

Henry Stanhope

Foreword by H.R.H. The Duke of Kent

HAMISH HAMILTON
London

First published in Great Britain 1979
by Hamish Hamilton Limited
Garden House, 57–59 Long Acre, London WC2E 9JZ

Copyright © 1979 by Henry Stanhope

British Library Cataloguing in Publication Data
Stanhope, Henry
  The soldiers.
  1. Great Britain. Army
  I. Title
  355'.00941   UA649
  ISBN 0–241–10273–1

Printed in Great Britain by
Ebenezer Baylis & Son Limited
The Trinity Press, Worcester, and London

'The Army is not like a limited liability
company, to be reconstructed, remodelled,
liquidated and refloated from week to week
as the money market fluctuates. It is not
an inanimate thing, like a house, to be
pulled down or enlarged or structurally
altered at the caprice of the tenant or owner;
it is a living thing. If it is bullied, it
sulks; if it is unhappy it pines; if it is
harried it gets feverish; if it is
sufficiently disturbed, it will wither and
dwindle and almost die; and when it comes
to this last serious condition, it is only
revived by lots of time and lots of money'

WINSTON CHURCHILL, *Daily Mail*, 17 December, 1904

To Alison and Owen

Contents

I*

Illustrations

Photographs are reproduced by kind permission of the following: The Ministry of Defence, Numbers 2a, 2b, 3a, 3b, 4b, 5a, 5b, 6a, 6b, 7, 8, 9b 10a, 10b, 12, 14a, 14b; The Central Office of Information, Numbers 4a, 6a, 11a, 15b; *Soldier* magazine, Numbers 1a, 1b, 9a, 11b, 13, 15a; The Cavalry and Guards Club, Number 16a; The Union Jack Club, Number 16b.

Foreword

by H.R.H. The Duke of Kent

I doubt whether any period in British history has seen such fundamental changes as those of the last 25 years. Certainly nobody who joined the British Army in the early 1950's as I did can be unaware that this is now a very different creature from what it was when he was a recruit and one which evidently possesses extraordinary powers of adaptability.

For there is scarcely a single physical aspect of Army life that has not altered dramatically. In 1953 not only was the Army some three times its present size, but it was still largely a conscript force. A regiment or battalion was more likely then to serve overseas than not and, apart from garrisoning at least a dozen, chiefly colonial, outposts, British troops were still actively fighting two major and several minor campaigns. Today's regular soldier will be very lucky if he serves anywhere outside Britain and West Germany during his six-year engagement.

The Army of the 1950's was, moreover, housed mainly in pre-war barracks, it wore war-time uniform and still used almost exclusively the weapons and equipment of the Second World War or earlier. In material comforts it was none too well provided for, with cookhouse fare which gained an almost legendary if doubtful reputation and barrack-rooms of frequently Dickensian squalor. The attitude towards even minor disciplinary matters was also far more rigid than would be acceptable in today's society.

Standards of training too were highly uneven, since the limitations of Salisbury Plain or Soltau were no conceivable substitute for the active service in which many battalions were engaged.

In contrast, today's soldier is not only incomparably better housed, fed, paid and equipped but he displays towards his soldiering an attitude of cheerful professionalism which would certainly have surprised his National Service predecessors. If discipline is also more relaxed, that probably implies a higher degree of mutual confidence and respect between leaders and led.

What has emerged, from the evolutionary processes of the last quarter-century, perhaps especially of the last fifteen years, is an organism which, although much smaller and with naturally more restricted horizons, shows a higher state of proficiency than probably any previous British peacetime Army. Its standards and methods are widely imitated and, I suspect, secretly envied by many other armies who readily send their officers and soldiers for training at Sandhurst, the Staff College and other British establishments.

To have reached and maintained such standards would have been a remarkable achievement under any circumstances, but to have done so against the background of natural apathy towards the armed forces, even occasionally of anti-militarism, which always occurs in peacetime is not far short of a miracle. Undoubtedly the long years of service in Northern Ireland, for all their tragedy and frustration have been valuable to the Army in terms of a common experience, but above all I think what has been achieved is a tribute to the extraordinary spirit and dedication of the officers, NCOs and soldiers of the Army.

One of the cheapest jibes made about soldiers in the past used to be that they had joined the Army because they were not fit to do anything else. Even if this was ever true of a tiny minority in the nineteenth century, a visit to any unit of today's Army immediately dispels any such idea and leaves one considerably reassured that young men and women of such quality are still coming forward to take up the profession of arms. Rightly, these young soldiers feel a pride in the job they are doing and a pride in belonging to an organization with such a long and glorious history.

Whether or not ours is the best Army in the world is, as Mr. Stanhope says, a matter of opinion. What is not in doubt is that it is a very special body of people, of tradition and of professional skill to which I feel extremely proud to belong.

The modern British Army's achievements and its place in society are I believe too little understood and for this reason I warmly welcome this most interesting and informative book.

Introduction

The relationship between the British and their Army resembles that between a family at home and an uncle in Australia, affectionate but distant. Few British institutions seem so familiar and at the same time so remote. This book is an attempt to bridge the gap. It is not a history of the Army, still less an analysis of its military strengths and weaknesses. It is rather an explanation of how the Army works, and a description of the lives of those who serve in it.

This seems an appropriate time to present it, just ten years after soldiers were tasked to keep order on the streets of Northern Ireland. For the volunteer Army, re-created in the early 1960s, Northern Ireland has been a proving ground. Despite some dramatic errors of judgement and a tragic list of casualties, Britain's soldiers have so far emerged from this test with their reputation enlarged rather than diminished.

It is an Army which has become increasingly technical. Already nine of every 100 soldiers belong to one corps, the Royal Electrical and Mechanical Engineers, born in the last war to cope with the attendant problems of mechanized warfare. Gunners in the Royal Artillery now use computers, and tank crews in the cavalry measure the ranges for their 120mm guns by laser beam. Even in the modern infantry, the term 'foot soldier' or 'rifleman' no longer seems appropriate for a soldier who travels in an armoured personnel carrier and fires guided missiles at the enemy. Because of advances in night vision aids, all have to be prepared to fight for twenty-four hours of every day, and in all weathers.

Partly because of this, it is an Army whose soldiers have to be selected and placed with care. The practice of hammering square pegs into round holes, familiar to those who served in the war and the years immediately following, has had to be abandoned. The Army needs to ensure that soldiers can do the jobs required of them. Moreover the square pegs are no longer prepared to have the edges shaved off them. As volunteers they have to be encouraged to join, then persuaded to stay.

Manpower has presented the Army with its most persistent problems since conscription ended. So far it has managed to find the right answers in time. Bad recruiting years have been followed by good ones, and the Army has been able to maintain a bumpy balance.

In recent years its main worry has been that of wastage rather than recruiting. Because of high unemployment outside, enough young men have come forward to fill the ranks, particularly those at the junior training establishments, and the Army has been able to pick and choose. But it has proved difficult to retain them for as long as the Army would like, particularly during a period of government pay restraint when soldiers have felt themselves underpaid and over-worked in comparison with their civilian counterparts. And although raw recruits continue to take their places, these are a second-best substitute for the trained men who have left.

Manpower difficulties are likely to grow worse in a few years' time as a result of the falling birth-rate in the 1960s. The Ministry of Defence has sponsored a study of pay and conditions in the Armed Forces to ensure that when the time comes, it will be able to compete with industry for the young men available. But however attractive a package the Army might offer, the number of those who would seriously consider a regimented, disciplined life in uniform, will always be limited.

Still the Army has to keep up with the times. It has to consider whether the familiar officers' mess meets the needs of young men in the 1980s; whether soldiers should be encouraged to join a trade union—or to form one of their own; how best to fill its married quarters when so many soldiers prefer to invest in private houses and leave their wives behind; and whether the present system for assessing military pay is the right one.

It is after all an increasingly married Army, whose wives and children, on most camps, outnumber the troops. Many of these wives are accustomed to working, and would like to continue doing so to supplement the family income. Nor is it only Judy O'Grady who feels that way. The colonel's lady too is just as likely to be out of the house by 9 am, on her way to the office, or hospital or school.

It is an Army whose horizons have shortened since the war, even during the last ten years. India, Singapore, the Persian Gulf are among the imperial outposts from which it has retreated. Even in Hong Kong the garrison has been recently reduced and the average British, as opposed to Gurkha, battalion can now expect to be posted there only once in ninety-nine years.

This does not mean that soldiers no longer travel. They still fly all over the world on exercises. But they are usually away for short periods, and their families stay behind. Their wives have to reconcile themselves to camp life in England, West Germany or Northern Ireland, with a rare glimpse of Cyprus or Gibraltar if they are lucky. Many soldiers' families have travelled further as civilians, on package holidays in Spain and Yugoslavia, than they ever will for Queen and country.

It is an Army which has shrunk along with its commitments and Britain's diminishing role in the world. By 1978 it had strunk so much that despite an extensive restructuring, the process had to be reversed and 6,000 troops added to its strength. Even so, it still has to 'borrow' units from the British Army of the Rhine (BAOR) to maintain a large enough presence in Northern Ireland.

Some famous old regiments have been forced into shotgun marriages during the period of postwar contraction. Even the Royal Horse Guards, one half of the Household Cavalry, have not been immune. Others have been swallowed by new, large regiments like the Royal Anglians and the Light Infantry, with three battalions each.

Although most regiments have retained their own recruiting areas, few seem as local as they used to be. On the other hand, British civilians are also less 'local' than they used to be. So the weakening of territorial links has not seemed as traumatic as it might have been before the war.

As an all-professional force it is very different from the Army which National Servicemen remember. Soldiers spend less time on the parade ground, less time with the regimental barber, wince at the term 'cookhouse' and drive to work in their own cars. They are better fed, better clothed, better trained, better paid, better equipped —and they expect to be so.

On the other hand, the Army has preserved much from the past, and its soldiers are still identifiable. Loyal, disciplined, conservative, sometimes snobbish and curiously vain—they are all these things. Whether they are trooping the colour on the Queen's official birthday, or patrolling the squat Belfast streets, they frequently earn the commendation that no other Army in the world could do as well. It is certainly an Army with a unique sense of occasion.

Whether it is better than any other Army is a matter for fruitless debate. What is beyond question is that it is unlike any other. Just as no British regiment is quite like the next, so the British Army is distinct from its contemporaries in other countries.

Acknowledgments

During the three years that it has taken me to research and write this book, I have become indebted to more people than I can individually mention. The Army has been cooperative beyond the call of duty and I am grateful to all those soldiers who have given me their help, their hospitality and above all their time.

I am particularly in debt to Major General Martin Farndale, Director of Military Operations, who was Director of Public Relations for the Army throughout 1976 and 1977, to the present Director of Public Relations, Brigadier Derek Boorman, and to all those members of the Public Relations staff who have provided me with so many facilities in this country and abroad. I must also acknowledge the assistance I have had from the Ministry of Defence Library, the Picture Library and the Army Historical Branch, and from Mr. Peter Wood, the editor of *Soldier Magazine* and his staff.

Others whom I can mention without, I hope, embarrassing them are Mr. Richard Shields, editor of the *Hereford Times*, and Mr. George Thomas of the *Hereford Evening News*. The general secretaries, and many members, of service clubs in London, have been more than helpful. So have the officials of all those other organizations covered by this book, including the Soldiers', Sailors' and Airmen's Families Association, the Women's Royal Voluntary Service, Naafi, the Council of Voluntary Welfare Work, the British Forces Broadcasting Service, the Services Kinema Corporation, the Regular Forces Employment Association, the Officers Association, the Army Benevolent Fund, the British Legion, the Royal Hospital at Chelsea, and the National Army Museum.

I am grateful to the *Daily Mail* for giving me permission to quote from Winston Churchill's 1904 article, and to the *Sunday Express* for allowing me to reproduce the cartoon by Giles. The Central Office of Information has allowed me to use the recruiting advertisement illustrating the Army's regimental badges and all other Crown Copyright material appears by kind permission of the Controller of Her Majesty's Stationery Office.

PART ONE

THE ORGANIZATION

'Spivs!' from the *Sunday Express*, November 16th, 1947

1

War and Peace

Peace in 1945. When the Second World War ended in August 1945
the British Army had 2,900,000 men and women in uniform. In
different shades of camouflage they wound around the world,
stringing together the red blobs of Empire like a necklace. The Army
had been less well prepared for war in 1939 than it had in 1914. Yet
it had once more ended up on the winning side. Its image was that
personified by the cartoonist Giles of a man in baggy trousers and a
funny hat whose cheerful perseverence had finally overcome the
military machines of Germany and Japan. It is this image which the
Army ever since has been trying to erase.

Those who fought in the Second World War saw themselves as the
spiritual heirs of Cromwell, Marlborough and Wellington, and in
one sense they were. Their strengths and weaknesses, tenacity and
good-humoured indolence, were the characteristics that had
identified their forefathers on the battlefields. In another sense their
pedigree stretched back only to January 1916 when the exigencies of
the First World War had forced Britain to overcome its distaste for
mass conscription.

This history of the British Army had been a stop-go sequence of
foreign campaigns which had impinged little upon the day-to-day
lives of the population at home. The Royal Navy had defended the
British Isles and inspired its national mythology. Given a strong
Navy the nation could leave the greater part of any European land
war to its allies, if it had any.

The British Army meanwhile could be plumped out to meet a
sudden emergency, then deflated again when the crisis had passed.
Its story had been one of hasty improvisation, distinguished less by
the flair of its commanders than by the national qualities of inventive genius and determination, the inventive genius that produced
the tank and the determination of the thin red line.

There had been exceptions to this general rule. In 1914 Britain
had contributed, and lost, the best expeditionary force it had ever
constructed. At the Armistice, however, the military machine had
been broken up again. Conscripts had been sent packing to their old

jobs, or to no jobs at all, while regulars reverted to their introspective lives within the regimental system. To most civilians between the wars the Army meant little more than the chance of a job during the economic depression.

Years of muddle and indecision ensured that when the Army emerged from its inter-war period of 'stop' to enter a new cycle of 'go' in 1939 it was unprepared to do so. In 1938, a year after Britain had started to rearm, it was only 220,000 strong. When the war began only four divisions were ready to be sent to France.

Many of the tactical lessons learned by the Army during the war should have been taught before it had even started. The British now absorbed them empirically, the hard way. As the First World War had introduced the aircraft and the tank to the battlefield, so the Second World War showed Britain how to use them.

Mechanization brought a new mobility to the battlefield after the fortifications and artillery barrages of 1914–18. The Royal Electrical and Mechanical Engineers (REME) was formed in 1942 in recognition of the change. Between 1939 and 1945 the number of armoured brigades in the Army rose from five to twenty-eight.

Nor was it only the equipment that had changed. The soldiers were better informed and educated than those who had died on the Somme. They were aware of what had happened in 1914–18, and often embittered by what had not happened thereafter. They did not have the endurance of the soldiers in the First World War; General Wavell once remarked that while the soldier of 1914–18 was tough, his successor in 1939–45 had to be toughened.

All this meant that soldiers in the Second World War expected higher standards of medical and social care. Greater mobility and the new involvement of the civilian population at home meant that these expectations could to a large extent be met. So it was a war remembered for its tank battles and air raids on the one hand and its cups of Naafi tea on the other.

It was also a war which left Britain financially and emotionally drained. Even in the elation of victory, the nation was aware that it would never had made it without the help of powerful allies like the United States and the Soviet Union. Britain had won through after a bad start, but only just and at a price. In 1918 the Army had been anxious to return to the ordered life it had known before Sarajevo. But in 1945, in a world which had seen guided missiles and atomic bombs there could clearly be no going back. Not everyone wanted to anyway.

The Regimental System. The regimental system which identified the British Army in 1939 had been designed to cope with the needs of

Empire. It was largely the work of Edward Cardwell who was Secretary of State for War between 1868 and 1874. Cardwell is best remembered for abolishing the buying and selling of commissions. (It cost Gladstone's government around £7,000,000 in compensation for aggrieved officers deprived of their investment.) But he also reorganized the infantry so that it could do two jobs at the same time—defending Britain on the one hand and policing the Empire on the other.

He paired off most of the 141 battalions so that one could stay at home while the other was stationed abroad guarding one of Britain's new places in the sun. He also gave these new battalion groups permanent homes and recruiting areas by dividing the country into sixty-six zones, each one approximating to a British county, and linked them with local militia and volunteer battalions.

His successor Hugh Childers in 1881 carried these reforms to a logical conclusion by converting the two-battalion combinations into large regiments, and re-christening them with county titles. Until then they had been known only by numbers—and in the eighteenth century had been called by the name of the colonel, usually a nobleman, who raised and commanded them. The loss of the numbers caused a terrible furore at the time.

Cardwell, for all his creative energy, tackled only some of the weaknesses in the Army's structure. It was left to Lord Haldane, War Secretary in Asquith's pre-1914 government to prepare it for a European war, as opposed to Imperial campaigns. Haldane not only planned an expeditionary force of six infantry divisions and a cavalry division for service on the Continent, but also dismantled the old militia and volunteer units. From the remains of these he constructed the Territorial Army which came into being on 1 April 1908.

The Army which entered the Second World War still bore the stamp of Cardwell and Haldane, as well as that of Leslie Hore-Belisha who became Secretary of State for War in 1937. After all, its dual role of protecting Britain and its Empire had not changed all that much. Of the 220,000 soldiers in 1938, about 122,000 were in Britain itself, 55,000 were in India, 19,000 in the Middle East, 8,000 in Gibraltar and Malta and 16,000 in the other colonial outposts.

This red ribbon which encircled the Pax Britannica nearly snapped under the strain of global war. The regimental system which was woven into its fabric stiffened and strengthened morale. But its tendency to compartmentalize the Army into small, semi-independent groupings failed to provide enough flexibility in wartime. Since the first year of the war the cavalry and the Royal Tank Regiment had been formed into the Royal Armoured Corps, which centralized recruiting and administration while preserving the separate identities of the regiments. The avant-garde at the War Office in 1945 were hoping that another Cardwell might emerge to find a similar compromise for the infantry too.

Post-War Troubles. The history of the Army since 1945 has been shaped by the threat to Western Europe from the Soviet Union, the winding-up of the British Empire—sometimes peaceful and sometimes not—and by economic constraints at home. It has also been punctuated by a series of campaigns associated with Britain's historic responsibilities as a world power. Any hopes of peace, perfect peace which soldiers may have cherished in 1945 were soon dashed by involvement in Trieste that same year or by the Communist uprising in Greece in 1946.

Counting only the more important campaigns since the Second World War, the Army has lost 223 dead and 478 wounded in Palestine 1945–48; 489 dead and 961 wounded in Malaya 1948–61; 865 dead and 2,589 wounded in Korea, where Britain contributed a brigade and other troops to the Commonwealth Division, 1950–53; twelve dead and sixty-nine wounded in Kenya 1952–56; seventy-nine dead and 414 wounded in Cyprus 1955–58; twelve dead and sixty-three wounded at Suez 1956; fifty-nine dead and 123 wounded in Malaysia 1962–66 (during confrontation with Indonesia); and ninety-two dead and 510 wounded in Aden 1964–67. But between 1945 and 1970 there were fifty-eight other campaigns.

Because the Army became actively involved on the streets of Northern Ireland in 1969, 1968 remains the only year this century in which no British soldier was killed in action. The most significant decision since the war was taken in 1948 when Britain, as a member of the new Brussels Treaty Organization (later to become the Western European Union), agreed to keep a peacetime army, the British Army of the Rhine, on the Continent. Field-Marshal Viscount Montgomery, the most famous folk hero produced by the Army during the war, left his job as Chief of the Imperial General Staff to head the organization's military command. He was the first British officer to be appointed to an international command in peacetime.

The Brussels Treaty Organization was largely superseded by the North Atlantic Treaty Organization (Nato) which was formed in April 1949 with the United States as the dominant member. In 1951 Nato began its own command structure under the Supreme Headquarters Allied Powers in Europe (Shape) with General Eisenhower in charge as the Supreme Allied Commander in Europe (Saceur). Field-Marshal Montgomery moved over to become his deputy again, just as he had been during the war. The Warsaw Pact was not formed until 1955, when it was originally christened the Eastern European Mutual Assistance Treaty.

The peace which was won in 1945 has thus remained durable, but uncertain. It has also been expensive. If anyone in 1945 had doubted that this would be so, the events of the next few years, notably the 1948 Communist coup in Czechoslovakia and the seven-month Berlin blockade, soon convinced them. In 1946 Winston Churchill had added a new epithet to the language when he said at Fulton, Missouri: 'From Stettin in the Baltic to Trieste in the Adriatic, an Iron Curtain has descended on the continent.'

In such circumstances it seemed hardly sensible for the British Army once more to sail off into the sunset after the battle, leaving its allies to sort out the rest on their own.

National Service. In 1947 the Labour Government decided to continue with peacetime conscription. The war had exposed Britain's need for a large reserve of manpower, and the general public reluctantly agreed with the government's decision. But the length of service was reduced to twelve months as a concession to the government's left wing.

When the new National Service Act came into force in January 1949, the Army was 380,000 strong. It included 184 major combat units consisting of thirty armoured regiments, sixty-nine artillery regiments, seventy-seven battalions of British infantry and eight battalions of Gurkhas—those little mercenaries from Nepal who had been fighting for the British Crown since about the time of the Battle of Waterloo.

The Army had been growing steadily smaller since the war. This was partly because Europe was at peace, more or less, and partly because of shrinking commitments elsewhere. India, the brightest jewel in the British crown, had rolled away in 1947. Palestine had been evacuated a year later. But the Army was still fatter than it had been before the war, and more pear-shaped.

The infantry which had absorbed about half its total strength before the war, now took up no more than a fifth. By contrast the less glamorous corps who supplied the fighting men with their food, fuel and ammunition, needed forty per cent of the manpower. There were also large headquarters and depots because of the need to train and organize such a large, ever-changing force of conscripts. The Army which had once proudly pushed out its chest, now stuck out its stomach.

Within two years of victory most infantry regiments had been reduced to one battalion. The Guards were the only notable exception, the Grenadiers and the Coldstream keeping three battalions each and the Scots Guards two. The 1st battalion of the Royal Warwickshire Regiment which was once commanded by Monty himself was among those made to amalgamate.

The conscripts still had a good chance of acquiring a suntan. There were three infantry battalions and two armoured regiments in Egypt and a similar garrison in Libya, a brigade in Cyprus, two battalions in Somaliland and one in the Sudan, thirteen battalions including eight Gurkha units in the Far East, one battalion in Jamaica, two in Gibraltar and eighteen battalions and eight armoured regiments in West Germany. About thirty infantry and seventeen armoured units remained in Britain.

The public attitude to National Service was stoical rather than enthusiastic. A public opinion poll which asked people if conscription should continue, discovered that fifty-seven per cent thought that it should while thirty-three per cent thought that it should not. Most people saw it as a necessary evil.

The period of service was increased to eighteen months in 1949 and then for two years in 1950. As a consequence of the Korean War the Army started to expand again, and it continued to do so until it reached a peak of more than 440,000 in 1953, the year of the Korean Armistice. The public once more approved of the extended service. An opinion poll in 1950 showed very similar figures to that of the previous year.

The regular forces would have preferred the age for National Servicemen to be higher than eighteen, because this would have provided them with more mature trainees. In the second place, even two years of service was barely long enough for the forces to derive real benefit from the men they had trained. In the case of some specialist skills it was clearly not long enough.

The conscripts themselves regarded their two years in uniform with fortitude. Most had some memory of the war, however remote. This helped them to accept National Service as a fact of life—for the time being anyway.

Many tried to by-pass it. Anecdotes persist of the ingenious methods which they devised to defeat the system. But it was difficult to do so. About one in every six failed the medical examination for genuine reasons. Others tried to fail for reasons which were less than convincing. But examining doctors were so wary of 'artful dodgers' that a government report in 1956 complained that they were passing many boys who were clearly unfit.

In the eleven years between 1949 and 1960 some 1,132,872 young conscripts were introduced to the realities of military life. At any one time they constituted about half of the Army's total manpower.

In one sense the Army enjoyed being able to deploy such a wide range of talent—far wider than it could ever have hoped for in an all-professional force.

But it was also a prisoner of the system. National Service had to be continued because regular recruiting was poor. Yet everyone realized that it would remain poor as long as National Service continued. Pay was raised a number of times during the 1950s in an attempt to make the job of the long-term soldier seem more attractive. But it was not until after about 1957 that pay stopped being considered a disincentive to potential volunteers.

The chances of a conscript being sent abroad, even if only to Germany, were assessed at one in two during the early 1950s and one in three later on. But one was not supposed to enjoy National Service, wherever one went. It was a duty to be performed. Conscripts were subjected to similar disciplines to those which their fathers had known in the war. Indeed they were often tougher because training sergeants could devote more time to imposing them. After training the discipline was often replaced by debilitating boredom. Many conscripts saw active service on location in Korea, Malaya or Cyprus. But others spent long hours in the Naafi, or lay on their bunks listening to Radio Luxemburg and designing 'demob' charts on which they ticked off the days. Some charts were quite imaginative examples of graphic design.

It was all very British with much grumbling but little open revolt. Most later forgot the bad times and remembered only the good, upon which they have looked back with nostalgia. Whatever anyone thought about his part in this unique period of British history, none could forget it.

The End of Conscription. In 1955 Field-Marshal Montgomery declared that 'National Service is an essential factor of modern defence.' So at the time it must have seemed. The Korean War, the Malayan Emergency, the Cold War at home, the patrolling of what colonies remained—all made a large comprehensive army and reserve seem like a permanent feature of post-war Britain. But it was not to be.

In 1956 there was the Suez crisis. The attempt by Britain and France to wrest back control of the Suez Canal from Egypt and at the same time topple the revolutionary Colonel Nasser was ill-planned and badly managed. It needed a swift decisive strike. The British Army, still equipped with the residue of the Second World War was in no condition to conduct such an operation. Diplomatically isolated, Britain withdrew from Suez and the Prime Minister Mr. Anthony Eden withdrew from power. In came Mr. Harold

Macmillan supported by a Defence Secretary Mr. Duncan Sandys with a plan for the forces which did not include National Service.

The plan relied upon Nato's current 'tripwire' strategy. This involved the tacit threat that if the Russians placed one foot over the frontier they would bring down upon themselves the terrible might of Nato's nuclear forces. There was thus no longer any need for a large, short-service Army. It would be more sensible to return to the idea of a small, highly skilled team of regulars. That was how the argument went.

Under the new plan the Army was to be reduced from 385,000, half of them conscripts, in 1957 to only 180,000 without any conscripts at all by 1963. The public had by now grown tired of National Service despite Montgomery's confident assertion of two years before (in fact they had grown a bit tired of him too) and the so-called Sandys White Paper made for a popular start to Mr. Macmillan's administration.

The plan included a larger strategic reserve in Britain, backed up by an improved RAF transport fleet. At the same time Britain's colonial garrisons would be slimmed down. In effect Britain, policeman of the Third World, was moving away from the village 'bobby' and investing in a flying squad.

The shape of the Army was changing in other ways. Although it would be smaller, it would be relatively more fierce. The infantry with 45,000 would make up a quarter of the strength instead of a fifth while the size of the supporting services would go down. The administrative 'tail' could be shortened too, because with an all-regular force there would be less coming and going. And more civilians would be employed to do the hum-drum jobs at home, releasing as many troops as possible for front-line duty.

However, all parts of the Army were to be reduced in size. The number of infantry battalions was to fall from seventy-seven to sixty-four, the armoured regiments from thirty to twenty-three and the Royal Artillery, now equipped with American nuclear weapons, was to be literally halved from sixty-nine regiments to thirty-four. (All fourteen anti-aircraft regiments were to go.) But in general it was decided to merge regiments rather than scrap them altogether, so many were forced into shotgun marriages.

The number of Royal Tank Regiments went down from eight to five, and eight cavalry regiments were paired off, including Churchill's old regiment the 4th Queen's Own Hussars which was to move in with the 8th King's Royal Irish Hussars to become the Queen's Royal Irish Hussars (4th and 8th). Casualties among the infantry included the third battalions of the Grenadier and Coldstream Guards, while a number of other regiments were told to amalgamate.

Some of the mergers were fairly obvious. The North Staffordshires joined the South Staffordshires, the Devons joined the Dorsets, the East Yorkshires linked up with the West Yorkshires to become the Prince of Wales' Own Regiment of Yorkshire, the Norfolks joined the Suffolks and the Northamptonshires joined the Lincolnshires.

The regiments faced up to the surgery with a stiff upper lip in most cases—but not in all. The merger of the Highland Light Infantry with the Royal Scots Fusiliers—to form the Royal Highland Fusiliers—was accomplished only after the involuntary resignation of the two recalcitrant regimental colonels.

In BAOR the number of divisions was cut from four to three. Together with the Berlin brigade there would be twenty infantry units and fourteen armoured regiments in West Germany. After reductions in the Far East and the Middle East, Britain itself would be left with twenty-three infantry battalions to cope with home defence and the obligations of the new strategic reserve.

The days of the troopship, filled to the gunwhales with seasick soldiers, were also over. In future troops would be moved where possible by aircraft. The Army would be smaller than it had been, but faster and fiercer. Britain would have a New Model Army—again.

There were changes at the top too. A Chief of Defence Staff (CDS) was created, a tri-service overlord to sit in judgement over the other chiefs of staff, in theory anyway. Tri-service headquarters were also established overseas, although the Government was careful to defer to service prejudices by allowing them to take it in turns to appoint the tri-service chief.

In 1963 Mr. Peter Thorneycroft as Defence Minister announced an even more fundamental change. There had been a Defence Minister since 1946—following the war years when Churchill had taken the job under his own wing. But the postwar Defence Minister had been only a co-ordinating link between the three separate service ministries, the War Office, the Admiralty and the Air Ministry. He had no real authority over them. Mr. Thorneycroft, later Lord Thorneycroft, announced that henceforth there would be only one Ministry of Defence for all three services with a Secretary of State to look after the lot—and only junior ministers beneath him to represent the separate service interests.

The Chief of the Imperial General Staff dropped the anachronistic 'Imperial' from his title and moved from the War Office across Horse Guards Avenue to the old Air Ministry building which became the new Ministry of Defence. A heavy slab of concrete dotted with windows, like tiny black currants in a cake, it seemed to symbolize the new dedication to geometric precision and cost-effectiveness.

Contraction in the 1960s. In 1964 the first Labour Government for thirteen years came into power under Mr. Harold Wilson. Economic difficulties forced it to continue the process of rundown and re-structuring. Moreover the Secretary of State for Defence, Mr. Denis Healey, was clever enough and strong enough to push through a series of radical reforms whose impact at least matched that felt under his Conservative predecessors. The Army which had pre-viously regarded Mr. Sandys as the bogeyman in postwar military evolution, now re-focussed their discontent on the beetle-browed Mr. Healey.

Faced with the perceived need to reduce defence spending from more than seven per cent to less than six per cent of the country's Gross National Product (GNP) he initiated yet another series of amalgamations. One could save money from the naval budget by abandoning plans for a new aircraft carrier, or from the RAF budget by scrapping the TSR-2 aircraft. It was more difficult in the case of the Army, a labour-intensive organization whose money is spent upon a diversity of smaller items of equipment and on the soldiers themselves.

Some of the amalgamations were still more traumatic than those which had gone before. Even the Household Cavalry was involved, with the Royal Horse Guards fusing with the 1st Dragoon Guards to form the Blues and Royals in 1969. Two more old cavalry regiments, the Royal Scots Greys and the 3rd Carabiniers went into partnership in 1971 to form the present Royal Scots Dragoon Guards. Three battalions of Gurkhas went, as did another of the Royal Tank Regiments.

Infantry regiments were grouped into divisions for recruiting and administrative purposes, and a number were encouraged, though not forced, to amalgamate as large regiments with up to three battalions. Thus the old Northamptonshire and Lincolnshires, the Norfolks and Suffolks and the Leicestershire Regiment were all lumped to-gether under the Royal Anglian Regiment. The Royal Regi-ment of Fusiliers swallowed the Royal Northumberland Fusiliers, the Royal Fusiliers, the Royal Warwickshire Fusiliers and the Lancashire Fusiliers.

The Royal Irish Rangers absorbed the Royal Inniskilling Fusiliers, the Royal Irish Fusiliers and the Royal Ulster Rifles; the Queen's Regiment took the Queen's Royal Surreys, the Queen's Own Buffs the Royal Sussex and the Middlesex; and the Light Infantry was formed by four separate light infantry regiments, the King's Own Yorkshire, the Somerset and Cornwall, the King's Shropshire and the Durham. The Royal Green Jackets took over three regiments, including the Rifle Brigade, the King's Royal Rifle Corps and the old Oxfordshire and Buckinghamshire Light Infantry—although all three had been renamed Green Jackets regiments since 1958.

The most emotive decision of all was to disband the Argyll and Sutherland Highlanders. The regiment had caught the public imagination by its uncompromising attitude in Aden under its colourful commanding officer, Lt.-Col. Colin Mitchell—dubbed 'Mad Mitch' by the newspapers. To the disgust of other infantry regiments which had had to succumb to Mr. Healey's axe, the Argylls launched a successful publicity campaign on their own behalf. It was so successful that 'Save the Argylls' was made an election promise by the Conservative Party in 1970—one which they ultimately fulfilled. If the Press had reason to be grateful to the Argylls for the material which the regiment provided while in Aden, the Argylls now could thank the Press in return.

Mr. Healey stirred up still more trouble, however, by scrapping the old Territorial Army, Haldane's creation, and the Army Emergency Reserve. From the remains he constructed the new Territorial and Army Volunteer Reserve (TAVR). The old TA had been 120,000 strong, an army in its own right. The new TAVR was 50,000 strong and had the job only of reinforcing BAOR if war broke out—apart that is from helping to defend the British home-land. Mr. Healey's critics argued that the reorganization was inappropriate at a time when Nato had just changed from the old tripwire strategy to a new one of flexible response, in which conventional forces would need to play a bigger part. In 1939 the TA had provided fourteen divisions. On the other hand, most of the critics came to agree in time that the TA had become moribund and that the restructuring had not come too soon.

Most of all however, Mr. Healey will be remembered as the Defence Secretary who ordered the withdrawal of British forces from East of Suez. The troops pulled out of Aden during his time. But the 1967 Defence White Paper also announced that they would leave Singapore and the Persian Gulf by the end of 1971. In the Far East only Hong Kong would then remain—an isolated red blob on Mercator's projection.

Britain's defence effort would now be concentrated upon Nato and Western Europe. The country had been moving in that direction since the end of the Second World War, but slowly and painfully. Mr. Healey put his not inconsiderable bulk behind the wheel and finished the move in one shove.

Actually he did not quite manage that. The Conservative Government which came to power in 1970 brought the aristocratic Lord Carrington to the Ministry of Defence. Lord Carrington outlined his policy in a Supplementary Statement on Defence four months after taking over. The aim was 'to enable Britain to resume within her resources a proper share of responsibility for the preservation of peace and stability in the world.'

Although most of the troops left Singapore in 1971 Britain kept a battalion group there for five more years as part of a joint Australian–New Zealand–United Kingdom (Anzuk) brigade. Lord Carrington also added 10,000 more men to the strength of the TAVR and halted the rundown in the Gurkhas. Not only was there trouble in Northern Ireland, which stretched the Army's manpower, but there was also a need for some stability after years of almost constant change. Lord Carrington did not reverse the policies introduced by Mr. Healey, but he introduced a pause before some of them were carried through to a logical conclusion.

The Defence Review. The Labour election victory in February 1974 brought Mr. Roy Mason, a junior minister under Mr. Healey, back to the ministry as Defence Secretary. Mr. Mason immediately began a Defence Review prompted partly by left-wing agitation for more cuts in defence spending and partly by genuine economic problems. The Heath administration had been forced to make a number of short-term cuts in planned spending towards the end of its short life, and it is generally recognized that it would have probably been forced to prune its programme still further had it been returned to power in 1974.

The target set Mr. Mason by the Labour party manifesto was to take several hundred million pounds off the budget 'over a period', and to bring down the percentage of Britain's Gross National Product which was spent on defence from 5½ to 4½ per cent—more in line with that of the main European allies.

This was well down on the 11·8 per cent which was being spent on defence in 1952 during the Korean War, and the seven per cent at which it remained for a long time afterwards. But it was still higher than the three per cent which Britain had needed to spend before the Second World War—except when some emergency had forced the Government to dig more deeply into its pocket.

The resulting White Paper which was published in 1975 covered the period up until 1984. It announced the final withdrawal of the battalion group from Singapore—although as the Australians had already pulled out of the Anzuk brigade this was largely academic anyway. It confirmed the withdrawal of the small garrison from

Malta in 1979 on the expiry of the 1972 agreement between the two governments. The garrison was to be reduced in Hong Kong and the Hong Kong government was to be asked to pay more towards its upkeep.

Two pieces of Army equipment were cancelled. One was the Vixen armoured car which did not matter all that much. The other was the RS.80 rocket launcher. This mattered more but was not a disaster in itself.

Far more serious was the loss of 15,000 men (the RAF lost 18,000 and the Royal Navy 5,000). The manpower cut was drastic enough to force the Army to carry out its own review of how best to accommodate the loss. The result was a programme for restructuring the whole Army, which was presented to the Press by Major General John Archer (now General Sir John Archer), Director of Army Staff Duties in 1975. General Archer described the shake-up as the most fundamental since that of Cardwell more than a century before. He also defended it on the grounds that it was long overdue anyway and would have been necessary, manpower cuts or not.

The restructuring proposals were detailed and complex, and some have already been modified because they did not work too well. Basically they involved keeping as many regiments and battalions as possible, reducing the manpower in each of them and doing away with brigades—and the headquarter staffs which went with them.

Difficulties soon became apparent. One was that the ratio of men to weapons had gone down so much that there were simply not enough men to cope with the workload. Another was that without brigade commanders operating under them, divisional commanders found that they had too much to think about at the same time.

But the real problem was that by reducing the size of the Army by 15,000, at a time when troops were still involved in Northern Ireland, the Government had expected too much. Accordingly in 1978 it was announced that the Army could claw back 1,900 of the 15,000. Some of the men would be used to form a special demonstration battalion at the School of Infantry at Warminster. The others would flesh out those corps which were still having to find men to work on headquarters staffs in Ulster.

That was in February 1978. But the 1,900 extras never looked like being enough. Soldiers still complained of being 'overstretched'—particularly in BAOR. Morale was low, partly because of discontent over pay and partly because of the cumulative effect of defence cuts and regimental mergers.

So the Army fought for more, encouraged by a three per cent rise in Britain's defence budget in 1979–80. The result was as complete a victory as the most sanguine general could have hoped for. In

August 1978 the Government not only added 4,000 more, but cancelled a 1,000 reduction in the size of the Gurkha Brigade. Half of the 4,000 would be sent to BAOR. Some would take over 300 jobs previously done by the Mixed Service Organization, a force of 3,000 uniformed civilians, displaced from Eastern Europe at the end of the war. These civilians who do a variety of jobs from labouring to guarding military installations, are reaching retiring age and have no obvious successors unless the Army takes over.

Others formed a battalion to carry out special duties in BAOR, which had previously been done by an infantry battalion on a normal posting. This would release the infantry battalion for duties elsewhere. But most of the 4,000 would plump out regiments which had been thinned down beyond the point of endurance as a result of the 1975 manpower cuts.

Together with the 1,900, these additional increments meant that the Army had won back nearly half of the 15,000 it had lost three years before. Senior officers reflected that after a long period of 'stop', the lights had changed to red and amber if not yet to green.

The Army had come a long way since 1945—or rather, it had come back a long way. Designed to police an empire it had been re-drawn for duties nearer home. To say that an era had ended would be to encapsulate time too neatly. But life had changed for Britain in general and the Army in particular, and soldiers were adjusting to it slowly and painfully.

2

New Model Army

It is not very new and not much of a model. As might be expected from its jerky evolution, the Army today is a compromise between accident and design. But it still manages to look different from its contemporaries in other countries.

Although it has over 167,000 members, only about 160,000 including 6,000 women, signed on in Britain. The others consist of 6,400 Gurkhas and about 1,000 locally enlisted personnel—who rarely serve away from home in Hong Kong or wherever. All are divided between 107 combat units and twenty-one supporting corps, which care for the Army's military, physical and even spiritual needs.

The combat units consist of nineteen armoured and armoured reconnaissance regiments, twenty-two regiments of artillery, nine of engineers, one regiment of the Special Air Service and fifty-six infantry battalions, including three of paratroopers and five of Gurkhas.

Who runs the Army? The hierarchy of the Army resembles a pyramid, but an imperfect one full of bumps and indentations. Like the pyramids of ancient Egypt it has been weathered by the years. It is not even very clear who sits on the top of it. Constitutionally it is the Queen who as sovereign is titular head of the Armed Forces. But her annual ride up the Mall in front of the Guards after the ceremony of Trooping the Colour is only a symbolic, vestigial relic of monarchical command. No sovereign since George II at the Battle of Dettingen in 1743 has actually led his or her troops into battle.

Political power over the military stems from the Prime Minister and the Government or, more specifically, from the Defence and Overseas Policy Committee of the Cabinet. A realist might argue that the most influential single person is the Chancellor of the Exchequer who pulls the purse strings. On the other hand, Cabinet battles over defence spending, like those of the mid-1970s, have often been fierce and have not always been resolved in the Chancellor's favour.

Day-to-day control over the Armed Forces is in the hands of the

Secretary of State for Defence who sits on the Defence and Overseas Policy Committee. He is aided and abetted by a deputy, the Minister of State for Defence, and by three Parliamentary Under-Secretaries —one for the Royal Navy, one for the Army and one for the RAF. The Under-Secretary for the Army is in some ways little more than a figurehead, a concession to military pride and a residual legatee of the old system under which the Army had its independent Secretary of State for War and its own budget. On the other hand he does provide an important link between the Army and its political masters.

An ambitious young Under-Secretary has the opportunity to inject ideas of his own into the veins of one of the country's largest organizations. A less ambitious individual might spend an agreeable time, chairing committees, opening new barracks or judging cake competitions for the Army Catering Corps. To a large extent it is up to him to make what he can of the job. But like so much else in the British Constitution the Army is controlled by a system of checks and balances, and no single person would find it very easy to call out the troops in a crisis.

The country's top soldier is the Chief of the General Staff (CGS) a full general who normally becomes a field-marshal on half-pay on retiring from active service after his two-year tour of duty. (General Sir Peter Hunt who left as CGS in 1976 declined the promotion because he felt that it would have been improper after a period during which defence cuts had made so many soldiers redundant). Every six years the CGS ascends an even dizzier pinnacle as Chief of the Defence Staff (CDS), the Army taking its turn with the other two services. But this is a tri-service appointment and the CDS has to forget what colour uniform he wears, however difficult this may be.

The CGS has a large comfortable office overlooking the River Thames on the sixth floor of the Ministry of Defence. The ministry with a careful eye on protocol sites him between the Chief of the Naval Staff and the Chief of the Air Staff.

But even the CGS for all the apparent grandeur of his job has become more of a figurehead over the years and it needs a determined man to make the post seem three-dimensional. Sir Michael Carver (now Lord Carver) CGS 1972–74, belonged to that exclusive group known rather grimly as 'Whitehall warriors' who are capable of standing up to the combined forces of the Government, the Civil Service, the Royal Navy and the RAF when the Whitehall in-fighting is fiercest. Not all fall into this category and by no means are all well known outside the Army.

A succession of household names served as Chief of Staff after the war, Generals Montgomery (1946–48), Slim (1948–52), Harding

(1953–55) and Templer (1955–58)—who had distinguished himself as High Commissioner in Malaya during the Emergency in the early 1950s. They are not such glamorous figures today although the Army like the other two services still tends to pick men who have won their reputation as brave and resourceful commanders in the field rather than brilliant staff officers. Soldiers like to have a father figure to look up to, so high integrity probably counts for more than intellectual capacity when the choice is made. Of the eleven Chiefs since the war seven have been infantrymen, one has been a Gurkha officer, two won their spurs in the Royal Armoured Corps and one has come from the Royal Artillery—although Viscount Alan-brooke, who was Chief of Staff during the war, was also a former gunner.

Even a strong CGS soon finds that power at the top is limited. The Army is administered within the Ministry of Defence by the Army Board much as a large company is managed by its board of directors. Officially the Board's chairman is the Defence Secretary himself, and Mr. Denis Healey and Mr. Roy Mason exercised their privilege from time to time. But this is unusual and the chair is usually taken by the Parliamentary Under-Secretary with the CGS as his principal adviser. Others who attend the monthly meetings are the Vice-Chief of the General Staff (VCGS), a lieutenant-general, and three full generals, the Master-General of the Ordnance (MGO), the Adjutant General (AG), and the Quartermaster General (QMG), the ministry's Second Permanent Under-Secretary, the Deputy Chief Scientist (Army) and the Deputy Under-Secretary (Army)—the Army's top civil servant who acts much as a company secretary to the Board. There is also an executive committee of the Board, which meets once a month under the CGS to deal with lesser decisions which do not need the approval of the full team.

The Board's duties vary widely. In 1975 it was involved in the re-structuring proposals for the Army, made necessary by the Government's Defence Review. It has also dealt with the QMG's new logistic system for the Army involving millions of pounds worth of stores. The perennial problems of pay and conditions are brought before it by the Adjutant General, and the MGO is constantly seeking its approval for new equipment. Although it does not have to decide how much money the Army will spend, it does say how the money allotted to the Army is spent. When the Army needs more money, and it always does if only because of inflation, the Board can make its views known, primarily through the CGS as a member of the Chiefs of Staff Committee and to some extent through the Under-Secretary to the Secretary of State and thence to the Cabinet. In theory it could resign *en bloc* if it felt that the ultimate sanction was called for. But the machinery is very flexible, and the CGS on returning from a visit to Northern Ireland, for example, could report directly to the Defence Secretary if he wanted to.

The Units. 'Not so much an Army as a collection of regiments' is among the caustic comments that have been passed upon the British Army over the years. Soldiers wear the epithet proudly, like a badge of distinction—which indeed it is. The tribal independence of the regiments with the territorial links and local jealousies has advantages and disadvantages. But at least it is different, and helps to give the British Army its distinctive character.

The infantry is not as different as it used to be. Post-war reorganization has weakened these local affiliations with their feudal overtones. A Shropshire lad who thirty years ago might have served in the King's Shropshire Light Infantry, in a company commanded by the son of his local squire, now has to make do with a place in the ranks of the more anonymous Light Infantry regiment, with its three battalions, commanded perhaps by an officer from Durham or Cornwall, half a world away. The same applies to those other large regiments like the Queen's, the Royal Regiment of Fusiliers, the Royal Anglians and the Royal Green Jackets, each of which has three battalions, or the Royal Irish Rangers which has two.

Since 1968 the infantry has also been divided into six recruiting and training divisions. These are the Guards, the Scottish, the Queen's, the King's, the Prince of Wales' and the Light Division. Although a recruit can specify which regiment he wants to serve in, he now reports not to the old regimental depot but to a divisional depot for initial training, along with other young men from all over the country.

It is a compromise between the old system of semi-autonomous regiments and the alternative option of mixing up everyone and everything in a single corps of infantry. Like all compromises it pleases no-one very much, but it has become acceptable over the years.

On the other hand, the artillery has become more tribal than it used to be. Like the infantry and the Royal Armoured Corps, the Royal Artillery now consists of what are very much county regiments. For example, the 22 Light Air Defence Regiment is all Welsh, 19 and 40 Field Regiments are Scots, 4 Field Regiment draws its men from Tyneside, 20 Medium Regiment from Hampshire and 1 Royal Horse Artillery from South Yorkshire and Nottingham.

The structure of the Army can seem confusing because of the various organizations superimposed upon it. Although infantry units have their recruiting and training divisions they are administered on a day-to-day basis under a system of military districts when they are serving in Britain. So are all other sections of the British Army when in the United Kingdom. Then in wartime the units join up with the field forces or operational divisions with which they would fight the enemy. Needless to say, the operational divisions—four armoured divisions in Germany—are quite separate from the recruiting divisions of the infantry. Similarly the Royal Armoured Corps is a different kind of corps from the 1st British Corps which contains the four divisions in Germany. To a soldier it is all very simple. But a layman might feel that he needs a computer to work it all out.

The oldest unit in the regular Army is the Royal Scots, a Scottish lowland regiment which is also thought to be among the oldest in the world. It is directly linked to those Scottish soldiers of fortune who served the French crown from the early fifteenth century and from whose ranks the French formed the Garde du Corps Ecossais. The regiment itself dates from 1633 when Louis XIII allowed Sir John Hepburn of Athelstaneford to form a regiment from the independent companies of Scotsmen then serving in the French Army.

The newest is the Army Air Corps which was born in 1957. It was constructed out of the old Glider Pilots Regiment which had been killed off in 1950 and a number of air observation pilots of the Royal Artillery. But it is only during the last few years that the corps has been able to recruit directly instead of transferring soldiers from other parts of the Army.

In age, origins and military roles the Royal Scots and the Army Air Corps represent the opposite ends of an Army which has become increasingly technical throughout this century. They are also very different in their internal organization. One is made up of companies and platoons, the other of squadrons and flights.

In most of the Army soldiers are called privates before they win their first promotion. But others are called guardsmen, or fusiliers or riflemen in the infantry, troopers in the Royal Armoured Corps, sappers in the Royal Engineers, craftsmen in the Royal Electrical and Mechanical Engineers or gunners in the Royal Artillery. The Royal Artillery is still more perverse by dividing its regiments into batteries instead of squadrons or companies, and calling its corporals bombardiers.

The Front Teeth. The 'teeth' arms of the Army are the Royal Armoured Corps, Royal Artillery, Royal Engineers, Royal Corps of Signals, the infantry and the Army Air Corps. Together these make up more than sixty-four per cent of the total strength. The rest of the Army is sometimes described as the 'tail'. But most people think of

2*

the 'front teeth' as being the armour, the artillery, and the infantry, because these usually have to take the first bite.

The Royal Armoured Corps, which is made up of the old cavalry regiments and the four Royal Tank Regiments, absorbs nearly seven-and-a-half per cent of the Army's manpower. Thirteen of its regiments are in BAOR and six are kept in the United Kingdom. A typical Type 'A' armoured regiment in BAOR consists of 464 officers and men plus ninety-two more in a REME Light Aid Detachment. It is equipped with seventy-four Chieftain main battle tanks as well as other vehicles. In 1977 it cost around £22,000,000 to equip it and £3,600,000 annually for its manpower. Two of the tanks belong to regimental headquarters but the other seventy-two are divided between four armoured squadrons. Each squadron has two tanks in its headquarters and four more in each of four troops. But a Type 'B' armoured regiment in Britain has only forty-six Chieftains and has slightly fewer men, so in 1977 it cost only £15,500,000 to equip and £2,300,000 for its manpower.

Of the nineteen RAC regiments only ten are fully armoured at any one time. The other nine are armoured reconnaissance regiments equipped mainly with Scorpion and Scimitar tracked vehicles. An armoured recce unit in BAOR has 485 men including fifty-six in the LAD and 154 vehicles including ninety-eight on tracks. In 1977 the total value of its equipment was £7,500,000 and its annual manpower cost was about £2,800,000. But an armoured reconnaissance regiment in Britain was again slightly smaller, and cheaper to equip.

The Royal Artillery, which includes the Royal Horse Artillery, represents nearly a tenth of the whole Army. It has fifteen of its regiments in BAOR and seven in Britain. But the regiments vary a great deal in their size and organization according to where they are based and what kind of regiments they are. A general support regiment in BAOR, firing its big guns in general support of an attack by its division has 670 men and is divided into two medium batteries, each with six 155mm guns, a heavy battery with three 203mm guns which can fire nuclear shells and a light air defence air battery with Blowpipe missiles.

A close support regiment, however, whose Abbot self-propelled 105mm field guns are directed to the more specific support of units has only 642 men, split between four field batteries each with six Abbots. Batteries are sub-divided into troops—a term which the artillery shares with the RAC.

The infantry is also divided into regiments. But a regiment in the infantry is mostly an administrative, even ethnic term, and it is the battalion which is the fighting unit. As most infantry regiments have only one battalion, the two mean very much the same thing. It becomes complicated, however, when referring to the new large regiments and the Parachute Regiment each of which has three battalions, or the Grenadier Guards, Coldstream Guards, Scots Guards and the Royal Irish Rangers which have two apiece.

There are eighteen infantry battalions stationed in BAOR, thirty, including one Gurkha battalion, in Britain and seven including four Gurkhas in other parts of the world. An infantry battalion like other Army units varies according to where it is based. A typical mechanized battalion in BAOR has about 650 men. It costs £7,000,000 to equip and £4,200,000 a year to run. The battalion contains a headquarters company and four mechanized companies of 100 men each whose basic vehicle is the FV 432 armoured personnel carrier. A company has its own headquarters and three platoons, each with an officer and twenty-seven men. Then a platoon is in turn split into three sections of eight men commanded by a corporal and a sergeant. In fact, a battalion is more complicated than that because it also includes a fifty-man mortar platoon and a fifty-eight-man anti-tank platoon equipped from now on with Milan anti-tank missiles.

An armoured division in BAOR contains a mixture of teeth arms and tail. A typical blend might be two armoured regiments, one armoured reconnaissance regiment, two artillery regiments (one general support and one close support), an artillery battery with guided missiles, three mechanized infantry battalions, an engineer regiment, an Army Air Corps regiment, a transport regiment, a medical unit, an ordnance unit and a REME field workshop. In battle, however, the division might be given more guns, engineers or helicopters depending on the job in hand.

Postings. Which unit finds itself in BAOR, or Britain or anywhere else is the responsibility of the Director of Army Staff Duties (DASD), who is a major-general at the Ministry of Defence. It is a complicated business, because like so much else it varies from one part of the Army to the other.

Infantry battalions move usually, but by no means always, at two-yearly intervals and accompanied by their families. They do so according to a number of duty rotas, one of which includes the 'plum' postings like Gibraltar, Hong Kong, Berlin and garrison duty in Cyprus. Belize in Central America does not count as a plum because soldiers are on active service in an awful climate for six months' unaccompanied tours.

There used to be the unique job of serving as nuclear escort battalion in BAOR. The nuclear escort battalion has the wartime role of escorting the Royal Corps of Transport trucks which transfer warheads from Nuclear Ammunition Supply Points (NASPS) to the launching sites. But a permanent battalion has now been formed to do the job, and soldiers are posted to it as individuals.

A decision on what constitutes an attractive posting is bound to be arbitrary. Wives seem less anxious to travel than they used to be, partly because they are younger and partly because so many have been abroad on holiday anyway. The glamour of foreign travel has to some extent been lost. A two-year posting in Gibraltar might mean living in overcrowded quarters on a lump of rock, far from 'Mum' and British television. Soldiers often seem to prefer travelling alone for short exercises, while their wives stay behind with the children. Before 1969 a posting in Northern Ireland was an attractive concept, but not any more.

The rotas are calculated over a fourteen-year period. During that time a battalion might expect to spend eight years in Britain, four years in BAOR and only two years on a plum posting.

But that is only for the infantry. The RAC and RA regiments have a seventeen-year rota which takes account of the opportunity for a RAC squadron to spend two years in Cyprus or Berlin or, less exciting, a spell as demonstration regiment at Bovington in Dorset, which is the RAC's headquarters.

RAC regiments have less chance of travel than the infantry. They spend most of their time in BAOR, where a regiment might be in one place for as long as six years. This allows them to settle down for a while, but it is a far cry from 'join the Army and see the world'.

A regiment spends about half of its time in an armoured role with Chieftain tanks and the other half on armoured reconnaissance which is the job that most of them prefer. For most of the time, a switch from one of these roles to the other is the most exciting 'move' that a unit can expect.

The Royal Artillery regiments now move by units in much the same way. But again there are few places to go. Indeed, apart from Britain and West Germany there have been none since the artillery was withdrawn from Hong Kong in 1976. Missile regiments and 94 Locating Regiment never leave West Germany anyway because of their specialized roles. A tour of duty of three years or more at the School of Artillery, Larkhill, Salisbury Plain, is as ripe a plum as the Gunners can look forward to. On the other hand, individual Gunners are often sent on secondment to Third World armies which need Western expertize to help build up their artillery.

The Royal Engineers and most other soldiers move around on 'trickle' postings, joining and leaving units in ones and twos. This system is more economical, but it is hard to build up an *esprit de corps*.

The actual movement of regiments is difficult, even when one has decided where they should go. School holidays limit movements to certain times of the year. The DASD issues what is called an Arms Plot every April with the object of giving units twelve months notice of where they will be going next. Once issued, it is very hard to change. The whole system is apt to crumble if one does.

Uniforms. Moving the Army is one headache. Clothing it is another. For one thing soldiers come in all shapes and sizes. The mean height is 5′ 8½″ and the mean weight is 10 stones 7 ounces. But there are wide variations, and it is Army policy that this should be so. After all one wants big, strong guardsmen on the one hand, but compact little drivers on the other—who can be squeezed into the confines of a tank. Not that the Army can afford to be very selective. Within reason it takes what it can get, and puts up with the fact that some are shorter, and fatter, or longer and thinner or broader in the beam than others.

The headache would be less painful if soldiers were content to dress alike. As it is, the Directorate of Clothing and Textiles, manipulating a £50 million budget from its headquarters in the old War Office building, has to cater for a number of almost feminine idiosyncracies among the regiments. It is all part of the tribal system, and the Army Dress Committee meets three times a year to consider applications from one unit or another for a new colour of beret, or lanyard, or sweater or a new kind of badge. In general the Army looks tolerantly upon such whims, arguing that if the cost can be kept to reasonable proportions, then the benefit in terms of military morale pays off in the end.

The basic kit issued to soldiers at present includes:

2 Combat suits (camouflage jacket and trousers)
1 No. 2 dress (single breasted khaki jacket and trousers)
2 Pairs of green barrack-room trousers
2 Pullovers
2 Khaki poplin shirts
1 Beret
1 No. 1 Dress cap (peaked cap, usually dark blue)
1 Gaberdine raincoat (rarely worn)
3 Thick khaki shirts (for combat wear)
2 Pairs of directly moulded sole (DMS) boots
1 Pair shoes
4 Pairs of socks

Badges of the British Army

But that is only a basic list. The number of extras and variations is considerable. The Household Cavalry, the Foot Guards and the King's Troop Royal Horse Artillery have their ceremonial finery. Scottish Lowland regiments wear plaid trousers, or trews, as part of their Number 2 dress and Highland regiments have to be provided with trews and kilt. Scottish regiments also wear brogues instead of the plain walking-out shoes issued to other units.

Since the 1960s the day-to-day wear of soldiers in barracks has consisted of green barrack-room trousers and khaki sweater—or 'woolly-pully' as officers cosily describe it. But almost every regiment has managed to preserve some variation on the official theme. The Royal Signals have dark blue sweaters, the Royal Hampshires black, the Cheshire Regiment brown and the Intelligence Corps green. Others wear different shades of blue, green, maroon and grey. None so far has chosen purple or yellow. All wear canvas belts in regimental designs, and some have even affected distinctive cravats to lend a little 'je ne sais quoi'.

The official Army colour for soldiers' berets is dark blue. But again there are many exceptions. The Foot Guards wear khaki, the Special Air Service sand, the Light Infantry green, the Parachute Regiment maroon, the Army Air Corps sky blue, the Royal Hussars chocolate, the Intelligence Corps cypress and the Royal Tank Regiments black. The Royal Anglians were also given permission recently to change to khaki like the Foot Guards.

Number 1 dress is now worn only by soldiers who have special ceremonial duties—forming guards of honour for instance. Those who do use it have managed to keep a similar number of variations on the official navy blue. Scottish regiments wear glengarry hats with it, the Royal Irish Rangers have big floppy berets and the Royal Hussars, 'the cherrypickers', are still identifiable by their cherry red trousers.

The DCT is privately hoping that some of these idiosyncracies might disappear if and when the new Army bottle green uniform comes into use in the 1980s, replacing both Number 1 and Number 2 dress. Worn with a white belt and a red band round the hat, the uniform should, it is hoped, please everyone. But soldiers are so notoriously difficult about how they appear in public, that the DCT bureaucrats keep their fingers crossed.

With price rises of sixty per cent for wool, 100 per cent for cotton and forty per cent for boot leather, the Army has been struggling for some time to find room for economies in the clothing budget. It costs £180, for instance, to buy an officer's jacket and two pairs of trousers. A guardsman's bearskin costs £150 and a guards' officer's bearskin £175. But there are limits to what one can do. Scientists at the Stores and Clothing Research and Development Establishment at Colchester have been quite successful in standardizing the coloured threads used in making Scottish tartans.

But attempts to find a substitute for bearskin, taken from real live bears (male bears in the case of guardsmen, and the soft side of female bears for officers) have so far proved a failure. The International Wool Secretariat have been trying to persuade the Army to opt for sheepskins. But sheepskins do not behave well in wind and rain. Nor does man-made fibre, so the Canadian bears (and Russian bears in the past) will have to continue to provide the necessary.

One problem is that soldiers grow out of clothes. They enter as slim young men—and at first are kept so by plenty of running about. Then they get married, settle down to a family life, perhaps eating

too well on cream and potatoes while serving in West Germany, and
soon the clothes they were issued with no longer fit them. An astute
quartermaster will hire a tailor to carry out alterations, or will
re-issue the outgrown uniform to the next slim young recruit who
comes along, after cleaning, pressing and general refurbishing. But
at the very least it costs tailors' and cleaners' bills.

The DCT is hoping to save something on their budget by extending
one experiment which is now being carried out at Aldershot. There,
one large stores for the whole garrison has taken over from the
individual regimental quartermaster's shops. Although there are
twenty-three different sizes of Number 2 dress jackets and a similar
number of trouser sizes, quartermasters are always having to turn to
tailors to help achieve the kind of fit that soldiers nowadays expect.
The relatively small size of regiments restricts the size of the stores
anyway—and so does the endless variety in the shades of khaki. A
jacket and a pair of trousers do not necessarily make a good colour
match. By centralizing Army clothing stores, the size of stocks
should be increased and the choice enlarged, thus further cutting
down on tailoring charges.

Then there is a policy of signing, where possible, longer contracts
with the textile manufacturers who supply the Army. This should
not only help to stabilize prices but should enable the manufacturers
to plan their labour requirement more efficiently. There should,
therefore, be savings all round. The Army's bargaining power has
been strengthened too in recent years, partly because of the
recession and partly because of increasing competition from overseas
which is affecting the civilian markets for clothing firms. Turning out
khaki uniforms for HM Forces may not count as a glamorous image
for the company concerned. But it is steady, lucrative trade with a
customer who is unlikely to go bankrupt before paying his bills.

The Military Salary. The manner in which soldiers are paid changed
fundamentally in 1970. Apart from the ending of conscription, it was
probably the most significant alteration to military life since the war.

Until 1970 soldiers were paid relatively low basic wages. But these
were supplemented by free board and lodging and such extras as
marriage allowances. Not only was it very complicated, but it was
difficult to persuade young men to join when so many of the cash
benefits were hidden. The doubtful pleasure of a free bed in a barrack
room did not have the same appeal as a fat pay packet. Anyway it
was not much use exhorting young men to 'join the professionals'
when they would be paid in a manner totally unlike that enjoyed by
professionals in civilian life. The system more closely resembled that
for domestic servants, or farm labourers.

The present scheme, known as the Military Salary, began in April 1970 after a recommendation by the National Board for Prices and Incomes. It is complicated enough but it is infinitely simpler than the old method—and rather more dignified. Instead of earning a low wage and free keep, a soldier receives a reasonable salary, comparable with equivalent civilian trades, out of which he pays something back to the Army in return for his food and bedspace—or quarter.

Comparability is a difficult concept. It is hard to find a civilian job which equates with that of a paratrooper or a tank gunner. But a system has been worked out under which military trades and a number of civilian jobs are awarded points in respect of the training needed, experience, supervision, the danger, working conditions and the likely consequences of any errors. The civilian jobs used for the comparison include those of bricklayer, barman, car worker, waitress, secretary, coal miner, engineer, electrician, traindriver and fireman. A similar system works for officers and even takes account of fringe benefits like company cars, free telephones and reduced mortgage rates.

Once the right amount has been decided, the Armed Forces Pay Review Body which makes annual recommendations to the Government on service pay, adds an 'X' factor. This is an extra ten per cent for servicemen, five per cent for servicewomen and six-and-a-half per cent for doctors and dentists—to compensate them for the disciplines and discomforts of Army life.

The salaries of officers above the rank of brigadier are the responsibility of the Review Body on Top Salaries, which also decides how much judges, higher civil servants and other public figures should be paid. The Armed Forces Pay Review Body (AFPRB), a voluntary eight-man committee, looks at the pay of all other soldiers.

The structure is complicated. Officers up to the rank of brigadier are paid according to how long they have served in that particular rank. A major for instance starts at so much, then sees his pay rise by a series of increments to a maximum after eight years.

For non-commissioned soldiers it is more complex. Their pay depends upon how long they have served in the Army and how long they have signed for. There are increments after nine, twelve, fifteen and twenty-two years. But there are also differences between trades so that a qualified craftsman would earn more than an unqualified infantryman, although both had served for the same time in the same rank.

The Military Salary worked well at first and was popular with the services. But weaknesses began to appear in the early 1970s and again in the years after 1975, when the Government was operating a pay policy for everyone.

Soldiers bitterly complained that their incomes had fallen behind those of civilians because unlike other people they could not make up their depleted earnings by working overtime, living on expenses or signing productivity agreements—which were permissible for industrial workers.

In 1977–78 all the services became so discontented that recruiting and wastage started to suffer and morale began to fall. Some soldiers even started to talk of the need for them to start a trade union of their own to persuade the government that they should be treated as a special case. They were particularly angry after acting as auxiliary firemen during the national firemen's strike in the long, hard winter of 1977–78. They pointed out that some of them were even worse paid than the firemen.

The AFPRB largely agreed with them. Its report in April 1978 acknowledged that their pay had fallen behind that of comparable civilian workers by an average of thirty-two per cent. The government responded by giving the services a thirteen per cent rise in basic pay, an extra one per cent in improved allowances and a guarantee that full comparability with civilian earnings would be restored by April 1980. However, the award was not enough to end all the criticism. Moreover, it made many soldiers wonder if they could ever regain their confidence in the system. In 1978 a number of officers were arguing that something would have to be done to ensure that a similar incomes gap did not widen again. After all, the X-factor was supposed to make sure that servicemen were paid above the general level, not below it. As a result, full comparability was restored by the new Conservative Government in May 1979.

Fringe Benefits. Married and single soldiers are now paid the same. But there are still a number of allowances. Soldiers have travel allowances, separation allowances—after more than thirty days away from home—boarding school allowances for their children and local overseas allowances (LOAs) when serving abroad.

In 1978 boarding school allowances were £1,062 a year for the first and second child, £1,266 for the third and £1,387 for the fourth and any other children. Many soldiers complain that although the school allowances go up to keep pace with rising fees, they still have to pay a significant amount themselves to make up the difference. And they prefer to send their children to boarding school rather than cart them around from school to school as their postings change. Still, it does help them to provide their children with a good education and must be counted as something of a perquisite.

LOAs tend to go down as the cost of living in Britain goes up. They are intended only to make up the difference between living in Britain and anywhere else. They vary, of course, from country to country. In 1977 the Ministry of Defence decided not to lower the LOAs for soldiers in Germany, although it would have been justified in doing so. Soldiers were so unhappy over their pay and conditions that it was felt wiser not to upset them any further.

Soldiers also receive free uniforms, or at least the non-commissioned ranks do. Officers have to pay for most of their clothes but receive a 'once only' grant to help them. Only their combat kit is free. The allowance for an officer is supposed to cover two sets of service dress, a Sam Browne—that leather harness which officers wear over their Number 2 dress—and a Mess kit, which is the officers' equivalent of dinner dress.

In 1975 the basic grant was fixed at £637·50. But there are many variations because some regiments need more than others. Highland officers, for instance, receive £719 because they have to buy a kilt. The Foot Guards drew £740 and the Household Cavalry £776. (A pair of made-to-measure riding boots in 1977 cost £300—although many officers buy second-hand boots for much less.) But the ceremonial dress for the Guards, the Household Cavalry and the King's Troop RHA is issued free.

Uniform allowances are paid only once. Officers who need replacements through normal wear and tear have to pay for them themselves, helped by a tax allowance. But they qualify for further grants if they need new specialized kit on changing jobs.

The uniform allowances are fixed after an annual review of the prices charged by ten leading military tailors. They are surrounded by acrimony. One officer required to buy a Number 6 dress, a special light grey outfit worn by officers posted to the United States and several other locations, complained bitterly that the £197 he received fell short of the £240 he had to pay. But the Army argues that the allowance is meant to cover the average cost, and that those who complain have indulged their own vanity by patronizing the most expensive tailors. Many buy second-hand uniforms, so they often make a profit, not a loss.

Soldiers also receive a non-contributory pension. It is payable to officers who have completed sixteen years service from the age of twenty-one, and to other ranks after twenty-two years of service from the age of eighteen. The amount ranges from one third to one half of his salary on retiring, depending upon how long he has served. He can also take part of his pension in the form of a lump sum if he gives the Army enough notice. He receives a gratuity when he leaves anyway, tax-free and equal to three times his annual pension, and if it turns out that he really did have a field-marshal's baton in his knapsack, he leaves on a field-marshal's half-pay rather than a pension. But not many recruits can count upon that.

3

The Queen's Shilling

Boy Soldiers. Outside, workmen were digging up Whitehall with a pneumatic drill. Inside the Central London Recruiting Depot, a stern and formidable building in Great Scotland Yard, Ritchard Goldman, aged sixteen, of Kensal Rise, was joining the Army.

A pleasant, eager boy in an open-necked shirt, he sat in the first-floor office of Lt.-Col. Richard Hearn (ret'd), Chief Careers Officer for Central London, beneath Annigoni's painting of the Queen, an Army calendar and a multi-coloured wall-map. Recruits from Central London and by tradition, potential Guards and Household Cavalry officers from all over Britain, enlist in these same rather ordinary surroundings.

The short ceremony was something of a formality. Ritchard Goldman had decided to join the Army several weeks before and the Army had already decided to accept him. His enlistment was the final act in a process whose checks and complexities would have amazed some of Col. Hearn's more distant predecessors. How formal the formality is depends upon the officer concerned. Some of the more regimental turn it into a solemn ritual, the recruit standing to attention in his crimplene trousers and suede shoes as he re-nounces his days of philandering. Col. Hearn ensured that it was kept as informal as possible. He called Ritchard Goldman 'Mr. Goldman' as he came in and if he felt any temptation to address him as 'Fusilier' on the way out he certainly resisted it.

First came the ceremony of the money when three crisp pound notes and 20p, representing one day's basic pay of £2·50 plus 70p expenses, were pushed across the desk. Ritchard Goldman signed the B271B Attestation Form, then was handed a small blue Bible.

He stood facing Col. Hearn, the Bible in his right hand, and re-peated the Oath phrase by phrase: 'I Ritchard Goldman swear by Almighty God that I will be faithful and bear true allegiance to Her Majesty Queen Elizabeth the Second, her heirs and successors, in person, crown and dignity against all enemies and will observe and obey all orders of Her Majesty, her heirs and successors and of the generals and officers set over me.'

At that moment Ritchard Goldman, a civilian and until a few days before a schoolboy, became a member of HM Forces, 'subject to military law' as the Attestation Form sternly puts it. He shook hands with the man who had enlisted him and who now wished him well, and walked off into the sunshine. In a month's time he would take the train from King's Cross to Royston, Herts., from where along with other boys he would be conducted to the Queen's Division Junior Infantry Training Regiment at Bassingbourn to begin a year's preparation for adult service in the Royal Regiment of Fusiliers.

About one in three soldiers now joins the Army like Ritchard Goldman, as a junior straight from school. The brightest might go to a Junior Apprentice Regiment, with a view to training for one of the Army's more technical trades. The next-best tend to join Junior Leader regiments in the expectation that they will flower into non-technical NCOs after graduating to the adult ranks at the age of seventeen. Others simply enter as Junior Soldiers.

Many advance beyond the level of NCO. At the last count the Army had two brigadiers, fifty-four colonels and lieutenant-colonels, and 805 majors and captains who began their military careers as juniors. The Royal Navy is even more dependent upon the system than the Army, with about two out of every three seamen starting their service in this way. General Forsyth who had the job of planning the all-volunteer American Army after the Vietnam War said at the time that he would have liked to buy all Britain's junior regiments and ship them back to the United States. Saying it as he did, soon after some Americans had bought London Bridge and carried it back across the Atlantic, there are some who might even have feared that he meant it.

Junior enlistment has given the Army some anxious moments. One of these occurred in late 1970 when a committee under Lord Donaldson recommended that boys who had signed on at the age of sixteen should be given a second chance to change their minds at the age of eighteen. They could give three years notice and leave at the age of twenty-one. The recommendation, which was accepted by the government, does not now seem very revolutionary. Less than two years later all adult soldiers were given the right to take up an eighteen-month notice engagement, which reserved for them the right to leave the Army at any time provided that they gave eighteen months' notice. None the less the Army was afraid at the time that it would wake up one morning to find a third of its recruits decamping —and with government approval.

This fear has not been realized. Although two years ago an eighteen per cent wastage among boy soldiers was being attributed to the effects of the Donaldson Committee reforms, the benefits these conferred upon the Army's image ensured that the number of boys who joined in the first place actually went up. The main September intake in 1971 recorded a record number of 4,900 and a year later this rose to 5,700.

Then there was the government's decision to raise the school-leaving age from fifteen to sixteen in September 1973. In the short term this meant that the flow of juniors between September 1973 and September 1974 would virtually dry up. In the long term the Army wondered if sixteen-year-old school-leavers would be as ready to join the forces as fifteen-year-olds had been. At sixteen a boy would be that much more likely to have found a girl-friend, or perhaps to have developed an adolescent antipathy to discipline and the establishment.

During 1973–74 only 2,890 juniors came forward—as had been expected. But in 1974–75 the total bounced back to 8,093—not as high as the 10,000 schoolboys who had applied to join the colours in 1971–72, but not far from it. It was certainly more encouraging than the most optimistic officers had dared to hope for.

One important reason for this was the success of the Guaranteed Vacancy Certificate—a 'See now, join later' brainwave. Under this scheme schoolboys on reaching the age of fifteen can apply—perhaps through the Army's own Schools Liaison Officers (SLOs) to spend two days at one of two Youth Selection Centres in England, one for the North and one for the South. After two days of mutual examination they might be invited to 'book a place'—preferably in the regiment of their choice—which they can then take up on leaving school in the following year. In extolling the virtues of the scheme the Army argues that by booking early in this way a boy can have a much better chance of ending up in the regiment he likes. This sounds like the guileless innocence of an insurance salesman, because the scheme was conceived to help the Army, not the boys.

But the scheme has benefits for both parties. The Army, sensitive to the charge that it is cradle-snatching in schools, insists that it is doing no more than providing career opportunities and guidance—as do a number of industries. Moreover, the commitment is binding only on the Army. The Army has to honour the Guaranteed Vacancy Certificate when the boy produces it a year later—but the boy himself can reject the option when the time comes.

One proviso stipulated by the Army is that a boy should continue to be of good behaviour during the rest of his schooldays—a proviso which, for obvious reasons, has been welcomed by headmasters. Meanwhile those boys who do not come up to the Army's standards when tested at the Youth Selection Centre, may soon be offered a kind of compensatory certificate which offers them a place as adult recruits at the age of seventeen-and-a-half. This should take away some of the sense of failure felt by a boy returning to school empty-handed, and by so doing should help the Army's image as a benevolent employer. If it resulted in a number of sub-standard recruits turning up at the age of seventeen-and-a-half it would have to be re-examined. But the general expectation is that relatively few will take up the option.

Recruiting Patterns. The Army has been battling to fill its ranks ever since National Service ended. At no time have its recruiting officers been able to sit back and take it easy. On the other hand, it has always been so. Morale was so low during part of Charles II's reign that the old and infirm were welcomed to the colours. Men for Marlborough's wars were virtually kidnapped. In the mid-nineteenth century a recruiting crisis was caused by the Irish famine. The Army has always recruited heavily in Ireland, even during the early years of the present troubles.

Since the end of National Service in 1962–63 the history of recruiting has been one of peaks and troughs. During the peak periods there have been smiling faces at Lansdowne House in Berkeley Square where the Director of Army Recruiting (DAR) and his staff plan their strategy. But the optimism is always guarded. Similarly a year or two of poor returns no longer plunge everyone into the depths of depression. Experience has taught them that sooner or later things will start to pick up again.

For some years the Army has relied upon an intake of about 18,000 adult soldiers a year. This, however, has been very much an average figure. The total has swung from a record haul of 19,800 in 1971–72 to as few as 10,000 in the calendar year of 1973. (A recruiting year now runs like a financial year from April 1.)

There are several reasons for the ups and downs. The defence cuts of the 1960s resulted in poor recruiting totals because confidence in a military career was eroded. Only 11,300 joined up in 1968. Figures improved as confidence returned, with 13,500 in 1969 and 15,650 in 1970. The 1970 and 1971 returns were helped by the introduction in 1970 of the Military Salary, which meant a big pay rise for the troops.

At first the troubles in Ulster seemed to help recruiting. Soldiers were in the news again and were seen every night on television. Some people sympathized with the Catholics and others with the Protestants, but everyone sympathized with the Army. By 1973, however, the rising total of deaths and injuries was bringing disenchantment. Its influence is still debatable. In 1976, about thirteen per cent of boys questioned in a survey said that the prospect of serving in Northern Ireland would put them off joining the Army. But twenty-three per cent still mentioned 'military discipline' as the biggest disincentive.

The most telling influence on recruiting and on the wastage caused by soldiers quitting the Army early, seems to be the economic climate in Britain. The Army argues that there is no direct correlation between unemployment and recruiting. Men do not walk from the dole queue to the nearest Army Careers and Information Office (ACIO). Statistics show that three out of four adults who enter Britain's recruiting offices have already got jobs.

But unemployment breeds uncertainty. When there are plenty of jobs around, young men stroll pass the local ACIO without a second glance. In hard times, however, their mothers often steer them towards the security offered by HM Forces with three square meals a day and warm clothing. A recruiting graph for the last fifteen years would show an exact correlation with economic trends. In fact, recruiting tends to rise several months before a crisis as if the young men or their parents can scent the approaching storm. Economic uncertainty also makes soldiers already in the Army think twice about leaving.

The poor recruiting returns for 1973 coincided with the trebling of civilian job opportunities. But rising unemployment brought about an improvement in 1975–76. By August 1975 the Army was enlisting 500 a week. By the spring of 1976 this was down to 300 a week, but the Army was still able to pick one out of every three adult applicants and one out of every four juniors.

There were signs, however, of another trough in 1977–78 when only 11,635 adults were recruited, which was below expectations. Moreover, the Army was suffering from a high wastage rate, although there was still high unemployment in Britain. The number of officers seeking Premature Voluntary Release (PVR) doubled in twelve months because of discontent over pay and conditions, and the number of other ranks who left the Army totalled 4,643 between April 1977 and February 1978 compared with 3,401 during the same period in 1976–77.

Manning the Army is not a case of simply finding as many young men as possible. Requirements are constantly changing. The DAR, a brigadier, has the job of finding the right men at the right time. But the Director of Manning (Army)—known as the DM(A)—a major-general, tells the DAR how many are wanted and when. The two men and their departments, work in close liaison.

The best known piece of machinery run by the DM(A) is the

Standing Committee on Army Manpower Forecasts (SCAMF) whose membership includes officers from the staff of the DM(A) and the DAR. There are four SCAMFs, one for officers, one for adult soldiers, one for juniors and one for women. They meet at varying intervals. The junior SCAMF, for instance, gathers only once a year but the adult soldier SCAMF once every six months, when the committee decides on the manpower requirements for the next six months. But to say that they meet 'once' is misleading because one session of the adult soldier SCAMF might mean as many as six full day meetings.

Each SCAMF has to work out what proportion of recruits should go to each corps or infantry division. These percentages are passed to the corps or divisions who then divide their ration into the Army trades they need—so many drivers, signallers, riflemen and so on. These new figures go to the Army's Chief Personnel Selection Officer who in turn passes them on to the various Recruit Selection Centres. But the process is even more complicated than that. All findings of the SCAMF have to be endorsed by the Standing Committee on Army Organizations, which meets at major-general level under the chairmanship of the Director of Army Staff Duties.

Image-making. The hardest post-war battle for the Army has been to establish a new identity for itself in a changing world. The picture of a cheerful corporal giving the 'V' sign from his three-ton truck during the Second World War is no more apposite to an age of guided missiles than that of Colonel Blimp, the pre-war creation of the cartoonist David Low. Moreover, many of the old incentives which it relied upon in the past have gone for good. Not only has the chance of travel diminished, but so has the soldier's place in the scale of importance. While at home defence has dropped several places in the order of priorities, abroad the contribution of BAOR to the security of Europe has been made to look small beside that of the West German Army or the United States Seventh Army in West Germany.

Furthermore, the wartime image of the Army persists, nurtured by television programmes like 'It ain't half hot mum' and 'Dad's Army'. The image is half affectionate. But it is not the kind best calculated to inspire boys to join.

To some extent this is the job of the Army's Director of Public Relations, a brigadier, who helps to inform the nation about the shape, size and role of the Army through the newspapers, radio and television. The picture which the media present includes 'warts and all'. But it helps to create the right climate for the DAR's recruiting campaigns.

Before the Army can bring a young man to the point of making a decision it has to promote 'target awareness'—an advertising phrase which officers, fond of jargon, splash into their small talk like tonic into a glass of gin. The Royal Navy and the RAF can project their life-style through a picture of a warship or a jet fighter. The Army can counter with the picture of a tank, but it is not quite the same. The equivalent military attraction is in a sense the 'esprit' of a regiment, which is difficult to put across to a teenage boy.

But the Army also spends heavily on advertising. Around 1976 it was costing up to £2,000,000 a year. The money does not come out of the defence budget but belongs to a sum allocated by the Government every year and administered by the Central Office of Information. Allowances have been made for inflation, but the allowances have never been quite enough and in real terms the money spent on selling the Army image has tended to go down slightly.

Advertising contracts are awarded for three-year periods and are eagerly sought by advertising agencies. The campaigns are fairly continuous, particularly for officers who seem to be persuaded by a build-up of pressures over a period rather than by any sudden impulse. But there are also peak periods. Adult soldier advertising increases in late summer and after Christmas when there are more young men looking around for a career.

Army advertising is particularly sensitive. The more controversial it is, the more positive the response. But the response in terms of recruiting may be matched by a hostile reaction in Parliament. There is also a thin dividing line between a glossy tongue-in-cheek appeal and gross misrepresentation. The Army has to be careful about keeping on the right side of it because it is dealing in men's careers not tins of soup and it may have to sort out those careers if they are ruined.

To assert that 'there is no bull left in the regular Army' would be counter-productive because of the reaction from young recruits the first time they are told to brush their boots or even their teeth. Similarly the officers in DAR-3, the section of the DAR's department responsible for advertising, have to be careful not to place too much stress on travel. It is advisable not to make too much about visits to Hong Kong, because they are not very frequent. It does no good for a soldier on a wet Sunday afternoon on Salisbury Plain to pick up a newspaper and see a recruiting picture of a colleague stretched out on a palm-fringed beach, improving his tan, beside a slant-eyed Suzie Wong. It might simply make him feel cheated.

Advertising for adult soldiers, juniors, the TAVR, and the Ulster Defence Regiment includes buying space on commercial television.

About two or three films might be running on any one of these at the same time. But TV advertising tends only to whet the appetite for more information. It is very much a case of creating this 'target awareness'. Ideally a television campaign is linked to a series of good hard factual advertisements in newspapers and magazines. Hence the ad. which appeared in newspapers in 1976 headed 'The Ten most asked questions about the Army', which dealt in turn with Northern Ireland, 'bull', haircuts, toughness, discipline, fears of redundancy, availability, travel, time off and the fear of irrevocably committing oneself.

Boys reading the advertisement are invited to send off a coupon in the right-hand corner to Lansdowne House where a couple of secretaries respond by sending a packet of glossy information booklets to complement the information in the advertisement. About 900 inquiries might be received in a good week, 400 in a bad one. The girls also notify the local Army Careers and Information Office (ACIO) and return the coupon to the boy with the literature. This enables a boy to use it as a form of introduction if he pursues his interests by calling at the ACIO himself. 'A boy who might be a little inarticulate finds it a great help to be able to brandish his coupon and say: "I've come about this" ' one colonel explained.

Advertising is always geared to the state of recruiting. If recruiting is going through one of its 'trough' periods the advertisements concentrate upon, say, the range of attractive jobs that the young man can look forward to in the Army, upon the promotion prospects or perhaps the pay and conditions. When the graph is rising the emphasis shifts to 'the challenge' of the job. 'Are you good enough for the Regular Army?' is the kind of message which attracts the kind of keen, well motivated boy that the Army wants. It also might deter the less enthusiastic young man whom the Army can afford to do without in times of plenty.

A television film in 1976 which was indeed a time of plenty was called 'If'. It showed three picture sequences. One was of jeeps speeding over rough ground in Cyprus, another of a patrol in Ulster with the bricks and bullets flying thick and fast and the third showed soldiers in arctic gear in Norway. 'If you are man enough to cope with this we would like to meet you', said the commentator grimly.

This is the sort of gritty advertising that the Army prefers. This is not only because it reflects all that the Army likes to stand for, but also because it is more satisfying for those young men who are already serving. A soldier likes to impress the people at home that he has a hard life. The Army also insists that all soldiers depicted in advertisements are real-life soldier, not bit-part, spear-carrying actors or male models who have never even seen a tank let alone driven one.

'Target research' polls are held regularly among boys aged between fifteen and twenty-three to find out what might attract them to the colours or, still more important, what might deter them. If it is found that a high proportion are worried about service in Northern Ireland at that time the Army will make a point of concentrating upon Ulster in the next series of advertisements. Northern Ireland is a different subject because the Army cannot afford to glorify service there. But a vigorous effort has been made to portray soldiers as members of a highly professional skilled team in Ulster. This can help to dispel the awesome image of a young twenty-year-old stuck on his own in some isolated observation post—a prey to an IRA sniper.

In the same way the Army, while it cannot pretend that discipline is no part of its life, makes a conscious effort to rationalize the need for it. An advertisement in 1976, when the Army could afford to be brutally honest, explained, 'There is discipline there is drill. But it is all designed to help you work as an efficient member of a team. When you are relying on your mates and they are relying on you, there's no room for slackness or sloppiness. If you're not prepared to accept the rules you're better off where you are.'

Officer advertising is more philosophical. Potential officers, according to Army research, are more conscious of political, patriotic motives. Hence the advertisement in 1976 which announced: 'Volunteers are needed for three years National Service.' The illustrations showed soldiers facing angry crowds in Northern Ireland, peace-keeping in Cyprus and guarding the border in West Germany.

Target research does not always tell the Army what it wants to hear. A poll amongst students several years ago suggested that they were less likely to be attracted by some patriotic appeal than by practical bait, like career opportunities and pay. In another, a potential junior recruit poured scorn on a television film which showed a tank lumbering through the undergrowth with the commentary: 'if this man is fit to drive a tank, he is fit to drive anything.' He said that it sounded 'silly' because it was simply not true.

The enormous costs make it important that the message should be the right one. In 1976 a series of colour advertisements in *TV Times* for three months cost the Army £60,000, and a black-and-white series in the *Sun* and *Daily Mirror* totalled £130,000. The average cost of a sixty-second TV film then cost £15,000, and a three-week spring campaign for the TAVR was £60,000.

With this kind of investment the Army also has to ensure that it reaches the right people. A film is less likely to be shown in an area where recruiting is going through a bad patch. And the Army also has to think twice about showing TV films in London, not because London is a poor recruiting area, but because television time there is so expensive.

Part of the budget is fed to recruiting staff in the districts, for buying space in the local Press—usually to advertise local displays. District recruiting officers often complain that they should have a bigger share. But national recruiting staff in London say that the Army is now seen to be a national institution, whatever the strength of local regimental pride. When boys enter an ACIO it is usually on the prompting of national rather than local advertising.

Army Careers and Information Offices. The ACIOs, or recruiting offices as they used to be known, are in more senses than one the Army's shop windows. So many famous old regiments have disappeared that in parts of the country the ACIO is all that remains—and as often as not even that is in a county town some miles away.

Local knowledge is important. This is why the DAR keeps recruiting staff in each district headquarters. The DPR(A) also keeps public relations staff in the districts to link up with the local Press.

South Wales, for instance, is known to the Army as a matriarchal society. Whoever is in charge of recruiting there should realize that it is the mother in the family who will probably decide whether or not the son and heir joins up. It is also important to know where the tribal areas begin and end. A suggestion from Lansdowne House that part of the Black Watch recruiting area in Scotland should be handed over to the Gordon Highlanders was met with horror by officers in Scotland. Aghast, they pointed out that the two regiments had fought on different sides in the 1745 Jacobite Rebellion.

There are now 222 ACIOs ranging in size and importance from large city offices with a retired lieutenant-colonel and possibly another junior officer, to those manned by a couple of sergeants. London itself has twenty-one, five main ones in the Strand, Finchley, Surbiton, Forest Gate and Blackheath, and sixteen others in Holloway, Acton, Marble Arch, Fulham, Crayford, Camberwell, Penge, Romford, Wembley, Harrow, Edgeware, Hornsey, Tottenham, Norbury, Battersea and Hounslow.

Sergeants, the so-called 'backbone of the British Army', certainly form the backbone of this recruiting organization. Most are Long Service List NCOs (LSLs)—soldiers who after completing a full twenty-two years, remain until the age of fifty-five, renewing their contract by mutual consent every three years. But most ACIOs also contain special recruiting sergeants—regulars contributed by the regiment with a recruiting interest in that area to ensure that the regiment secures a fair share of the likely lads. In Acton, for instance, a busy but otherwise typical ACIO which covers the whole London borough of Ealing, there are two LSLs, one from the RAOC and one from the REME, and two special recruiters, a sergeant from the London-based Queen's Regiment and another from the Royal Irish Hussars who have been forced to take a particular interest in the London Irish because of the dearth of recruits from Ireland during the troubles. These special sergeants who complete a normal two-year posting in the ACIO are usually carefully chosen, bright young NCOs, likely to capture the imagination of the casual callers.

Potential recruits who call at the ACIO have to sit the Army Entrance Test, which involves ticking the right answer in a list of alternatives marked A, B, C, D and so on. If he fails this he will be told he can try again in six weeks' time. If he passes, he can try a second test, the RO21 which consists of spelling, verbal reasoning and some basic arithmetic. On the basis of his showing in this he can be told what jobs in the Army he could *not* enter. A boy who cannot do straightforward arithmetic, for example, is not going to be very welcome in the Royal Army Pay Corps. This gives the recruit a chance to walk out at once without wasting his time any further. On the other hand, he can decline to try the RO21 and to leave all such detail until he visits the Army's Recruit Selection Centre.

He is also interviewed by the recruiting sergeant, who will need to identify any criminal record. In the lean days of 1973, three crimes was the maximum permitted level for a boy to be considered by the Army. In 1976 the limit was two—depending on the nature of the crimes. As a result of the Rehabilitation of Offenders Act in 1975 the Army cannot accept any boy who is on probation—a change which some recruiters regret. One LSL told of a boy who was admitted to the Royal Green Jackets while on probation and who recently returned to pay a friendly call. 'He had smartened up and was so fit and keen that he was just going on a PT Instructors' course. But had he come in to us nowadays we wouldn't be able to help him—and I think that's a pity,' he said. Another problem involves finding references. Many aspirants simply do not know anyone who fulfils all the criteria, especially in the cities and especially in an age of enormous schools where the headmaster or even form master might have only the haziest notion of a boy who left school two years before. Most are reluctant to ask their employers because to disclose their intentions would be tantamount to giving in their notice.

The procedure for juniors is similar. But the boy's parents have to sign a B6711 form, a headmaster's report has to be procured and the boy has to sit both the ACIO tests—instead of having the option on the second one. Some boys, juniors and adults, ask the sergeant to go to their homes to talk to their parents. But sergeants are wary of this in London and other large cities as a result of the Irish troubles, and some insist on going there two at a time.

Business varies. Acton, the second busiest ACIO in London (after Wembley) received 250 serious enquiries during the first three months of 1976—twice as many as the year before. These were in addition to about 500 more casual calls. From these totals there eventually emerged ninety-one adult recruits to the Army and twenty-four juniors. Many boys withdraw after being 'put off by their mates in the pub that night'. Recruiting sergeants often try to paint a bleaker picture of Army life than is necessary so that the recruit is pleasantly surprised when he joins his training regiment. Otherwise the boy leaves at the first opportunity and returns to his home area, complaining to his circle of friends. 'Then we have a rotten apple in our barrel,' one LSL said. Discipline, 'bull', and the length of hair are the subjects that most recruits seem to ask about.

The DAR sometimes uses the ACIOs to control the flow of recruits, especially during a peak period. To call a halt to recruiting altogether or just to stop advertising for several months, for instance, is considered counter-productive. Once the operation has stopped it is difficult to restart it. A better way of controlling any headlong rush into uniform is to instruct the ACIOs to raise the standards required in the I.Q. tests or perhaps to impose stricter limitations on criminal records.

Part of the ACIO's work consists of arranging local displays or band concerts or Army participation in local carnivals. About a third of their time, however, is monopolized by the 'Information' role suggested by their title. Because the offices often represent the only military presence within miles, people tend to use them as a contact point for any inquiry relating to the Army or even HM Forces in general. Recruiting sergeants will reminisce for hours about some of the more bizarre inquiries they receive. There are widows who call about their pensions, men who want to recover the medals they mislaid twenty years before and even one request from a soldier's widow who wanted his old regiment represented at his funeral. But all ACIO's are instructed to help provide answers or at least to put the caller in touch with the right authorities. Some complain that the words 'Information Office' above the door bring them foreign students wanting to know the times of buses or flights from Heathrow Airport.

Choosing a Trade. After being tested and interviewed at the ACIO the recruit attends a medical and assuming he passes it, he is enlisted

in the Army. Manchester like London enlists boys at one central
office but elsewhere the enlistment is carried out at the ACIO.

In the bad old days the recruit decided on his regiment at the
ACIO and was then sent to the regimental depot where perspiring
NCOs had the job of hammering square pegs into round holes.
This changed in 1971 when the Recruit Selection Centre (RSC)
opened for adult soldiers at St. George's Barracks, a former RAF
Station, Sutton Coldfield. Some juniors go there too when their own
Youth Selection Centres at Harrogate and Blackdown are over-
stretched.

The recruits spend two-and-half days doing tests, presentations
and interviews, then place in order of preference the three jobs in the
Army they would most like to do. Nearly half have decided which
regiment they would like to join before they arrive and as many as
eighty per cent get their first choice. Those who do not are free to
discharge themselves without obligation, regardless of the fact that
they have already enlisted. About nine per cent do discharge themselves for this and other reasons. (One boy said recently that he had
decided he did not like getting up at 6.30 a.m.) For some trades
there are simply no vacancies at the time. There is a certain amount
of luck involved in turning up at the right moment—a fact which
officers are unhappy about.

There are certainly some jobs which the Army has no difficulty in
filling—and conversely there are some where the difficulty is acute.
The attraction of acquiring a heavy goods vehicle driving licence at
the age of eighteen instead of twenty-one—the minimum age for
civilians—means that the Army is rarely short of drivers. This may
not sound like a very romantic motive for serving Queen and
Country, but at least it provides the Army with the driver manpower that it needs. Nor is there ever any shortage these days of
cooks—a trade which has acquired an entirely new image since the
days of the conscripts' cookhouse. On the other hand the Army is
always desperately short of clerks because few boys apparently
think it worth donning uniform to push a pen.

Up to 320 boys can go to Sutton Coldfield at a time and eighty-
five per cent of these are fixed up with jobs by the time they leave.
The others, apart from those who discharge themselves, fail to meet
the Army's standards for a variety of reasons, including physical
fitness.

The Army has its own system for evaluating physical fitness, as it
does for almost everything else. The infantry demand a grade A
which means a score of 110 in a series of tests. The main supporting
corps want grade B, other corps like the Medical and Catering
Corps demand either grade C or D while grade E is what every

3

recruit should be able to reach during the fifth week of basic training. This is a score of fifty. The RSC, however, requires a recruit to
come up only to grade P which means that he has to heave himself
up to a bar in the gymnasium three times, perform three 'dips' on
the parallel bars and sit up seven times on an inclined bench.
Between five and ten per cent fail, which is astonishingly high, and
about one per cent cannot even do a single exercise. Even rugby
forwards are said to have failed. The Army nowadays rejects those
who cannot do a single exercise as being beyond redemption. They
represent a challenge which the Army has not the time or the money
to accept. But those who score between zero and the minimum
number to pass are given the chance to attend a special physical
development course at the barracks. After three to four weeks of
diet and physical exertion most pass the test satisfactorily.

Still more important are the intelligence tests which the recruit has
to take soon after his arrival. There are five of them. One is a
domino test which entails recognizing sequences and patterns, one a
mechanical aptitude test, one verbal, one involving classifying and
coding, and the fifth basic mathematics.

The lower the score, the better the recruit has done. The boy who
scores top marks in all five tests is given one mark for each totalling
five. This is called his total selection grading or TSG. This TSG is
then converted to a Sum Selection Grading in the following way: All
TSGs of five to eight are graded SSG-1, a TSG of nine to thirteen
becomes SSG-2 and so on. The lowest TSG rating is thirty and the
unfortunate recruit who collects this kind of rating will be classified
in his records as SG30·5 which means he is TSG30 and SSG-5. The
brightest and best, on the other hand, emerges as SG-5·1.

There are a total of six SG gradings. These are SG-1, SG-2,
SG-3 plus, SG-3 minus, SG-4 and SG-5. SG-1 represents the top
ten per cent of the national population, SG-2 the next twenty per
cent, SG-3 plus the next twenty per cent above the median level of
intelligence, SG-3 minus the twenty per cent immediately below the
median, SG-4 the twenty per cent below that and SG-5 the final ten
per cent.

Only about seven per cent of the Army's intake belong to the
SG-1 grade. On the other hand, only 1·5 per cent are SG-5. More
than twenty per cent are SG-2 and another twenty per cent are
SG-3 plus, which means that forty-seven per cent of the average
intake are above the national intelligence median line. The proportion of SG-2s tends to rise during times of economic difficulty as
the brighter boys are forced to look to the Army for secure employment.

Recruits at the RSC are offered a choice of about 140 or so jobs in theory, but in fact their medical condition, physical fitness, character record or their SG rating might preclude them from a number of these—whether or not there are any vacancies. A boy with only second-class eyesight would not, for instance, be suitable for the infantry.

No Army trade demands a SG-1 rating and, in fact, the highest minimum required for any jobs is SG-10·2—in other words, a TSG of ten and an SSG of two. This standard is required for a range of specialist trades including those of student nurse, laboratory technician, radiographer, photographer and ammunition technician (the men who form the bomb disposal squads in the RAOC.)

A high proportion of SG-1s end up in the Royal Military Police. This is because the RMP demand a high standard of verbal ability for writing reports. Because it is rare to find somebody of that standard who is not an SG-1 they tend to receive a high number of recruits who have all-round excellence. Paratroopers by contrast need to be no higher than SG-23·4.

Recruits who are particularly weak on verbal ability are given a special reading test. If they fail that they may be sent on a 10½-week course at the Army School of Preliminary Education. The school's target is to improve reading age by at least two years so that a boy who enters with a reading age of 9·3 could emerge with one of 11·5.

Since 1975 the RSC has had the right to reject a soldier for no particular reason other than that they do not think he would be suitable. But the officer in that case has to write a report of formidable detail, explaining at every point why the recruit has been rejected for each of his three choices.

The Army has been considering whether an adult soldier should be enlisted before he attends the RSC. Juniors, officers and girls for the WRAC, all attend their selection centres before actually enlisting. The argument for retaining the present system for adult soldiers has been that the RSC at Sutton Coldfield needs the back-up of military discipline to keep 200 to 300 young men under control. If they were not already members of HM Forces they would be able to do what they liked and the Army might require a civil police detachment at St. George's Barracks to uphold order.

Soldiers attending the RSC receive £7 pay for their 2½-days stay and seven articles of kit: a pair of battle-dress trousers, a shirt, a sweater, PT kit and a kit bag to carry it all. Those who pass out successfully retain the kit when they leave and go straight to their training units.

Leadership Potential. Since the end of National Service there have been times when the Army has seemed in danger of having too much room at the top. Although there has been no shortage of boys who have fancied themselves as future field-marshals, most of those applying for commissions have been simply not good enough.

There are several ways in which to win a commission and the problem does not apply to all of them. It does not apply, for instance, to schoolboys who win Army scholarships. There are sixty such scholarships every year, each of which was worth £385 a year in 1976 for a maximum of two years. Scholarship boys either go straight to Sandhurst, or to university first. About five times as many apply, so the standard of those who win them is usually very high. The scheme has been so succcessful that the Army now awards a number of reserve scholarships which do not involve any money, but at least promise the boy a place at Sandhurst without his having to run the gauntlet of the Regular Commissions Board (RCB).

A high standard is also needed to win one of the seventy-five places every year at Welbeck College, the Army's own sixth form college near Worksop, Notts. Again, nearly five times as many apply and a large number of 'O' levels is the minimum pre-requisite. Like Army scholarship boys, those who go to Welbeck are chosen by interview not by the RCB, and have to sign on for a minimum of five years. But most Sandhurst cadets are chosen by the RCB which since 1949 has been based at Leighton House, a modest, Georgian mansion at Westbury, Wilts. This is the direct descendant of the old War Office Selection Board (WOSB), which was introduced in 1942. During the first six years of the 1970s as many as 11,308 tried their luck beneath the scrutiny of selection officers at the RCB. But after three days of intensive testing, only 3,040 were judged good enough.

The Army has long been careful about whom it chooses for its officers, but not always for the right reasons. Twelve years ago, however, when there was admittedly a bigger demand, it found itself able to accept about half the candidates who came forward. But the success rate fell back to only one in four in the late 1960s, causing a shortage of about 120 boys a year at the Royal Military Academy Sandhurst. The Army has been struggling ever since, although there has been a slight improvement during the last year or two.

The Army sometimes wonders if the kind of boy it is searching for is just not around any more. The other services after all make the same complaints and so do the so-called captains of industry. All are looking for that elusive 'quality of leadership' which cannot be measured in terms of academic achievement. A 1st Class Honours degree is not enough in itself, particularly when a cadet could find himself leading a platoon in Belfast within a year or two.

Regiments complain that the RCB is failing too many. The RCB complain to the Director of Army Recruiting (DAR) that he is not providing the right material. The DAR complains in turn that the right officer material is not being produced by the schools. Many officers attribute the shortage of suitable candidates to a lack of emphasis on discipline, at home, in school or in civilian employment.

The big public schools, the old reservoir of 'the officer class' now try to send not only their best but also their second and third best to university not to Sandhurst, as was often the case in the past. Eton has recently been supplying more boys than any other single school, followed by some of the large Roman Catholic schools. Officers say that Catholic schools are more disciplined than most—so they produce the material that the RCB is seeking.

The Army has fought back by offering university cadetships, in-service degrees and a direct-entry scheme for graduates, thus encouraging boys to join the Army while still having the benefit of a university education.

University cadets join the Army before going to college, where they are paid by the Army throughout their degree course. In 1977 they earned £1,800 a year. In return they have to serve for a minimum of five years after graduating. But it has not always proved easy to find enough university cadets of the right standard. In 1976 ten of the ninety places were left unfilled.

A new bursaries scheme began in 1977 in an attempt to attract a wider circle of candidates. Bursary boys receive only about half as much as university cadets while they are studying, and they do not actually join the Army until after they have graduated. They then undertake to serve for a minimum of three years only. The Army thinks that in time this could turn out to be the most cost-effective solution.

A select number of bright young sixth-formers are also chosen each year for Short Service Limited Commissions (SSLCs). These serve for a few months before going up to university. The scheme was started more as a public relations exercise than anything else, and SSLC boys have to reapply if they decide after their short experience that they would like to make their careers in the Army. But a surprising number have done so.

The RCB argues that the most important distinction is not between public school and state school, but between boarding school and day boys. Between 1970 and 1976 a total of 1,685 boarding school boys passed the RCB, out of 4,307 who tried. But the number of day boys who passed was only 1,355 out of 7,001. For graduates the ratio was only 269 passes out of 815 applicants. Officers say that boys who have spent most of their schooldays away from home have the confidence and authority to get them through. The Army, conscious of the general expectation that its demographic spread should appear more even, is not entirely happy about all this. But it has not so far found a foolproof solution.

The RCB weeds out the failures by a group selection method first used by the German Army in the Second World War. The Germans, however, watched their candidates off duty as well as on duty, with the help of two-way mirrors and 'bugging' devices. The RCB does not resort to this, despite sinister rumours which always percolate through the candidates own Mess.

Each intake, or board, consists of up to forty-eight candidates divided into groups of eight. Each group is identified by a colour (red, blue, green, yellow, brown and black) and each candidate is known only by his number which he wears on his chest like a speedway rider.

A major-general serves as president of the RCB. Under him come three brigadiers, each one responsible for examining two groups. Each group also has a leader who is a serving major.

The candidates spend three days at Leighton House, in buildings in the grounds. They write essays, complete intelligence tests, deliver lecturettes, take part in group discussions, run round obstacle courses and negotiate at least two interviews. But the most famous test is the command task when they take it in turns to lead their group across imaginary ravines and less imaginary obstacles with the help of barrels, ropes and planks.

After they have left, they are 'boarded', which means that their potential is assessed on the basis of seventeen different qualities. There are five gradings for each quality—strong, good, adequate, limited and weak. One 'weak' can be enough to fail a candidate because it implies one weak link too many. He is also likely to fail if he has five or more 'limits'. The qualities are divided into three main sections. One is called training potential, another is practical ability and the third is 'character'. Two 'limits' out of the three qualities which make up 'practical ability' can also be enough to dash his hopes.

The officers base their assessment of the candidates on evidence from three kinds of source. One is their performance at the RCB itself. Another is their record in life so far, including academic qualifications. The minimum qualifications are five 'O' level passes for a short-service commission and a sixteen-year special regular commission, and two 'A' levels for a long-term regular commission. But serving soldiers applying for commissions from the ranks are admitted with less than this. Reports from headmasters and university tutors are also taken into account. Some of these reveal more about the headmasters and tutors than they do about the candidates but others are delightfully unequivocal. 'If this boy becomes a regular officer I hope to God he joins the other side' one master wrote fervently.

A third source of evidence is the series of three intelligence tests which confront candidates soon after their arrival. One is an 'intruder's' test, so-called because it involves picking the odd one out in a selection of shapes and patterns. Another consists of verbal analogies and the third entails verbal reasoning. On the basis of these the candidate is given an Officer's Intelligence Rating (OIR) on a scale of 0 to 10. For the purposes of 'boarding' at the end of the three days, an OIR-10 and OIR-9 are classed as 'strong', an OIR-8 as 'good', OIR-7 as 'adequate', OIR-6 as 'limit', and OIR-5 and below as 'weak'. The OIR-7 or 'adequate' candidate might be equal to IQ rating of 120 to 125 on the national scale.

The OIR scores are perhaps the most important single source of evidence, rightly or wrongly. The general RCB belief is that a boy who 'loses his head' or, more graphically, 'blows a fuse' on, say, his command task, is usually found later to have a 'weak' or 'limited' OIR. An OIR-5 has occasionally scraped through, an OIR-4 rarely and an OIR-3 never. The son of a notable peer of the realm turned out to have an OIR-3—'about the standard of an average lance-corporal'—and 'blew a fuse' the next day. The RCB acknowledges that with that kind of intelligence a boy should not have been trying in the first place. On the other hand, while a low OIR almost automatically rules out a boy, a high OIR does not necessarily qualify him. One brigadier recently pointed out that in nearly two years at the RCB he had been unable to pass a single OIR-10—although one or more might be on each intake.

Some of the failures at Westbury have been quite spectacular. Headmasters aghast at what has happened to their brightest and best, occasionally write to query the Board's judgement. In that case the RCB agrees to take a second look—but in ninety-eight cases out of 100, the end result is the same.

Candidates receive the RCB's verdict by letter within a day or two of their return home. There are basically three kinds of message —either they have passed or they have failed or they have failed this time but are invited to try again, with perhaps a recommendation on how to spend the interim. In fact though the final 'profiles', which are confidential, define the candidate's potential more closely.

An 'A' final grading means that he should make an outstanding officer—a dazzling prediction which, perhaps understandably, is hardly ever made. A 'B' indicates to Sandhurst that he should make a 'very good' officer—and even these appear nowadays only once in

five or six months. On one recent intake a Scots boy who was at once
recognized as a potential 'B' might have wondered why on the final
obstacle course a small clutch of officers and guests were clustered
round, looking at him with awe. A 'C' candidate—likely to make a
good officer—emerges on average every two weeks or so. But the
most common pass-grade is 'D' which carries the rather half-
hearted appellation 'adequate'.

There is, however, yet another pass-grade 'E' which signifies that
the candidate has been given the benefit of the doubt but that
Sandhurst should consider him as something of a risk. There are
three kinds of 'E'-types—an 'E-Immature' an 'E-Education' or an
'E-Character'—denoting the area in which the RCB detects a risk.
A survey of the E-type system indicated that eighteen per cent
blossomed into 'thoroughly good officers' and fifty-five per cent
proved adequate. Only twenty-seven per cent continued to be
considered a risk.

A candidate who fails is marked 'F' on his profile, and the rare
candidate who scores 'FF' has proved so disastrous that the RCB
never wants to see him again. But only the president himself can
deliver such a drastic judgement. (The president also becomes
involved by interviewing 'grey' candidates—and perhaps giving the
final 'yes' or 'no' on these doubtfuls.) Yet another grade is DW or
'deferred watch' which means that the candidate has failed but is
invited to come back again—an encouraging pat on the back for a
boy who might well improve. But it is rare for a boy to be invited
back if his OIR is low. Intelligence is classed as a gift of God which
one either has or has not—and cannot improve with time.

One suggestion made by frustrated adjutant-generals, anxious
about over-manning levels, has been that the RCB should take more
risks by perhaps passing more 'Fs' as 'Es'. On the other hand, the
RCB argues that it is flexible enough already. The 'E' system works
with three out of four emerging successfully—so why risk spoiling it?

Another suggestion has been that the RCB should take a second
look at its methods, which have changed little since the war. Officers
revisiting the RCB nowadays gaze nostalgically at the same command task exercises which they had to perform—and often wonder
how on earth they ever passed. Indeed the RCB itself is sometimes
concerned over the mystique which surrounds the command task
part of the three-day operation and wonders if the fear of having to
get seven other men, barrels, rope and planks across some obstacle
with the emotive name of Zambesi or Treasure Island, overwhelms
some candidates to the extent of being counter-productive.

On the other hand, officers at Westbury tend to make allowances
while compiling their reports. The system is usually admired rather

than derided by other organizations and seems to let through the kind of young man whom the Army, rightly or wrongly, seeks.

One reason for the high failure rate might simply be that the Army makes it too easy for boys to get as far as Westbury. This does not apply in the same way to ordinary soldiers. As soon as a potential soldier enters an ACIO he is being scrutinized and has to prove at almost every step that he is worth considering. But potential officers go more or less straight to the RCB, although recruiting officers sometimes try to discourage those who are manifestly unsuitable.

One solution has already found favour with a number of regiments. An increasing number of candidates now join the Army on officer-type or 'O-type' engagements. They enlist as private soldiers but with the proviso that if they fail at the RCB after two months' special training, they can discharge themselves without obligation. It means that when they go to Westbury they have at least experienced Army life and have toughened themselves physically and mentally for the tests ahead of them. The Guards have operated a training scheme for these potential officers with considerable success for some years and others like the Royal Green Jackets, the Royal Engineers, Royal Artillery, and Royal Armoured Corps are now trying to fill their messes by a similar expedient.

The 'O-type' system has its critics who maintain that these courses are merely crammers designed to get doubtful starters—'wet Wykehamists' as one officer unsympathetically described them— past the keen scrutiny of the RCB. On the other hand they do enable a candidate to show his potential and the RCB itself is satisfied that it can tell when it is being taken in. RCB officers are, however, wary of some 'O-type' courses which are geared rather too specifically to the tests at Leighton House.

Soldiers have a right to expect their officers to be at least as intelligent as they are themselves, and this would not be the case if all the candidates who have been turning up at Westbury were accepted. Soldiers may not have worried about 'the reason why' at Balaclava in 1854, but they are unlikely to be so indifferent today.

3*

4

The Making of a Soldier

Sandhurst Past. The most famous piece of real estate in the British Army is the Royal Military Academy Sandhurst, where officer cadets have been groomed like thoroughbreds since 1812. Roberts, Haig, Wavell, Alexander, Montgomery, Winston Churchill and a selection of royal princes first learned about the military arts amid its 650 green acres. The success of the RMAS in picking future winners has been mixed. Haig and Wavell passed out top of their respective classes and Churchill was 8th out of 150. But Alexander was only 85th out of 172 and Montgomery was 36th. In describing Montgomery in his final report as a 'troublesome and erratic figure' the Sandhurst establishment was, however, not far out.

More colourfully the Academy has trained an impressive number of visitors from distant lands. King Hussein, Ayub Khan, Prince Lek of Albania are among those who have been pleased to acknowledge their Sandhurst origins. When Cyril Phillips retired in 1970 after seven years as Academy Sergeant-Major, it was calculated that 6,000 cadets had been trained there during his stewardship, including nine foreign princes, three sheikhs and a sultan. No Third World revolution since the war would have been complete without its quota of Sandhurst men on one side or another—and sometimes on both. 'It's nice to be back,' said General Gowon of Nigeria on re-visiting Sandhurst in 1975 after being overthrown in Lagos. But he resented suggestions that Col. Odumegwu Ojukwu, his military opponent during the Nigerian civil war which broke out in 1967, was also a RMAS man. 'Dammit, he was only at Mons' he complained. King Hussein on private visits to Britain, often finds time to call on his old Alma Mater on the Surrey-Berkshire border, and recently took his family on a conducted tour of the place.

For someone trying to capture the flavour of the British Army, as it is and as it was, Sandhurst remains a good place to begin. Physically it is a seductive setting with its wooded grounds, the Wish stream with its stepping stones, the lake, partly shaped by French prisoners during the Napoleonic Wars, and the classical frontage of the Old Building looking over the Surrey hills. Despite all the changes that have been willingly or unwillingly absorbed, it still reflects a traditional picture. Drill sergeants, recruited mainly from the Guards, still scream 'Pick up your feet SIR!' at sweating young patricians who, straight as gun barrels, slam their boots down on the gravel. Sovereign's Parade when cadets finally pass out into the Army at the end of their course is still one of the Army's prettier spectacles, with the band, the uniforms, the profusion of summer frocks and occasional glimpse of Arab robes and sunglasses. The bands still play 'Auld Lang Syne' as the Army's latest batch of Second Lieutenants march up the steps of Old Building, followed by the Adjutant clattering up behind them on his white horse—an uncomfortable experience as any RMAS adjutant will confirm.

But for all that it has managed to conserve, Sandhurst is not what it was. It has evolved with the Army, reflecting the vicissitudes of its parent body for a century and a half, and officers still argue over how much it has gained and lost during the years since the Second World War.

The history of the Royal Military Academy Sandhurst goes back only as far as 1947, when after half a century of debate the Royal Military College at Sandhurst was merged with the Royal Military Academy at Woolwich—hence the present amalgam in the title. The RMC had previously trained officers for the cavalry, the infantry and the Indian Army. The RMA had trained them for the Royal Artillery and the Royal Engineers.

Both Sandhurst and Woolwich had acquired an unpleasant reputation for bullying and upper-class hooliganism—although officers who remember them in the Thirties protest that many of the accounts have been exaggerated. One legendary episode of indeterminate date involved a fight between two companies of Sandhurst cadets, so fierce that two boys were injured for life. A newspaper reporter investigating the incident is said to have been thrown into the lake.

Field-Marshall Lord Montgomery, despite his petite size, was the ringleader of one dubious coterie who set fire to a cadet's shirt-tails before the First World War—an episode which did neither the cadet nor Montgomery's reputation much good. Some of the more sensational stories of life at the RMC seem to have been founded on hearsay, but by no means all of them. Meanwhile the college authorities while lamenting those incidents which resulted in permanent damage to cadets, the fabric or the RMC's reputation, tended to take the philosophical view that future leaders on the battlefield should be taught how to look after themselves anyway. Nor were all the excesses pre-war. An officer who was at the modern RMAS in 1960 recalled one fight in which cadets were being flung out of first-floor windows. A member of the instructing staff who drove up in his car to quell the riot was promptly and anonymously knocked insensible with a blow to the jaw and left under a fountain to cool off. Now a prominent general he is said to have no idea to this day who or what hit him. The guns outside Old College have had to be moored in concrete.

One interesting difference between Sandhurst and the American Academy at West Point involves the teaching of loyalties. At West Point cadets are expected to obey the Honour Code which compels them to unmask wrongdoers to the authorities. At Sandhurst it is the English public school tradition of 'don't split' which prevails. Even Montgomery's scorched victim did not name his assailant at the time—though this might have been due to fear of retribution rather than any honourable feelings.

One important reform introduced by the Labour Government after the war was the ending of the old distinction between gentleman cadets—largely public schoolboys whose father paid for their tuition at the RMC—and Army cadets who had risen through the ranks. (Even gentleman cadets had needed to pass into Sandhurst—Churchill failed to do so three times—but at least they had been able to attend expensive crammers to beat the system.) Since the war all have been officer cadets, paid by the Army not their families.

Sandhurst Present. A far more controversial change was introduced in 1971 when the Officer Cadet school at Mons, formerly a training ground for National Service officers and latterly for cadets taking Short Service Commissions, was merged with the RMAS. The cadets moved out of their hutted camp at Aldershot into Sandhurst's New College—'new' in that it was built in 1911. The merger with Mons, however, was not purely physical. The Army also changed the course —and echoes of the argument which followed still rumble round many an Officers' Mess. Under the old system a Short-Service cadet at Mons completed a five-month course of practical military skills— weapon training, map-reading, drill, fieldcraft and so on. Regular Army cadets at Sandhurst stayed for two years, half of which was military training and half purely academic—including compulsory language training.

Henceforth all cadets would start at New College for a six-month Standard Military Course (SMC) which resembled the old Mons course. Then the SSC cadets would leave as Second Lieutenants in the usual way. while the regular Army cadets would move over into Old Building for a further six months Regular Commission Course (RCC) before following them. Meanwhile those who wished to take in-service degrees but had not got the requisite number of adequate

'A' level passes, would move over to Victory College (established in 1947) for a six-to-nine months course of Pre-University Studies (PUS).

What incensed critics of the system was the lower emphasis on academic training for the regular officer. Although the RCC was, and is, predominantly academic, there is time only to teach vocational studies, like War Studies, international affairs, 'communications' and social studies. Because of shortage of time even War Studies has had to be restricted to post-1945 wars. The Army's argument was that the shorter course would prove more attractive to potential young officers, and at a time when the Army was desperately short of them. But conservationists bitterly protested, particularly over the end of compulsory language training.

The courses were slightly lengthened in 1975, with the effect that regular officer cadets would spend fourteen not twelve months at the RMAS. But the curricula remained the same combination of physical activity and vocational studies. The change was introduced simply because the pace had been too fast for the more modestly endowed cadets—with the result that nearly one in every five was being relegated during the course to take some subjects a second time. It did little to assuage the criticism of those who complained that Sandhurst had been turned into an officer factory—and nothing to ruffle the calm of the system's defenders who pointed out unofficially if not officially, that this was exactly what they wanted.

Another casualty of the 1971 revolution—for so it seemed to many—was the system of cadet government. Under the pre-1971 regime Sandhurst resembled a public school in that much of the day-to-day discipline was administered by the cadets themselves. Some of the senior cadets were made under-officers and others were made NCOs. Before the war when the entire staff at the RMC numbered fewer than forty, these privileged young men for better or worse, more or less ran the place. Now cadets take it in turns to act as orderly for a week—and shortly before the end of the SMC a chosen few are promoted in advance. But Nemesis is all too obviously poised to strike at he who interprets his role too enthusiastically given that sort of timescale.

The RMAS now has about eighty-five military staff and seventy-five academic who are responsible for about 630 cadets on the SMC, 470 on the RRC at any one time and 130 graduates. These are in addition to other temporary birds of passage like TAVR officer cadets—as many as 200 at a time perhaps—who do a two-week course, eighty or so doctors, dentists, lawyers and other professionals on their own specialist course, about sixty on a pre-University Cadetship course, sixty on a Short Service Limited Commission course and so on. All the specialist and graduate courses are housed in Victory College.

In the first ten years of the new RMAS two out of every three cadets had been to public school and one out of every eight had been to either Wellington or Eton. Nowadays only about forty per cent have been to public school—and while Eton is still the most prolific single source, Wellington's output has been reduced to a trickle. After Eton it is the big Catholic schools who do most to keep the public school spirit alive. On the other hand, the proportion of public school boys has shown signs of rising again. Every November the RMAS hold a headmasters' conference at which headmasters or sometimes careers masters from a wide variety of schools are assiduously courted and questioned. But it is those from the public schools to whom the RMAS looks with most hope. The new generation of large comprehensives has not produced enough of those boys with the 'leadership potential' that the academy wants.

About nine out of ten pass the course—although those twenty per cent who are relegated will have done so after taking a longer run at it. About half of those who fail in the end have lost their motivation and have opted to leave. The other half have been rejected by the RMAS for lack of something or other—most often that elusive quality of leadership. Most of those who fail have been borderline cases all along. The final examinations, however, are only about 'A' level standard.

SSC cadets have to decide after eight weeks which unit they want to join, if they have not decided before they arrive. This is generally thought to be too soon. Regulars can defer their decision until the tenth month. Curiously, given the options open to them and the varying demands of all the regiments, the right vacancies seem to get filled without much trouble. Only about three per cent have to be directed into one particular arm or another.

Cadets are divided up into companies with suitably evocative names. Companies in Old College are called Waterloo, Dettingen, Inkerman and Blenheim. New College has Ypres, Amiens, Somme and Gaza, while Victory has Alamein, Burma, Normandy and Rhine. Each company is commanded by a major with a captain as second-in-command. But the basic teaching unit at Sandhurst is the platoon of around twenty-eight or thirty boys. A typical SMC platoon at New College might have eight Short Service cadets, eight regulars, four or five who have been promoted from the ranks, four or five who have come directly from Welbeck College and four or five from overseas.

Each platoon has a captain as its instructor—a job held by

Captain Mark Phillips after his marriage to Princess Anne. But a large part of the instruction is carried out by a colour sergeant, or staff sergeant—a system which makes Sandhurst unique. French officers from St. Cyr where officers are trained only by officers shake their heads in disbelief over the British habit of using NCOs. These sergeants are called 'Staff' by the cadets—and they call the cadets 'Sir' or perhaps 'Mr. Bloggs' in return—but without much obvious respect. The Academy Sergeant Major is called 'Sir' and as the most senior NCO in the British Army probably deserves it. Most ASMs stay at Sandhurst for up to ten years or so before retiring at the age of fifty-five. But then most have chosen the unique appointment in preference to being promoted from the ranks and ending as a major. There are after all plenty of majors, but only one ASM—and the prestige attached to the job is enormous.

About forty per cent of all RMAS cadets come straight from school and about fifteen per cent are overseas students who might need to go to the Army School of Education at Beaconsfield first to learn English. Some fourteen per cent come from Welbeck. The others come from the Army itself—some of them promoted from the ranks but many of them now the product of O-type courses. Major-General Robert Ford when Commandant in 1974–76 believed that a preliminary period in the ranks for all cadets would be of benefit to Sandhurst and to the cadets themselves. But this would mean expanding Army training units and the Treasury would view this with alarm.

Changes in the course and in the background of the cadets have all had their influence on the atmosphere of the place. At one time old hands in Camberley, the charmless town which has grown up around the Army and the railway, thirty miles from London, could not only tell a Sandhurst boy by looking at him but could even tell which company he belonged to. Boys from Blenheim, who affected a languid air of effortless superiority, were particularly distinctive. But most of these idiosyncracies have been eroded, if only because cadets are not there long enough to imbibe them and have no opportunity to bequeath them to their successors. On the other hand, the bullying and the muscular approach to life has also largely vanished.

Cadets are more critical of the system. General Ford, an amiable, popular commandant, said he was sometimes surprised, though not shocked, by the ease with which cadets seated near to him on company mess nights would question a system, which in his time as a cadet during the war was regarded as sacrosanct. Cadets now have their own cars, invite girlfriends to mess nights and after the first four weeks—when they are not allowed outside the campus—can stay out all night if they wish to. Women, though, are not allowed into the cadets' own rooms.

Some older officers regret the changes. In defence of them the RMAS point out that the overall standard has not been allowed to slide. About three per cent of those who pass out each year into the Army are considered to have been sub-standard who somehow or other have slipped through the system. But, officers say sagely, 'they will be found out in time'. The majority, they insist, are as good or as bad as their precursors. The system by which they have been tested has changed, but the level they have been asked to reach has not.

Staff College. Sandhurst represents only the opening process of a training machine which grinds away almost continuously throughout an officer's career. The Army argues that no other organization takes so much care over the selection and preparation of its higher management, and the claim is not unjustified.

For the unambitious there are few problems. For the unambitious it is always so—but in the Army the distinction between high and low fliers is codified and explicit. The average young regular officer leaves Sandhurst as a Second Lieutenant at the age of about twenty, and after joining his regiment, is sent on a special-to-arms course which educates him in skills which the RMAS has no time to teach.

The artillery officer goes to Larkhill on Salisbury Plain, the Royal Corps of Signals officer to Blandford in Dorset, the Royal Armoured Corps man to Bovington, the Royal Army Ordnance Corps to Blackdown, the Royal Engineer to Chatham, the Royal Electrical and Mechanical Engineer to Arborfield, the infantryman to the School of Infantry at Warminster, and so on.

He will be promoted to lieutenant at the age of twenty-one, and given command of a rifle platoon—or similar appointment in the non-infantry arms. He then becomes captain at the age of twenty-six and major at the age of thirty—unless he fails his captain-to-major promotion examination, which is rare. He can then look forward to a relatively unbroken career until retirement at the age of fifty-five. Many leave earlier of their own accord, anxious to pick up a reasonable second career as a civilian before it is too late.

But in recent years more officers have tended to stay until the bitter end—though how bitter it is depends upon their own feelings of frustration and disappointment. Before the war many young men regarded a commission in the family regiment as a temporary experience before leaving to join the family business or to become something in the city.

Nowadays an officer faced with a mortgage, school fees and no job to inherit, is more likely to settle for an adequate, though by no means extravagant major's salary within the comforting embrace of the devil he knows. During his career he will fill a variety of regimental posts—adjutant perhaps, then company commander—and an assortment of junior and middle-grade staff jobs. He will also attend a number of courses.

The most important of these is arguably the Junior Division of the Staff College at Warminster. It started in 1969 and is attended by all young captains at about the age of twenty-six. The objective is to prepare them for an appointment as, say, adjutant in their regiment, or a grade three staff job like that of brigade-major. On the other hand, it is a fairly relaxed course which has no direct bearing upon an officer's later career—although a report is later submitted to his commanding officer. The Army is very proud of it and likes to emphasize its importance. But it is not among the higher hurdles that the ambitious young man must vault in his progress to the top.

There are enough high hurdles as it is—so many that the ambitious young man marching off the square at Sandhurst to the tune of 'Auld Lang Syne' must sometimes regard his future as more of an assault course than a career.

He might start, for instance, by going to university to take an in-service degree—unless he has a degree already. About eighty young officers a year take an in-service degree, twenty going to various universities and sixty moving to the Army's own Royal Military College of Science at Shrivenham. Shrivenham has between ninety and one hundred places but the others are filled by civilians and by soldiers from overseas.

The 1975 report of the Committee on Army Regular Officer Training (CAROT) emphasized the importance of regimental duties in an officer's career—and the importance of an officer joining his regiment at as early an age as possible. There is a need to strike a balance between the training of more and more graduates, and the demand for ordinary, uncomplicated commanders in the field.

A study made of young officers at staff college several years ago indicated that while graduates did no worse there than those who had spent more time with their regiment, they did no better either. The Army not unnaturally demands that the subject to be studied at university is relevant to an officer's career. The CAROT report was critical of the standard of literacy among young officers in the 1970s, which made some wonder if the emphasis on higher education was really paying off. On the other hand, it would take a brave man to argue that the three years spent at university or Shrivenham amount to a waste of time. Most other Western armies award degrees or diplomas as a matter of course at their officer training establishments. Britain has always insisted that the time and money absorbed by a degree course should be spent only on those who want to do it and are good enough to derive some advantage. But the policy is still to make the Army more, not less, academic. The fact that one in every three regular officers now reads for a degree at some time or another and that half of all the regular officers at the age of twenty-five now have degrees, give cause for satisfaction not dismay.

The water jump in an officer's career, if he is able and ambitious enough to take it seriously, is the Command and Staff course at the Staff College, Camberley. Everyone attends the Junior course at Warminster. By no means everyone goes to the Italianate building which is adjacent to the RMAS. Yet without the magic letters 'psc'— short for 'passed staff college'—after one's name, one's chances of advancing beyond the rank of major are diminished.

The Royal Navy by contrast regards its six-month course at Greenwich as an interlude in an officer's career. A higher proportion of senior officers tend to have attended it than in years gone by, but it is far from being a prerequisite for those seeking high command. Nor indeed was it always regarded thus in the Army. Before the war, in the heyday of the regimental system, an officer who chose to go to Staff College was regarded as something of a heretic—someone who was implicitly questioning the accepted order of priorities in which the regiment came first. Colonel Blimp frowned on these intellectual poseurs.

Nowadays an officer qualifies for selection for a place at Staff College when he sits the captain-to-major promotion examination at the age of twenty-nine. This is the 'crunch' in his career. The examination itself is not all that difficult. There are three papers, one on international relations, one on war studies and one on military law—from which he is exempt if he has reached the status of 'linguist' in a foreign language. To be promoted to major he has to score forty per cent in each, but can sit the papers one at a time and on failing, can try, try and try again. To qualify for Staff College he has to score fifty per cent in each of the first two and has to take them all in one shot. Moreover, he can only try twice. If he succeeds, his name goes before the Staff College Selection Board who sift though his Commanding Officer's report and other records in an attempt to reduce a list of 300 young hopefuls to a final selection of 135.

The CAROT, aware of the strain on the examinee and the inequality of a system which took no account of where the officer might be serving at the age of twenty-nine, first suggested scrapping the examination requirement. Candidates instead could score points progressively throughout their early career until they reached a certain number. But rather to their surprise most young officers whose opinion was sought, rejected the proposal and voted to keep the examination. The Army then tried to make the best of both worlds by linking the papers in the Captain-to-Major exam to those in the Lieutenant-to-Captain exam, and even to the subjects studied at the RMAS. It is called the Progressive Qualification Scheme (PQS). The Lieutenant-to-Captain test is now called the PQS-1 and the Captain-to-Major examination the PQS-2, but it is the latter which really counts. However, the Army also introduced more flexibility into the timing so that officers who might be in Northern Ireland at the time, with no opportunity to study, might not feel hard done by.

The staff course itself consists of two parts. Part one entails a course on military technology at Shrivenham. Science graduates and those who have good 'A' levels in science go there for a year and fifteen months respectively. These are the men who might later become technical grade officers. Others who have only hazy memories of Boyle's Law and the colour of litmus paper, join them for the final three months.

Then all go to the Staff College at Camberley for the best part of a year. This second part of the staff course is quite intensive with homework every night and officers hardly find it a relaxing grove of academe.

They go to Staff College between the ages of thirty-one and thirty-three. This tends to sort out the high-fliers. Officers who have failed to get to Staff College can now become 'staff qualified'. This means that by doing very well in a series of staff jobs, as a captain and as a major, they have proved their ability to do senior staff work anyway. But lieutenant-colonels with 'sq' after their names are less likely than those who have been to Staff College to be given command of a regiment or a battalion. The 'sq' scheme has not been going long enough for the Army to say how well they will compete with 'psc' officers in the future battles for senior promotion. But they will probably find it harder going, if only because they will be two years behind.

It is hard enough for anyone. After leaving Staff College the high-flier does two two-year jobs before being promoted lieutenant-colonel at the age of thirty-seven. He used to be called a 'brevet' but is now often referred to as a 'two-shotter'. His more average colleague might not get his promotion until the age of forty or even forty-two. By that time the high-flier might well be collecting his second pip to become a full colonel.

Three boys who left Sandhurst together at the age of twenty, might reflect at the age of forty-two upon their differing career prospects. One could be a colonel, with hopes of one day wearing the crossed sabre and baton badge of a general. Another might be a lieutenant-colonel wondering if he is going to make the next fence, while the third, still only a major, glumly decides that he has reached the end of the road. By studied attrition the Army has thus opened a gap in the ranks.

High Command. Army promotions above the rank of major are decided not by examination but by a combination of reports and promotion boards. The system is not in itself unique. But what makes the Army's use of it unusual is that the reports are shown to the officer concerned at the time. A commanding officer will not only show one of his junior officers what he has written on his annual report but will discuss the points with him. This system is constantly under review. But officers always opt to retain it, arguing that they prefer to know what has been written about them rather than have some unfriendly CO compiling nasty things behind their back. It all seems to work anyway, with the acknowledged weakness that a CO, embarrassed by having to show what he has written to the man he has just been drinking with in the mess, tends usually to over-mark. But the Military Secretary's department which handles the complex career structure always says that over-marking is a fact of life that it has learned to live with.

Each report gives a grading, as follows:

Outstanding (only 0·8 per cent ever merit this)
Excellent   (not very much less sparing)
Very good   (the officer has done more than asked of him)
Good   (the officer is worthy of promotion)
Adequate   (not much hope of advancing further)
Weak   (this means what it says).

The reporting officer also has to say whether an officer is worth promoting, according to one of the following timetables:

Yes now
Yes in his turn
Not yet
No

A high-flier after two two-year tours of duty as, say, lieutenant-colonel, one commanding his regiment and one in a staff job, might hope to get a 'Yes now' on his latest and a mix of four 'out-standings' and 'excellents' if he is to continue his rapid progress to the top.

Competition is intense. In 1976 there were 500 possible candidates for seventy vacancies as full colonels. The Military Secretary's department had the job of weeding out a top 300, whose reports would be worth the promotions board considering. This still meant four or five possibles for every job. It follows that an officer needs four 'very goods' at least to give him much chance of winning through.

Throughout his career there are chances for the high-flier to move still higher, widening the space between him and his more pedestrian colleague. There are also plenty of opportunities for him to come crashing to earth with a bump—and the shires are full of wistful looking gentlemen in tweeds who were once regarded as a hot favourite for a divisional command but who, for a variety of reasons, fell at the last fence.

The Army is always looking for high-fliers, opening up short cuts for them to move on to the next section of the course. An officer can be promoted to full colonel for instance at any time between the ages of forty-one and fifty-two, and to brigadier between forty-three and fifty-two. But the high-flier who wants to win one of the more illustrious brigadier command jobs—as opposed to some ad-ministrative post—must win promotion to his one-star rank by forty-three. In other words the officer who is really going places would become a lieutenant-colonel at thirty-seven, colonel at forty-one, brigadier at forty-three—and then major-general at forty-eight or forty-nine. There are sixty-six major-generals in the Army, and the number of brigadiers competing for each ranges from two to eight depending on the nature of the job. A plum appointment is the command of one of the Army's operational divisions, followed perhaps by a post as Director of Military Operations or Director of Army Staff Duties at the Ministry of Defence.

But there are only eleven lieutenant-generals, which makes it obvious to most officers that a major-general's badge of 'star above crossed sword and baton' is the highest to which they can realistically aspire. The lucky ones become lieutenant-generals at the age of about fifty-two, but the others have to retire after two postings as a major-general.

There are three promotion boards. The Promotion Board-3 con-sists of five major-generals and brigadiers who decide on the pink list—those majors who are to be promoted to lieutenant-colonel. The PB-2 includes five major-generals under the chairmanship of the Director of Army Staff Duties, who go through the blue list—

promotions to full colonel, and also the green list, from colonel to brigadier. The PB-1 with five full generals selects the major-generals. Above that rank all promotion is decided by the Chief of the General Staff himself, who knows them all anyway.

It is a complex, painstaking business, the boards meeting for five days at a time, first grading each candidate, then making the final selection. Some jobs are tied to a particular branch of the Army. Others are tied to certain age brackets, and the Army anyway tries to achieve a mix of ages to avoid blocking the promotion ladder at various points along it. For those officers who have not made it, there is the prospect of what the Army calls a 'little or no chance letter'—a regretful note informing them that there is now little chance of their advancing higher in rank. The idea is that these officers will at least then know their future, and can make provision accordingly. A lieutenant-colonel for instance would get his 'little or no chance letter' at about fifty. He can then get out if he wishes, or he can join the Special List—perhaps filling a major's post—until the age of fifty-five. He draws his ordinary pay for the first two years, but then remains at that level of salary for the next three years—regardless of any further pay awards that the rest of the Army might receive. Officers say that at least in the Army one knows where one stands.

Higher Defence Training. Those on their way to the top are likely to be sent for courses on Higher Defence Studies at one or both the Ministry of Defence's joint service colleges for senior officers. There used to be three but the number was reduced to two in 1977.

The first is the National Defence College whose six-month course is attended by a mixture of Naval, Army and RAF officers, together with civil servants and policemen. It is centred on an old house on a hill above the mellow Buckinghamshire village of Latimer. It used to be known as the Joint Services Staff College and overseas officers were also admitted. But it was restricted to British nationals when it became the NDC in 1971.

Army officers attend as lieutenant-colonels, and sometimes majors, but only after being to staff college. The chief complaint which has been made by the Army in the past has been that NDC training has come along at an awkward time in an officer's career—just when the brightest and best are wanted for important jobs elsewhere. The CAROT report argued that it should come either sooner or later—or not at all.

In 1978, however, the course was shortened from ten to six months and made more intensive. The basic idea is to encourage these budding young senior officers to look at defence in depth and in the company of their colleagues from the other services.

The symbol of the NDC is a cormorant—which lives on the land, in the sea and in the air. Cynics point out that the bird does not walk, swim or fly very well—and moreover smells very fishy. But the NDC, and the JSSC which preceded it, has inspired great loyalty among those who go there. The Cormorant Club to which old students belong, has branches worldwide, with its own sports teams.

The Higher Defence Training Establishment which closed was the Senior Officers War Course at the Royal Naval College, Greenwich. It was founded in 1900 by the First Sea Lord 'Jackie' Fisher and remained all naval until the 1960s when it was opened to the other services too.

In 1977 it was proposed that the NDC should move from Latimer to Greenwich on the closure of the Senior Officers War Course. The announcement dismayed the NDC Cormorants, present and past. For one thing they were reluctant to leave Latimer, which had been 'home' since the JSSC started in 1950. For another, they feared that at Greenwich the college would fall too much under the influence of the Royal Navy.

However, the proposal was dropped. Instead it was decided to close down another Ministry of Defence establishment, at Old Sarum in Wiltshire, and transfer the Joint Services Warfare school which had been there, to Latimer. In 1979 the Joint Services Warfare school, which runs a series of short courses for officers of various ranks, was combined with the NDC under one commandant— although the two have kept their separate identity. So the NDC has gained rather than lost from its brief encounter with bureaucracy.

The other Higher Defence Studies centre which thrives is the Royal College of Defence Studies in London. Only one in seventeen officers in the Army make it to the NDC. But only one in fifty go to the RCDS.

It was founded in 1927 as the Imperial Defence College, after a committee chaired by Winston Churchill decided that senior officers should study the defence of Empire. A promising young lieutenant-colonel called Auchinleck was among the officers on the first course. It was suspended during the Second World War. But it re-opened in 1946 because officers insisted that its teaching had contributed to the allied victory. Before the war it had been housed in Buckingham Gate. But since 1946 it has been at Seaford House, an early Victorian mansion in Belgrave Square. It changed its name to the present one in 1970.

About seventy-five attend the year-long course. Only forty are British—ten from each of the three services and ten from the civil

service. The others come from overseas; the Foreign and Commonwealth Office regard it as a useful way of winning friends and
influencing people.

The Army officers are brigadiers, apart from the occasional
colonel, and the assumption is that these will be modern major-
generals in a few years' time. There is no attempt to teach them their
jobs. The RCDS assumes that if they do not know them by that
time they never will. The purpose is to equip them for high command
by broadening their outlook. They attend lectures, take part in
seminars, engage in debates, read innumerable books on international relations and counter-insurgency and even on industrial
relations. They claim to do several hours homework a night. They go
to some lengths to 'hear the other chap's view' and travel widely—
including one prolonged overseas tour. But the lounge-suited
brigadiers who ascend the marble staircase at Seaford House for the
first time might well reflect that they are about to begin a rather
relaxed and enjoyable year.

There has been disagreement over how relaxed it should be. At
one time the courses contained an obligatory thesis of 10,000 words.
Brigadiers trained to précis everything down into simple Staff College
prose found this a tall order. The authorities came to the conclusion
that it was taking up too much time. So the thesis was pruned to
3,000 words, to the relief of those who had to write it—but to the
disgust of some academics.

Other Ranks. There is a less intense but equally complicated career
structure for non-commissioned ranks. It was introduced after a
report by the Committee on the Structure of the Army in 1964 and
is now well established. About 180 different career patterns are
woven into it, like a honeycomb.

Basic training for soldiers is less arduous than it is for officers if
only because it is shorter. It starts with eight weeks of instruction
on the Common Military Syllabus (CMS), as opposed to the six
months Standard Military Course (SMC) at Sandhurst. Then
soldiers like officers, begin special -to-arm courses of varying length.
The Army says that the more technical the corps, the longer the
training. But this is not immediately apparent with the infantry
spending twice as long on training as the REME and nearly twice as
long as the RE. It is also interesting that it takes most time of all to
train a cook in the Army Catering Corps and least time to train
gunners in the Royal Artillery. The list is as follows:

ACC	17	weeks
RAPC	15	weeks

RCT	10	weeks
R. Signals	10	weeks
Infantry	10	weeks
RMP	8	weeks
RAC	7	weeks
RPC	7	weeks
RE	6	weeks
RAOC	5½	weeks
REME	5	weeks
RA	3½	weeks
RAMC	3½	weeks

Promotion to lance-corporal is decided by the Commanding Officer and could come after only six months for the kind of young man seen on the recruiting poster, full of fire and determination. The average soldier is more likely to have to wait three years or more for his first stripe.

After that, the promotion ladder is held firmly in place by the records office of the corps or infantry division. Who climbs up it is decided after consultation between the records office and the CO. Relations between the two are usually close because the records office staff make a point of visiting units at least once a year to keep in touch. There is rarely any disagreement.

The Army has its own ideas about how long a soldier should serve before reaching a certain rank. The results are not far off Army targets. In 1973–74, the last year for which figures are available, the system worked as follows:

Rank	Target		Actual
Lance-Corporal	3	years	4·6 years
Corporal	6	years	6·8 years
Sergeant	11	years	10·1 years
Staff-Sergeant	14	years	13·2 years
WO2	16	years	15·9 years
WO1	18½	years	18·7 years

Soldiers' education was also examined and revised in 1971. Out went the Army Certificate of Education One, Two and Three. In came the Education Promotion Certificate (EPC) which a soldier has to pass for promotion to sergeant and the EPC (advanced) which he has to pass to become a warrant officer. The subjects are the same in each case—communications skills (English), military calculations (anything from measuring angles to keeping the bar accounts), military administration and contemporary world affairs. But the EPC (advanced) sets a higher standard.

Some soldiers realize after a year or two that their chances of promotion are slender, and these tend to leave after six years or even less. This has been made easier since 1972 when the Ministry of Defence brought in the notice engagement, allowing servicemen to leave at any time after giving eighteen months notice. The average length of stay for a soldier is now six years and has been going down gradually. But this is very much an average. In fact more than half leave after three years. But of those who stay for six years seventy per cent go on further, and after twelve years eighty-five per cent decide to make a career of it. They can even stay on after their full twenty-two years, joining the long serving list (LSL), for example, and continuing to serve until the age of fifty-five.

Others, however, may find a field-marshal's baton in their knapsack, or if not quite that then at least a passport to the officers' mess. Between 1967 and 1975 as many as 31·9 per cent of all officers had come up the hard way through the ranks. This percentage is fairly constant. The variety of commissions open to ambitious NCOs is bewildering. There are twenty-three types of Quartermasters' commissions alone.

The opportunities vary. Throughout most of the Army a number of soldiers who become Quartermaster officers ranges from below one per cent to four or five per cent. But in some of the smaller corps the chances are very much higher—up to nineteen per cent, for instance, in the Small Arms School Corps. There are similar discrepancies in the promotion structure for other kinds of commission. It is far easier to win a commission in the supporting corps than in the infantry, for instance, or in the cavalry, where the tribal system largely inhibits a man's chances of being promoted outside his division or even his regiment. In the REME, on the other hand, as many as 24·1 per cent of the soldiers are eventually commissioned. For some years the Army has been worried by the thought that the number of senior NCOs being promoted might lower the quality left behind in the sergeants' mess. So far, however, their worst fears have not materialized.

In some ways the Army resembles a gigantic training establishment dedicated to passing down the art of warfare from generation to generation. Training virtually never stops. Altogether some 2,236 officers and 10,490 soldiers are employed in training establishments, compared with only 755 officers and 6,565 soldiers who are actually on basic training at any one time. It is a costly business, although the expense of training particular trades varies almost unbelievably. On the one hand, an infantry soldier at the Scottish Infantry Depot at Glencorse can be manufactured for £1,605. It is slightly cheaper to train soldiers in Scotland than in England. On the other hand, it costs an incredible £137,400 to train an air gunner in the Army Air Corps, because of the cost of missiles and helicopter flying time. It is because the Army has to find this kind of money that it is always so concerned with getting its training schedules right.

5

Military Hardware

Weapon Procurement. The job of finding enough soldiers for the Army is hard enough. That of finding the right weapons for them to fight with is, if anything, worse. One reason for this is the widening gap between rising costs and shrinking resources. Another is the pace of technological change. At around £250,000 in the mid-seventies a Chieftain tank cost more than twice as much as the Centurion which preceded it. A Rapier anti-aircraft missile launcher costs eight times as much as the L40/70 Bofors gun which it is replacing—but is so much more effective that the Army cannot afford not to buy it.

The Army spends about a quarter of its annual budget on equipment. But only half of this goes towards buying new weapons or other needs. Ten per cent is devoted to research and development, and the rest goes on maintaining equipment already in service. Because it costs so much to look after an Army composed entirely of professionals, it seems unlikely that the share of the money which can be spent on equipment will rise. If anything the reverse has been true in the past. It follows that the Army has to be 200 per cent sure that the weapon it gets hold of is the right one.

Ironically the difficulties have increased in parallel with the need. Modern tanks are much more efficient than those which fought it out in North Africa during the Second World War. But how will they compare with those that armies might want by the end of the century—if indeed they will still want any at all?

The question is not just academic. It now takes between ten and fifteen years to produce a front-line weapon—the first four years to research on paper what the Army wants and the rest of the time to develop and make it. The services must try to make an expensive piece of equipment like a tank, a gun or a new missile last for between fifteen and twenty years. So a research programme which starts from a gleam in the eye in 1975 will result in a weapon which might still be in use in the year 2010. The Army sometimes reflects that what it needs most is a crystal ball.

It has been particularly difficult for the British Army since 1945 because of the country's changing role in the world. The £43,000 airportable 105mm light gun has a range of 17,500 metres, 7,000 metres more than that of the Italian made 105mm pack howitzer which it started to replace in the British Army in 1975. But it is doubtful if the Ministry of Defence would have gone to the trouble and expense of development had it known that Britain's presence East of Suez would have dwindled away by the time that the gun was ready for use.

There is also the question of money. Britain's resources have vanished along with its role. In time of financial hardship, the services usually have to look for savings in their equipment rather than their manpower. This is more difficult for the Army than for the Royal Navy or the RAF, because the Army is more labour intensive. Equipment used in the land battle is smaller and cheaper than ships and aircraft. But military equipment is more inter-dependent. If you take away one card, the whole pack falls down.

The 1974/75 Defence Review enforced cancellation of the Vixen, a small scout car similar to the Fox which survived unscathed. It also ended development of the RS80 rocket launcher—designed to deal with long-range targets. But savings have also forced the Army to coax a few more years service out of its FV432 armoured personnel carrier, and also its Ferret Scout car. Some of the money which would have been spent on replacing them will now have to go towards keeping them on the road.

A new dimension has been added to military procurement by the need to standardize Nato equipment. The most agreeable way to achieve standardization is for a number of the allies to make their new equipment together, in collaborative projects. A new family of helicopters has been bred by the mating of British and French expertise. A still more glowing example is that of the 155mm Field Howitzer (FH70) which has been produced for the British, West German and Italian artillery. These joint projects do not save as much money as was originally hoped, and they certainly take longer. Moreover, the Army has to be prepared to accept compromises to fit in with allied demands. But there are military, political and some economic advantages to be won and everyone is obliged to explore the possibilities.

The Army tries to decide in advance how its resources should be divided over the next ten years. Under existing plans, for instance, about a fifth of the equipment budget during the next decade will be spent on armoured warfare, about seventeen per cent on logistics, sixteen per cent on command and control equipment, eleven per cent on the infantry, six per cent on air defence, one per cent on electronic warfare and so on. There is very little stopping and starting in any of these programmes. It is more like painting the Forth Bridge. Nor can the Army afford to be capricious. Its progress has to be slow and methodical, not fast and intuitive.

The man most in need of a crystal ball is the Director of Combat Development (DCD) a major-general who plays the part of Merlin to the General Staff. He lives in the world of twenty years hence, drawing upon the experience of domestic and foreign intelligence as well as a number of arms specialists in the Ministry of Defence, to forecast what the battlefield then might look like.

It tends not to be a very abstract picture, and owes more to statistics and to war games carried out by the Defence Operations Analysis Establishment at Byfleet in Surrey, than to any reading of tea-leaves.

It is the job of the DCD to ask rather general questions about the direction in which the Army should move when shopping for the future. The man who has to answer such questions is another major-general, the Assistant to the Chief of General Staff (Operational Requirements)—or as he is usually known, the ACGS(OR).

The first phase in the procurement of new equipment is the preparation of a General Staff Target (GST) which outlines the job which the equipment should do, rather than the kind of equipment needed. It is prepared under the aegis of the ACGS(OR) but only after soundings have been taken of a number of other major-generals. He would, for instance, confer with the Director of Army Staff Duties (DASD), the Director of Military Operations (DMO), the Director of the Royal Artillery, Director of the Infantry, and allied counterparts, before presenting any papers to the appropriate committees at the ministry. (The Combat Engineering Tractor, a mechanized work horse for the Royal Engineers, started as an idea among the Sappers themselves.) Any important new programme would also be passed on to the Master General of the Ordnance at this early stage, so that the MGO, a full four-star general, can commission a preliminary study from one of the country's research and development establishments, or from private industry.

There are a number of committees. After the GST has been approved by the Army's own Weapons and Equipment Policy Committee (WEPC) it goes before the Operational Requirements Committee (ORC) a central body which is chaired by the Deputy Chief of Defence Staff (OR)—a post which rotates between the three services. Then it bounces back to the MGO who passes it on to the R and D establishment again for a feasibility study—a more detailed scrutiny of the technical prospects.

The principal establishments involved are the Military Vehicles and Engineering Establishment (MVEE) at Chertsey, Surrey, the Royal Signals and Radar Establishment (RSRE) at Malvern in

Worcestershire, the Rocket Propulsion Establishment at Westcott, the Explosives R and D Establishment at Waltham Abbey, the Summerfield Research Station at Kidderminster, Worcs., and—one of the most important—the Royal Armaments R and D Establishment (RARDE) at Fort Halstead, near Sevenoaks, Kent. But the MGO could again choose private industry for the study if that is where the expertise obviously lies.

It is on the basis of the feasibility study that the ACGS(OR) prepares his General Staff Requirement (GSR) which is the stage at which the project moves from the realms of fantasy into fact. The GSR sets out precisely what the equipment should be capable of doing, establishes the time it will take and estimates the cost, and supplies enough detail for a designer to start work on the weapon. Before being accepted the GSR has to run the gauntlet of more committees, including now the Defence Equipment Policy Committee, chaired by the ministry's Chief Scientific Adviser, which examines in depth the industrial potential and the budgetary prospects for the equipment, while the ACGS(OR) pleads his case. It might take a major piece of equipment four years to get this far. On the other hand, a small, inexpensive addition to the inventory might take only a few months—and it would also take rather less if the weapon was being bought off the shelf from some other country.

Whether the equipment is made by private industry or by one or more of the government's own eleven Royal Ordnance Factories (ROFs), production is managed by the MGO and his staff in the Ministry of Defence's Procurement Executive. One might say that the Director of Combat Development points to the need for a new weapon. The ACGS(OR) decides what weapon is required and the Master General of the Ordnance produces it—although in practice the division of labour is not as clear cut as that.

The MGO works through a trio of major-generals—the Director General Fighting Vehicles and Engineer Equipment, the Director General Weapons (Army) and the Director General Guided Weapons and Electronics. Beneath these come project management teams, one for each new piece of equipment. A team may be headed by a civilian or, more commonly by a serving officer—usually a colonel but sometimes a lieutenant-colonel.

The first objective of the development programme is to produce a number of prototypes. It is on the performance of these that the MGO decides whether or not to approve the new addition to the Army's offspring. Then the ACGS(OR) formally accepts it on behalf of the General Staff.

While the procurement machine moves forward slowly and ponderously, like an elephant, it can still put a foot wrong. One unhappy story is the development of the Rarden 30mm cannon, which was first designed by the Royal Armaments R and D Establishment at Fort Halstead. The contract was given to the Royal Small Arms Factory at Enfield in 1965, and the gun when completed was to be fitted to the Army's new Fox and Scimitar armoured vehicles, as well as the FV432, the main armoured troop carrier in service with BAOR. Seven years later after tortuous progress, the first production models failed their tests at the Proof and Experimental Establishment, Pendine in South Wales. The difficulties were dismissed as 'minor', however, and the project team cheerfully pressed on—only to discover twelve months later that there were basic faults in the design drawings and factory errors in some of the parts.

Production started again in 1974. But the Army then found that when the Rarden was fitted to the FV432 they could not squeeze all the ten men inside as well. That part of the plan had to be abandoned and several hundred guns erased from the Army's order. The trials did establish that the Rarden would be a valuable weapon, and it was eventually accepted into service. But the heady optimism which had accompanied them earned the Army a stern lecture from the House of Commons' Public Accounts Committee.

Not all new equipment takes a long time. Some of the ingenious gadgets developed for the Army in Northern Ireland have been rushed through, stamped 'Operational Emergency'. The Wheelbarrow robot for dealing with bombs was developed without a hitch for only £8,000 within a few weeks. But in general the Army has learned from experience that it is best to avoid cutting corners.

The Tank. Particular care has to be taken to ensure that the Army is equipped with the right kind of tank. Since before the Second World War the main battle tank (MBT) has been the Queen of the battlefield, the most important piece on the board. The Royal Armoured Corps has more than 900, which makes it a poor relation of the West German Army which has 4,000 or the United States Army with 10,000. But the tank is still the Army's biggest single investment.

The tank has recently looked more vulnerable than it used to. The development of anti-tank guided weapons (ATGW) and of missile-firing helicopters has led a number of pundits to conclude that the days of the tank as a primary weapon are numbered. On the other hand, there is still the need for a vehicle armed with a big gun to win space on the battlefield, so until some more ingenious solution is found there is little alternative to the tank as we know it.

Britain's MBT is the Chieftain, a 54-ton monster which began to replace the long-serving Centurion in the mid-1960s. The RAC loyally insists that it is the best tank in the world, and in many respects it certainly is. Its 120mm gun is not only the most powerful in Nato, but it is also very accurate with its new laser rangefinder. Moreover, the crew are well protected, with armour estimated to be about 150mm thick in the front, where it matters most.

The first priority in designing a tank is to give it a good gun and plenty of room for ammunition, so that it can carry firepower close to the enemy. The second priority is to coat it with thick armour so that it can survive on the battlefield. In both these respects Chieftain is well endowed. The third, however, is to make it as agile and mobile as possible, so that it can move quickly into action, and then get out of trouble.

In this respect Chieftain has looked less impressive. For one thing it has always been under-powered, because of its huge gun and weighty armour. The Mark-5 Chieftain has a 840 hp engine— similar to that in the highly successful West German tank, the Leopard-1. But while the 42-ton Leopard has a power-to-weight ratio of 21 hp for every ton, the Chieftain's is only 15:1. As a result the Leopard can trundle down a road at 40 mph, while the Chieftain can manage only 30 mph.

The L-60 engine in the Chieftain has also had a long history of trouble. Not only does it give off a lot of smoke, which has earned it the nickname of 'Smoky Joe' but it has broken down depressingly often. After continual research and a series of trials, colourfully called the 'Sundance Trials' the Army announced in 1978 that it had cured the L-60's overheating trouble and that the Mean Miles Between Failure (MMBF) rate had been improved by a third. But the RAC tank crews who had heard such reassurances before were keeping their fingers crossed.

Meanwhile they can look forward to Main Battle Tank-80 (MBT-80), the tank, so far only on the drawing board, which will replace Chieftain in the late 1980s. Originally it was planned to build a joint tank with the West Germans. Talks about the joint project called Future Main Battle Tank (FMBT) went as well as could be expected and the two armies came quite close to one another in their thinking. But they broke down in 1977, partly because the time-scales of the two armies were different.

So Britain is now building its own new tank, the MBT-80, details of which were announced in 1978. It will cost £1,000 million to develop and build 1,000 over the next fifteen years.

It will be fitted with Chobham armour, a new kind of armour pioneered by Britain in 1976, which offers protection against the latest anti-tank missiles. It will also have a 1,500 hp engine which should give the tank a top speed of 40 mph and a power-to-weight

4

ratio of about 27:1 which is more than twice as good as that of Chieftain.

More controversial has been the decision to fit it with a new British 120mm rifled barrel gun—an advance on that carried by Chieftain. The Germans have switched to a 120mm smooth-bore gun for their new tank the Leopard-2, and have succeeded in persuading the Americans to fit a similar weapon to about two-thirds of their new tanks, the XM-1. They had hoped that Britain might do so too in the interests of standardizing Nato tank ammunition. But Britain has politely declined.

The arguments over smooth-bore and rifled-bore revolve around the ability of tank shells to penetrate armour. By fitting fins to the shells and using a smooth-bore gun you can make the shells more streamlined. On the other hand, the Americans and now the British have developed a shell with a slipping driving band, which means that you can fit it with fins and still fire it from a rifled barrel. So the Army has argued that there is no advantage in changing to a smooth-bore gun. A rifled-barrel gives one more flexibility in using ammunition, so Britain has discarded German arguments.

MBT-80 will be assembled at the Royal Ordnance Factory, Leeds. The gun will be made at the ROF in Nottingham, and about six other ROFs will make ammunition for it. But MBT-80 will have a conventional turret, and to the uninitiated will look much like any other tank. It will also have the traditional crew of four. The alternative was to have an automatic gun loader and only three men. But automatic loaders can go wrong in the heat of battle. Moreover a four-man crew is less likely to suffer from fatigue.

Armoured Vehicles. Tanks were first used in 1916 to support the infantry on the Western Front during the First World War. Now the infantry support the tanks. Because they too need to survive in an armoured battle they travel in armoured personnel carriers (APCs).

Like tanks these vary in type according to differing military philosophies. The Russians and Germans have long held that an APC should be a fighting vehicle in its own right, with a substantial gun, and portholes in the sides through which troops can fire their rifles. Vehicles like the German Marder or the Russian BMP-76 roll into battle like porcupines, bristling with weapons.

The British and the Americans have looked upon APCs as taxis—a means of transporting troops to the battlefield and dumping them there to fight on their feet behind natural cover. For instance, the British FV-432, which since 1964 has been the standard APC with mechanized infantry battalions in BAOR, needs only a crew of two and can carry as many as ten men in the back. But its only armament is a single 7·62mm machine gun. The Marder by contrast has two machine guns and a 20mm cannon and is more thickly armoured. But it needs a crew of four and has room for only six more in the back. The BMP-76 can take eight in the back and still finds room for a 76mm gun—but is a more expensive vehicle anyway.

The attempt to fit the Rarden gun to the FV-432 was a sign that the British, like the Americans, have moved some way towards the Russo-German thinking. On the other hand, they had not moved so far that they were willing to compromise the APCs function as a battle taxi.

An APC is vulnerable to the new ATGW that armies are now acquiring. This is something which worries the Russians. An APC with a big gun needs to expose itself to fire the gun—but one hit from an ATGW could kill all the men inside. Britain is now developing the Mechanized Infantry Combat Vehicle (MICV), which will succeed the FV-432 in the 1980s. But it is likely to lean more towards the battle taxi concept for these reasons. It is all a question of how one sees the role of the modern infantryman.

While the tanks and APCs are fighting it out in the centre of the battlefield, reconnaissance and flanking operations will be left to another family of fighting vehicles which were brought into operation in the 1970s. Their official group name is Combat Vehicles Reconnaissance (Tracked) or CVR(T). But they are more commonly referred to as the Scorpion family, after the Scorpion light tank, their paterfamilias.

The Scorpion is made of aluminium armour, weighs less than eight tons and can drive down a road at around 55 mph. It also exerts a ground pressure of only 0·35 kilograms per square inch, which is less than that of a walking man—so it is very agile. Aluminium provides only about a third as much protection as does conventional armour so it is unlikely to be used for a MBT. But it should be good enough for a reconnaissance vehicle like Scorpion, which is fast and agile enough to get away from trouble.

Other members of the family are Striker which carries five Swingfire ATGW launchers instead of Scorpion's 76mm gun; Scimitar which has the Rarden gun—and would be used for short rather than long range reconnaissance; Spartan which is an APC; Sultan, a command post vehicle; Samson, a recovery vehicle for breakdowns; and Samaritan, an ambulance.

In the past Britain has had to produce a mix of tracked and wheeled vehicles because of the role she had to play in policing the Empire. But the role has now so diminished that wheeled vehicles like the Saladin armoured car and the Saracen car, which have trundled round the world since 1955, are unlikely to be replaced.

Artillery. Artillery is the oldest source of long-range firepower in the world. It has been used since ancient times when soldiers hurled rocks by catapult at siege fortifications. The operative word in the motto of the Royal Artillery is 'Ubique'—or 'Everywhere'. Napoleon, an artillery officer, said that it could decide the fate of nations—and 100 years later the big guns tried to do just that during the barrages of the First World War. This was the old French principle that artillery conquers while infantry occupies. Now armies appreciate the need for combined operations throughout.

It was the costly failure of static bombardment to enable infantry to break out of their trenches during the war, which caused artillery to enter a period of relative decline after 1918. Generals searching for mobility on the battlefield turned their attentions to the tank. Now the tank itself is finding its powers curtailed, and with advances in accuracy and range the Gunners believe that their power and prestige might once more be on an ascending graph. The armies of the Warsaw Pact seem to have reached the same conclusion, and their guns not only outnumber Nato artillery by three to one but tend to have longer ranges.

The most obvious development during and since the Second World War has been the pre-eminence of the self-propelled gun, reflecting the emphasis on mobility. At least this is so in Western armies, while the Russians still favour the towed gun. Divisional artillery in BAOR now consists of forty-two guns comprising thirty Abbot 105mm guns, six of the elderly 155mm American M-109s and six 175mm M107 howitzers. All are self-propelled. Within one minute these could drop a total of $7\frac{1}{2}$ tons of high explosive within a 100-metres square. The M107 on its own can drop its 135-pound shells on to targets twenty miles away.

Some changes are on the way. The most fundamental will be the introduction of the SP70, a self-propelled 155mm gun which is being developed jointly by Britain, West Germany and Italy and will replace the Abbot and the M109 in BAOR in the 1980s. This is part of a Nato decision to make 155mm the standard short and medium range calibre on the central front. The SP70—which should be called the SP80 because of the time it has taken to develop it—will fire a shell nearly three times as heavy as that of the Abbot. Using rocket assisted rounds developed by the Americans, it will also hit targets nineteen miles away—nearly twice as far as the Abbot. Another feature which pleases the Gunners is its ability to pump out three shells in the first fifteen seconds. This 'burst fire capability' is important because about eighty-five per cent of artillery casualties are caused within the first ten to fifteen seconds—before the troops on the other end have had time to get away.

Two more new guns are the FH70 and the 105mm Light Gun. The FH70 is a towed version of the SP70. Britain is buying only seventy of them at £300,000 each, and none will be stationed in BAOR. Only one regiment in Britain, and two volunteer regiments will be equipped with them. The Light Gun is an even more peripheral weapon, originally planned as a light airportable gun for the artillery in the days when Britain was still patrolling the far-flung outposts East of Suez. It still has a part to play with British troops sent to reinforce the flanks of Nato but it is arguably more valuable as an export commodity than as a British weapon.

Artillery like everything else has become computerized. Gunners who once sweated in their command posts working out range tables and measuring the effects on ballistics of changes in wind direction or speed, now talk blandly of FACE (Field Artillery Computer Equipment), or AMETS (Artillery Meteorological System), or PADS (Position and Azimuth Determining System) or even BATES (Battlefield Artillery Target Engagement System). Meanwhile Cymbeline, the latest mortar locating radar, can tell a battery almost at once the location of an enemy mortar position. The emphasis has been on accuracy because of the need to hit the target before it has had time to move.

Guided Missiles. So far the history of conventional artillery since 1945, like that of the tank, has been one of evolution, not revolution. Revolution has been brought to the battlefield by the guided missile. If the First World War belonged to the artillery and the Second World War to the tank, then the last quarter of the century seems likely to be the Age of the Missile. Men have been hurling missiles at each other since they discovered how to throw stones—but most of them have missed. Now with the coming of precision guidance they are more likely to hit.

The British Army has, or will soon have, seven different kinds of missile. Three are anti-aircraft weapons or surface-to-air missiles (SAMs) used by the Royal Artillery. Three are anti-tank guided weapons (ATGW) used by the RAC and the infantry and one is a tactical nuclear weapon or surface-to-surface missile, which adds a new and terrible dimension to the Royal Artillery.

The three SAMs are Thunderbird for medium range air defence, Rapier for short range and Blowpipe for close range. Thunderbird is being phased out after eighteen years service with the Army and it is not yet clear what, if anything, will replace it. With the enemy aircraft being forced to fly low beneath radar screens, more emphasis is placed on fast reaction missiles like Rapier—which is effective up to 15,000 feet—or Blowpipe, which is the kind of weapon soldiers will rely upon in the battlefield. Blowpipe is Britain's answer to the American Red Eye or the Russian Sam-7, though it works on different principles. In other words it is man-portable and is fired from the shoulder. Blowpipe which was developed privately by Short Bros. in Belfast, is the only weapon of its kind with an Identification Friend or Foe (IFF) device built into it—an important addition when a soldier has to decide in a second or less whether or not to shoot down a supersonic jet aircraft. Another advantage is that it is guided to its target by the soldier through a series of radio command signals. Red Eye and the Sam-7 are guided by infra-red. The missile homes on to the aircraft's jet exhaust, which means that the soldier has to wait until the aircraft has passed him—and no doubt bombed him—before he can hope to bring it down.

Meanwhile Rapier which is being brought into service with the RAF as well as with three Royal Artillery Light Air Defence regiments, instead of the old Bofors L40/70 anti-aircraft gun, is already a successful export product. It was narrowly defeated by the Franco-German missile Roland, in a contest to supply the United States forces with a low-level anti-aircraft system—and many Americans think it should have won.

The Army's ATGW are Swingfire (long range) which is used by the Royal Artillery, Milan (medium range), which is coming into service with the infantry and the SS-11 which is fitted to the Army Air Corps Scout helicopters. Swingfire has a thirty-four kilogram warhead with a range of up to 4,000 metres. Milan's warhead weighs only a fifth of that and has a range of up to 2,000 metres. Swingfire is a British development. But Milan is a Franco-German invention which Britain is making under licence. The Army decided to buy Milan after the 1973 Middle East war in which Arab infantry dented the prestige of the Israeli armoured columns with the Russian-made Sagger missile.

The Army was so impressed that it pushed Milan to the top of the shopping list—ahead of a new ATGW to replace the obsolescent French SS-11. However, it has now decided to buy the American TOW missile as a successor to the SS-11. The TOW which is already in service with a number of Nato armies will be fitted into the new Lynx helicopter which will shortly come into service to replace the Scout. The helicopter armed with TOW will provide an armoured commander with the ability to re-deploy his anti-tank defences rapidly if the enemy does the unexpected.

It is the development of ATGW which has encouraged some prophets to conclude that the tank has met its match. But armoured experts argue that ATGW are mainly defensive weapons which can offer little in the way of a counter-attack. Moreover, less than a quarter of the tanks destroyed in the 1973 Middle East war were destroyed by them. Most tanks fell victim to other tanks.

A missile controller needs a steady hand and if he is under bombardment from aircraft and artillery his hit rate can be very low. So he does not have everything going his way. He is likely to make life difficult for tanks, but not impossible.

The Army's other missile is Lance, the tactical nuclear weapon which has been bought from the United States. It has replaced Honest John which has been in service since the 1950s. Like Honest John it has its nuclear warheads maintained under American guard in a Nuclear Ammunition Supply Point (NASP) with a regiment of the Royal Corps of Transport and a nuclear escort unit to carry the warheads to the launchers of 50 Missile Regiment of the Royal Artillery if and when necessary.

But Honest John was a free-flight rocket with a range of only twenty-five miles and an accuracy no better than that of conventional artillery. Lance is a fully guided missile which flies at twice the speed of sound to its target more than seventy-five miles away. There are twelve of the launchers in the regiment. But Lance like Honest John comes outside the normal field of military operations. The artillery can be taught how to fire it. But when to fire it, is a decision they are happy to leave to others.

There is another newcomer to the artillery in battle called Precision Guided Munitions (PGM). This is a way of guiding an artillery shell by laser beam. The observing officer locates his target, orders a gun up to twenty miles away to fire, then fires a laser gun to illuminate the target. The shell picks up the laser beam and follows it to the target. This technique will again improve the first round hit capability and enable artillery in future to knock out tanks. It has been developed by the Americans following the success of the guided bomb in Vietnam.

Another new device is the pilotless aircraft, sometimes called a drone which can locate targets in depth. Very soon anything that moves or fires or emits electronic waves will be located and destroyed.

Helicopters. A newcomer to the battlefield, whose credentials are still being scrutinized, is the helicopter. It arrived on the scene too late to make an impact during the Second World War. Even in the Korean War it was used only for reconnaissance and for evacuating wounded men. Britain and France exploited its potential during the Suez Operation of 1956, and the French fitted cannon and rockets to it during the Algerian campaign to create the first helicopter gunship.

But the first true 'helicopter war' was that in Vietnam, where the American air cavalry and gunships like the Huey Cobra fired the military imagination.

Most of the arguments during recent years have concentrated upon the relevance of the helicopter to any war in Central Europe. Nobody doubts its value as a means of enabling one's soldiers to see what is happening in the enemy camp on the other side of the hill. But how much more can it do? In Vietnam the helicopter operated in skies which were controlled by the United States Air Force—but this is unlikely to be the case in Europe. Air space will at least be hotly contested.

The helicopter 'lobby' has proclaimed it heir apparent, destined to rule the battlefield in succession to the tank. To support its claims, a famous series of trials held at Ansbach, Germany, in 1972 ended with helicopter gunships scoring an eighteen to one 'victory' over an American armoured unit. Other trials have ended in favour of the missile-armed helicopter, with a superiority ranging from seven to one to as much as thirty-three to one.

These trials have almost invariably been 'loaded' in favour of the helicopter because not enough attention has been paid to the lethality of anti-aircraft missiles. But the Army Air Corps argues that even when this is taken into account the margin of superiority has been enough to demonstrate its advantages. A Cobra can after all fly in at around 250 knots, fire its anti-tank missile from a range of 4,000 metres while lurking among the tree-tops, then dart out of range again.

The potential of the helicopter as a weapon of war is beyond all doubt. On the other hand, some British estimates have suggested that in Central Europe helicopter losses could be as high as fifty per cent, even ten miles behind the front line. Moreover, bad weather and the number of high buildings and telegraph wires could restrict its treetop operations. For this reason attention is being given to making the helicopter less vulnerable. The helicopters can be designed to show a lower silhouette to any anti-aircraft missile unit. Body armour for the crew, better camouflage, pressure sensors to warn the crew of enemy fire might all help. Defence scientists are even trying to reduce the glint from the canopy, which could warn a distant military unit of an approaching helicopter.

As a result most soldiers acknowledge there is a role for the missile-armed helicopter. But it will be a restricted role. The helicopter can help to break up an enemy armoured offensive by sweeping in fast and low and unleashing its stand-off missiles. But it cannot afford to stay around for long because the tanks will be accompanied by troops firing anti-aircraft missiles—in addition to close support aircraft. It is one's own tanks and infantry who will still have to slog it out down below.

Britain has so far resisted the temptation to invest in a specialized gunship helicopter. The Army is equipped with two types, one a small reconnaissance helicopter and the other a general purpose aircraft—armed with an anti-tank missile. The first until recently has been the Sioux, which is now being replaced by the Gazelle, which can carry five men, including the pilot at around 150 knots. The Gazelle is a French-designed helicopter, one of three types developed under the Anglo-French agreement between Aerospatiale and the Westland company at Yeovil. The general purpose helicopter is the Lynx, bigger brother of the Gazelle, which has been designed by Westland. This can carry ten troops at around the same maximum speed as the Gazelle.

The Army is buying 158 Gazelles and 100 Lynxes. About sixty Lynxes will go to BAOR where they will probably be deployed in teams of six to complement the tanks, using their new TOW missiles. The Army is disappointed that it cannot get more men inside it. As a troop carrier it has severe limitations. But at least it is small enough to be carried long distances in the belly of RAF Hercules aircraft.

Moreover, there are two other helicopters which are being supplied to the RAF to support the troops on the ground. One is the Puma, big brother to the Lynx and the Gazelle. The other is the CH-47 American aircraft, better known as the Chinook. The Chinook, an old Vietnam veteran, can hold up to fifty troops, depending upon how much kit they are carrying. A Puma can take around twenty. One would need up to sixty Pumas to move a battalion—but the same job could be done by twenty Chinooks.

More relevant, a team of medium lift helicopters like the Chinook could be used to ferry heavy equipment—at least, in the rear areas of the battle where they would be less exposed to enemy fire. The RAF, however, will not have many of them. The total purchase in 1978 was only thirty, and about half of these will be used in West Germany, where they might be needed to support operations by the RAF Harrier. So its meaning for Army operations has yet to be assessed.

Small Arms. If the tank is the queen of the battlefield, the infantry-man with his rifle is the pawn—not the most powerful piece but at least the most ubiquitous.

For the last twenty years or so British soldiers have been armed with the self-loading rifle (SLR) a variant of the Belgian FN, which fires a 7·62mm bullet. Only about a sixth of a man's body represents

4*

the fatal area, in which a single hit is likely to kill him. From a soldier's point of view it is important to have a gun which will at least incapacitate the enemy if its bullet lands on the other five-sixths instead. One solution is to use a big, heavy round which will stop a man in his tracks even if it wings him. Cowboys in the American Wild West who were no better shots than soldiers, placed their faith in the Colt 45. Nato armies, after a series of trials in 1954 chose a similar answer with the 7·62mm bullet as the standard round. The SLR can stop a man at 1,000 yards if necessary—and if the soldier hits him.

However, the SLR is a heavy, cumbersome weapon with a fearful bang and recoil. The Americans soon found this out in Vietnam, and switched instead to the M-16, or Armalite, which is a much lighter rifle, firing a lighter 5·56mm round. This ended the brief honeymoon period during which Nato countries had managed to standardize their small arms—but soldiers in other armies have envied their American allies nonetheless. The British Army itself bought a number of Armalites for its troops in Borneo during confrontation between Malaysia and Indonesia during the 1960s.

Times have changed. At the turn of the century an infantryman had to learn how to bring down his enemy with a rifle shot at 1,000 yards simply because there was no alternative. Then came the machine gun to do the job for him, followed by the mortar and by advances in artillery. A graph published in *Jane's Infantry Weapons* in 1975 showed that ninety-six per cent of modern rifle engagements took place within a range of 400 metres, eighty-six per cent within 300 metres, seventy per cent within 200 metres and twenty-eight per cent within 100 metres. This bears out the Army's argument that 300 yards is about as far as one might reasonably expect a soldier to shoot from, given the stress of the battlefield, poor weather and uneven ground in Europe. In common with the allies therefore, the Army has been searching for a rifle which might be more serviceable at that range than the old SLR with its outdated 'overkill'.

Nato countries are once more trying to find a common solution. A series of trials are now taking place in Britain and West Germany, with the idea of deciding on a new general rifle which will come into service in the mid-1980s. The British Army hopes that the judgement of Brussels will fall on the British candidate at the trials. This is a buttless, stubby gun which has been designed by the Royal Small Arms Factory at Enfield. When fully-loaded it weighs only nine pounds and one ounce compared with the twelve pounds two ounces of the SLR. It is only 30·3 inches long, whereas the SLR is 44·5 inches, has much less recoil and makes far less noise. More important, 100 rounds of the new rifle's 4·85mm ammunition weighs less than half as much as 100 rounds of the 7·62mm bullets in the SLR.

Because the Army had emphasized the need for something cheap and practical the 4·85 cost only £180 at 1976 prices, compared with the SLR's £200. For a weapon to be actually cheaper than that which it is designed to replace must be in itself something of a record. It is also very flexible. Because it is light, short and capable of automatic fire, it can dispense with the need for a separate sub-machine gun like the Sterling. With a longer barrel and other modifications, it can also replace the general purpose machine gun (GPMG). And a soldier can be trained to use it more quickly than he can the SLR.

Sceptics point out that Britain had high hopes of winning the 1954 trials with a rifle not dissimilar to the 4·85—but failed to do so for a number of reasons, political as much as military. But the infantry is so enthusiastic about this latest development that it hopes that it may come into service whatever the outcome of the Nato competition. The most important objective of the allies is to standardize on small arms ammunition. A way might be found of keeping the new British rifle, even if Nato armies vote in favour of a different round from the 4·85mm. In that case the Royal Small Arms Factory would have to design a new barrel and magazine. But they might be able to retain the main characteristics of the gun.

The Engineers. The engineer is often the forgotten man on the modern battlefield. In fact, like the infantryman he helps to form the framework of the battlefield itself, denying areas to the enemy and forcing him into those directions that one wants him to take.

But military engineering like almost everything else has been affected by the search for bigger guns and faster movement on the battlefield. The old Bailey bridge—whose name is known to those who have never seen one—needed 100 men working for twelve hours to span a 100-foot gap. The Royal Engineers' medium girder bridge today, needs only thirty men working for less than one hour to do the same job. Someone should invent a better name for it.

Minelaying is another example. To sew a 1,000-yard line of mines in the Second World War required twenty-five soldiers working for sixteen hours. But the modern barmine vehicle enables four men to cover the same ground in an hour. Moreover, the Ranger multi-barrelled mine-layer can fire anti-personnel mines over a wide area in one burst to help delay an enemy advance.

Then there are general purpose vehicles like the Combat Engineer Tractor and the Light Mobile Digger (MMD). The LMD can dig a thirty-foot slit trench to the regulation depth of four feet six inches within a minute—a job which would have taken a soldier all day and probably longer. On the other hand, it needs to. The SP-70 gun will need a hole eleven metres square to sit in, which suggests a need for some mechanical aid. Actually engineers complain that soldiers have lost the art of digging themselves in—if only because they have not had to do so since the Korean War. (It is difficult to practise on exercises because it upsets farmers and ecologists. Soldiers, who detest digging themselves in anyway, are only too glad of the excuse.)

Not only is the battle more mobile, but it is likely to go on all night and in all weathers. Image intensification gunsights, night-driving goggles, alarm systems and surveillance radars are all being introduced to enable one's own troops to move while preventing the enemy from doing so. These devices are expensive, with an individual weapon sight, using light from the stars and the moon to 'illuminate' the target, costing around £2,000. But their effect on the conduct of the war could turn out to be as fundamental as that of the tank or rifle. An army must be able not only to move, but to see where it is moving—to know where it is going, in all senses of the phrase.

PART TWO

DEPLOYMENT

6

The Home Front

Troops in Britain. Up to sixty per cent of the Army is at any one time stationed in the United Kingdom. About thirty per cent is in BAOR and Berlin and the other ten per cent is scattered round the globe. It was not always so. Until 1967 the reverse was true, with most soldiers serving overseas. Their return has reflected Britain's diminishing role in world affairs, and the realization by successive governments that Britain could no longer afford to play the role of an international police force, even if it wanted to.

The change has been met by mixed reactions within the Army. Most soldiers stationed at home wish that they were overseas, while those who are overseas wish they were at home. That is a cynical commentary upon human nature rather than upon the average soldier, who has as much right to be contrary as anyone else. Experience suggests that married men, accompanied by their families, enjoy serving abroad. Single men prefer life at home. This is the reverse of what one might assume. But single soldiers find it harder to enjoy themselves when off-duty overseas, partly because of the language barrier and partly because they can no longer afford the high life of postings like Berlin and Hong Kong.

The military population in Britain, including wives and children, is about 230,000, and it is widely scattered. Fewer than one in three of the 43,000 married quarters in this country are to be found in the four main garrison areas of Aldershot, Catterick, Colchester and Bulford/Tidworth on Salisbury Plain. The others are spread over 160 different towns. Statistics bear out the old observation that soldiers are recruited in the North to serve in the South. While nearly half the soldiers, as opposed to officers, come from the industrial North of England and Scotland, only fifteen per cent are stationed there at any one time.

Only the Parachute Regiment and the Household Division have established garrison headquarters to which the families automatically return after a period overseas. The rest can be posted anywhere, which means that soldiers can have little chance to put down roots.

They belong only to the Army, which feeds them, houses, clothe them—and moves them on again when the need arises.

Since 1972 all troops at home have come under the Commander in-Chief United Kingdom Land Forces (C-in-C UKLF), a ful general. A senior officer on his way to becoming Chief of the Genera Staff (CGS) might expect to command either UKLF or BAOF before reaching the very top. There are still anomalies. Troops i Northern Ireland do not come under UKLF for instance, but those in Belize, Central America, do—and so do the training units at the Suffield exercise area in Canada.

The C-in-C has his headquarters at Erskine Barracks, Wilton—a minute but ancient town on the fringe of Salisbury Plain. The Army's interest in Salisbury Plain and its open windswept grassland dates from the middle of the last century when the growing scale o warfare forced regiments to search for more space to practise in In 1902 Southern Command was set up at Salisbury, and in 1940 early in the Second World War, it moved to Wilton several mile away. The present barracks was opened in 1964, first for Souther Command, then for Strategic Command and finally for UKLF, a successive administrations have struggled to reorganize the Army for its changing job.

Until 1968 Britain was divided into five geographical commands each under a lieutenant-general, and these were sub-divided into a total of twelve military districts under major-generals. In 1968 thi pattern was changed to four commands and ten districts, with a ne outfit called Strategic Command to control these operationa formations which were stationed in Britain, like 3rd Division an 16 Parachute Brigade. Then in 1972 came the next big reorganizatio when the geographical commands were abolished altogether and th C-in-C UKLF was created as a new overlord, with a lieutenant general as deputy. Under UKLF come only nine districts, each wit more autonomy than before. South-East District and Scotland ar commanded by lieutenant-generals, for slightly differing reasons while the others come under major-generals as before.

The present districts and the number of troops in each, as a June 1976, are as follows:

District	Regular Army	TAVR
South-East	17,500	8,000
South-West	19,500	3,000
London	12,000	7,000
North-East	9,000	10,000
Eastern	8,500	7,000
West Midland	5,000	4,500

Scotland	4,000	8,000
North-West	2,000	7,000
Wales	1,500	3,500
Total UKLF	89,000	58,000

(Figures for the regular Army include adults, male and female, junior soldiers, Gurkhas and Ministry of Defence headquarters staff. Units on emergency tours in Northern Ireland are included in their parent districts. TAVR strengths include regular soldiers posted to TAVR units.)

There are inevitable variations between the districts. Annual spending on such items as civilian pay, local purchase of stores, local repair contracts, fuels, electricity, gas, movement by road, rail and air, telephones and so on, varies from about £25 million for South-East District to £4 million for North-West District. But this does not include such items as soldiers' pay, civilian pay and spending on building works.

Such is the system through which the Army carries out its peace-time administration. If war broke out the picture would look rather different, although the organization is more relevant to the Army's operational plans than it used to be.

Fighting Formations. Until the 1974–75 Defence Review, the main fighting formations stationed at home consisted of the UK Mobile Force, the Joint Airborne Task Force (JATFOR) and Britain's contribution to the Allied Command Europe Mobile Force (AMF)— which Nato's Supreme Allied Commander in Europe (SACEUR) would immediately dispatch to any part of the European flanks in a crisis.

The UK Mobile Force comprised the 3rd Division headquarters and three airportable brigades, the 5th, 19th and 24th, a total force of nine battalions. JATFOR contained the headquarters of 16 Parachute Brigade with two battalions of the Parachute Regiment, while the AMF contingent was a battalion group totalling about 1,500 men. Other troops in Britain were simply earmarked for reinforcement of BAOR or for protecting the home front.

The economies introduced by the Defence Review forced the Army to take a long hard look at its shape in Britain as well as in West Germany and other parts of the world. Although the administrative organization was left more or less unchanged, the operational formations were altered once again.

First the Army sent 3rd Division headquarters to West Germany to form a fourth armoured division in BAOR. Then it abolished brigades as such to save manpower at operational headquarters. Finally it looked at a more economical way of organizing the troops in Britain in the event of war. The idea it came up with was to superimpose the operational formations on the district organization, so that some headquarters would be made to do two jobs. Although the new pattern was forced on the Army by its straitened circumstances, a number of senior officers—chiefly those who had designed it—argued that it was long overdue anyway.

So now Britain has three field forces, the 6th, 7th and 8th, each with a different role. The 6th Field Force, which is really a reorganized 16th Parachute Brigade, will take over from 3rd Division as the strategic reserve for SACEUR. It will only have five battalions instead of nine, and will be superimposed upon South-East District with its headquarters at Aldershot. It is commanded by a brigadier but when mobilized will be bigger than a division in BAOR which is headed by a major-general—so one wonders if the Army has yet got it right.

It means that Nato's Supreme Allied Commander will be able to use Britain's 6th Field Force wherever he thinks it is most needed. It consists of:

> One armoured regiment
> One armoured reconnaissance regiment
> One Royal Artillery regiment
> One Royal Engineer regiment
> Three Infantry battalions
> One squadron of the Army Air Corps
> Logistics Units
> Two TAVR battalions.

But not all the three Field Forces in Britain are quite the same. The 7th consists of a reconstituted 19th Brigade and has the job of reinforcing BAOR in wartime. This has been superimposed on Eastern District at Colchester, in much the same way. The 8th is centred upon South-West District at Bulford where it will form the nucleus of the C-in-C's reserve to defend Britain itself. The AMF battalion group has remained virtually unchanged, however, while the other airportable brigade, the 24th, has been scrapped.

One result of the changes is that for the first time in peacetime, the TAVR battalions, and some supporting units, will be in regular field formations alongside their professional comrades-in-arms—which pleases them immensely.

Each field force will eventually be equipped on the same level as the field formations in BAOR. But there will be variations in, for instance, artillery, APCs and other vehicles, depending upon the job each of them has to perform.

Another change took place at the end of 1977 when the Army centralized its 'tail' in Britain by forming a new Logistics Executive at Andover, Wilts. This combined under one roof a number of directorates which had previously been scattered in and around London. The directorates were those for transport, ordnance and electrical and mechanical engineering, so now the men who work out the Army's transport needs, its engineering support and its shopping list for food, clothing and ammunition, can work together for a change.

'Home of the British Army'. Anyone searching for the soul of the British Army is unlikely to find it at Wilton. He would probably not think of looking there, anyway. Most Englishmen associate the name of the place with carpets rather than soldiers—though as some soldiers lugubriously observe, they both get trodden on.

Wilton could hardly be described as its nerve centre either. This clearly resides still in London where about thirty buildings are given up wholly or in part to the Army, including the Ministry of Defence itself, the colossal War Office building next door and the lordly (from the outside) labyrinth (on the inside) at Horse Guards—where the major-general commanding London District inhabits one of the Army's more elegant offices. In terms of top brass London is certainly the most heavily weighted with a total of twenty-three major-generals, three lieutenant-generals and four full generals controlling different parts of the military machine.

The only town which actually lays claim to being the 'Home of the British Army' is Aldershot, which announces it on the road signs just as other towns welcome careful drivers. Few other garrisons could seriously quarrel with this. Aldershot and the Army are associated together in people's minds as easily and as inseparably as spit and polish or bugle and drum. The association goes back to 1854 when the Army put up a line of tents near the Basingstoke Canal at the start of the Crimean War.

In about 1961 the Army started to rebuild Aldershot military town, a community of about 20,000 people. It was to be its third incarnation. Down came the old barracks and the grim, Victorian terraced quarters. Up in their place went newly-married estates— situated in town for the convenience of the families—while the soldiers trained in new exercise areas on the outskirts.

The new buildings include the headquarters of the Parachute

Regiment, the Duchess of Kent barracks for the Women's Royal Army Corps and the new Buller barracks for the Royal Corps of Transport. Even the Royal Pavilion has been pulled down to make way for the new home of the Queen Alexandra's Royal Army Nursing Corps. Queen Victoria would not have been amused by that. But the most spectacular new development is the £3,500,000 fourteen-storey training centre for the Army Catering Corps, which is said to be the world's most up-to-date catering school with fifty-six training kitchens in which young would-be Army cooks can do their worst.

Aldershot also represents home for the Royal Army Dental Corps, the Army School of Physical Training and the riding school of the Military Police. The headquarters of the Army's blood donors' scheme, together with the abattoir where the Royal Army Ordnance Corps trains its butchers, are there. So, of course, is the headquarters of South-East District. The Royal Army Medical Corps, the Royal Army Ordnance Corps and the Royal Engineers all have head-quarters or units nearby. Even the Royal Military Academy Sand-hurst and the Army Staff College at Camberley fall within the official garrison area.

Aldershot is the Army's spiritual rather than its physical home. The garrison church of All Saints is known as the Army's cathedral and the superb sporting facilities represent the Army's Twickenham, Wembley, White City and Lords, where most of the big fixtures take place. The now biennial military display at the Rushmoor Arena is watched by about 250,000 people. Regiments which have been given the freedom of the town include the Parachute Regiment, the Royal Hampshires, the Army Physical Training Corps, the Royal Corps of Transport, the Army Catering Corps and the Canadian Army Overseas who were stationed there during the last war.

Nowadays Aldershot probably means less to the Army than the Army means to Aldershot. Most soldiers might end their careers without ever going there—except to attend a resettlement course on leaving. Although the 7th Regiment Royal Horse Artillery was based there as part of the old 16th Parachute Brigade, Aldershot means little to the Royal Artillery, not much more to the infantry and virtually nothing to the cavalry and the tank drivers in the Royal Armoured Corps.

On the other hand, the Army is the largest single employer in Aldershot with 3,500 civilians working for the Ministry of Defence and 2,500 more for the Department of the Environment. It is also the largest single ratepayer in the area providing about a quarter of Aldershot's rates and also a substantial percentage of those in Farnborough. Until 1974 three Army representatives sat as co-opted members on Aldershot council. While this right has been lost under local council reorganization, a number still serve as non-voting members on council committees.

The Cambridge Military Hospital is the main hospital in the area. as well as the best-known military hospital in the country. About forty per cent of the patients are civilians. The Louise Margaret maternity hospital has a similar dual function. Aldershot people join the Army's golf club and the Aldershot Officers' Club has as many as 700 local civilian members. Even the thousands of acres of training land on the edge of the town serve Aldershot well as a green belt, a defensive bulwark against the invasion of suburbia.

Colchester and Catterick. A far older military centre is Colchester, though the town is more famous for its oyster beds than for the 4,000 or so troops who are stationed there. It has served as a garrison for nearly 2,000 years, first for the Romans, then for the Normans and more recently for the headquarters of Eastern District and the units of 19th Airportable Brigade. Apart from three infantry battalions and an artillery regiment, Colchester accommodates the Ministry of Defence's Stores and Clothing Research and Development Establishment—about half of whose work is for the Army—a 114-bed military hospital and the Military Corrective Training Centre which serves as prison for miscreants from all three services. More than 1,250 Colchester civilians work for the Army in one way or another, and the annual military tattoo which makes money for local and military charities is one of the most colourful in the country.

A younger but better-known garrison is that at Catterick Camp in Yorkshire. If Aldershot can call itself the home of the British Army, then Catterick might be described as its northern annexe.

The history of Catterick goes back only as far as 1914–15 when a collection of huts was hastily erected to meet the exigencies of the First World War, at a cost of only £15,000. The decision to site a camp at Catterick was founded on a survey carried out under Lord Baden Powell, hero of Mafeking and founder of the Boy Scouts, who commanded the Northumbrian Division between 1908 and 1910. But the actual construction was carried out so hastily, without the Army waiting for proper roads to be built, that the first units moved into their new homes across a sea of churned-up mud. The image of Catterick as a muddy wilderness has persisted to this day. The garrison was originally called Richmond after the small, mellow, stone-built town down the road—but the name was changed because everyone mixed it up with Richmond, Surrey. The name Catterick actually comes from a local fall or cataract, in the nearby River

Swale—said to be the fastest-flowing river in England. (Army canoeists shoot its rapids—and the river wins as often as not.)

There are now between 11,000 and 12,000 at Catterick. But this includes only 5,000 soldiers. The others are families. The average soldier now has, statistically speaking, 1·9 children. Some 3,000 civilians also travel to work there every day, some of them driving the ten miles or so from Darlington. Although soldiers from a wide variety of units have served there, the camp is very much a stronghold of the Royal Corps of Signals. It accommodates two signal training regiments and the commander of the Signals Training Brigade usually doubles up as garrison commander. At any one time a quarter of the entire corps—among the biggest in the Army—are stationed there.

But the garrison also contains the training regiment of the Royal Armoured Corps (the unmistakable squeaking of tanks is a familiar sound in North Yorkshire), two infantry battalions, an artillery regiment and a number of smaller units. There is also a hospital and a resettlement centre for soldiers leaving the Army in the northern half of Britain.

The Army likes to think of Catterick as a town rather than a camp. Its population after all is twice that of Richmond. Public roads bisect the place and there is no all-encircling perimeter fence. There are clusters of shops and one or two banks, and certainly the 1,000 or so soldiers who moved into the muddy site in the First World War might have difficulty in recognizing the more permanent structure which arose from the Yorkshire Moors before the Second World War broke out. There are churches, a cinema, innumerable societies and sports clubs—all the trappings of twentieth-century urban living.

Richmond several miles away is undeniably a delightful little town which has managed to preserve its identity pretty well, considering that it has been overshadowed by Catterick for more than half a century. The Property Services Agency of the Department of the Environment has landscaped the camp itself as part of a £20 million rebuilding scheme, opening up walks and planting more than 6,000 trees to break the skyline.

Not only is the garrison being rebuilt, but changing lifestyles have helped to make Catterick more habitable. Soldiers now share taxis to and from work when the married quarters are shrouded by mist and rain, and the local hire car service reports a roaring trade. Troops are paid by cheque, like their officers, so that their wives have money in the bank—in theory, anyway—when the men are away from home. (There were nasty moments when the local banks first started to issue cheque books to the long, the short and the tall, but most soldiers now handle their money intelligently.) Soldiers grow to like the place so much that many have settled nearby after retiring from the Army. The local fish and chip shop is run by a former sergeant-major—and a number of other shopkeepers have the familiar short-back-and-sides haircuts of their military generation.

But if Catterick does not resemble everyone's preconception of a camp, it is still far from being a town. Its architecture would always give it away. While pleasant enough on a summer's day, when the birds are perched high in the PSA's trees and the air is clear and bright, its 21,000 acres—including training areas—can look forbidding in wet weather. This might be true of most places, But in Catterick the charms are obvious mainly to those with a taste for the outdoor life. The PSA admits sadly that thirty-five per cent of the trees that it plants every year fail to see their first spring. About fifteen per cent are destroyed by vandals, because Army fathers are no better than civilian fathers at controlling their children. The others give up the unequal fight against the Northern winter. Even Richmond, for all its picturesqueness, can present a depressing prospect to a forlorn young single soldier on a Saturday night, a long way from home. Many soldiers now have cars, and can venture farther afield, driving to Darlington, Middlesborough, South Shields, or even Newcastle in one direction, and Leeds in another. But the picture which many former conscripts still have of a windswept colony in the middle of nowhere, is not entirely without foundation.

Accommodation. Army life in Britain is being changed physically and socially by new accommodation programmes. In London the best-known rebuilding programmes since the war have included new barracks at Chelsea and Knightsbridge, for the Foot Guards and the Household Cavalry respectively. But on Salisbury Plain, too, new blocks have mushroomed at Bulford, Tidworth and Warminster. Elsewhere barracks put up before the Second World War are being de-gutted and modernized.

Instead of building the old type of dormitory accommodation for single soldiers, the Army is trying to move towards a system of self-contained flats for a dozen or more men. These should provide single rooms for NCOs and four-man bedrooms for private soldiers, with shared sitting rooms, kitchens, bathrooms and even ironing rooms. But shortage of cash and the uncertainties involved in planning for the future have hindered the programme, which involves 150 existing barrack blocks.

And soldiers still complain, sometimes bitterly. Soldiers always do complain, of course. But now their expectations are far higher than in the past, and young men demand more privacy and bed space than their ancestors were used to. Moreover, with so many of their companions married, single soldiers often feel they are becoming an under-privileged minority. In some stations hutted camps have been kept in use long after their time, storing up problems for the future. There is a long way to go before the Ministry of Defence can satisfy itself and its critics that the work has been completed. Perhaps it never will be.

Some relief has been supplied by the closure of a number of RAF airfields after the 1974–75 Defence Review. This has provided some ready-made accommodation for the other two services. The airfields are not always where the Army would like them to be. But it has made use of some of them, saving itself capital investment on new building programmes, by shuffling the pack. Thus the Royal Corps of Transport's driving school has been moved to an airfield in Yorkshire, and a unit moving from Salisbury Plain to join the new 6th Field Force has gone into the driving school's old quarters at Aldershot.

Married quarters cause continuous trouble for the Army. This is partly because it has to pacify wives, who tend to be more critical than their husbands, and partly because the whole system of providing married accommodation is complex.

The total number of 43,000 married quarters in Britain is about right, given that the Army now has a married strength of about fifty-five per cent. But the houses are not always in the right place. There are always more than enough houses where the Army does not want them, and an awful shortage where it does. Even when the Army puts up families in privately rented accommodation, some wives complain of having to hang around for more than six months in temporary quarters before being settled. There is even a married families hostel at Corsham, Wiltshire, where these nomadic people have to live while the Army finds them a more permanent home. But the standard of accommodation there is not up to much and the Army cannot leave them there for long.

It is not as if soldiers all had the same kind of married quarter. There are variations in size, quality and rent. Private soldiers and NCOs are awarded houses according to a complicated points system which takes a number of factors into account, including rank and seniority but most of all the size of family. A regimental sergeant-major is entitled to a four-bedroomed house, however large his family—and in 1976–77 was paying an annual £474 for it, including the cost of hiring the furniture, maintenance and what is the Army's equivalent of rates. But other ranks have to put up with the points system. A family with no children or with one child would be entitled to a two-bedroomed house (£380), a family with two or three children to a three-bedroomed house (£438) and a family with four children to a four-bedroomed house—just like the RSM.

The grumbling is constant. There are complaints about the standards of maintenance and the furniture, about the points system—which is said to lean too far in the direction of seniority—and complaints about the cost. The Army has tried to make the rents comparable to what a soldier might have to pay as a civilian; at least this has been the custom since the Military Salary was introduced. Opinions vary on how fair this is to the soldier concerned—but the soldier concerned, not unnaturally, always thinks that he pays too much.

Officers' houses are allotted according only to rank. Lieutenants and captains live in three-bedroomed houses (£610), majors (and captains with more than three children) in four-bedroomed houses (£723) and lieutenant-colonels, colonels and brigadiers in five-bedroomed houses (£821). Generals live in up to six-bedroomed 'residences' rather than houses, classified by the Army as Type-one or Type-two according to grandeur. A Type-two in 1976–77 cost a total of £923 and a Type-one £1,033. But there are not many of these around. HQ UKLF at Wilton has only one Type-one for instance—and that is for the commander-in-chief.

Home-buying. Housing problems both in the Army and in the country at large have encouraged an increasing number of soldiers to buy their own homes. Since 1973 there has been a seven per cent increase in house ownership among majors and lieutenant-colonels and a nine per cent rise among junior officers. So far there has been no similar increase among private soldiers and NCOs, but the Army is biting its finger nails with the fear that one might come along.

In mid-1976 about sixty-two per cent of all officers owned their own homes, although they were not necessarily living in them at the time. So did fifteen per cent of other ranks. Broken down into ranks, the figures were:

Officers: Brigadiers 79 per cent; Colonels 78 per cent; Lieutenant-Colonels 72 per cent; Majors 69 per cent; Captains 50 per cent; Subalterns 35 per cent.

Other ranks: Warrant Officers 44 per cent; Staff Sergeants 28 per cent; Sergeants 21 per cent; Corporals 8 per cent; Lance-Corporals and Privates 5 per cent.

One might have thought that the Army would encourage soldiers to buy their own homes if only because this relieved the pressure on married quarters. But there are disadvantages too—sometimes for the soldier himself but nearly always for the Army.

The 1974 Rent Act made it more difficult for house owners to regain possession of property they had rented out. Maintenance can be expensive, and income tax relief on mortgages is not allowed unless the house is let at a commercial rent or is occupied by a dependant relative. These difficulties might cause financial worries for the young officer who has bought a house for his family to return to on leaving the Army, and might distract him from his regimental duties. At least—this is one argument put forward by the Army. It must be said that the same young officer might be more easy in his mind after buying his house because of the comfortable feeling that he has invested in his future.

Many leave their wives and children at home, while they live a bachelor's life in the camp, miles away, staying in the single soldiers' barracks or officers' mess. This is the trend which most worries the Army. A soldier is allowed twelve 'leave and separation' travel warrants a year. But he would have to pay for all other journeys home to see his family at weekends. This means he is faced with the choice of paying this commuting expense every week, or staying on camp, drowning his sorrows in the bar with his bachelor colleagues.

The divorce rate is rising in the Army, as it is everywhere else. Although there is no certain correlation, the tendency among soldiers to join their families only at the weekends, cannot help. The Army has enough separation problems already without having any more heaped upon it.

But even if the family does not suffer, the regiment does. The Army is not only a collection of regiments. It is also a collection of little communities, in which the wives have their place. If more and more wives are to forego the doubtful pleasures of following the regiment around, trailing their children with them, something will be missing. Moreover, as more officers' wives than other ranks' wives are involved, the whole balance of social life on camp could be affected. However difficult it may be to sort out married quarters, the Army would prefer its families to live in them, so that the regiment, or battalion or squadron, can live together—like one big happy family.

It is easy to see why so many soldiers prefer to ignore this argument. Many have already been caught by rocketing property prices. Like clergymen, policemen and even some bank managers, they have watched in dismay as the cost of a new house has climbed beyond their reach. Meanwhile they have had to pay rent for married quarters, with nothing to show for it except a lifetime of living in someone's else's house, eating off Ministry of Defence tables and sitting on Ministry of Defence chairs.

It is also an age of working wives. Even officers' wives often work, as teachers perhaps or secretaries, to supplement the family income. Again the Army would prefer them not to, but there is little it can do about it. Many of these wives find it difficult to get the jobs they want when travelling with the regiment—partly because the camp may be some distance from the nearest town and partly because employers are reluctant to hire women who are certain to move away again after a year or two. So many wives find it more convenient to stay in one place, in the family home, guarding and improving the nest for the husband to fly back to at the weekends.

Then there is the constant worry over education. Even if soldiers take advantage of the grant which is paid to them on a flat rate, they still have to pay substantial fees when they send children to boarding school. There are two boarding schools in Britain, sponsored by the Ministry of Defence, which offer free board and education to service children. These are the Duke of York's Royal Military School at Dover, which is for the sons of privates and NCOs, and the Queen Victoria School for the sons of Scottish Sailors, Soldiers and Airmen, North of the border at Dunblane. But selection standards are said to be high.

As a result forty-two per cent of officers' children in Britain and only four per cent of privates' and NCOs' children attend boarding schools. For the Army as a whole the figures are forty-five per cent (about 8,800) officers' children and six per cent (4,700) other ranks' children. The rest have to go to day schools, trudging from one school to another as the regiment moves on, often moving in the middle of a term—since the Ministry of Defence can hardly plan every military re-deployment to coincide with the school calendar.

The Plowden Committee in 1966 drew attention to serious backwardness among Army children because of frequent school changes—and even the loss of schooltime altogether. Not surprisingly many wives opt to stay at home and send their children to the local school.

Training Areas. Keeping the soldiers happy is one thing. Keeping them up to scratch in their military skills is another—particularly in an age of precision-guided munitions, when the demands on their specialized skills are growing day by day. The Army is not only having to cope with the quickening pace of technology; it is also having to combat pressures from environmentalists and conservationists who see no reason why large tracts of fine British countryside should be defiled by the sound and fury of mock battlefields and by barbed-wire fences, punctuated by stern warning 'Ministry of Defence—Keep off!'

Of the 88,982 overcrowded square miles in Britain, the Arm either owns or leases 588 square miles for training—or about 0·6 per cent of the whole. How large or how small a percentage th represents seems to depend upon whose side one is on. Thes training lands are distributed as follows:

District	Square miles	Percentage of district area
South-West	199	2·16
North-East	127	1·37
Wales	71	0·89
South-East	53	0·73
Eastern	42	0·32
Scotland	41	0·13
North-West	37	0·65
West Midland	12	0·24
London	6	0·79

Some of these lands are major training areas used by units from all over Britain who need to practice large-scale manoeuvres an live firings of weapons. Others are local areas for use by particula garrisons, establishments and units.

The major training areas in the United Kingdom are:

Salisbury Plain	91,000 acres
Otterburn, Northumberland	56,000 acres
Sennybridge, Wales	30,000 acres
Catterick	21,000 acres
Aldershot	11,000 acres
Stanford, Norfolk	18,000 acres
Warsop, Cumbria	24,000 acres
Dartmoor	15,000 acres
Cinque Ports	10,200 acres
Castlemartin, Wales	5,900 acres
Cultybraggan, Scotland	5,100 acres

All Ministry of Defence lands in Britain were studied by th Nugent Committee 1971–73, which was set up to review th Ministry's holdings after pressure from conservationist groups. Mos of the committee's recommendations were accepted by the Govern ment, although these fell far short of pleasing the environmentalis lobby. But its main recommendation, that the Royal Armourec Corps should surrender its gunnery school area at Lulworth, a beautiful stretch of Dorset coastline, and move to Castlemartin instead, was turned down. One reason for the Government decision was the cost. Another was the difficulty of accommodating the Army at Castlemartin, which for much of the year is given over to the German Army for tank training—a kind of *quid pro quo* for the German lands used by BAOR. But the Army has been obliged to make the land around Lulworth more accessible to members of the public. Not all environmentalists object to the Army's presence in some of the country's beauty spots. By keeping the public away it allows the flora and fauna to flourish undisturbed. The Ministry of Defence has now appointed a conservation officer, a retired lieutenant-colonel, in response to a recommendation by the Nugent Committee and an important programme of cataloguing the wild life on its training grounds is well advanced.

There are severe limitations which worry the Army's training officers. One is the shortage of space for live-firing exercises, involving, for instance, long armoured battle runs. The other is the lack of variety in terrain and, of course, climate. To some extent these can be overcome by training overseas. The most important addition in recent years has been that of the training area at Suffield in Alberta, Canada, where the Army really can exercise large battle groups, deploying realistic armoured formations. The eyes of RAC commanders light up when they talk about it, and the Ministry of Defence is anxious to renew the lease from the Canadian government when this expires in a few years' time. How far the discovery of large mineral deposits under the same land will affect this issue has still to be determined.

The Army also sends units to a variety of overseas locations during the year, testing them in arctic wastes one time and primary jungle the next—although the loss of the Jungle Warfare School in Malaysia following the withdrawal from Singapore is one which has always been lamented. Units also, of course, have to train with their allies in Europe.

But the recent defence cuts have made things more difficult again. Not only has the Army's own budget been tightened, but the RAF's capacity to lift large forces for a training exercise has been affected by the dramatic reduction in the fleet of transport aircraft. This in turn has thrown the Army back upon its resources in Britain. Not only are the major training areas limited in the scope they offer to military combat units, but there is now a danger that they will become over-used.

7

The Front Line

The Development of BAOR. The British Army of the Rhine (BAOR) was carved out of the forces occupying Germany in 1946. At first there were to be only two divisions, the 7th Armoured (the Desert Rats) and the 2nd Infantry, whose emblem consisted of two crossed keys. But it was expanded during the Cold War in the early 1950s.

In 1950 itself the 11th Armoured (the Black Bull) was re-formed and dispatched to West Germany, and in 1952 the 6th Armoured (the Mailed Fist) followed it. In 1951–52 the four divisions were grouped into the 1st British Corps which had just been re-formed with its headquarters at Bielefeld, and in 1954 the headquarters of BAOR was switched from Bad Oeynhausen to the village of Rheindahlen, five miles from Munchen Gladbach, where a familiar maze of Officers' Messes, office blocks and short-back-and-sides lawns quickly appeared.

Since then BAOR has continually changed in size and shape. From a strength of 77,000 during the Cold War it has been reduced to around 55,000. This is the minimum figure required by the various protocols to the Revised Brussels Treaty of 1954, but it does not include the troops in Berlin.

In 1956 the 11th Armoured Division was replaced by the 4th Infantry—whose flash shows a red circle with a displaced segment. But by the early 1960s the pattern had changed again, from two armoured and two infantry divisions to three combined arms divisions with a little bit of everything, including nuclear artillery. Then came the restructuring of the Army after the 1974–75 Defence Review, which gave BAOR the four smaller armoured visions that it has today.

If one adds up everyone, the total number of British soldiers on the Continent is around 61,000. This includes 55,000 in BAOR, the brigade, or field force, with about 3,000 in Berlin, and 3,000 others who are scattered in small pockets at various Nato headquarters and at Emblem, the village outside Antwerp—which would be the main port of entry for British reinforcements during any future war.

BAOR itself can be split into two main parts. The better known is still the 1st British Corps at Bielefeld with about 9,000 troops, commanded by a lieutenant-general. This is by far the biggest operational command job in the Army and the man who gets it usually moves on to become a full general with a seat on the Army Board. The other part of BAOR is the Headquarters of Rhine area at Dusseldorf, which is a geographical command including mostly logistic troops.

The divisions of 1st Corps are now the 1st, the 2nd, the 3rd and the 4th, all armoured divisions with only 8,500 soldiers each in peacetime and nearly 14,000 after being plumped out by wartime reinforcements. The 1st has its headquarters at Verden, the 2nd at Lubbecke (this is the only division which has been there from the start) the 3rd at Soest and the 4th at Herford. The headquarters of 3rd Division, which once formed the most part of Britain's strategic reserve, moved there from England in the autumn of 1977 as the extra division after restructuring.

Two other formations were created in the 1st Corps under the restructuring programme. One is the 5th Field Force, an infantry formation of 4,000 men with its headquarters at Osnabrück. The other is an artillery division, the first ever to be formed in the British Army. This has replaced the two artillery brigades which once divided the 1st Corps artillery (as opposed to the divisions' own artillery) between them. Instead of having one brigade to protect the corps with anti-aircraft fire and another to look after long-range general support bombardment, there is now the one division. The idea is to save on headquarters staffs.

Each of the new armoured divisions contains two armoured regiments with Chieftain tanks; one armoured reconnaissance regiment; three mechanized infantry battalions with armoured personnel carriers; a close-support artillery regiment with four batteries of Abbot 105mm self-propelled guns and a battery of Swingfire anti-tank missiles; one medium-range general support artillery regiment with two batteries of M-109 155mm guns, a battery of M-110 203mm howitzers—which have nuclear shells—and a battery with Blowpipe anti-aircraft missiles; one Army Air Corps regiment with twenty-four helicopters, half of which will be Lynx helicopters armed with the American Tow anti-tank missile; a regiment of Royal Engineers—and all the other supporting bits and pieces. (The armoured reconnaissance regiment will have two squadrons of Scorpion light tanks, with its 76mm gun, for long-range work, and one squadron of Scimitars which are armed with the Rarden 30mm cannon for closer range reconnaissance.)

The new artillery division contains: one general support regiment with four batteries of the M-107 175mm long-range gun, capable of destroying tanks twenty miles away, if they have not moved by the time the shells arrive; two regiments with Rapier anti-aircraft missile; a regiment of four batteries with the Lance nuclear missile; and 94th Locating Regiment which is the largest artillery regiment in the Army.

The 5th Field Force consists of three infantry battalions with wheeled vehicles as opposed to tracked APCs; an armoured reconnaissance regiment; one artillery close support regiment and a squadron of engineers. It has no tanks.

The original plan to restructure BAOR has already had to be slightly modified. Brigades were abolished, as they were elsewhere in the Army. As the divisions in Germany had been made smaller the Army thought that a divisional commander and his headquarters staff could cope on their own without subordinate commands to parcel out the tasks. But a series of trials showed that this was not so —particularly as the existing communications equipment was not comprehensive enough. The staff complained that they were overwhelmed by the flow of detail.

So the Army has been forced to compromise. Each divisional commander can use two Task Forces in wartime, which would be commanded by brigadiers. The same brigadiers work as garrison commanders in peacetime. Cynics have suggested that the Task Force is a face-saving invention to cover the fact that the restructuring scheme had partly failed. But the Army has argued that a Task Force headquarters is smaller than that for the old brigade—so there is still some manpower saving. It is also a very flexible formation and can vary in size or scope according to the situation.

BAOR then ran into another problem—that of overstretch. As an army it has been overstretched for some time because of the Ministry of Defence's need to 'borrow' up to seven units at a time for duty in Northern Ireland. But restructuring made this worse. The main cause was the Army's decision to cut the manpower in the regiments while keeping the same amount of equipment—or even increasing it. In armoured regiments, for instance, the number of tanks went up by fifty per cent, while the number of men went down. The overall ratio of weapons to men was raised by thirteen per cent—which at the time sounded like something to boast about. But for the men who had to share the extra workload, it was not so funny.

The burden was heaviest on those units which man heavy equipment. As weapons become more complicated troops have to be sent on longer courses to learn the new technology—so regiments have a number of men away from camp. In wartime it would not be so bad because many of the peaceime jobs with which the soldiers have to cope would quickly disappear. There would be no need to look after married families or to find a steward for the Officers' Mess. The married families would return to Britain and the regiments themselves would move out of their bases to battle positions.

However, in peacetime conditions these simple daily chores have to be looked after. Commanders complained of soldiers in REME workshops working seventy-hour weeks, and at one time up to fifty Chieftain tanks had to be withdrawn from day-to-day use because there were simply too few men to man them. The increases in manpower announced for the Army in 1978 were designed partly to end the difficulty. About half of the 4,000 extra men given to the Army in August 1978 were destined for BAOR—most of them to add some fat to the bones which had been scraped clean by the reductions imposed by the Defence Review. This still left BAOR with some manpower problems, but at least it helped to relieve some of the strain.

War Plans. If war did break out, there would be bigger problems than overstretch to worry about. For instance, the job of dispatching the families back home would be more complicated than it sounds. There are 76,000 women and children, which is more than the number of men. There are contingency plans for moving them all. But no one envies those who would have to put the plans into practice.

The moves involved in restructuring were bad enough. Some twenty-three major units and forty minor ones had to be uprooted so that the headquarters of 3rd division could be fitted into the jigsaw. This meant shifting 18,000 soldiers and 23,000 dependents. Schools, Naafis and all the other paraphernalia of camp life were suddenly found to be not exactly where they were most needed. At least, this was true in some cases.

Moving the families in wartime would be much more difficult. They would probably have to be transferred along roads, railways and air routes already jammed with military reinforcements moving one way and refugees the other. So it would be important to get them out at precisely the right moment. Not too soon, because that might worry the Russians; not too late—because then the families would never make it in time.

Not only would the families be on the move, but so would the troops. In some cases they would have to move quite far. Most of them are stationed where they are, not because that is the most convenient place for them in wartime, but because that is where there were empty barracks after the Second World War. To re-locate

5

them now would be far too expensive, even if alternative sites could be found nearer to the front line. So the units have resigned themselves to having to travel some distance across country, through teeming towns and picturesque German villages, before they reach the front line.

BAOR belongs to Nato's Northern Army Group, which in wartime would have to defend the Northern part of West Germany. Northag consists of four corps, one Dutch, one Belgian, one German and the 1st British Corps. Its Commander-in-Chief is traditionally—though not necessarily—the C-in-C of BAOR wearing his wartime Nato hat.

The condition of Northag pleases no one very much. Most people expect that if the Russians really did decide to invade Western Europe they would do so across this North German plain where the ground is open, rather than in the South. It is arguable, therefore, that the two superbly equipped American corps should be stationed in the North, not in the South. One and perhaps two American brigades are indeed being moved to the North to bolster the Northag hotch-potch.

There are also worries about getting Northag's heterogeneous forces into the right places by the right time. BAOR troops may not be ideally located, but the locations of the Dutch and Belgians are much worse. Moreover, BAOR itself would need reinforcements from Britain to bring it up to its wartime strength—which is more than double its present size. And its scattered units may have to be brought back from various places—from Northern Ireland for instance, or the tank training grounds at Suffield in Canada.

The 1st Corps' four divisions would fight in what is called the Forward Combat Zone (FCZ). The artillery division would be deployed in the corps area according to need, while the 5th Field Force would operate behind the divisions, protecting their flanks and rear, ready to counter any breakthroughs. (This saves the 1st Corps commander from having to draw back some of his front line strength to do the same job.)

BAOR as such would disappear along with its C-in-C. He would promptly put on his Northag hat and move to his wartime head quarters, a secret location still further west than his present one at Rheindahlen. From there he would commute to his mobile head quarters in the battle zone as he felt necessary. Meanwhile logistical troops would be grouped into yet another organization called British Logistics Support Command under the present BAOR Chief of Staff, a major-general. This command, operating in the Rear Combat zone (RCZ) would be responsible for getting the 50,000

British reinforcements into line and for ferrying back up to 2,000 casualties a day.

If the Russians really did attack, Nato troops would conduct what is called a mobile defence. Instead of being met by a thin red line the Russians would find themselves confronted by a series of red blobs. With the help of the local terrain, these red blobs, or allied battle groups, would try to impede and divide the enemy, funnelling his advancing forces into prepared 'killing zones' where they would be engaged on all flanks by mobile allied units.

In other words, the Russians would run into not so much an oak tree as a willow which would bend but not break. It would give a little here, whip back a bit there, absorbing and containing the shock of the onslaught.

Mobile defence as opposed to positional defence—like the Maginot Line and the trenches of the First World War—has a long pedigree. It can be traced back even to Genghis Khan. When your borders are long and when your enemy has large, highly mobile forces, you have little choice. The alternative is to stretch your own troops thinly along the frontier. But then the enemy has only to bunch his forces in two or three places and smash his way through— after which there is nothing to stop him. Mobile defence is more flexible.

However, it sounds easier than it is in practice. Nor has it been helped by the allied plan to engage the enemy as far to the East as possible. Militarily there is a good argument for making one's stand on the Rhine, which is a wide and swift-flowing obstacle for the enemy to cross. But the Germans have understandably persuaded the allies to push the front line far to the East. First the allies planned to make their stand on the Weser. Now they will have to fight still further to the East, probably along the banks of the Leine, which is not a very effective barrier to a determined invader.

The generals would prefer to lie back, forcing the enemy to declare himself—and then react accordingly—even with tactical nuclear missiles if necessary. In other words they would prefer to ride the punch rather than thrust forward their chin to meet it. But the German argument is natural enough, and the allies have got to make the best of it. Britain, for instance, has had to move ammunition dumps further forward to adjust to the changes in strategy—something which is in itself a complex and expensive operation.

Battlefield terminology these days needs some explaining. Soldiers may serve in battalions and companies in peacetime, or perhaps in squadrons or batteries and troops. In wartime they would actually fight in battle groups and combat teams which are combinations of infantry, armour and artillery—pre-packaged little armies on their own.

As things now stand the four British divisions would be divided into eight Task Forces—two for each. Each Task Force would be divided into battle groups, each of which is roughly the size of a battalion. An armoured battle group might consist of an armoured regiment headquarters, three tank squadrons and an infantry company with artillery support—while an infantry battle group would be more or less the reverse. But you could have two companies and two squadrons if necessary—according to taste. The idea is that it should be a flexible, *ad hoc* mix.

Each division should manage to provide five battle groups. One Task Force might have three and the other have two or, in theory, one could have four and the other one—or they would have two each and leave one with the divisional command.

A battle group, though, would not consist of companies and squadrons, but of combat teams—mixed packages of tanks and infantry. In other words, the various military skills would be jumbled together all the way up. One of the attractions of the restructuring proposals was that by some extraordinary feat of legerdemain they managed to raise the number of combat teams available in wartime from seventy-two to ninety-two.

It is arguable that with so much emphasis on combined arms in war, one should divide the Army this way in peace. But to scrap the old distinctions between infantry, armour and artillery would mean a tremendous upheaval not only of traditional loyalties but of training, equipment and accommodation. And the Army, which is never a very radical organization, has had enough change for the time being. Anyway, the whole point of battlegroups and combat teams is that they should be flexible. A permanent battle group in peacetime may not be the right mixture for a particular situation in war.

Living Quarters. In peacetime, life in BAOR is certainly very regimental. Troops live in their garrisons, quietly preparing for a war which will probably never happen. It is a bit like India in the old days of the Raj—a big foreign country where a large number of soldiers can expect to spend most of their service. With only four RAC regiments stationed at any one time in Britain, and a few scattered squadrons elsewhere, the average armoured unit can expect to spend thirty-six years out of a forty-two-year cycle in West Germany.

There are fourteen major garrisons and a number of minor ones. The largest is Osnabrück where there are 14,000 soldiers and dependants. The smallest is Lubbecke where there are only 3,000. Lubbecke, a small, mellow town, is also one of the prettiest places to be posted to. There are 8,500 in Rheindahlen itself, although only 2,100 of these are soldiers while the rest are dependants and UK-based civilians. Other BAOR towns include Detmold, Lippe, Soltau, Dortmund, Hildesheim, Celle, Munster, Fallingbostel, Hameln, Minden, Menden, Hohne, Sennelager, Lippstadt and Paderborn. They vary a lot. While those in Lubbecke, Celle and Hildesheim can count themselves fortunate, those in Hohne and Osnabrück are not so well endowed.

Accommodation is something of a problem. It is not too bad for married soldiers, although there never seems to be quite enough quarters for what is now largely a married army. Tall blocks of flats have been built in some garrisons and troops seem reasonably content with the results.

For single men, 'home sweet home' often sounds like a joke. Some regiments live in Kaiser barracks, built for the German Army before the First World War. Others live in 'Ophumane' accommodation—hutted establishments hastily built from prefabricated materials to house troops during the sudden expansion of BAOR in the 1950s. The name given to them comes from 'Operation Humane' which was the name of the building programme at the time. A few live in modern post-war camps, like that at Rheindahlen.

But most are in Hitler barracks, so called because they were built by the Nazis for their rapidly growing armed forces between the two world wars. They were very good in their day and compared favourably with contemporary British barracks. But they are showing signs of age, and at a time when soldiers' expectations have risen. Troops today are more fastidious than their fathers were.

A party of MPs touring BAOR in 1975 were appalled by the bare floors, bleak rooms and noisy corridors of Belfast Barracks at Osnabrück—even after the Queen's Own Highlanders had redecorated the place under a self-help scheme. They were still more horrified when the C-in-C of BAOR confessed that sixty per cent of BAOR accommodation was no better.

The need for improvement has been apparent for some time. An £80 million programme covering 17,000 beds was begun in 1972. The objective was to de-gut existing single accommodation blocks and turn them into apartment blocks. A dozen or so men might share one compartment, which would consist of several bedrooms, a living-room where they could install their own television, a bathroom with several showers and a utility room where they could wash and press their clothes. There would even be cooking facilities for those who wanted to get their own meals. (Few of them do.)

Ideally the Army would have liked to provide each soldier with his own bedroom. But this never looked feasible. So they have settled for a compromise under which up to four will share a room, depending upon its size. This does not sound like luxury.

But it would be a substantial improvement if only the Army could get on with it. The programme was due to be completed within ten years, but three major cuts in the accommodation budget in three years after the Defence Review have not helped.

Similar difficulties affect working conditions in Rhine Army. Some regiments enjoy very good working conditions. But others have to put up with facilities which are ludicrously bad. Two infantry battalions did not even have any garages for their vehicles until a few years ago. As it is, because of cost, they have had to make do with opensided shelters.

Exercises. On the face of it, West Germany has plenty of land set aside for military training. Apart from smaller garrison training areas, there are larger ranges at Soltau-Luneberg, Sennelager, Haltern, Bergen-Hohne, Vogelsang, Munsterlager, Putlos and Todendorf. Soltau-Luneberg is allotted solely to BAOR, although any damage there still has to be paid for. But most of the exercise areas are used by all the other Nato countries; troops in Sennelager, for instance, have excellent facilities and are actually administered by BAOR. But Britain has to take its turn in using the area and its annual entitlement works out at no more than about fifteen weeks. This is not very long when shared out among the regiments.

The training year has to be planned to fit in with the German crop cycle. German farmers while anxious to be defended, are unenthusiastic about having their wheatfields flattened by Chieftain tanks. Conservationists can also make life difficult and the German Nature Reserve Association has recently been locked in litigation with the West German government over the training space allotted to Britain at Soltau-Luneberg.

In the spring units keep to individual training and exercises up to combat team level. In the summer they move up to battle group operations. Then in the autumn when the crops have been harvested they are able to manoeuvre with larger forces, at Task Force or even division level, across country. But these big exercises over cultivated land can only be conducted with special permission from the German government and a 443 requisition order. The exercises are sometimes referred to as 443s in consequence.

Exercises all have a damage budget which has to be kept to. If there is any sign that the damage bill is about to exceed the limits imposed, then the whole thing has to be scrapped. One important restructuring exercise in 1977 had to be abandoned for this reason, and the operation was written off as a costly failure.

Some German farmers try to get a number of long-standing repairs carried out at the expense of the British taxpayer, by claiming that the damage was done during a military manoeuvre. The haggling over Soltau-Luneberg can become very bitter and pressure to reduce the amount of training space grows every year.

It is because of these difficulties that BAOR officers are enthusiastic about the facilities at Suffield in Canada. About seven battle groups go there every year, for a month at a time. No other army in the world, it is claimed, has better facilities—except perhaps the US Army. The extent of the Suffield battle run for tanks can be judged by the fact that it takes between three and four days for a tank to get round it. The equivalent at Hohne can be negotiated in forty-five minutes.

Off-duty Problems. On duty a soldier spends his time preparing for a war which he does not seriously think will ever happen. Off duty he tries to amuse himself in a strange land where they speak a foreign language and eat funny food. Alternatively he gives up the unequal struggle and retreats behind his own camp gates, drinking beer with the lads in the Naafi. Like any institutionalized society BAOR can become very boring. Like his ancestors in India Tommy Atkins today has to learn how to take advantage of his circumstances. But he often fails to do so. Social problems are complicated by a number of special factors. If you include British civilians employed by the Ministry of Defence, BAOR contains about 145,000 souls, which is roughly the population of a moderately large British city. But the population is also very scattered. Army welfare officers say that their parish stretches from Antwerp to Berlin. Rhine Army sprawls over a chunk of the North German plain which if superimposed upon a map of Britain, would cover quite a large part of England and Wales. It is as if one took the town of Bournemouth, divided its population into small segments and scattered them over Southern England—then tried to look after them.

But it is worse than that. BAOR has some social workers belonging to the Soldiers', Sailors' and Airmen's Families Association (SSAFA) and there are the facilities supplied by Naafi and a variety of other welfare organizations. But for the most part it has to cope with family problems on its own, without the back-up of local authorities.

In some ways this brings out the best in the British military system. When thrown upon its own resources, the regiment develops the *esprit* for which it is famous. Soldiers, their wives and their children look to the regiment for moral support. On the other hand, the colonel's lady cannot provide for Judy O'Grady as well as she used to fifty years ago. Mrs. O'Grady, like her husband, expects rather more than kindly patronage.

It is a young Army. Three out of every four soldiers are under the age of thirty. More than half the girls in the WRAC are under twenty-one, which itself places quite a lot of responsibility upon their elders.

It is also an increasingly married Army. Between 1967 and 1977 the number of married soldiers rose from forty-two to fifty-eight per cent. The total of dependants went up by 20,000. Because they are young married couples, they also tend to have young children. Altogether there are 45,000 children, or forty-seven per cent of the dependent population. The number of those under ten years old is well above average.

It is a big job to provide schools. There are as many as 104 of them, nine of which are secondary schools (four of them with room for boarders). Seven are middle schools for those aged between seven and thirteen and eighty-seven are for children between five and eleven. At Brunssen in Holland there is also an all-age school for the children of British Servicemen stationed at Nato's Armed Forces Central Europe (AFCENT) headquarters.

But a survey of children at one secondary school in 1976 showed that seventy per cent had been to more than four primary schools and that some had attended as many as ten while accompanying their parents round the globe. About seventy-five per cent had to travel for more than an hour each way to get to school. More disturbing for the Army and for that matter the RAF families in Germany is the rapid turn-over of teaching staff. About half of these leave after one tour of duty and few stay longer than six years. Women teachers either get married, or leave their jobs when they find themselves short of companions of their own age. Rather than lead a lonely life in a BAOR officers mess, they get out and move back to Britain.

The falling birth rate is likely to have repercussions. According to one estimate the child population in BAOR could be halved in the 1980s. One might think that this should make it easier. But it could make things more difficult because many schools might become hopelessly uneconomic. As a result some might close and the remaining children might have to travel still greater distances.

In these circumstances the separation of families causes trouble. Because of Northern Ireland, about 3,000 wives in BAOR have been separated from their husbands at any one time in recent years. If one added up the time spent in Ulster one would find that out of a six-year period some soldiers have been absent from their families for between two and three years.

Despite the determined efforts of regiments to make the wives feel at home, Army camps are not the homeliest of places to live in. This is particularly so for those young wives who are away from home for the first time—and many of them are. The size of some of the Naafi shops in BAOR, like that at Rheindahlen or the new, colossal supermarket at Detmold, encourages the agoraphobia of many young wives who lead a confined existence in a big country, buying British, eating British and meeting British. Like American Air Force bases in Britain, Army camps in BAOR often seem like island communities—corners of a foreign field that are forever England.

The Army would like soldiers and their families to get out more. There are ski-ing trips, sailing expeditions and a wide variety of less organized pastimes which they could enjoy. At least the number of soldiers who can speak German has gone up. In 1978, 512 junior officers had reached a 'colloquial' standard in one Nato language, and 327 of these were proficient in German. But most soldiers can still say no more than 'Zwei biers bitte'.

One of the greatest success stories in recent years has been the introduction of a British television service for the troops. Ironically this has taken away one of the incentives for soldiers to learn German. Now even their soap operas come in English. Still, it was never much of an incentive. And certainly the availability of television programmes, selected from the BBC and ITV schedules at home, has been a big source of comfort to soldiers' families. The standard of the programmes has also been far higher than had been feared. The only complaint has been that shortage of money has slowed down the introduction of the service throughout BAOR since it began in 1975.

The change to a married Army has not been without its benefits. At least it has helped keep young soldiers out of trouble. The number of Courts Martial has gone down steadily from 1,000 in 1972 to fewer than 600 in 1977, although this may have had more to do with the increased power of a battalion commander to dispense summary justice. Still, in six months of 1977 only 599 soldiers out of 61,000 were mixed up in serious crime. This compares quite well with the rates for civilians in Munchen Gladbach. They included eighty-nine cases of theft and fifty-six of assault—of all kinds.

The rise in car ownership among soldiers has brought some problems. In the ten years between 1967 and 1977 the number of car owners went up from 24,281 to 57,398—a rise of 138 per cent. So most soldiers in Germany would now seem to have their own transport.

5*

This rise in car ownership coincided with a West German Police campaign against drinking and driving several years ago. As a result the number of British soldiers convicted in the West German courts rose alarmingly from 185 in 1969 to 333 in 1971. Over the ten years, however, the conviction rate was only fourteen for every 1,000 soldier-drivers against twenty in every 1,000 German civilians.

BAOR has also welcomed the Standing Civilian Courts which were introduced in 1977 to deal with juvenile offenders. Soldiers' children can be as destructive as any other children. But until the new courts started, commanding officers could do little more than haul the young offenders before them for a magisterial reprimand. Now they can receive a full range of punishments including detention at juvenile detention centres in Britain.

Costs. BAOR is expensive to maintain. In 1977–78 it cost £779 million. For British Forces Germany which includes the RAF, it meant a cost of £544 million in foreign exchange. The West German Government has traditionally made 'offset' payments to Britain to alleviate this burden on the British economy. The latest agreement provided for the Germans to make £114 million available in this way over a three-year period from April 1977. Most of this would go towards improving barracks and other facilities—which could revert to West Germany in the long term.

But the Germans have become more grudging in their provision of offset payments, complaining that they now provide equivalent benefits for Britain in other directions—like the EEC. So perhaps the last offset agreement, which was negotiated only after a great deal of haggling, will be the last.

British forces abroad also have to be helped with Local Overseas Allowances (LOAs). These are paid to close the gap between the cost of living in Britain and the cost of living in whichever country they are stationed. This is to ensure that they will not be worse off while serving abroad.

The allowances are reviewed every three years after extensive research by the Ministry of Defence. A small team of Civil Servants visit local shops and places of entertainment to assess the difference, and also take into account those benefits which soldiers in BAOR can enjoy, like duty-free alcohol, tobacco and motor cars.

For many years the LOAs paid to soldiers in BAOR were gratifyingly high. The cost of living in Germany was that much more than in Britain. But in recent years inflation at home has narrowed the gap and in April 1975, soldiers faced their first big drop in LOAs. In 1977 the Ministry of Defence decided that a cut of between thirty and forty per cent would again be justified. But this would have meant a fifteen per cent drop in the take-home pay of many soldiers, already smarting over their latest pay rise. So the Ministry decided that discretion was the better part of valour and that LOAs in BAOR would be left as they were, at least for another twelve months. BAOR troops had something to smile about.

Berlin. The Army always supposes that Berlin is one of the most desirable postings that a soldier can covet. And it is probably right. Berlin is not as popular as it was in the days when soldiers could afford to enjoy the shops on the Kurfurstendamm or the night-spots with their winking neon. But at least it is different.

Berlin is the one place where a troop of tanks could still rumble down the main street in the rush-hour without causing more than passing protest—assuming that is that they were Western tanks, not Russian. Nature conservationists in Berlin might still remember the 1948 blockade when the Soviet Union blocked Western access by road and rail and the city depended upon an allied airlift for its supplies. Those who cannot remember have only to gaze upon the 103 miles of wall and fence which since 1961 have ringed West Berlin, emphasizing its island status. At least twenty-five refugees still cross to West Berlin every month, by some means or another.

Militarily the position of West Berlin is untenable. Within a twenty-mile radius of the city are 95,000 Soviet and East German troops with 1,300 tanks, tactical nuclear missiles and 300 heavy guns. The 11,600 allied troops calculate that they could not hold out for more than a week against such a force—and that sounds over-optimistic.

On the other hand, they might help to tie down three Warsaw Pact divisions, so their position is not without some military value. Moreover, their presence sustains the moral courage of the 2,000,000 West Berliners. So soldiers who seek some *raison d'être* should find it without too much difficulty.

Not that many of them try. Most of the 3,000 troops in the British Field Force were still in their perambulators, or perhaps in primary school when the Berlin Wall was built. To them the bizarre situation is a fact of life. They accept a posting to the city as something of an adventure—marred by the routine of irksome guard duties. It is rather like household duties for a guards regiment in London, except that there is less magic and more meaning.

When soldiers do stop to think about it, most cannot understand why the Russians do not march in and take over the place. Their own resources seem so slender. The British Field Force consists of three infantry battalions and one armoured squadron. They live in

barracks with evocative names—the infantry units at Wavell and
Brooke and Montgomery (which is ten miles out of the city centre)
The RAC squadron is based at Smuts and the various supporting
units like the 120-strong company of Royal Military Police, at
Alexander. Exemption from tours of duty in Northern Ireland is one
of the perquisities which they enjoy.

The Army goes to some lengths to bring home to soldiers why they
are there. Units take them on guided tours of East Berlin—which
they are free to do—in seventeen-seater coaches, often with an
intelligence officer in charge. Regiments try to demonstrate for their
soldiers the contrast between East Berlin's drab streets and half
empty shop windows and the teeming affluence of the Western half
of the city. They take them to the Soviet Military Museum and
include Soviet barracks on their tours, parking outside so that
Tommy Atkins can take a good look at his potential enemies inside.
Sometimes the Russians have taken exception to the practice and
have nudged the British bus ever so gently on its way.

The Army also encourages soldiers to visit the East during their
time off. A sergeant can take up to eight men across the wall and a
corporal can take four, but only a sergeant and above can go there
on his own. If a soldier visited the East every night, British Intelligence officers might start to wonder why. But they seldom have
cause to do so because comparatively few non-commissioned ranks
take full advantage of the opportunity to pass through Checkpoint
Charlie into the East.

This could be because West Berlin has more to offer. It is after all
a city which is full of pleasant surprises. Not only does its night life
cater for most tastes, but its day life, too, has multiple attractions.
With its lakes, rivers and forests which one can get lost in, it is a
place where the feeling of being besieged can be quickly forgotten.

But the language barrier makes it difficult for single soldiers to
find the blonde frauleins that they dream about. Another more
recent difficulty is that Berlin can be expensive. The frauleins can be
entertained more lavishly by Berliners, or perhaps by young men
from West Germany itself—lured to jobs in Berlin by the promise of
exemption from National Service.

Married soldiers enjoy life rather more. For one thing they are
slightly better off than in BAOR. This is because of the Families
Ration Issue Scheme (FRIS). It is official policy to keep up to
twelve months stock of food and clothing in West Berlin in case the
1948 blockade is ever repeated. Because the food needs to be
rotated, it is sold to service families at cheaper rates than those at
which they can buy food elsewhere. In recognition of this Berlin
soldiers receive slightly lower LOAs than their comrades in BAOR.

But even after allowing for this the families in the Berlin garrison are slightly better off.

Work in Berlin for much of the time means performing a selection of guard duties. Every four months, for instance, the British garrison takes its turn with the Americans the French and the Russians in mounting guard at Spandau where Rudolph Hess, last surviving Nazi war prisoner, remains the most grossly over-protected man in the world. The three infantry battalions share the month's tour of duty, each one doing about ten days. This does not sound too burdensome. But each guard demands a platoon of one officer and twenty-one men, and actually involves two platoons because one is coming on duty as another is going off. So it can be quite intensive, particularly when men are away on courses or on leave.

Then four or five times a year a soldier might find himself in the 'alert platoon' at Field Force Headquarters, ready to be called out at fifteen minutes' notice in case of an emergency.

While one infantry platoon is on 'alert' duties, the same battalion's reconnaissance platoon does a turn on border patrol around the wall. Its members drive along a section of the wall in a Land Rover or a Ferret Scout Car, dismounting from time to time to climb an observation tower and stare over the border at their East German counterparts. The East Germans stare back, so there they are— friend and foe staring into the whites of each other's eyes through binoculars and to not very much purpose. One might call it confrontation. Meanwhile the battalions' intelligence section does a flag tour round East Berlin, driving round in a car, thereby exercising the allied right of access to all parts of the city.

The most popular duty for soldiers is the train guard. The company which provides the alert platoon on any particular day has also to find an NCO and three privates to ride on the British military train. This runs daily, except on Christmas Day, between West Berlin and Brunswick in West Germany. The French Army also has a train which runs from Strasbourg and the Americans have two, one from Hamburg and the other from Frankfurt.

The British military train is another example of Britain exercising its rights. As a means of transport it is hardly an essential. As often as not a long line of coaches carry a mere handful of people, who travel in one section, eating freshly boiled eggs for tea accompanied by buttered cream crackers.

The scenery is hardly picturesque. The train trundles through the flat German fields with few natural features to catch the eye. But it is full of interest and atmosphere. It is all rather like a film from the late 1930s in which Marlene Dietrich might be expected to come slinking through the corridors. The Army thinks so too—to the extent that it distributes a special hand out to travellers explaining what to look out for on the way.

The points of interest include anything from the Soviet tank-training area at Kirchmoser and a political prison at Magdeburg, to an engine shed near Werder where the Kaiser's personal engine was once kept. The day is a long one for the four-man guard who leave Berlin at 6 a.m. and do not return until 9 p.m. But there is a three-hour break at Brunswick in the middle and it is all a bit of a change.

The British headquarters are at the Olympic Stadium, built by Hitler for the Olympic Games of 1936. Those were the games at which Hitler refused to shake hands with the American negro sprinter Jesse Owens—who paid the British Army a nostalgic visit there several years ago. It makes a very grand headquarters. Its bare, echoing corridors still give one the feeling that the Army has just moved in. But it all adds to the general atmosphere of some-where rather special.

The man who must be most conscious of this atmosphere is the major-general who is General Officer Commanding in the British sector. Berlin after all is still officially under military government, although to all intents and purposes daily life is managed by the civil authorities.

The GOC is usually an officer with some diplomatic skills and probably some linguistic ability. His life is a nice mixture of the sublime and the ridiculous. He has enormous responsibility in such a sensitive city where the simplest act could have important political undertones. In 1977 the GOC Roy Redgrave had to intervene after four Welsh soldiers had exchanged some copies of a well-known girlie magazine for a fur hat from some of their Russian comrades in the East. The Russians later made an official protest, not because they objected to the infiltration of Western decadence but because the Welshmen had thoughtfully removed the centre-page spread of Miss Whatsit-of-the-month. General Redgrave had to order a search of barrack room walls to recover the elusive ladies before the Red Army could be mollified. It is that sort of job.

When not on duty at the Olympic Stadium, the GOC lives with his family in some style at the Villa Lemm, a riverside residence built by a boot polish manufacturer in the early years of the century. The grandson of the original owner recently returned to ask for some of the family furniture back—but was politely refused. As the GOC stands on his balcony overlooking the river, feeding the ducks on a crisp autumn morning, he might reflect that Berlin is not at all a bad place to be—for major-generals anyway.

The British Mission to the Commanders-in-Chief of the Soviet Forces in Germany, better known as Brixmiss, is also located in

Berlin. This is headed by a brigadier and has its Mission House at Potsdam, just outside Berlin itself. Brixmiss officers have the right to travel around East Germany—an important facility for British intelligence. It is another institution which has survived since the occupation of Germany after the war, and the American and French forces have a similar privilege. So has the Soviet Union, and a Soxmiss car is usually observed, hovering around any large military exercises in West Germany.

8

Peacekeeping in Ireland

The Start of the Troubles. On 14 August, 1969, this Army which had policed an empire was ordered to keep the peace at home for a change. After ten months of violence which had exposed inadequacies in the Royal Ulster Constabulary (RUC) and the Special Constabulary—the so-called 'B' Specials—the decision to use troops on the streets of Northern Ireland was controversial but not very surprising. Lieutenant-General Sir Ian Freeland who had arrived to take over as General Officer Commanding (GOC) earlier that summer gloomily predicted that the campaign would last for between five and ten years. It now looks as if he was over-optimistic. Nobody could have forecast that by the end of that time nearly 300 soldiers would be dead and more than 3,000 wounded.

There had been troubles before. Between 1956 and 1962 the Irish Republican Army (IRA) had tried to shake the foundations of Protestant power by a series of attacks on government buildings, mainly in the country. But the flames of revolution failed to engulf the towns and flickered out without much military involvement—although a barracks was attacked near the border and a truckload of weapons seized.

For the rest of the time the Six Counties had remained a relaxed backwater for soldiers lucky enough to be posted there. There were 2,168 of them when the troubles began in 1968. There were infantry battalions at Holywood Barracks, Belfast. and at Ballykinlar in County Down, and an armoured regiment at Omagh. There were also 308 in supporting base units and seventy-seven at Lisburn, where the GOC's Northern Ireland headquarters stood next door to the HQ of 39 Brigade at Thiepval Barracks.

The brigade had a reinforcement role in BAOR, and the odd battalion was often away on exercise. Even the brigade headquarters was borrowed for one overseas emergency. The soldiers spent the rest of their on-duty time preparing themselves and their equipment to face the Russians rather than the IRA. Off duty they hunted, shot and fished, sailed on the Ulster loughs, drank in the Ulster bars and chased after Ulster girls who were as plentiful as they were pretty.

The troubles began in October 1968 after a series of protest marches organized by the Northern Ireland Civil Rights Association, largely on behalf of the under-privileged Catholic minority. With growing unease the Army watched them escalate. Senior officers hurried between Lisburn and London as contingency plans were taken down and dusted. Then in April 1969 the first reinforcements arrived when the 1st Battalion The Prince of Wales' Own (PWO) was ordered in to guard installations like power stations and government buildings, after a series of attacks.

It was a company of the PWO, a battalion of cheerful, down-to-earth Yorkshiremen, who were first to be involved on the streets when they marched into the Bogside Catholic ghetto in Londonderry on 14 August. Reinforcements now started to arrive in waves: 15 August brought the 3rd Light Infantry, 17 August the 1st Queens, squadrons from the Life Guards and Royal Engineers and companies from the 1st Grenadiers and the Duke of Edinburgh's Regiment, 19 August the 1st Royal Hampshires, 20 August the 1st Royal Green Jackets and 23 August the 2nd Grenadiers.

By 5 October when the first soldier was shot there were 8,000 troops in the province. On 6 February, 1971, when the first soldier was killed, the number of troops had fallen to 7,300. But it had risen to 12,300 by 9 August, when internment without trial was introduced and 300 men were arrested. Since then the number of troops has gone up and down like the Irish temper, but has never fallen below five figures.

Tours of Duty. The number of soldiers rose steadily until 31 July, 1972, when the Army launched Operation Motorman. Then, with 21,266 troops on hand, it 'invaded' the so-called 'no-go' IRA hideouts in Belfast and Londonderry, forcing out the gunmen and establishing a military presence which has remained. Operation Motorman was a turning-point in the campaign, because however much damage has been caused since then, the IRA has never regained all of its old power in the ghettoes.

During the last few years the number of soldiers in Ulster has hovered between 13,000 and 15,000, according to need at any particular time. About thirteen major units and a number of minor ones have usually been posted there, grouped into three brigades. (In 1978 they were still being called brigades despite the new term 'Field Force' which was being used elsewhere in the Army.)

The brigades are 39 Brigade which covers Belfast, 8 Brigade in the City and County of Londonderry, and 3 Brigade at Portadown—

from where it polices 3,500 acres of rural Ulster including most of the border with the Irish Republic.

Some of the units have been on eighteen-month garrison tours of duty, accompanied by their families in the usual way. Most, however, have been posted to Northern Ireland on four-month emergency or roulement tours—while their wives and children remain behind in Britain or BAOR.

For most of the time there have been only five garrison units. These have been at the old camps of Holywood, Ballykinlar and Omagh, and two others, at Ebrington Barracks in Londonderry and at Ballykelly. However, a sixth was added in 1978, at Aldergrove beside Belfast Airport. There are also plans to add a seventh under government policy to shift the emphasis away from the emergency tours to more permanent bases.

The roulement units tend to be based in the more troublesome areas, where they work an average ninety-two to 100 hours a week. Garrison battalions in 1978 were on duty for between seventy and eighty hours—which sounds punishing enough. But the very fact that the Army has been able to rely upon them to an increasing extent, reflects the slow decline in the level of violence.

Only those regiments with Irish connexions have been excused Ulster duty—for obvious reasons. For everyone else it has become an occupational hazard. For instance, between 1 January, 1974 and 30 June, 1976, as many as fifty major units and 80,000 men served in the province at one time or another. By mid-1978 one battalion, the 2nd Light Infantry had served seven emergency tours there, and three others, the 1st Queen's, the 1st Royal Green Jackets and the 2nd battalion of the Parachute Regiment had been there six times. And these figures did not include shorter postings—as reinforcements perhaps to strengthen the Army during July or August, when the traditional Protestant marches through the towns and cities have threatened to provoke a degree of violence unusual even for Northern Ireland.

The length of the roulement tour was decided on after much thought and proposals to alter it have always been rejected. A shorter tour might not give troops enough time to settle in and exploit the local knowledge so painfully acquired. It would also mean that units would have to serve there that much more often. As it is by mid-1978 the time for Ulster duty had been stretched to fourteen months for units based in Britain and to twenty-two months for those 'borrowed' from BAOR. The policy of relying increasingly upon garrison units should mean that the interval between Ulster tours for the roulement battalions should become even longer.

The alternative has been to lengthen the tour from four months to six. But four months is felt to be as much as the average soldier can stand, given the tensions of the job. There is little time to do anything but work, sleep, eat and watch television in the makeshift barrack rooms. Soldiers are so exhausted that they have little inclination to do anything else anyway. Commanding officers particularly, after carrying a burden of such responsibility for four months, are ready for a break by that time.

Training schedules have been badly disrupted as it is. A unit is out of commission for longer than the four months actually spent in Ulster. It needs at least a month in which to prepare for the specialized job of peacekeeping, a month in which to revert to its normal programme on return and a month's leave for the men—a fortnight before going and a fortnight after coming back. Thus one tour in Northern Ireland takes more out of the year than it leaves. The House of Commons Defence and External Affairs Sub-Committee was shocked to discover on a visit to BAOR several years ago that troops were short of brigade and divisional exercises, partly because of restrictions on fuel and finance, but partly also because of Northern Ireland. Not only have the Royal Artillery and Royal Armoured Corps had to climb down from their self-propelled guns and tanks to take their place beside the infantry in Northern Ireland, but up to seven units at a time have been 'borrowed' from BAOR, after first asking for permission from Nato's Supreme Allied commander Europe (Saceur). The RAF Regiment, as well as the Royal Marines, have helped out in their time—which is some indication of how stretched the Army has been to fulfil this latest, unexpected commitment.

Along with most people in Britain, soldiers sympathized with the oppressed Catholic minority when they were first given the job of preventing sectarian riots in 1969. Their initial task was seen to be that of protecting the poor Catholic areas from vengeful Protestant mobs, and the Catholics gave them an enthusiastic but temporary welcome. It was about the middle of 1970 that the troubles began to grow more sinister as the Provisional IRA (PIRA), a breakaway IRA movement dedicated to ending British rule in Ulster by whatever means, emerged as the principal threat to the forces of law and order.

Living Quarters. When the first wave of reserves arrived in 1969 they were billeted in schools, factories, community halls and, for a time, outside in the streets. Since then conditions have slightly improved. Where land has been available and the makeshift accommodation has been particularly miserable the Army has built semi-permanent camps of prefabricated huts, which are more comfortable than they look. Seven have been constructed since 1971, the most notable examples being the fort-like complex above the Creggan housing estate in Londonderry and the camp at Portadown which has enabled 3 Brigade Headquarters to move out of its old home in a deserted 'Knickers' factory at Lurgan. The Army has also tried to add some home comforts, like weather proofing and central heating to those dark satanic mills and mission halls which are still in use.

The soldiers themselves have done their best. Officers thoughtfully chew cottage pie and beans in gloomy upstairs rooms, at tables decorated with regimental silver, and drink their beer from gleaming tankards flown over from their mess in Germany or wherever, as they flick through copies of *Punch* and *Country Life*.

Army accommodation is always controlled, as one might expect, by careful regulations on time and space. Thus soldiers posted there for eighteen months or two years can take their families with them to married quarters. If they have no families they are entitled to 'Synopsis' accommodation which means a minimum of ninety-one square feet of bed space in the barracks. This compares with a council house at the new town of Craigavon which provides only seventy square feet per person at an economic rent of £30 a month. Soldiers on four-month emergency tours are entitled to camp scale accommodation or sixty-five square feet of bed space. The philosophy is that they do not have to bring all their worldly possessions with them.

There is a third type called emergency accommodation which means sixty-five square feet but with two-tier bunks. The minimum standard is about sixteen square feet for each man and some soldiers endure this at times, sleeping in old bomb trailers, for example. But the Army regards such conditions as being tolerable for only two months at a time. On the other hand, soldiers are remarkably resilient and often seem happiest in such conditions, cheerfully helping each other like Londoners during the blitz. Most serious complaints about accommodation come from those on eighteen-month and two-year tours whose expectations of comfort are naturally higher. A temporary failure in the hot water supply at, say Omagh where a Cavalry Regiment lives with its families in comparative comfort, brings down far more wrath on accommodation officers than the privations endured by troops in such notorious billets as Albert Street Mill or the Cromac Mission Hall in the Markets area of Belfast. A thirty-foot prefabricated hut with three bunks is classed as synopsis accommodation. With four bunks it becomes camp scale and with four more it gets 'bloody uncomfortable'. Soldiers sometimes make curious use of available space.

One accommodation officer, who called to investigate a complaint of inadequate room in a prefabricated camp, found that soldiers had squashed all four bunks into one corner while they used the rest of the room to play cards.

In general Ulster accommodation is better than it was and in some cases could not be improved without considerable expense. The modernization of Albert Street Mill would cost one million pounds. Some units have even pointed out that their temporary quarters in Northern Ireland have been better than their permanent homes in Germany—a back-handed compliment which has given the Army food for thought.

Equipment. In August 1969 the stores contained anti-riot shields, wooden truncheons, and plastic visors which when fitted to steel helmets made the helmets flop forward over the face. The troops had little else except surprising reserves of patience and fortitude. They had not even any experience to guide them in the specialized job of peace-keeping at home where minimal force was from the first a necessary doctrine.

They did have CS gas which was first used to control a hostile crowd in Belfast on 7 September. After angry protests a Home Office investigation reported in September 1971 that the gas was safe in all but exceptional circumstances. In consequence it is still available for occasional use at the discretion of the commanding officer.

On the other hand, there are doubts over its effectiveness. Resourceful Irishmen soon discovered how to cope with it by wearing handkerchief masks soaked in vinegar and water—the solution having been placed in the streets by sympathetic housewives. Then again soldiers once inadvertantly gassed a squad of policemen who came marching round a corner at the wrong moment. On another occasion they accidentally immobilized the entire congregation of the Rev. Ian Paisley, the Protestant politician, as they were leaving chapel one Sunday morning. While still making it available to battalions senior officers now tend to discourage its use.

By contrast to the situation in 1969 soldiers in Ulster now have well over 200 different items of equipment ranging from the plain and practical to the weird and wonderful. All have their limitations and none has proved a panacea. The water cannon for instance made an impact when it was introduced. But the leaders of rioting crowds soon appreciated that it did no more than soak them and as they did not wear their Sunday best clothes at a riot this did not matter too much. Moreover, the cannon runs out of water from time to time and has to be refilled, making the operator, unprotected by armoured plating, a vulnerable target.

A more dramatic innovation has been the rubber or plastic bullet. The idea has been not only to scatter hostile crowds but to bring down the ringleaders so that lightly armed 'snatch squads' containing the fastest and the fittest can rush forward and arrest them. The original practice was to bounce the missiles off the ground so that they hit the target like a cricket ball on the legs or in the groin. Again it has had its limitations. In the first place it has been inaccurate at more than fifty metres so that it has sometimes hit the wrong target. In the second place it has sometimes inflicted permanent injury. The worst case was that of a housewife who was hit in the face and blinded while watching a riot from her council house window.

Now the bullets are fired direct without being bounced off the ground. The introduction of an anti-riot gun with a rifled barrel instead of the old smooth-bore also promises accuracy up to seventy metres which means that troops can stay out of stone-throwing range.

The Ministry of Defence has tried to respond to every twist and turn of the Irish campaign. In some cases existing equipment has simply been improved. Thus the old Humber one-ton armoured personnel carrier, better known as the Pig because of its ungainly shape, has been more heavily armoured to withstand high velocity bullets from American and East European rifles which have gradually come to replace weapons like the old Thompson sub-machine gun in the IRA inventory. The more effective Saracen introduced for Operation Motorman in 1972 has had a new turret fitted to enable the crew to fire its gun without opening the hatch. A close fitting, purpose-built Northern Ireland helmet, lighter than the old one and equipped with a proper visor, has been introduced and the Army has even designed a new boot with a plain sole that leaves no tell-tale military treadmark.

In other cases new equipment has been bought off the shelf and sometimes improved in later marks. Thus a whole range of image-intensifying and seismic surveillance equipment—proven in Vietnam —has enabled soldiers to see and sometimes hear their assailants at night. There are 'sniffers' to detect traces of explosives on suspects, 'nitesun', an 800-candle power searchlight which can illuminate the ground from a patrolling helicopter, hand-held metal detectors, radar sets and so on.

The normal development time-table for new equipment is too long for a soldier who is struggling to combat a new threat in Northern Ireland. Any new development for Ulster now has 'Operational Emergency' stamped on it which means that it is given high priority and that scientists may be taken away from other projects to work on it. For anything which is already available on the open market the Army has an alternative stamp 'Urgent Operational Requirement', and some pieces of kit have been sent to Ulster within a week.

The Army has been impressed by the speed with which scientists and engineers have responded. One scientist suffered a nervous breakdown through trying to get his project completed on time and another is said to have killed himself by overwork. Industries sometimes complain that they get no feedback from Northern Ireland. But one prominent electronics company was gratified recently to have a letter from a sergeant in Northern Ireland who thanked them for developing the equipment, which the previous day had saved his life.

One area of research which has so far failed to produce the hoped-for results has been that covering protective armour for soldiers. Throughout the campaign troops have been issued with the flak jacket or fragmentation vest. It weighs only one pound per square foot which means that it is light enough for soldiers to move around in without undue discomfort. However, while it has undoubtedly saved many soldiers from serious injury from missiles and even low velocity bullets, its padding of ballistic nylon fabric cannot stop the high-velocity bullet which has inflicted some hideous injuries. The only kind of jacket which can, is one packed with ceramic armour which weighs more than six times as much. While offering valuable protection for soldiers on static duty, it is too heavy for them to move around in. Moreover it covers less of the body than does the flak jacket, although it does effectively protect the heart, the lungs, and backbone. A similar jacket was used by helicopter gun-ship crews in Vietnam. But for most soldiers in Northern Ireland the flak jacket remains the only suitable compromise between armour which is light but ineffective and armour which is effective but intolerably heavy. This is despite occasional complaints in Parliament from politicians who do not fully understand the situation. Meanwhile the search at the Stores and Clothing Research and Development Establishment at Colchester for a lightweight fully protective body armour continues—as it has continued since about the time of the Battle of Crecy.

Bomb Disposal. Even if chemists do perfect a material it is unlikely to be of more than peripheral comfort to the Royal Army Ordnance Corps' Ammunition Technical Officers (ATOs) who have the unenviable job of bomb disposal in Northern Ireland. ATOs already have an Explosives Ordnance Disposal (EOD) suit which makes them look like moonmen and is now compulsory wear. It offers useful protection while the ATO is approaching or walking away from the explosive device—but virtually no protection at all while he is bending over it. A Mark-2 version which has ceramic armour over the chest and lower abdomen has now been brought into service. But even this offers protection against only one pound of explosives at close quarters—and few bombs are as small as that. Moreover it weighs fifty pounds and is uncomfortable to wear. ATOs who have a distinctive taste in humour say that if the bomb goes off one would end up looking like striped toothpaste.

Of more obvious benefit to them has been Wheelbarrow, the remote control robot which can inspect, remove or detonate a bomb at the command of the ATO—waiting in relative safety 100 yards or so away. The Mark-1 Wheelbarrow was designed by inventive engineers at the Military Vehicles and Engineering Establishment near Chobham, Surrey. Built round the concept of a bath chair, Wheelbarrow is a marvellous example of British ingenuity under pressure. Each new model has seen refinements added to the boom which it extends like an arm, smashing car windows, poking round inside, and relaying television pictures to the anxious controller. Mark-8 is now in service with a manipulative 'hand' which can even pluck out detonators. Each model costs more than £5,000 and is worth every penny. The robot can now handle six out of every ten explosive devices in Northern Ireland, which gives some indication of the number of lives it must have saved.

The Army has only 250 ATOs qualified to carry out EOD work in Ulster. Fifty are officers and 200 are sergeants and warrant officers, who are officially called Ammunition Technicians (ATs) but are always referred to under the blanket term of ATO in the present campaign. All are carefully selected on the basis of confidential reports and psychosometric tests, and are still more carefully trained. Officers do a fourteen-month course, consisting of six months at the Royal Military College of Science, Shrivenham and eight months at the Army School of Ammunition at Kineton, near Banbury.

But most of their work is very unglamorous and until the current wave of troubles in Northern Ireland few people had ever heard of them. They are basically ammunition experts who supervise the storage of Army ordnance, inspecting ammunition dumps, and advising on maintenance.

They are not in fact the Army's official bomb disposal experts, responsible for dealing with, say, the odd 1,000-pound bombs which still emerge from time to time in South-East England—survivors of the blitz. That role belongs to the Royal Engineers. But RAOC ATOs began to look after improvised explosive devices (IED) in

Cyprus during the 1950s and had done so in Hong Kong and Aden before turning to Northern Ireland.

They have since become one of the best known bodies of men in the British Army. Virtually all of them have now served four-month tours of duty there at least twice. The chief ATO, a lieutenant-colonel, evocatively known by the acronym Cato, always serves there for a year, with an office at the headquarters in Lisburn.

At any one time there are fifteen ATOs working on EOD in Northern Ireland. (Each brigade also has an ATO working in intelligence, keeping an eye on the bombers.) The EOD men work in teams of five. One of the five is the ATO himself. Another is his assistant, usually a corporal who although an AT is not qualified to do EOD himself. The others are a driver, a signaller and an armed escort who keeps guard while the bomb is being dealt with. There are four teams in 39 Brigade, four in 8 Brigade, five in 3 Brigade—because of the enormous area which it covers—and two at the Lisburn headquarters. All come under 312 Ordnance Disposal Unit which is commanded by a major—himself second-in-command to Cato. Apart from Cato all are kept away from the television cameras and their names are kept out of newspapers, for fear that their work would make them particular targets for the IRA.

Each ATO has about three weeks special training before being posted to Ulster. This may not seem very long. But he knows everything there is to know about explosives before starting. So he needs only to be brought up to date with the latest IRA techniques.

When in Northern Ireland his schedule can be a tight one. The average response time to a bomb alert is seventeen minutes. The ATO is told where the bomb is and what kind of bomb he must expect—a car bomb perhaps, a suspect parcel or a culvert mine. Then the team climbs into its vehicle—which is already packed with equipment including Wheelbarrow and the EOD suits. ATOs say they have little time to think about the approaching confrontation until they are in the vehicle, driving at high speed to the scene, and even then they are too busy contemplating the techniques to be used to worry about the danger.

This is a good thing because some of the situations they have to deal with are terrifying. Wheelbarrow cannot, for instance, deal with mines hidden beneath the road in some dark, narrow culvert. An ATO has to wriggle towards the device, knowing that a terrorist may be waiting 200 yards away behind a hedge, waiting for the appropriate moment to detonate the bomb by radio. In ninety-five per cent of the cases dealt with, ATOs can accurately distinguish between an IRA device and one which has been made by Protestant extremists.

The first ATO to be killed was a young married captain, caught by a booby-trapped bomb which he was investigating on the steps of an Orange Hall at Castlerobin between Lisburn and Belfast. His death caused the name Castlerobin to enter common parlance as the shorthand for a bomb which has been designed to kill the ATO himself. It also forced ATOs to adopt a more cautious approach, and led in time to the invention of Wheelbarrow.

By mid-1978 a total of sixteen ATOs had been killed—one more than the entire complement of 312 EOD Unit at any one time. Four had been officers (one major and three captains) and twelve had been sergeants and warrant officers. Two died in 1971, six in 1972, two in 1973, three in 1974, two in 1975 and one in 1977. One man returned to the British mainland in 1976 after dealing with 190 separate incidents without mishap. On the other hand, another was killed in a motor accident on his way to Belfast Airport at the end of his tour of duty.

By mid-1978 103 decorations had been won by these extra-ordinary men. They included a George Cross, awarded to Lieut.-Col. George Stiles, perhaps the best-known Cato of all, for his work in defusing a bomb in the lobby of the Europa Hotel. The others were twenty-four George Medals, twenty-two Queen's Gallantry Medals, thirty-one Mentioned in Dispatches, three OBEs, six MBEs and sixteen BEMs.

By temperament cool and phlegmatic, ATOs talk philosophically about the dangers of their job. None are glory-seekers and few are flamboyant extroverts. The only complaint that they make is that they earn no extra money, apart from the daily Northern Ireland bonus which has been paid to all soldiers serving there since 1974.

Ulster Defence Regiment. One regiment has owed its very existence to the campaign in Northern Ireland. This is the Ulster Defence Regiment, a force of locally recruited, part-time volunteers who help to guard important installations, carry out searches, man vehicle checkpoints and, on an increasing scale, play a more active role in support of their all-regular colleagues.

It was formed in April 1970 with the object of freeing regular soldiers for front-line duty. It also offered a means of channelling the energies of former 'B' Specials, 'redundant' following the disbandment of the force in 1969, into a disciplined organization under Army control. Regular British officers fill key posts like those of commanding officer, adjutant, regimental sergeant-major and quartermaster. In both these respects the UDR has been successful. Its senior officers like to argue that it conducts searches and checkpoints with more expertise than the regular battalions because it has by now had more experience.

It has been less successful in preserving its non-sectarian image. When it started, under the command of a regular brigadier, it had eighteen per cent Catholic recruits. This did not quite reflect the divisions in the population, which is about one-third Catholic. But given the prevailing climate it was a promising beginning. However, this Catholic proportion has shrunk to only three per cent. This is hardly surprising given the pressures on young Catholics not to join, but it is still a disappointment. More seriously the UDR has been suspected of harbouring Protestant extremists who thus not only receive their military training and their weapons from the Army, but are actually paid as well. There is a very careful security net, more tightly meshed than that for soldiers joining the regular Army. But most senior officers acknowledge that a number of shady characters slip through, and suspicious eyes have been levelled at the UDR after the odd arms raid on its own stores or the disappearance of weapons.

Recruiting has been progressively more difficult as the Catholics have slipped away and as the RUC and police reserve have fiercely competed for the same kind of young man. In mid-1978 the UDR had just over 8,000 members, formed into eleven battalions, two of them in Belfast. But the ceiling was 10,000, so there was some way to go. Recruiting was just good enough to keep pace with wastage.

Regular soldiers have sometimes regarded the UDR as a bunch of amateurs. But the butchers, bakers and candle-stick makers on whom it relies manage to plump out the Army's strength in Ulster, to make a more comfortable profile. Between 1,200 and 1,500 are on duty every night and about 2,000 turn out at weekends.

A number of families serve together, including one family of six in Fermanagh—a mother, father, grandmother and three children. The system is flexible, so students can drop out altogether at examination time. But most are on duty two or three nights a week and on two or three weekends a month. Not only do they relish the chance to 'do their bit' but they like the money. They earn the same rates as regulars, but only get paid when on duty. A single eight-hour shift merits one day's pay. A husband and wife team might find that while it does not do much for married life, at least it helps pay off the mortgage.

Their bravery has at least been indisputable. By mid-1978 eighty-six had been killed and 159 injured.

Marksmanship. Northern Ireland duty has disrupted training schedules, interrupted promotion courses and imposed a heavy workload on the troops. But it has probably made better soldiers out of them. The hiss of a bullet fired in anger can do more to train a man in a minute than a whole fortnight in front of a blackboard or on the plains of West Germany, fighting imaginary Russians.

One positive result has been a revision of small arms training. When soldiers first came under fire in Ulster they found that they had little time in which to line up their assailants in the sights of their SLRs. They had still less time to drop into the classic prone position. Previous campaigns had questioned soldiers' ability to shoot straight. Northern Ireland confirmed the doubts and forced the Army to do something about it.

Statistical analysis showed that seventy-five per cent of shooting was at ranges of 150 metres or less, seventy-five per cent was at night and fifty per cent was at moving targets. Only twenty-three per cent was carried out from the prone position. Several reforms were introduced after careful study at the School of Infantry, Warminster. Soldiers have been taught how to fire kneeling down, standing up, in the dark, at fleeting targets and at a variety of ranges.

The whole philosophy was changed. A training pamphlet 'Shoot to Kill' introduced new concepts. A soldier had been taught how to fire a variety of small arms and he practised once or twice a year on the ranges. Now he would be taught to fire one weapon, in most cases the self-loading rifle (SLR), but he would be taught to fire it really well and would practise throughout the year. Most soldiers would regard the SLR as his personal weapon—and this would apply to all ranks up to lieutenant-colonel. Every year he would have to score seventy per cent in shooting trials or face remedial training if he failed. But those who scored over eighty-five per cent would qualify as marksmen, with a badge to prove it. The result of all this has been a dramatic improvement in shooting standards, particularly at night, when marksmanship has also been helped by the introduction of the Sight Unit Infantry Trilux—a night sight with four-times magnification, usually referred to as the Suit.

Special courses have been held at the School of Infantry. Some soldiers have even dressed up as women, swearing obscenities at the trainees in the manner of Irish street crowds. (The Army has always said, virtuously, that its men have been shocked by the language of women in Ulster.) The need for this kind of preparation has diminished over the years because most soldiers have learned it all at first hand. But it indicates how suddenly and how thoroughly the Army had to adjust to a new kind of threat, which had not been seriously envisaged. Meanwhile the Ulster patrols have been helped to some extent by a new mobile radar set, called Claribel, which when carried in the back of a Land Rover can immediately show the troops in which direction to shoot back when they have been attacked. The Army believes it will be of great value in the echoing Belfast side-streets, especially at night.

Common sense has been taught the hard way, with infantry sections covering one another as they patrol the towns, backing up at the sound of a shot and sealing off the narrow streets. In this sense Ulster has provided unique experience for junior officers and NCOs.

Publicity. Northern Ireland has also pushed the Army before the public eye. It has been a television campaign in every sense of the phrase. Off duty the soldiers have watched television. On duty the television has watched them. This has often been embarrassing for the Army as mistakes and indiscretions have been ruthlessly examined in the media. It has also forced it to pay more attention to its public persona. Every unit in the province now has to appoint a Press officer who is responsible for liaison between that unit and the reporters, and for communicating incidents to the central Press office at Lisburn for general dissemination. Officers and NCOs going to Ulster for the first time have been given lessons in the art of being interviewed, sitting before television cameras while Royal Army Education Corps officers have tried to play the part of aggressive young examiners, seeking to uncover embarrassing facts.

The Army has if anything moved too far the other way. From being totally insensitive about its public face, it has become over-sensitive, prickly over criticism. Senior officers have made themselves available to the Press for interviews, but have been bewildered by the ease with which reporters have then gone away to attend similar briefings from members of 'the other side'. On the other hand, relations between Army and Press have been generally good, certainly far better than those between the United States Army and reporters in Vietnam.

There have been errors of judgement. The most notorious was Bloody Sunday on 19 January, 1972, when the 1st Battalion of the Parachute Regiment shot thirteen Catholics dead after a riot. That incident has gone down in Irish folklore and has been well used by the Republican movement as a focal point for anti-British propaganda. But even that disaster has failed to scar permanently the general image of restraint and good sense which the Army has cultivated. Soldiers have not been gentle at all times when enforcing the law. But they have been under unbearable provocation. To say that no other Army in the world could have done as well in Northern

Ireland, has become something of a cliché. But it is probably true nevertheless.

The cost of military operations in Northern Ireland has risen steadily, partly as a result of inflation and partly because of the more sophisticated equipment which has been needed, and the accommodation programme. The statistics are as follows:

	£ million
1969–70	$1\frac{1}{2}$
1970–71	$6\frac{1}{2}$
1971–72	14
1972–73	29
1973–74	33
1974–75	45
1975–76	60
1976–77	65
1977–78	68·8

But it has kept the Army in the public eye. Its influence on recruiting has been debatable. At first the publicity probably helped recruiting. Later it seemed to have an adverse effect. But when the world recession brought high unemployment among school leavers in 1975–76, the Army was not short of applicants. Surveys have indicated that few young men were deterred from joining up by the thought of having to face danger across the Irish Sea.

There have been a number of campaigns to pressurize the Government into withdrawing the troops from Northern Ireland. But none has been well orchestrated and all have failed. The mother of one soldier who drove an armoured fish and chip van around Londonderry initiated a petition to bring the boys back home. Army wives have also protested, notably those of the 2nd Battalion of the Parachute Regiment who were aggrieved because their husbands during part of 1972 were in danger of spending more time in Ulster than they did at home. They had a point, and the Army quickly promised that the 2nd Paratroopers would not be returning to the province in the foreseeable future. A number of MPs, among them Mr. James Wellbeloved who later became Parliamentary Under-Secretary for the RAF have at one time or another and for a variety of reasons argued that the Army should pull out. Mr. Roy Mason, Secretary of State for Defence, in early 1974 warned the Northern Irish ominously that pressure was mounting in Parliament for a withdrawal. This was widely interpreted as a threat to the quarrelsome politicians in Ulster—although the Ministry of Defence issued a statement later that day, anxiously denying that any threat was intended. Mr. Tam Dalyell, the Labour MP claimed about the same time about half the Labour MPs in Parliament were in favour of withdrawal, and some observers thought that his estimate erred on the low side rather than the high. The Cabinet at one stage seriously considered the possibility of bringing back the troops, although not so seriously that it ever seemed likely. Pacifist groups have encouraged soldiers to desert, in some cases to Sweden where they could join American GIs who had absconded on their way to Vietnam. In 1978 the *Daily Mirror* urged the Government to plan for the withdrawal of troops in five years' time—the first major newspaper to do so.

The Army has responded by trying at all costs to keep morale high. Individual grievances have been dealt with more swiftly than usual and strenuous efforts have been made to keep the soldiers' wives happy with mid-term week-end leave for the troops, free telephone calls back home and video-taped messages from units relayed through closed circuit television at the home bases in West Germany and Britain. The only campaign which has consistently pressurized the Government has been the IRA's programme of violence. But this has not been as effective as one might have supposed and has stiffened rather than weakened Army resolve. In any case the troops have soldiered on.

Since 1976 the Government has pursued a policy of 'RUC primacy'. As the violence has gradually decreased the police have taken over the front-line role. This was partly made necessary anyway by the ending of detention without trial in December 1975. The RUC have had to investigate crimes like any other police force and prosecute the gunmen in the courts. But the IRA, reorganized on a tight cellular pattern since 1977, has been too strong to allow the Army to lower its guard dramatically. Moreover, there are still many areas in Ulster where the RUC cannot go without Army protection. Army bases in parts of Belfast and Londonderry and along the border in tough little towns like Crossmaglen and Forkill, have looked more like wartime dug-outs than peacetime police stations—and a series of attacks by electrically detonated home-made mortars and M60 machine-guns have made the precautions remain necessary.

Compensation. Some of the most deeply-felt grievances over Northern Ireland service have arisen from the compensation paid to injured soldiers or to the families of those who have been killed. There have been complaints that young soldiers have sometimes received less than the civilians for whom they have been fighting—included those who have supported, or at least sympathized with 'the other side'.

148   THE SOLDIERS

The Army says that much of the criticism has been based upon ignorance. Press and public, unaware of all the avenues to which a soldier can turn for help, have allowed their hearts to rule their heads in what has been throughout, an emotional campaign. It is true that the critics were more justified in the early years than they are today. But it is also arguable that the benefits would not have improved without them.

The most important improvement of all was in April 1973 when the services introduced a number of changes to the Armed Forces Pensions Act for those who had been invalided out of service, and for widows of those who had died. They included a system of 'attributable pensions' for servicemen disabled or killed in the call of duty. Special ex-gratia payments were also introduced for those who had been injured in Northern Ireland before the new pensions started.

The pension varies according to the disability and to the soldier's rank, and is adjusted every year to allow for inflation. It is based upon a percentage of the ordinary full service pension for that rank. In 1978 a major with 100 per cent disability (severe paralysis for instance) was entitled to an annual £4,135, while a private with a similar injury received only £1,175.

A major's widow was entitled to £3,527 a year and £844 for each child, while a private's widow received £1,529 and £400 for each child. They also receive lump sums ranging from £6,062 for a brigadier to £2,000 for a private with 100 per cent disability. A brigadier's widow in 1978 received a lump sum of £3,031, while a private's widow was given £1,000. These lump sums are given to widows in addition to the gratuities which they receive on the death of their service husbands, regardless of how they have died.

Apart from these Ministry of Defence awards, there are war widows' pensions and war disability pensions available from the Department of Health and Social Security. The idea is that the combined pensions should provide a minimum level of income. In addition, there are a number of allowances which the soldier can claim from the DHSS.

Finally, he can claim compensation from the Northern Ireland Office—and so can his widow. It is awarded in respect of financial loss, pain and suffering and expenses. The amounts have varied widely over the years, according not only to the extent of the injury but also to the career prospects of the soldier. One private who suffered a thirty per cent disability after multiple fractures and a partial amputation of his left foot in 1973, later received £13,500 through the courts. Another who was sixty per cent disabled had only £10,000 because his careers prospects had not been so bright.

Awards in general have ranged from about £50 given perhaps for pain and suffering after a slight head wound, through £74,000 for a private who was severely paralysed, to £88,300 which is the highest compensation so far paid to any soldier. It was awarded to Captain Ray Hazan, aged twenty-nine with a wife and two children, who was serving with the Royal Anglian Regiment when he lost his sight and his right hand in a parcel bomb explosion at Londonderry in October 1973.

The widow of a soldier who has been killed receives less than a soldier who has been badly disabled. Her husband's career prospects over the next sixteen years are examined on the basis of his annual reports. Then the authorities take into account how much he would have earned during that period and compare it with the pension which his widow will now receive.

From that sum they deduct a 'personal allowance' which is the money that the soldier might have spent upon himself had he lived. The average personal allowance is about twenty per cent. But it varies widely. Had a soldier spent a great deal upon himself, smoking forty cigarettes a day and drinking every night in the local pub, the widow might have a larger sum deducted. On the other hand, if her husband had been a quiet family man who handed over his pay packet every week, she might lose no more than twelve per cent.

In a few cases a widow has found herself entitled to no extra compensation at all, because attributable widow's pension has left her better off than she was when her husband was alive. But this is likely only in the case of a private soldier with little hope of promotion.

There have been complaints in the past about the time that the courts have taken to adjudicate on claims against the Northern Ireland Office. A soldier has had to wait up to three years because it has taken that time for the extent of his injury to be fully assessed. The case takes less time when a limb has been lost. He might therefore have his claim settled in nine months if he is lucky. Nor do widows have to wait quite so long. But the system, certainly in the early years, has seemed unsatisfactory to families who have suffered mentally and physically.

It was improved in August 1977. Since then all claims for compensation have been dealt with under the Northern Ireland (Compensation) Order 1977, instead of under the Criminal Injuries to Persons (Compensation) Act 1968. One effect of this is that when the back-log of cases has been dealt with, there should be less delay in dealing with claims because there will not be a queue for court time to deal with disputed cases. The 1977 Order also provided for a discretionary award of £5,000 to a widow.

In general the Army points out that soldiers injured in Northern

6

Ireland are not quite as hard done by as critics believe, in so far that any amount of money can compensate for some of the horrific injuries inflicted by high-velocity rifles or bombs. The benefit of the doubt, it says, has always been given to the soldier or his widow. And the great benefit which they get is the attributable pension, which, unlike the large sums of money sometimes awarded to plaintiffs in the High Court, allows for inflation and continues for life.

Much of the criticism has sprung from an impatience with bureaucracy and the subjection of wounded men to legal scrutiny. In that case, it will probably never be completely stilled.

9

Imperial Legacy

Hong Kong. Since the last British troops left Singapore the only whiff of the Orient which soldiers can look forward to is in the colony of Hong Kong. Even there the garrison has been so reduced that a British battalion can expect to go there only once in ninety-nine years. So a new recruit can hardly be guaranteed a visit.

Hong Kong island was seized by the British in 1841 after China had upset Victorian traders by banning the import of Empire-made opium. Kowloon, now a bustling city on the mainland, just opposite the island's main town, was added in 1860. Then in 1898 China granted a ninety-nine-year lease on the New Territories which consist of 235 more islands and a chunk of land behind Kowloon. What happens in 1998 when the lease expires is the 64,000 Hong Kong dollar question.

Still, it is not a question which bothers the soldiers overmuch. For one thing they are unlikely to be around themselves when the time comes. For another they have plenty to think of meanwhile.

This is partly because there are not all that many of them left. Under the Defence Costs Agreement of December 1975, Britain withdrew one infantry battalion, the artillery regiment and the armoured reconnaissance squadron and lumped all those units which remained into one brigade—or field force—instead of two. The Royal Navy and the RAF contingents were also reduced and the total military presence went down by nearly a third.

There are now nearly 8,000 soldiers in Hong Kong and they account for about ninety-three per cent of the entire British presence. But the majority are Gurkhas. Some are based at the headquarters on Hong Kong island, serving on the staff of the Commander British Forces (CBF)—who in a colony is bound to be a very important person. But the post of CBF has been downgraded to a major-general appointment since the rundown, instead of the lieutenant-general's post which it used to be.

About 7,500 however belong to the remaining brigade—or Gurkha Field Force as it is called. The Field Force should not be confused with the Gurkha Brigade, which is the old administrative term still used for the Gurkha organization itself. The Colonel Brigade of Gurkhas, for instance, in his office at the island headquarters, is different from the Field Force commander, a British brigadier who is unlikely to be a Gurkha officer himself—at his headquarters of the Field Force at Sek Kong in the New Territories.

The Field Force consists of three Gurkha battalions all stationed in the New Territories, a British battalion at Stanley Fort on the far side of the island, and three Gurkha supporting arms, the Gurkha Engineers, Gurkha Signals and Gurkha Transport regiments. There is also a squadron of the Army Air Corps with eight helicopters. Of the 7,500, about 5,000 are Gurkha, 1,500 are British and 1,000 are locally recruited Chinese who never move out of the colony. There are also 6,000 dependents, so it is something of a colony within a colony. The Royal Hong Kong Regiment however is only a locally recruited force of between 600 and 700 volunteers, rather like the TAVR in Britain, with British officers filling the key posts.

Under the same Defence Costs Agreement of 1975 the Hong Kong government promised to pay more towards the cost of maintaining the British garrison. Since April 1978 they have been paying three-quarters of the costs and will continue to do so until 1983 when the agreement expires.

In return Britain surrendered any land which had become superfluous after the run-down. This included the old headquarters at Victoria Barracks, a leafy complex which soldiers were sad to see go. The Army has had to move in with the Navy, in a new tower block in the grounds of the old naval headquarters, HMS Tamar, nearby.

There are several roles for the Army in Hong Kong. The best known but least convincing is that of deterring the Chinese from grabbing the colony back. (China regards Hong Kong as British-occupied Chinese territory.) No one seriously believes that the Army could do much to stop the People's Liberation Army if they decided that Britain has overstayed its welcome on the Chinese mainland. But at least the British garrison could make the Chinese use some force, instead of just marching straight in.

More important is the job of backing up the Hong Kong police if riots started up again on the scale of 1967—when Hong Kong was affected by the overspill of the Cultural Revolution in China. The troops are on twelve-hour alert, and frequent exercises test their readiness to respond to the instant crowd trouble, for which the colony is almost as famous as for instant suits and topless bars. They have Saracen armoured personnel carriers and a stock of anti-riot equipment like that used in Northern Ireland—although their stock has been in serious need of replenishment.

There is also a lot of community relations work—or there has been over the years. Troops have run youth camps, built roads and helped to fetch and carry water in times of drought, all to combat Communist propaganda. But this kind of work has been cut down because it all costs money, and soldiers have found that the residents are not very appreciative.

When they are not scanning the border for early warning of the Yellow Peril, troops are on the look-out for illegal immigrants. Up to twenty of them are caught every night as they try to slip from Communist China into capitalist Hong Kong, lured by the bright lights and the relative comforts of one of the most acquisitive communities in the world. Those caught are handed back to the Chinese border-guards because Hong Kong is in some danger of being swamped by too many people in too small a space. But the Chinese treat them quite leniently so nobody feels too badly about it.

One battalion at a time guards the Chinese border. The British and three Gurkha battalions take it in turns, and each border stint lasts from four to six weeks. The duty battalion sets up its headquarters at Fan Ling police-military station and divides the twenty-one-mile border into three sections, East, Central and West. Most illegal immigrants pop up in the Eastern sector, where the town of Sha Tau Kok has the frontier actually running down the middle of the main street. Battalions keep a tally of how many they have caught, which is one way of passing the time. But they also get more money because when up at the border they are operating in field conditions, which means that they enjoy free food and accommodation.

Battalions also take it in turns to supply an officer and twenty-five men for United Nations honour guard duties in Korea. This detachment has the distinction of being the Easternmost extension of the British presence. Based in Seoul they perform guard of honour duties for visiting VIPs. British soldiers say rather smugly that it takes a while to learn how to slouch along in time with the Americans. But Korean duty which lasts for two months at a time, is looked on as a nice perquisite.

Apart from regular training in Hong Kong itself, troops go to jungle warfare schools in Brunei and Fiji. Each company spends about six weeks on jungle training every year. 'It isn't the jungle that matters' as one officer said. 'It just happens to be a good opportunity for uninterrupted training of any kind.'

So life can be quite busy, what with one thing and another. British battalions in Hong Kong now complain of family separation for six months out of every year, which is higher than anywhere else, except for those units going to Northern Ireland.

This makes for familiar problems with the British wives. The battalion at Stanley Fort has its married quarters scattered round the colony in high-rise flats. Young wives away from home for the first time find themselves in isolated blocks among Chinese-speaking communities. This is particularly bad in the summer when the high humidity makes children crotchety. Most soldiers enjoy their posting in Hong Kong. But they do not all find life there very easy.

Even single men need organizing if they are not to become bored at the weekend. The day has gone when the British Tommy had plenty of money to spend. When the 1st Royal Green Jackets who went to Hong Kong in 1978, asked for volunteers to stay behind in Britain they had no great trouble in finding them, and all those who volunteered were single men.

Brunei. Brunei is the other Far East posting open to Gurkhas, but not to indigenous British units. And the Gurkhas will not be there for very much longer.

Brunei is a tiny oil-rich sultanate, the last remnant of a historic Moslem state which once ruled most of North Borneo. The original Brunei (which is another way of spelling Borneo) was gobbled up by British interests so that only 2,000 square miles are all that remain with a population of 160,000—rather less than that of Swansea.

Although Brunei ceased to be a British protectorate in 1959, Britain retained responsibility for its defence. Not only have British officers helped to train and command the Royal Brunei Malay Regiment, which is the Sultan's own army, but Britain has kept a battalion of Gurkhas at Seria, in the heart of the oil and natural gas fields which supply most of Brunei's wealth.

After the 1974–75 Defence Review the British Government announced its intention to end its commitment to Brunei and move the Gurkhas out. The reasons were political rather than financial. The Sultan already paid the full costs of keeping the battalion there, as well as those of the seconded officers in the Royal Brunei Malay Regiment. He could well afford to. But the British Labour Government was unhappy about the use of British troops to protect what is technically an autocratic regime, however benevolent it might be. Moreover withdrawal of the battalion would enable the size of the Gurkha brigade to be reduced.

The next few years were spent negotiating with the young Sultan and his father—both of whom proved skilful procrastinators.

Britain offered to keep the Gurkhas there for five more years. The Sultan held out for twenty years instead. The Hong Kong government watched with interest, hoping that the Sultan would win, because the battalion at Brunei provided a rapid means of reinforcing the Hong Kong garrison should trouble break out in the colony. The Gurkhas, too, were reluctant to leave because the two years in Seria made a nice change from the New Territories in Hong Kong—as well as providing a good opportunity for jungle training.

But the Sultan finally gave in and accepted the British compromise. Brunei will assume full sovereignty in 1983—five years after the agreement which was finally signed in 1978. The Gurkhas will remain there until then, and so will the seconded officers, who have the job of ensuring that the Sultan will have enough trained troops of his own to take over the defence of Brunei when the time comes.

Gibraltar. Gibraltar is another of those fine-sounding places which appeal most to those who have never been there. Soldiers in Catterick and Colchester look enviously at their colleagues as they pack their bags for a sunny posting on the Rock. But after two years in a parish measuring three miles by half-a-mile, few are all that sorry to return.

Gibraltar was uninhabited until the year 711 when the Moors under Tariq-Ibn-Zyad invaded Southern Spain and built a castle there. The name comes from Jebel Tariq—'the mountain of Tariq'. Britain captured it in 1704 during the War of the Spanish Succession and was granted sovereign rights under the Treaty of Utrecht in 1713. It has held on to it ever since, most notably during the siege of 1779–83, when the Rock was successfully defended against the combined forces of France and Spain. Now the Spanish, not unnaturally, would like to have it back.

During the Second World War the Army had 16,800 troops in Gibraltar. The garrison was gradually reduced after 1945 until it was down to 660. The run-down was reversed during the mid-1960s, however, when a Spanish campaign to freeze out the British, culminated in 1969 with the total closure of the border, the ending of the ferry to Algeciras and the cutting of the telephone link. Since then Gibraltar has been in effect an island, many of whose families have been isolated from relatives a few hundred yards away in Spain.

At one time during the period of tension in the 1960s the Army strength was raised to 1,100. Since 1972 it has remained at about 800. But although the atmosphere is more relaxed since the death of General Franco, the restrictions on the troops and their 800 dependants on the Rock, have not been lifted.

There is an infantry battalion, which is stationed in Lathbury Barracks on the southern tip of the Rock, a surveillance troop of the Royal Artillery and the usual bits and pieces including signallers and engineers. There is also the Gibraltar Regiment, a local volunteer force which provides an artillery battery.

The Army's role is to defend Gibraltar, although there is no imminent threat to it, even from the disgruntled Spanish over the border. In one sense the Rock is a natural fortress, strong enough to shake off a nuclear bomb and big enough to contain workshops and storerooms in twenty miles of cool, damp tunnels. Air turbulence is also said to make the Rock a difficult target for low-flying aircraft and paratroopers. On the other hand, one battalion of infantry would be hardly enough.

The troops man the Four Corners frontier guardroom and the three observation posts along the mile or so of wire which divides Gibraltar from the Spanish border town of La Linea. They also mount ceremonial guards like that outside the Convent, the Governor's official residence, and of course they train.

But training is limited on an 'island' with a total land area of only $2\frac{1}{4}$ square miles. They have an electronic target range within the Rock, and even a ruined village which has been recently built up into a useful practice ground for urban warfare. But each company has to return to Britain for more constructive training once a year, and the whole battalion returns once during its Gibraltar posting. Since 1976 the place of the missing companies has been taken by territorial units from Britain who spend their annual fortnight's 'camp' on the Rock—and the battalion is replaced by a regular battalion from home. But only the engineers who go around happily widening roads and maintaining fuel pipes find Gibraltar a useful place on which to exercise their military skills.

In the good old days Gibraltar was an enviable posting, because soldiers and their families could cross into Spain during their off-duty hours. Now they feel uncomfortably restricted in a community which must be one of the most parochial in Europe. Wives complain of high prices and lack of variety in the shops in Mainstreet—which is hardly one of Europe's more attractive thoroughfares. Fresh vegetables arrive ready-salted after their voyage across the straits from North Africa.

The Army has gone to some trouble to extend soldiers' horizons as much as possible. There are charter flights to Britain, and a special leave scheme for those who fancy taking their holidays in Morocco. The Moroccan authorities have welcomed them with open arms, and pockets. There are ski-ing and mountaineering expeditions in the Atlas Mountains, Dormobiles for hire and even permanently-sited caravans for service families.

Most take advantage of the opportunities. The alternative is to drive round and round Gibraltar's seven-mile perimeter—just as Gibraltarians do on a Sunday, like rats in a cage searching for the exit. Even the beaches become too crowded for comfort in summer, when tourists tend to raise local prices, and the services' own swimming pool is over-subscribed. They can still go to Spain, but only by visiting North Africa first then bouncing back to Algeciras or somewhere and doing the same complicated, expensive operation to return.

The worst influence of the border closure, however, has been on accommodation. It was never very easy anyway. The closure meant not only that the forces were cut off from the use of hired accommodation in La Linea to supplement their own limited resources, but also that more people came to live on the Rock. Spaniards who were previously employed in Gibraltar were forced to retire behind the wire curtain, while their place was taken by Moroccans—who snatched any spare houses and flats for themselves.

In 1972 only 227 of 490 Army families in Gibraltar lived in standard quarters. The rest had to make do with a selection of sub-standard houses, chalets and caravans, which did little for their morale. Since then 130 new quarters have been completed at Europa Point on the Southern end of the Rock, though after much delay and substantial cost. As a result fewer than 100 now live in sub-standard housing. But the situation is still far from satisfactory and the Ministry of Defence is faced with a dilemma over how best to improve it.

The dilemma is caused by uncertainty over the future. There is one question mark hanging over the naval dockyard and another over the dispute with Spain. The ministry is trying to improve existing accommodation but is reluctant to invest heavily in new building programmes as long as there is a chance that the border may be reopened.

There is also a question mark over the future ownership of Gibraltar. Gibraltarians still want to belong to Britain. But if they ever changed their mind in the face of Spanish pressure, Britain would probably let the Rock go—particularly now that Spain is once more governed democratically. It still has strategetic value to Nato. But Britain has largely withdrawn from the Mediterranean and would probably withdraw from Gibraltar too, given half a chance. However, that is an issue for the future. For the time being Britain has no plans to withdraw any of the soldiers who are

6*

stationed there, or avoid paying the annual cost of £32 million to maintain the Royal Navy, the Army and the RAF on the Rock.

Belize. Belize is the last British colony in the Americas. It is also among the less desirable postings that a soldier might receive. Until recent years there was little chance that he would ever see the place because one infantry company was enough to maintain the Pax Britannica on the Central American isthmus. But the aspirations of neighbouring Guatemala under its dictatorial regime have changed all that.

Belize which used to be called British Honduras was opened to British settlers in the seventeenth century but did not become a colony until 1862—first under Jamaica and later in its own right. But Guatemala which has a spurious claim to the place has been demanding ever since free access through Belize to the Caribbean. The constant bickering reached a head in 1963 when the Guatemalans, furious over the granting of internal self-government to Belize, broke off diplomatic relations with Britain.

Guatemalan sabre-rattling exercises on the border have provoked three crises during the 1970s. On each occasion Britain has reacted with astonishing speed, drafting in reinforcements to defend the mixed population of 120,000.

The last of these was in 1977 when Britain doubled the size of the garrison overnight by dispatching six Harrier vertical-take off aircraft and nearly two battalions of infantry with armoured and artillery to support them. In 1978 there were still nearly 2,000 British servicemen there, including 1,500 soldiers. These consisted of a battalion in the North, around Belize City, and two companies in the South—where the Guatemalans covet the natural harbours around Punto Gorda. (The Gurkhas provided the two companies in 1978). There is also an armoured troop with Scorpion and Scimitar vehicles and an artillery battery.

In the North where the land is flat and open they have to defend the Western highway which runs from the Guatemalan border, through the tiny capital of Belmoplan to Belize City on the East coast. In the South they patrol the frontier, moving from one Indian village to the next through some of the steepest, thickest jungle in the world. Patrols out on location from the jungle base camp at Salamanca have been known to take three days to cover three miles. In between these Northern and Southern battle zones the jungle is almost impenetrable for either friend or foe.

Soldiers who are first trained at the Jungle Training School at Sibun in the Maya Mountains, have to learn how to build a basha, a primitive shelter made of ground sheet, hammock, mosquito net and jungle wood—which might be their home for ten days while out on patrol. All water for drinking and washing has to be purified and shaving is banned.

The average rainfall is 170 inches in a year, and six inches have been known to fall in an hour. Soldiers complain of being constantly soaked, either from the monsoons or from the rivers which they have to wade—or through their own sweat in the steamy atmosphere.

Tracks are flooded as often as not, bridges are swept away during the worst of the rainy season, and the Army has to rely heavily on sea freighters for transporting supplies from North to South, or on helicopters. Helicopters also have to land in jungle clearings from time to time to evacuate soldiers overcome by heat exhaustion or bitten by snakes and insects.

The wild life is ferocious. There are coral and fer de lance snakes—which can grow up to eight feet in length—tarantula spiders the size of saucers, scorpions, clouds of the fiercest mosquitoes in the world, sandflies, a so-called beef bug which burrows beneath the skin, and fire trees which spurt blistering sap over the soldier who tries to strike one with his machette. There are also pumas and jaguars, and a four-man patrol which recently camped, unwisely, in a jaguar's lair had a sleepless night while two of the big cats prowled around outside in what might be described as a threatening manner. At least four men in every platoon have to be medically qualified and all section leaders carry morphine. There are times when the 'Guats' as they are called, dozing away in their own border outposts, seem the least of the Army's worries.

Off duty, life is if anything rather worse. Soldiers live in improvized tin huts with little to do in the evenings except wander round the local bars and brothels or swill beer in camp. Even Belize City, rebuilt after a hurricane in 1961, is a listless shanty town constructed largely of softwood and corrugated iron, surrounded by open sewers. There are not even beaches, only mudflats and mangrove swamps, although the Army takes parties of troops to a nearby atoll where they can get a feel for the real Caribbean.

All this creates problems. In 1978 a BBC programme about life in the colony upset the more puritanical among the television audience by portraying a beery Christmas party for the soldiers, and what looked suspiciously like a licensed brothel. The Army pointed out that it was only facing up to reality by ensuring that all the girls were medically checked. But the GOC Scotland, one of whose regiments was concerned, was so cross that he flew to Belize forthwith to see for himself what was going on.

Not all soldiers are disenchanted by their six-month unaccompanied tours in Central America. Some have liked the excitement of the jungle, and several regiments have been impressed by the opportunity for training. A number of officers have studied the wild life in their spare time and have made quite significant collections of butterflies. Others have gone shooting birds and iguana—which, they say, tastes not unlike chicken. Some have used their leave to tour the rest of Central America.

All manage to save some money. Because they are serving in field conditions they pay no food and accommodation charges. They would have reason to feel aggrieved if they had to. As a result some have saved up to £1,000 during their time there. On the other hand, few are reluctant to leave when their six months is up.

The Army has tried to improve facilities by building junior ranks clubs and installing air conditioning, and the engineers have had a busy time. But the Ministry of Defence is reluctant to pay more than the £11 million it now costs to keep the three services in Belize, because of the uncertainties.

While talks continue between Britain and Guatemala, preparations are well advanced for the happy day when the Army will be released from its task of guarding this so-called 'hell-hole of the Empire'. Since January 1978 British troops have been helping to train a home-grown Belize Defence Force which hopefully will one day take over the job. When that day dawns few British soldiers will be very regretful.

Cyprus. Cyprus became independent in 1960 after being a British colony for thirty-five years. But Britain retained its bases in the South, which became known as the Sovereign Base Areas (SBAs). There are two of them. One is at Dhekelia in the South-East and the other is at Akrotiri in the South-West, which contains not only the huge RAF airfield but the military headquarters at Episkopi. Separated by seventy miles, they together represent ninety-nine square miles of Cyprus territory.

It is just as well that Britain did hold on to them. The troubles of 1974 culminating in the Turkish Army's occupation of forty per cent of the island sent thousands of refugees from both communities into the relative safety of the SBAs. Akrotiri airfield also became the centre of a comprehensive RAF airlift of families to Britain—although many of the families were service people anyway.

There are not as many troops on Cyprus as there used to be because the RAF squadrons have been withdrawn and Akrotiri is now open only for a few hours each day. Those left are mainly soldiers, some of whom serve with the United Nations Force in

Cyprus (UNFICYP), but most of whom form a national garrison to guard the SBAs and the refugees still living there.

The UNFICYP was formed in 1964 after the civil war between the Greek and Turkish communities. Britain contributes about 770 soldiers, including a tactical headquarters, two infantry companies, an armoured reconnaissance squadron and a few logistics units.

Before 1974 the UNFICYP troops were stationed in small blobs in the more sensitive areas. Now they are stretched in a line along the buffer zone which keeps Greek from Turk. But the size of Britain's contribution has remained about the same.

The British contingent who cover Sector One to the West of Nicosia, are on active service so do not pay for food and accommodation—which is not very comfortable anyway. Most are on six-month unaccompanied tours. But there are 120 dependants who belong to a sprinkling of officers and NCOs on UNFICYP two-year staff appointments.

The garrison troops number 2,500, and are divided between the SBAs. An infantry battalion is stationed at Akrotiri and Episkopi. In the South-East at Dhekelia there are two infantry companies (the other half of the battalion involved in the UNFICYP) and a flight of helicopters. An armoured reconnaissance squadron, a Royal Engineers squadron, a transport and a signals regiment are split between the two.

The companies in Dhekelia are also on six-month unaccompanied tours like their colleagues further North. In fact since 1977 the two halves of the battalion have swapped jobs halfway through so that all get a change of scene. The UN commanders were reluctant to allow this. But the Ministry of Defence insisted that all should get a chance of some relative relaxation in the SBAs while out there— and that all should earn themselves a UN medal as a reward for their time in Cyprus.

The ministry has also tried to ensure that all battalions sent to Cyprus for six months see some sunshine while they are there. They used to change round in May and October every year, which meant that one battalion enjoyed the Cyprus summer while the other shivered in the winter. But the change-round dates have been adjusted so that the ration of sunshine is more equitable.

The logistics units at the SBAs also procure supplies for the UNFICYP soldiers—and for the UN force in Lebanon since 1977. Then the bill is sent to the UN for payment.

For a time after the 1974 troubles all troops in Cyprus were unaccompanied. But most of those in the SBAs have their families with them now and the number of dependants in 1978 totalled 2,560. Life for the wives and children is not quite as idyllic as it was.

Tourist spots like Famagusta and Kyrenia are no longer accessible. But there are still enough places to make Cyprus retain its reputation as a congenial posting, with good fruit and vegetables on hand, fine beaches and spectacular scenery.

Married quarters are good too, and so are the facilities on the bases. Single soldiers do less well. Barrack accommodation is described by the Ministry of Defence as 'not unsatisfactory' which means that the barracks are post-war—but old-fashioned in design. Nor are there any plans for converting barracks into flats for single soldiers—as is being done in West Germany. Cyprus hardly ranks as top priority.

How long the troops will remain in the SBAs in their present strength is an open question. The Army points out that those in Dhekelia are facing a Turkish army outside the base area, so they are in effect performing a similar job to that of the UNFICYP. There is also the long-range radar installation on top of Mount Olympus which is an important Western monitor in the Eastern Mediterranean and the Middle East. On the other hand, there is pressure from the Turks for Britain to relinquish the Dhekelia SBA altogether, in return for a guarantee that the area would be given to the local Greek Cypriot population. Much rests upon the outcome of Greek-Turkish negotiations over the future of the island.

It costs Britain about £43 million at 1978 prices to maintain all its servicemen in Cyprus. But this includes the salaries of the troops who are stationed there so withdrawal would not mean a saving of that amount. In 1978 there were no plans for any change in the deployment.

Training Teams. By 1978 few soldiers remained in Malta, where the entire British garrison was due to be disbanded by March 1979 at the end of the seven-year Defence Facilities agreement between Malta, Britain and Nato.

But there were still 440 Loan Service Personnel (LSP) scattered round sixteen different countries, 'hired' from the Ministry of Defence to provide technical expertize for local forces. In Bangladesh, Ghana, Kenya, Nigeria and the Sudan these consisted of full training teams involved in special projects. In Nigeria, for instance, they were running the staff college and the local school of infantry.

The other LSP who in some countries were additional to British garrisons, were stationed in Belize, Bermuda, Brunei, Hong Kong, Iran, Kuwait, Malaysia, Oman, Qatar, Saudi Arabia and the United Arab Emirates.

In Oman there were as many as 120 LSP, holding key positions in the Sultan's Armed Forces, three years after the end of the ten-year war against Communist rebels in the Southern province of Dhofar. They included the commander of the Sultan's forces and the commander of the brigade in Dhofar. But the sixty Special Air Service soldiers who had once helped to train the Firqat, the local militia on the Dhofar mountains, had been withdrawn. The other 120 were due to be phased out gradually as Omani soldiers assumed greater responsibilities within the Sultan's forces.

PART THREE

THE REGIMENTS

10

Corps D'Elite

Not everyone has seen soldiers policing the streets of Northern Ireland, driving their tanks across West Germany or peacekeeping on behalf of the United Nations in Cyprus. But most people have seen them trooping the colour on the Queen's official birthday every June or changing the guard at Buckingham Palace—if only in travel brochures or on television. 'All they have are generals, admirals and bands' grumbled General George Brown, Chairman of the United States Joint Chiefs of Staff, recklessly in 1976. He hastily withdrew when Britain's armed forces counter-attacked, but one can see what he meant. To an outsider it must sometimes seem like that.

Those soldiers whose scarlet uniforms, tall bearskins or silver helmets have made them the most famous ceremonial troops in the world, belong to the seven regiments of the Household Division. Five of them, the Grenadier Guards, the Coldstream, the Scots—each of whom have two battalions—and the Irish and the Welsh, are regiments of foot guards. The others are the Household Cavalry, the Life Guards and the Blues and Royals, the sight of whom riding down the Mall in full dress on a bright spring morning can still take the breath away.

All but the Irish and the Welsh Guards have a pedigree stretching back to the time of the Civil War in the seventeenth century, or the restoration of the monarchy which followed it. They are thus among the oldest in the British Army, and also among the most senior in status—which is not necessarily the same thing.

Tribal Distinctions. It is easy to distinguish between the Life Guards and the Blues and Royals—and not very difficult to pick out the Foot Guards. Although all Foot Guards apparently wear the same ceremonial uniform, or Home Service Clothing as it is called, they carry distinctive plumes in their bearskins. The Grenadiers wear a white plume or 'hackle' on the left side, the Coldstream a red one on the right, the Irish Guards a blue one on the right and the Welsh Guards a green and white one on the left, while the Scots Guards have no plume at all. The tunic buttons are arranged differently too. Grenadier buttons are evenly spaced in ones, the Coldstream's are in sets of two, the Scots Guards in threes, the Irish in fours and the Welsh Guards' in fives. One does not need to squint at their badges to decide whether it is a grenade (Grenadiers), the Garter Star (Coldstream), a thistle (Scots), a shamrock (Irish) or a leek (the Welsh). The tribal system is carefully preserved.

They also have their tribal areas, though this does not apply to officers and the areas are not as well defined as they used to be. The Welsh Guards are ethnically the purest in that virtually all their soldiers come from Wales. Nearly all the Irish, too, have Irish connections, though the Ulster troubles of the last ten years or so have forced the regiment to draw heavily upon the expatriate Irish colonies in London and Liverpool. But the Scots Guards have been forced to extend their catchment area to the North of England, particularly to Preston in the West and Darlington in the East, because of the large number of regiments who are drawing upon the youth of Scotland. And many come from London, sons of former Scots guardsmen who have married English girls and settled in the South. The Coldstream Guards who used to be a North of England Regiment now recruit heavily in Cornwall and the Grenadiers, once full of Birmingham boys take in men from all over the place, though with a strong London–Midlands–Manchester bias.

The Household Cavalry recruit nationally on principle. They actually try to be as heterogeneous as possible, so that all parts of the United Kingdom have a hand in guarding their sovereign. This is not always as easy as it might sound. Englishmen and Welshmen are not hard to come by. But Scotsmen are more difficult to net because Scotland is already so over-fished, and Irishmen, not surprisingly, have recently become more elusive.

Officers in the Household Division come from all over the place. A number of Coldstreamers still come from the North of England, perhaps the sons of Yorkshire landowners, and many of the Irish Guards have Irish ancestry—or more often, Anglo-Irish ancestry. But few Welsh Guards officers come from Wales and most look quite amazed at the suggestion that they might have done so. It is more likely that they have joined their particular regiment because their fathers or grandfathers had served in it. As Guards regiments spend most of their time in the South, their Northern or Celtic lineage impinges little upon the lives of their officers in the Mess.

The distinctions between regiments of the Household Division are insignificant when compared with those which set the division apart from the rest of the Army. In some ways it is like an army within an army, kept separate by virtue of the ceremonial duties it performs and the demands which these make upon its time and training.

It is, for instance, uniquely self-contained with its own Guards Depot at Pirbright in the Surrey commuter belt where everyone from officer to junior drummer begins his military career. It has its own duty rotas for battalions, and its centre of gravity rests so firmly and permanently in London that the division's commanding officer, usually a major-general in the Foot Guards, doubles up as the officer commanding London district.

For a soldier who yearns to put down roots in one part of the world, rather than lead a nomadic existence trailing from one barracks to another, life in the Guards may be what he craves.

The Foot Guards may be stationed in Chelsea Barracks, where there is room for two battalions, Pirbright (next door to the depot), Caterham—which actually was the Guards Depot between 1877 and 1969—and Victoria Barracks, Windsor. Wellington Barracks in Birdcage Walk, almost opposite Buckingham Palace, is now undergoing extensive renovations, and Victoria Barracks at Windsor will soon be temporarily vacated so that the builders can move in. There is therefore room for up to five of the eight battalions to be stationed in the London–Windsor area at any one time, and in the summer when ceremonial duties come thick and fast, they need that many. Otherwise guardsmen might wilt under the strain. Of the other three, one is always overseas (the Welsh Guards have been in Berlin for the last two years) and two more are usually in BAOR. Meanwhile the Army tries to free the Guards from emergency duties in Ulster during the summer months, although over the years they have certainly done their share.

The attitude of the Guards to their special position within the Army is somewhat ambivalent. On the one hand, they enjoy the glamour of the state occasion and their links, however formal and institutionalized, with the monarchy. On the other hand, they and the rest of the Army are sensitive to any suggestion that they are no more than painted toy soldiers, taken out of their box to make the place look pretty and then quickly replaced when the real fighting starts. They are, they protest, real soldiers, just like anyone else—only better.

The Household Cavalry suffer most of all. Poised on their huge black horses, their silver helmets gleaming and their white buckskin breeches spotless, they look too exquisite to do anything that matters. In fact though, most of the Life Guards and the Blues and Royals are khaki-clad members of service regiments in the Royal Armoured Corps. In most respects these Household Cavalry service regiments are no different from all the other cavalry units.

But there are certain distinctions, as one might expect. One is that the two regiments, typically enough, operate a rota of their own, alternating between two postings, Detmold in Germany and Combermere Barracks at Windsor. Until 1969 they enjoyed another privilege in that unlike the rest of the cavalry they always served as armoured reconnaissance units and never had to bother with tanks. But the Household Cavalry themselves began to feel that however noisy, dirty and smelly an animal the tank might seem, they were missing out by never serving in a fully armoured role. So now whichever of the two regiments is at Detmold is always armed with Chieftain main battle tanks while the regiment at Windsor remains an armoured reconnaissance unit with Scorpion light tanks and scout cars.

Another distinction is that whereas other cavalry units send their recruits to Catterick for basic training, the Household Cavalry send their people along with other members of the Household Division to the depot at Pirbright.

The depot, officially known as Alexander Barracks, was built in the 1960s and is thus quite a modern, breezy sort of place. At least it seems so to visitors who usually expect the Guards' training camp to look more formal and forbidding.

All adult recruits spend their first twenty weeks in the Army in Caterham Company, housed in an airy, open-plan block which would have amazed their fathers. It also sometimes amazes the Guards, who would have preferred the architect to have settled on a more orthodox design. The brand new gymnasium, the elaborate indoor shooting range, the assault course and the depot's extra-mural centres, the adventure training camp at Fremington in Devon and the battle camp at Stanford, Norfolk, all testify to the continuing success of the Guards in getting what they want.

The parade ground, affectionately called 'the Golden Acre' by Pirbright drill instructors, and the thirty-three daily bugle calls from Reveille at 6.30 in the morning to Lights Out at 11 p.m. seem more familiar. Basic training for recruits is a fortnight longer than for other infantry soldiers, because of the extra need for ceremonial drill. They have to learn how to slow march, for instance, and how to do double-sentry drill—in preparation for guard duty before tourists from all over the world at Buckingham Palace.

At the end of basic training the Foot Guards leave for their regiments. But the Household Cavalry go either to Catterick or to Windsor for more training, depending upon whether they are being posted to one of the two service regiments or to the mounted regiment, the ceremonial unit in London.

Household Cavalry. There are 1,600 men in the Household Cavalry, and recruiting is no great problem. In 1977 the height requirement was raised from 5′ 8″ to 5′ 9″, to regulate the flow of aspiring young household troops. Only 315, including eighteen officers belong to the mounted regiment and about two-thirds of the 297 or so troopers and NCOs, are ex-juniors—which is roughly double the proportion for the Army as a whole. They are asked when they join which part of the Household Cavalry they would like to serve in first and about fifty per cent opt for the mounted regiment with its pomp and pageantry. This is the life which most of them are expecting when they opt for the Life Guards and the Blues and Royals in the first place.

But very few of them can ride. However grand they look as they clip-clop down the Mall, one might reflect that most of them are still in their teens and have served in the Army for only a year or two. They are very much raw recruits, chosen specifically because the Army finds that the younger they are, the easier it is to teach them to ride.

The equestrian course which transforms them from nervous young men who have never even patted a horse before, into members of a Sovereign's escort, lasts only twenty weeks. The first sixteen are spent at Windsor, and the last four at London—where they wear their full-dress uniforms as much as possible and learn how to cope with the traffic. They are taught how to walk, how to trot and how to canter, and how to jump modest fences, up to three feet tall. The objective is to produce competent military horsemen, not virtuoso riders. Even so the course is very intensive and it used to last twice as long in the more leisurely days before the last war.

The regiment has its own riding master, a major who has risen from the ranks on a quartermaster's commission. The present riding master has been with the regiment at Hyde Park Barracks, Knightsbridge, for about twelve years and is an authority not only upon horsemanship but also upon every aspect of mounted cere-monial. The Prince of Wales recently attended the regiment's riding school for a refresher course, and the present Duchess of Gloucester, a Danish commoner before her marriage, was taught to ride there.

The young troopers have to learn how to look after their horses as well as how to ride them. They feed them, groom them and even learn how to detect minor ailments. There are 220 mounts, as well as those in training and ideally each man looks after his own. In practice it does not work out quite as tidily as that.

The mounted regiment is divided into three squadrons. One is the headquarters squadron which simply looks after administration.

The other two are the operational, or 'sabre' squadrons as they are called. One belongs to the Life Guards and the other to the Blues and Royals, and they remain quite distinct, with their own suites of offices and accommodation. But each has about fifty per cent more horses than men so each trooper has to care for about one-and-a-half animals during his time there.

Hyde Park Barracks was designed on contemporary lines by the late Sir Basil Spence, one of Britain's foremost post-war architects, whose buildings have included the rebuilt Coventry Cathedral. The stables are on two floors and visitors passing by on double-decker buses are sometimes startled to see a large black horse staring thoughtfully back at them over the wall.

Most of the troopers will spend only the first three years of their military career there. The Household Cavalry then posts them automatically to one of the two service regiments. By that time they are ready for a change anyway. But the three years of living in close proximity with animals is long enough to encourage quite a bond of affection between man and beast. Senior NCOs in the Household Cavalry, who may well have been posted back at some later stage as a Corporal of Horse (equivalent to Sergeant) can become quite 'horsey' people, and very knowledgeable.

An officer of the Royal Army Veterinary Corps (RAVC) is responsible for the horses' welfare. Most have to be re-shoed about once a fortnight after tramping along London's streets. This is done by young farriers, trained at the Army School of Farriery which is run by the RAVC at Melton Mowbray. But the farriers are more than just blacksmiths and assist the vet by administering medicines, rubbing on ointment and even giving minor injections.

The RAVC is also responsible for buying the horses, for the King's Troop of the Royal Horse Artillery and the Royal Military Police as well as for the Household Cavalry. Two RAVC officers, accompanied by an officer from one of the units involved, fly to Ireland to buy fresh supplies from dealers, who have been supplying the Army for many years. The mounted regiment orders its mounts a year ahead and always in the spring. By then they know how many of their older animals have failed to last the winter—which is, for obvious reasons, the time when most horses are called to their Maker. Usually the regiment needs between twenty-five and thirty replacements every year—and they remain grazing in the RAVC's paddocks at Melton Mowbray until the regiment summons them to the colours.

The daily routine for man and horse can be very tedious. It is also very long. Reveille is at 6.30 a.m. and by 7 a.m. they are out on the roads, exercising the horses either in Hyde Park or in West London.

Sometimes they are out on the streets earlier than that, if the regiment's commanding officer decides, in what are called the daily 'watering orders', that more exercise is called for. But they are always back by 8 a.m. before the rush hour starts—ready to feed the horses first, then themselves.

After breakfast, the troopers clean the stables and groom the horses until Naafi break at 11 a.m. Then they work on the riding equipment or 'tack' until 12.30 p.m. This is time for the daily 'Feed away' parade when the horses have their lunch. The squadron commander visits the stables, inspects the lunch boxes and, satisfied that the beasts are getting a fair deal, shouts 'Feed away', which is a signal for the horses to start munching. It is rather like an orderly officer striding around the cookhouse to ask if there are any complaints. In the afternoon the soldiers attend to their own kit, feed the horses again, clean out the stables once more and so on . . .

Much as a service regiment spends its time caring for its tanks or armoured cars, so the mounted regiment concentrates its energies on its horses. But unlike tanks, horses cannot be locked up in a garage and left there, so the routine continues on Sundays and at Christmas. This is why the regiment prefers to rely upon volunteers who actually want to spend all their working hours with horses. If they did not the days would seem endless.

Officers serve with the mounted regiment on rather a different basis. All begin their careers with one of the service regiments and then move to the mounted regiment at some later stage for a normal two-year posting. Their horses are called chargers, not horses—a little social distinction. Most of the officers are fond of horses anyway and nearly all can ride. But they still have to attend the riding school before starting service at Hyde Park Barracks. And they still have to be up at dawn, come fair weather or foul, to exercise their mounts before breakfast.

Officers also spend much of their off-duty time on equestrian pursuits, although this is not obligatory. The Blues and Royals are historically rather good at polo, the Life Guards at jumping or competing at point-to-points. Many if not most of them hunt. 'Most of our time is devoted to chasing or killing something or other,' said an officer. 'But we do not lose our military skills. You will find some of the best shots in the Household Division down at Hyde Park Barracks.'

But ceremonial duties are what life in the mounted regiment is all about. The trooper who tires of burnishing his cuirass or whitening his buckskin breeches has to be reminded that spit and polish is part of the regiment's *raison d'être*. The standards are high. The Army always uses a long stirrup for riding, which makes it more difficult for a soldier to retain his equilibrium and his dignity on horseback. Yet he is expected to sit up straight and resist the temptation to scratch his nose or to push back his heavy helmet from his brow. The helmet has a pointed forepiece which is not the most comfortable thing to have sticking into the bridge of one's nose. But it looks smarter when it does. It is therefore one of the uncomfortable facts of life that troopers have to learn to live with.

The long hot summer usually begins in late April or early May with a state visit to London by some foreign dignitary. In early June comes the Queen's Birthday Parade, followed by the Garter Service at Windsor and a second state visit in late June or early July. In September the regiment leaves London for its annual camp. Then on return, it starts preparing for the State Opening of Parliament and the Lord Mayor's Show in November.

Each ceremonial duty is planned like a military exercise. First, the regiment studies a list from Buckingham Palace which shows the number of carriages in the royal procession and the status of the royal family taking part. This status dictates how many troopers will be needed. The Queen for instance merits a full Sovereign's Escort of two divisions, each one consisting of an officer and twenty-four troopers. One division rides before the carriage and the other rides behind. The Queen Mother, however, gets only a Captain's Escort with Standard with two divisions of one officer and twelve men. Then there is a Prince of Wales Escort, a Captain's Escort without Standard, down to the Escort for the Speaker of the House of Commons, who has to make do with a single trooper to protect him.

After assessing the length of the procession, the regimental adjutant walks along the route, reconnoitring drains, lamp posts and pillar boxes by which the divisions can orientate their positions while riding. He takes notes and even prepares a series of sketches which are distributed to the officers on parade that day. Finally there is a full rehearsal at dawn.

Changing the Guards. Even when there is no special occasion, the regiment has to mount guard outside Horse Guards in Whitehall. When the Queen is in residence in London, this requires a guard of one officer and fifteen men, but only twelve men when she is away. Four men are on guard at any one time, two of them dismounted beneath the Horse Guards arch, looking curiously inept in their helmets, breeches and boots, like ducks out of water. But the other two sit on horseback outside the Whitehall entrance. This is the memory of the Household Cavalry that most visitors to London take home with them—which is one good reason why only the smartest men on guard that day are chosen for the chore. These are awarded 'the box'—which is short for sentry box—and they alternate throughout the day, doing one hour on duty and one hour off. Troopers strive to win 'the box' for other reasons than vanity. It lasts only from 10 a.m. until 4 p.m., so in effect the smartest men work the shortest day—and of course enjoy the more subjective pleasure of being photographed or filmed and incessantly stared at by every holiday-maker in town. In the summer, the troopers quite enjoy it, and the slow, stately walk on horseback down the Mall can be an exciting experience for a young boy in his teens. But the guard has to be mounted in the winter too, and on cold, bleak January mornings it is not so funny.

They do not, of course, wear their full regalia throughout the twenty-four hours on guard. Not only is it uncomfortable, but the soldiers do not want to crease the carefully pressed tunics and trousers by lounging around in them.

A visitor to the guard room at Buckingham Palace, where Christopher Robin went down with Alice, would be surprised by the transformation in the Queen's Guard within half an hour of the new guard coming on duty. The tall young guardsmen who look so impassive in their scarlet and bearskins are by that time sprawled on easy chairs, watching colour television in shirt sleeves, and drinking coca-cola or coffee from the slot machines installed there by Naafi.

The ceremony of changing the guard at Buckingham Palace is a much grander affair than that at Horse Guards with a Guards' band swaggering in and out of the Palace forecourt and sightseers standing on every available inch outside. Again most of the guardsmen rather like all the fuss, if only for the glamour associated with it and the admiring glances from wives and girlfriends. But it is unnerving for a young man on guard for the first time. One said: 'It does not matter how long you have practised back at the barracks. When you see all those people on the pavements as you come round the corner of Buckingham Palace Road your legs begin to shake with the fear that you might do something wrong.'

Foot Guards who are stationed at Chelsea Barracks have to leave precisely at 11.08 in the morning for the twenty-two minutes march to the Palace and the daily ceremony at 11.30. Battalions at Caterham, Pirbright or Windsor arrive by coach at Wellington Barracks first, then march to the Palace from there.

When the Queen is in London, the guard consists of fifteen guardsmen, one colour sergeant or pay sergeant (equal to a staff sergeant in other regiments), one lance sergeant, two lance corporals, a 'drummer' (who in fact blows a bugle) and a cook. All are commanded by the Captain of the Guard who may be only a lieutenant. Between them they have to mount three sentries—one of them positioned outside the guard room itself and the others at twin sentry boxes outside the front of the Palace. An NCO is always on duty in the guardroom, manning a radio link with the police and listening for the alarm bells which are connected to the sentry boxes for the use of sentries who see anything suspicious in the Palace yard.

Similar guards have to be mounted every day at St. James' Palace, the Tower of London and at Windsor. It follows that a duty rota has to be rigorously kept by the Brigade Major (a lieutenant-colonel) at the Horse Guards headquarters of London district. The rota is drawn up months in advance and can get quite complicated. Every effort is made to spread the load but even so guard duty can come round twice a week for some battalions in the summer months.

The sentries do two hours on duty followed by four hours off. It is a very comfortable guard room, brightly decorated in white and resembling the lodge of a grand house, which is in effect what it is. Guardsmen off duty can sit in the spacious television room, can play cards or simply doze on their beds in the large upstairs dormitory. There are double bedrooms for the NCOs, a small single room for the officer and an ample dining-room and kitchen below stairs. It was renovated very successfully several years ago.

But the senior guard room is that at St. James' Palace, where the Buckingham Palace officer joins his colleagues for meals. They can even invite guests for drinks up until eight o'clock at night and thereafter for dinner, which they eat in some style, surrounded by silver and numerous pieces of bric-a-brac bequeathed by a variety of regiments over the years. One heirloom is a snuffbox supposedly made from one of the hooves of Napoleon's horse Marengo— although Guards officers point out that so many mementoes have been made in similar fashion that Marengo must have been blessed with a dozen legs or more. It is not all fun and games, however, and the Buckingham Palace officer, back on duty for the night, is expected to be up and about several times, ensuring that all is as it should be.

Sentry duty itself is exacting. Some guardsmen who can remember the days when sentries stood outside the main gates of the Palace, say that it is more difficult now than it used to be. They were withdrawn to the comparative privacy of the forecourt to save them from over inquisitive tourists. But at least there was more to look at when the crowds were milling around them. They felt more involved.

There is still plenty to do, however tedious it may seem. Every passing officer has to be given a butt salute with his rifle and members of the royal family merit a full 'present arms'. A collection of royal photographs on the notice board inside the guard room ensures that a new guard can recognize the faces—often seen in the back of a fleeting car. If the major-general commanding the Household Division passes by outside the railings more than fifty yards away, the sentry is expected to recognize him and salute. An official arrival or departure of the Queen herself may mean a full turn out of the entire guard—summoned by the duty bugler. But the Palace sends a list of the Queen's engagements to the guard room in advance. So at least this does not come as a surprise.

A code of private but quite historic signals passed between the twin sentries outside the Palace ensures that they act in unison. The guardsman on the right in what is known as sentry box 'A' is always the senior of the two and as such has to make the decisions. He even has to decide when they will step out of their boxes and patrol slowly past each other on their beats—a drill which has to be performed every ten minutes or so, if only to stop the sentries from dozing on their feet. He cannot look at his watch so he judges when ten minutes are up, then taps his rifle butt on the ground to tell his partner that the next patrol is due. Two taps indicates the need for a butt salute and three for a 'present arms'. There is also a finger code which is used when the sentries are actually patrolling past each other. One extended finger means 'turn to the front and halt'. Two means a butt salute and three once more a 'present arms'. The code has been used successfully for many years and generations of puzzled tourists have stood curiously at the Palace gates, wondering how on earth the two men, without apparently speaking or turning their heads, have managed to synchronize so well.

Guard duty is not just a formality, particularly at the Tower where there is a large ordnance depot. Even at Buckingham Palace the occasional demonstrator or eccentric tries to intrude upon the royal privacy. And the sentry is not there simply to look pretty. If a man rushed past him with a gun in his hand, the guardsman would be expected to forget his dignity and tackle him.

Moreover at ten o'clock every night for the last six years or so, the Palace guard has gone 'tactical'—which means that it actually patrols the Palace grounds in earnest. The sentries abandon their boxes and their cumbersome bearskins. They draw walkie-talkie radio sets from the duty NCO and move along prescribed routes in front of the Palace and in the gardens at the back—which they enter by the policemen's gate in Buckingham Palace Road. They wear khaki forage caps, but keep on their scarlet jackets, so they can hardly be described as inconspicuous.

They are not the only barrier between the Palace and uninvited visitors. Policemen with dogs sniff out the dark corners of the Palace grounds at night, and patrol the wide expanse of lawns. One of the reasons why it is wise for guardsmen to keep to the known paths is that any unauthorized wandering might cause him to be attacked by the dogs.

A patrol has occasionally encountered the Queen—out for an evening stroll perhaps. 'But she always puts one at ease,' said a sergeant from the 2nd battalion Grenadier Guards. 'When I was on duty once as a young guardsman I suddenly noticed the Queen approaching with two of the younger children. I presented arms, shaking with nervousness when the children ran up to me. But the Queen called them back immediately, then chatted to me quite naturally. It was something to write home about.'

Guard mounting goes on every day except during the winter when it takes place every other day and the Queen's Guard stays on duty for forty-eight hours. There is always pressure on the Household Division from the British Tourist Board and from travel agents who would like the guard to be changed every day, and if possible twice a day, for the entertainment of foreign visitors. The Guards are flattered by the interest, but have so far not succumbed to the temptation.

Trooping the Colour. The most gorgeous spectacle of all is the Queen's annual official Birthday Parade when the Guards 'troop the colour' past the Queen, in a ceremony whose origins are older than their own. It takes place in early June. Travel agents sometimes wish that the Queen could have more than one official birthday. But the Queen herself, who has to ride side-saddle for the best part of two hours, has so far shown no sympathy with this view.

A regiment's colour or flag, at one time served as a rallying point on the battlefield, and was 'trooped' past soldiers at the end of a day's march to ensure that they recognized it. Because they symbolize the regiment's identity, the colours—with battle honours embroidered on them—have come to acquire a mystical significance. The Royal Artillery feels the same way about its guns, which have become officially recognized as its 'colours' and gunners have gone to suicidal lengths to save them from capture by the enemy.

The practice of trooping the colour developed into a ritual for special occasions. It was first performed on the sovereign's birthday in 1805, and has been repeated ever since, except during the period 1811–20 when George III was ill.

The eight battalions of Foot Guards take it in turns to perform the main part of the ceremony, which is the actual trooping of the colour. The battalion's commanding officer takes charge of the whole parade, under the superb, if temporary title of Field Officer in Brigade Waiting. But all those Guards battalions which happen to be in Britain, together with the massed bands, the Household Cavalry and the King's Troop Royal Horse Artillery, take part in the parade. Altogether sixty-two officers and 1,550 other ranks are involved.

There are two dress rehearsals on Horse Guards. Both are in public, and the second is attended by everyone except the Queen herself. Each rehearsal is video-taped, then replayed to officers and senior NCOs, who scrutinize every detail. But most regimental sergeant-majors are wary of over-drilling the soldiers beforehand. The aim is to bring them to a peak of perfection on the day itself.

The soldiers have to rise at 6 a.m. on the day of the parade, and do half an hour of physical exercises before breakfast, to tone them up for a tiring day. All those who faint on parade—a particular risk in hot weather—are medically examined. Those found to have stayed up late the night before, or to have gone on parade with too tight a collar or bearskin, can be charged and punished.

The ceremony has changed little over the years, which is just as well because some of the intricate drills demand plenty of practice. The most notorious is the spin wheel, a purpose-designed manoeuvre performed by the massed bands to get out of the way of the escort for the colour. One half of the band wheels to the right while the other half does an about turn and marches away on a left diagonal. Inexperienced musicians have sometimes found themselves quite lost amid a crowd of unfamiliar faces, all moving in different directions. It usually seems to work out in the end, but nobody understands how and attempts to write down the drill have so far failed.

The Household Cavalry too have some anxious moments, however impassive they might appear. The job of keeping in perfect line during the royal ride down the Mall is more difficult than it looks, and the size of the crowds can be unsettling even for soldiers and horses who are so used to ceremonial occasions. They also worry about steering their mounts round the tight corners of the Horse Guards parade ground. It is not as if Horse Guards formed a perfect square. An officer who tried to keep his troops parallel to the line of buildings could find himself charging too far off course.

Still, however tiring it is for the 360 musicians in the foot bands, however worrying for the cavalry squadrons, however irksome for the motionless guardsmen, the Queen's Birthday Parade is privately regarded by most of those who take part as a special experience which they would not like to miss. To be dropped from the parade is a very real punishment for offenders during the weeks leading up to it.

Research has been conducted into the use of prefabricated stands on Horse Guards. These might help to keep down the costs of mounting the Trooping of the Colour parade. By 1976 the annual cost was already £45,000, of which £38,000 had to be spent on hiring stands. This means that the Army has to charge for all the seats. Even the parents and wives of the men on parade have to pay for the privilege of watching them march past the Queen. There is also a charge for seats for the second dress rehearsal, although the first one is free.

There is never any difficulty about selling the seats. The Army could sell them to tourists for three times the price—and make a profit if it was allowed to. But it would like to prevent the price from rising too steeply, if only for the sake of relatives, some of whom might have to travel from Scotland and Wales, and stay overnight in London.

Social Elitism. The royal connexion is formal and institutionalized. But it is still quite close, Not only is the Queen the colonel-in-chief of all the regiments, but three of her family are honorary colonels of the Foot Guards, Prince Charles (Welsh Guards), the Duke of Edinburgh (Grenadiers) and the Duke of Kent (Scots Guards). The Coldstream whose colonel is Major-General Sir George Burns and the Irish who have General Sir Basil Eugster, seem quite proletarian by comparison.

The Household Cavalry is linked to the Court by three ancient appointments, two Gold Sticks-in-Waiting and their deputy Silver Stick. One Gold Stick is Earl Mountbatten, the Queen's uncle, who is Colonel of the Life Guards and the other is Field-Marshal Sir Gerald Templer, Colonel of the Blues and Royals. These are responsible for ceremonial and have a close relationship with the Lord Chamberlain's office. But most of the work is done by Silver Stick, a retired officer who is also known as Lieutenant-Colonel commanding the Household Cavalry.

Gold Stick and Silver Stick were originally the monarch's personal bodyguard, and they retain the right to have easy access to the Sovereign. After all it was not until 1951 that the Household Cavalry joined what was then the Guards Brigade. Before then they were

Sovereign's Parade at the Royal Military Academy Sandhurst

Potential officers undergoing command tasks at the Regular Commissions Board

General Sir Edwin Bram⌐
Chief of the General Sta
1979

Corporal Percy Broad,
handler, with the regim⌐
mascot of the Royal W
Fusiliers

A bedroom at the WRAC training centre at Guildford, Surrey

Soldier students parade at Welbeck College

An AFV-432 armoured personnel carrier

The 71st Regiment (TAVR) Royal Engineers, bridging the Rhine

Bomb Disposal Unit with their Wheelbarrow robot in Northern Ireland

A Black Watch piper in Hong Kong

Adventurous training in Norway

A border outpost in Cyprus

A camouflaged **TAVR** soldier in training

The Queen inspects the Irish Guards at Windsor

A soldier on the Brecon Beacons during a selection course for the Special Air Service

Dancers of the 1st Battalion The Royal Scots

Briefing for Gurkha patrol in Cyprus

Uniforms, old and new, of the Queen Alexandra's Royal Army Nursing Corps

Apprentice cooks at Aldershot

Special Air Service troopers on a combat survival course

The Women's Royal Army Corps band marching past the Kaiser Wilhelm Memorial Church in Berlin

NIGHTLY

1 · N° 1

SOLDIER

THE BRITISH ARMY MAGAZINE

MESSAGE FROM THE CHIEF

glad to have this opportunity of being
to speak to all soldiers in the B.L.A.
gh the first number of "SOLDIER".
and I have come a long way together ;
ave been through some very bad times
some very good times.

what is the situation to-day ?

o possible conceivable chance can
any win this war ; victory for the Al-
bsolute and definite victory, is cer-
All that now remains is the conquest
rmany itself.

re fighting on German soil and we
entered the ring for the last round ;
is no time limit for this round ; we
continue until our opponent has had
h.

what are we fighting for ?

emember the poem written in the
by a soldier of the Eighth Army, in
rse of which he gave his views as to
e were fighting for :

eace for the kids, our brothers freed,
kinder world, a cleaner breed."

ems to describe it very well.

o feel that out of the comradeship
great armies that are fighting in this
ll be born a new factor : a factor
d, which will be a powerful influen-
he difficult days that lie ahead
e fighting is over.

st see to it that this will be so.

r behalf I send our greetings to our
es serving in other theatres of war.
re many of our friends in Africa, in
India, in Burma, and in other pla-
all of them we send our best wishes,
the many thousands who garrison
ntain the lines of communication
ut the world.

te our comrades in the Royal Navy
Merchant Navy, and in the R.A.F. ;
ers know well that without their
e could have achieved little.

friendly greeting to the soldiers of
d nations fighting with us.

ur families and friends in the home
we send a very special word of

ften wished "Good luck" to sol-

ow to "SOLDIER".

Montgomery.

Field-Marshal,
21 Army Group.

2

FRANCS (B
IN FRANCE
IN HOLLA

The first day cover of *Soldier* magazine in 1945. An earlier 'dummy' run
was never distributed, although it was identical except for the goodwill
message from Field Marshal Montgomery

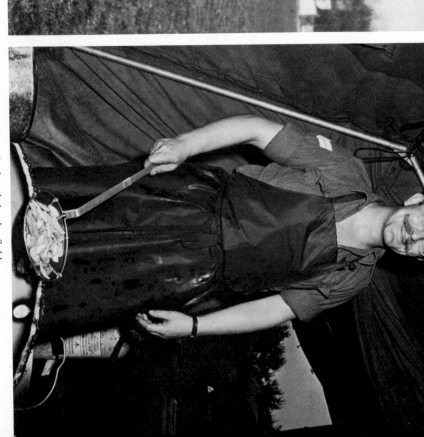

The bandmaster of the 4th/7th Dragoon Guards

A corporal cooks lunch in the field

Soldiers help civilians cope with flood relief in Surrey

nside a married quarter

The Cavalry and Guards Club, Piccadilly

The Union Jack Club, Waterloo Road

very much household troops, and the two Gold Sticks still have precedence over anyone else in the Army.

Silver Stick, although an officer on the Major-General's staff at Horse Guards, has the right to approach the Queen directly, ignoring Army protocol. It would be a grave discourtesy to do so, but there has been a precedent in modern times. It happened in the 1920s as an indirect result of the amalgamation of the 1st and 2nd Life Guards.

The Household Cavalry decided that it no longer needed two barracks in London, one at Knightsbridge and the other at Regent's Park, and after much humming and hah-ing, surrendered Knightsbridge to the Foot Guards. But it had reckoned without the rising popularity of the motor-car. Troopers on guard duty soon found themselves having to ride to Horse Guards through a West End full of honking traffic and exhaust fumes. Back to the major-general at Horse Guards went the cavalry to ask if they could change their minds after all and return to Knightsbridge with its easier approach to Whitehall. But the major-general, a Foot Guards officer, said 'No'. So the cavalry, unperturbed, took their case to King George V who immediately said 'Yes'.

The cavalry are still commonly regarded as being a notch or two above the Foot Guards in terms of social status, and the Life Guards are thought of as the richest and most aristocratic of all. Whether this is so is debatable. There is certainly not much to choose between the social background of officers in either of the two Household Cavalry regiments, and their counterparts in other cavalry regiments of the line are not exactly poor. Neither the Duke of Kent nor his brother Prince Michael, the two latest members of the royal family to make their careers in the Army, joined the Life Guards or the Blues and Royals.

The two cavalry regiments in the Household Division come into surprisingly little contact with the Foot Guards. So they tend to scoff at each other from afar, though without much acrimony. The Foot Guards call the cavalry 'pony soldiers' and the cavalry call the Foot Guards 'woodentops'—as do a number of other sections of the Army. 'The trouble with sending the Grenadiers to Belize,' said one officer 'is that you cannot tell them apart from the trees.' But the epithet 'the Guards have money but no breeding while the cavalry have breeding but no money' is more witty than it is accurate.

Virtually all are the products of public schools. Aberrations from this unwritten rule are certainly hard to find. There has been some marginal dilution of blue blood in that a wider variety of these schools are now represented. Before the last war most came from

7

Eton, Harrow and Winchester. Out of seventy-five applicants to join the Household Cavalry in 1977, roughly one in three had been to Eton, and a significant number were titled aristocrats. 'But we're not dazzled by titles' one officer insisted. 'We recently turned down an earl and a marquis.'

Most have private incomes or access to family inheritances in times of trouble. Some are extremely rich, particularly in the cavalry. 'But we don't all have grouse moors or private yachts' said an officer at Knightsbridge. 'Those of us who do not, rely upon the generosity of those who do. There is a pretty wide spectrum of wealth.' A young Scots Guards officer pointed out that he had no private means at all—'but only because my old man's a stingy old bugger.'

Applications for commissions, particularly in the cavalry, are carefully scrutinized to ensure that the boy would 'fit in' as they put it. A state school product, they acknowledge, would find it hard to 'fit in'. He would be unhappy, his colleagues would be unhappy and the system would suffer. The system works, so why change it, they argue patiently. There are other regiments which the state school boy can join.

'Parents often ask us how much money their sons would need' said a Life Guards officer. 'I tell them that it is not a question of how much money they have, but how wisely they spend it. He might have £3,000 a year in addition to his Army pay, and might spend it on women and gambling. But another boy might have only £500 and spend it more wisely, perhaps on polo or brushing up his ski-ing on the Continent.'

Full-dress uniforms and other ceremonial paraphernalia are free, issued to each man, officer and non-commissioned soldier, when he is posted on ceremonial duties. The shabrack, the richly embroidered saddle-cloth, costs £1,600 in 1976 and an officer fully attired, including his £800 charger is worth between £6,000 or £7,000. Few could afford that sort of expense on their own.

In theory an officer should be able to manage on his income. It is not as if life in the mess is always very hectic. In fact Guards and cavalry messes in Britain tend to be less sociable places than those of other regiments, if only because they are all near London. Officers either have homes nearby which they repair to in the evenings or at weekends, or they drive up to the West End to meet girl-friends and dine in town.

But extramural activities can be expensive. Household Division sports include polo, show jumping, hunting, shooting and fishing— most of which can make a large hole in a young man's pocket. There is no written rule which decrees that an officer should take part in these, but it is expected that he will—and if he does not he might well feel out of things.

Guards manners are impeccable. But their etiquette is exacting. It is not that their rules of behaviour are markedly different from those of anyone else. But they tend to observe rules which most other people have forgotten. 'Is it true that we never say 'cheers' when we have a drink?' said Major-General John Swinton, commanding the Household Division, a pained expression on his face. 'Well, you know, the kind of families that we come from would probably never say "cheers" anyway . . .' They also still use words like 'breeding' and 'class' and refer to a 'decent' regiment—all of which makes them sound eccentric. A young Guards captain described how he was shocked to find on attending an Army course, that he was expected to wear a dark suit for dinner. 'Here at Pirbright we wear what we like. Now it so happens that I *like* to wear a jacket of some sort and a tie—but that is what we like to think of as a difference of breeding. We don't need rules like that.'

How they get away with this studied social élitism is a matter for some surprise. One reason is that they are sufficiently detached from the rest of the Army to do what they like. Another is that the Army and even the general public, smile upon the Guards' peculiarities and regard them as endearing. Certainly nobody has so far felt strongly enough about them to do anything very positive about them—by, for instance, insisting upon a more democratic social mixture. 'They're a funny lot, the Guards' said one graduate Sapper, but more in wonderment than irritation. They represent part of the military mosaic in Britain, and perhaps the Army fears that if that part of the pattern were changed, the whole complex design would fragment to everyone's disadvantage.

The Royal Horse Artillery. One part of the Army which the Household Division can never look down upon is the Royal Horse Artillery (RHA). When on parade with its guns it has taken precedence over the cavalry ever since Queen Victoria decreed that it should. If the whole British Army paraded together, the man on the extreme right of the line would be the trumpeter of the Chestnut Troop, the senior troop of the 1st Regiment RHA and thus the senior unit of all. Even in the years following the Second World War when snobbery in the Army reached a particularly ludicrous level, the elegant cavalry officers still accepted their colleagues in the RHA as being of their own kind.

High standards, including quick thinking—and acting—have always been the hallmark of the RHA. After the last war the

Gunners decided to retain it as a *corps d'élite*, to which their best men would be sent. The theory was that if you put a crowd of good men together, they would compete against each other and force the general standard even higher. Over the years RHA men claim to have won more top appointments than almost any other corps, and most artillery regimental sergeant-majors are ex-RHA men.

Ordinary soldiers are posted directly to RHA regiments on joining the Army, and some stay in them for life. But others move to other regiments on promotion to sergeant or sergeant-major—to disseminate the high standards they have acquired. Officers who are posted to the RHA as subalterns, also have to move on promotion. But the lucky ones, assuming they have continued to impress, return to command batteries and even perhaps to command a RHA regiment later.

There are only three regiments of the RHA left. These are the 1st, the 3rd and the 7th Light Regiment—which was formerly the RHA parachute unit. But the 3rd RHA has been equipped with the Swingfire anti-tank missile, and parcelled out in batteries to the four armoured divisions in BAOR.

The King's Troop. The RHA unit which most people recognize is the King's Troop—those men in blue Hussar-style uniforms, busbies and gold braid, who gallop along with World War One guns on state occasions and fire royal salutes in Hyde Park. They provide detachments both in front and behind the state coach on state occasions, as they did on Jubilee Day in 1977 for the procession from Buckingham Palace to St. Paul's Cathedral.

One of the surprises about the King's Troop is that it was formed only in 1946. Originally batteries of the RHA had taken it in turns to perform ceremonial duties. But this became difficult after the RHA was mechanized. So King George VI decreed that one unit should be preserved with horses and fancy uniforms to act as a saluting battery for the Household Division.

So the new unit was formed at its present barracks in St. John's Wood, London. It was first called the Riding Troop. But the King on paying it a visit in 1947, spontaneously crossed out the word 'Riding' and wrote 'King's'—the kind of gesture that soldiers delight in. The Queen retained the name when she succeeded in 1952, in memory of her father, and it was one of the few British institutions to keep its masculine gender.

The use of 'troop' in this sense is a RHA term. The King's Troop is really a large battery with seven officers, 182 men and six guns. It is commanded by a major and is split into three sections of thirty-eight men and two guns, commanded by a subaltern.

The guns are 13-pounders dating from between 1905 and 1916. All saw service in the First World War. The design of uniforms has changed little since the turn of the century when it was the standard full-dress uniform of the RHA. Between 600 and 700 blank rounds have to be made especially for the guns each year at the ordnance factory in Glascoed, South Wales, to fuel the ten or so 41-gun royal salutes. The cartridge cases are sent back each time to be refilled.

There are 111 horses, thirty-two in each section. They are bought in Ireland like those of the Household Cavalry. But while the cavalry ride big, black mounts, the RHA use stocky, light draught horses, picked for their strength and manoeuvrability when trundling along the guns in teams of six.

Another surprising thing about the King's Troop is that most of the gunners are directly recruited. Some are attracted by advertisements in magazines like *Horse and Hounds*. Unlike the Household Cavalry, about half of them can ride before they join, and they spend most of their military careers with the King's Troop. Many of the NCOs though are posted from other RHA units.

It is altogether more specialized than the Household Cavalry. Not only do gunners tend to be horsey people before they join, but they spend six months on their equitation course, which is longer than their colleagues at Knightsbridge.

The standards of horsemanship are therefore higher. They need to be, because they have to do far more than simply walk or trot sedately in procession. They have to be able to gallop at twenty-five miles an hour on ceremonial musical rides, drawing a one-ton gun and a half-ton limber—and without any brakes.

Officers are sent to the troop on ordinary two-year postings from other artillery regiments. All are selected for their interest in horses. Like the cavalry they tend to come from the best schools. This, they maintain, is because with such a background, they are more likely to know about horses. Their relationship with the Household Cavalry is close, if only because they spend their summers competing against each other in equestrian events. But the social élitism tends to be more relaxed.

Gunners in the King's Troop certainly have to work hard. Apart from the usual round of summer occasions, with musical rides at the Royal Tournament, the biennial Army Display at Aldershot and so on, they appear at about half a dozen shows round the country every year. They would probably appear at more of them if the costs of hiring them were not so high. Even at 1976 prices it cost between £5,000 and £6,000, most of which was needed to transport the men, horses and guns from London. The cost of getting the

King's Troop to Newark in Nottinghamshire, for instance, was then assessed at £4,000. The men themselves might earn only a few pounds overtime, so it is very much a labour of love—or the call of duty.

Every September they take over the sentry boxes at Horse Guards while the Household Cavalry depart for their annual camp. Once a year they also forget their horses and move to the Royal Artillery ranges to fire modern guns for a change. In wartime they would become a light battery with the United Kingdom Mobile Force.

But for most of the time they are heard and not seen. For all their unique expertise they tend to be the forgotten men of Britain's state occasions.

11

The SAS and the Paras

The Job of the SAS. Anyone crossing the Brecon Beacons in South
Wales at certain times of the year might come across a young man,
a heavy pack on his shoulders, scrambling over the mountains in
lonely desperation. The chances are that one is looking at a potential
recruit to the Special Air Service, Britain's most secretive regiment.
It is better known by its initials, SAS, whose resemblance to the
more sinister SS, is unfortunate and unfair.

The SAS began life in the Western Desert in July 1941. It was
founded by Lieutenant-Colonel David Stirling, then a subaltern in
the Scots Guards, to carry out sabotage and intelligence missions
behind the enemy lines. A second regiment was later formed by
his brother Lieutenant-Colonel William Stirling. A Special Boat
Section was also developed out of the 1st regiment—although this
evolved separately and is now known as the Special Boat Service
of the Royal Marines. From 1944 until the end of the war the
two SAS regiments formed a brigade with French and Belgian
special forces, and the SAS's badge showing a winged dagger and
the motto 'Who Dares Wins' is still worn in the Belgian Army.

The British 1st and 2nd regiments were disbanded in 1945, but a
territorial unit the 21st SAS (Artists) was re-formed in 1947. The
'Artists' refer to the Artists' Rifles, a dashing and very fashionable
TA unit dating back to 1859 whose early volunteers had included
Holman Hunt, Millais and William Morris. The '21' was the result
of some tortuous logic. The original idea was to call it the 12th
SAS, incorporating the '1' and '2' of the 1st and 2nd regiments. But
this might have led to confusion with the existing 12th Airborne TA
unit. So the Army reversed the figures and emerged with '21'.

A post-war regular SAS regiment was not formed until 1952 in
Malaya. It was created out of the Malayan Scouts which had been
founded two years before to carry out SAS-type operations against
Communist terrorists in the jungle. It was called the 22nd SAS.
Then in 1959 the 23rd SAS, another TAVR unit, came into
existence, and these are the three Special Air Service regiments alive
today.

Apart from the years 1960–63, the SAS has been on active service continuously since 1952, including Borneo, Aden, Oman and Northern Ireland. Not so long ago there were as many as sixty in Oman, helping the Sultan to fight his ten-year war against Communist-inspired rebels in the Southern province of Dhofar. Their job was to train and lead the Firquat, a kind of militia formed by mountain tribesmen—many of whom once fought on the other side. SAS casualties were high before the virtual end of the fighting in December 1975. But the troopers suffered as always in silence. Living wild among the mountains they were often indistinguishable from the tribesmen they were training—which suited everyone.

It was partly their unpublicized presence which gave the Oman operation something of a clandestine air, leading to the epithet 'secret war' in the Press. The epithet did not please the British government. But it seemed to be one that they were prepared to put up with. Even when reporters were eventually allowed to visit British troops in the Sultan's front line, the SAS were always kept well out of sight.

The SAS are also still in Northern Ireland—for the second time since the Army began its peacekeeping role in the province in 1969. Again the hush-hush reputation of the regiment and its historic undercover role, encouraged both Irishmen and the British Press to see SAS troopers behind every tree in Ulster. Moreover, the fact that men are seconded to the SAS from other parent regiments made it easy for the Ministry of Defence to deny 'sightings'—or to identify soldiers by citing their parent regiments rather than the 22nd regiment. But in 1975 the Army admitted that a number of men who had 'just finished their SAS training' had been helping out in Ulster during a manpower shortage. The Press estimated their number as forty-five, all of whom returned to the British mainland after four months of intelligence gathering.

Then in January 1976 the government surprised its critics by openly announcing that the SAS were returning to the province on a rather more permanent basis. They were sent to the border areas following a rise in the number of terrorist attacks by gunmen operating from the Irish Republic. Up to eighty of them are still there, although they have since spread to other parts of Ulster.

For some of the time they wear plain clothes, and they are said to have acquired a very creditable Ulster accent to help them get by. But for most of the time they wear the uniform of the regiment in whose area they are operating, and are thus very hard to distinguish. They go on long patrols, setting up observation posts to watch border roads, or carry out raids on suspected hide-outs.

This is very much the kind of work that the resident unit does anyway, but the Army says that the SAS are better at it because of their special training.

There have been one or two embarrassing incidents. One involved the death of an IRA suspect who, according to his SAS captors, was shot while trying to escape after being detained near the Irish border. But more famous, or notorious, was the arrest of eight men from the 22nd regiment who crossed the border themselves in three cars in May 1976—and were promptly picked up by the Irish police.

Two of them, wearing civilian clothes, crossed the frontier by accident. When they did not return they were followed by six of their colleagues, four in plain clothes and two in uniform who had been sent along the same route in search of them.

The Army pointed out that the men had made a mistake in their map-reading. Sceptics pointed out that map-reading was supposed to be one of the skills for which the SAS were famous.

A Dublin court believed the Army and merely fined the men £100 each for possessing unlicensed arms in the Republic. It also sternly rebuked them for their mistake, before sending them on their way. The fines were paid by the Ministry of Defence.

It was an unhappy affair for all concerned. The error itself was simple enough, and the unfortunate troopers were not the first—or the last—soldiers to make it. But apart from its effect upon Anglo-Irish relations, it did nothing for the reputation of the regiment. A number of people in the Army think it would almost have been better to have pretended that the men had known where they were all the time.

The impact of the SAS on Northern Ireland has been hard to quantify, not least because the data relating to their presence is strictly classified. The Army insists that the impact has been considerable, if only because their fearsome reputation has had a psychological effect out of all proportion to actual numbers. Rumours have sometimes credited the regiment with more men in the province than they actually have there. But the Army is content to let the rumours run riot.

Captain Robert Nairac who was kidnapped from a public house near the Irish border, and killed, in May 1977, is generally supposed to have been attached to the SAS at the time—although this has never been confirmed by the Army.

Terrorism during the 1970s has added a new role or two for the SAS. In January 1975 a detachment was on stand-by at Stansted Airport, Essex, after a British Airways jetliner had been hijacked in mid-flight. They were not needed, but it was the first incident

7*

to reveal the SAS's job in the front line of Britain's counter-terrorist plans.

SAS men advised the Dutch Government in 1977 on how to tackle South Moluccan gunmen who were holding hostages in a school and in a hijacked train. And in 1976 a team of twelve troopers were said to have provided a secret escort for the Queen and other members of the Royal Family during the Olympic Games in Montreal. In 1977 two SAS men travelled to Somalia to advise West German Police Commandos on how to free hostages from a hijacked Lufthansa aircraft. In 1975 it was the reported presence of SAS marksmen in plain clothes which was said to have persuaded four young IRA gunmen to surrender after the siege in a flat in Balcombe Street, London. Whether this was true or not is unclear. But the very fact that it was considered possible by the Press at that time indicates the impression that the SAS have made.

The regiment remains very much a sharp instrument which the Army keeps concealed for as long as possible. Even allowing for this obsessive secrecy, the sensitivity which surrounds the SAS and the fears which they evoke are hard to explain. Perhaps it has something to do with their reputation for ruthlessness. Again perhaps it springs from a fear among trade unionists that the regiment could one day be used to spearhead a right-wing military operation in Britain. The involvement of Colonel David Stirling, long since retired, with a civilian organization which was founded in 1975 to help keep public order in the event of a general strike, did not help to dispel the paranoia.

Life at Hereford. How far the SAS's reputation is justified is hard to assess. This is because the Army keeps the 22nd regiment well away from the Press, or indeed from anyone else. It is a conscious policy which has been followed by successive generations at the Ministry of Defence.

The rationale behind this policy is complex and controversial. It rests partly upon the argument that some SAS work is genuinely classified, and that it would be counter-productive to let the world know how the 22nd regiment is planning to combat, say, a team of aircraft hijackers. But some SAS work is also politically sensitive, partly because it might be carried out in countries which do not want the troopers' presence to be known—and partly because the British Government itself may be uneasy over the status of one of two of these beneficiaries. Then there is also the argument that SAS soldiers should not be identified because of the danger to themselves and their families—and to the success of any future operations.

The secrecy surrounding the regiment is not entirely beneficial. It has encouraged such a cloak and dagger reputation that the Army has to think twice about using the SAS. Their presence, once it is discovered, might make a situation seem more mysterious than it is. But then again the Army argues that the mystique is in itself a benefit. It endows the troopers with such a reputation as supermen that enemies are psychologically beaten before the battle starts. This is an exaggeration, but the Army thinks that the policy has paid off in Northern Ireland. The SAS, too, probably enjoy the thought of being the Army's undercover unit. It adds a certain piquancy to what might otherwise be a tough and unrewarding life.

The desire for privacy is helped by the location of the regiment. When the 22nd regiment was first posted to Britain in 1959—the first time it had ever served at home—it was established at Malvern in Worcestershire. But it moved to its present home at Hereford, in the following year.

Not only is this a convenient base from which to mount exercises in the Brecon Beacons, but it is far enough away from any large metropolitan areas for the regiment to live their secluded existence.

The heavily guarded camp, Bradbury Lines, is in the middle of large housing estates to the south of Hereford. Helicopters drone constantly above the ancient town, transporting troopers to the training area at Pontrilas. Sometimes a balloon anchored over Hereford racecourse indicates that the SAS is carrying out parachute practice. But the local Press as well as the national Press are kept at a distance and recent visits by Prince Charles and Princess Anne, who were apparently judged 'safe', were not announced until after they had taken place.

A night-time anti-hijacking exercise which was carried out with police co-operation on a train on the Hereford to Worcester line during the autumn of 1977 was kept as one might expect, a closely guarded secret—even after it had taken place. The regiment denied all knowledge of it, and the operation came to light only because it was observed by local residents.

When SAS men are killed, as a number were in Oman, their bodies are flown back to Hereford, where they are quietly buried in a special plot at St. Martin's Church, near the camp. There are no military honours at the funeral. Nor are details released of how the man died. The regiment usually explains that he was killed 'during a training exercise' which is often untrue. Military honours are awarded, but without any citations.

Beside the empty asphalt drill square, which is used as a landing pad for helicopters, there stands a memorial clock tower bearing the inscription: 'We are the pilgrims, master: we shall go always a little further: it may be beyond that last blue mountain barr'd with snow, across that angry or that glimmering sea'. The names of SAS soldiers killed in action are added to the memorial, and those who survive some hazardous operation refer quietly to 'beating the clock'. But the life is not for those who would like their military glory to be made public.

In one sense the relationship between the regiment and the townspeople of Hereford is quite close. Soldiers marry local girls and drink in some local pubs—all of which have been carefully scrutinized for possible bombs since the regiment's involvement in Northern Ireland. In 1965 the regiment presented a silver statuette to the town, and in 1968 a regimental plaque which was handed to the City Council.

In 1976 Herefordshire people started a public fund to help three injured members of the regiment, all of them paralysed from the waist down as the result of an incident which the SAS refused to specify. They quickly raised a total of £35,000. There have in the past been visits to the local Rotary Club, and on every possible occasion soldiers and civilians have emphasized their close links.

But the fraternizing has its limits. All SAS men are careful not to discuss their military work, and even their wives remain tight-lipped. It is a fact of life which the people of Hereford have come to accept. Visits to the camp itself are at best infrequent, and local people say that security has been noticeably tightened as a result of the Ulster campaign.

In 1976 Hereford United began to hire off-duty soldiers to act as stewards to combat soccer hooliganism. But there were some complaints of rough handling by some of the troopers and the Ministry of Defence swiftly put a stop to it. The regiment has also had to stop some of its men from acting as 'bouncers' at a local dance hall in their spare time. It was embarrassing when one of the soldiers was charged with assault on a man he was evicting.

This was unusual, because few SAS soldiers appear before the local courts, although this probably reflects the tight discipline at Bradbury Lines rather than any attempt to place them above the law. Perhaps it is also because the average SAS man spends seven months of any year away from home, and half of that time abroad.

SAS Training and Organization. Not only is Bradbury Lines difficult for the public to enter. It is also difficult for other soldiers in that acceptance for the SAS eludes most of the hopeful young men who apply.

All are volunteers and all are already serving in other regiments. The Parachute Regiment supplies a large number, but by no means all. Others come from the infantry, the Royal Artillery and even the Royal Armoured Corps. They also come from the specialist supporting corps because even special forces regiments require doctors, dentists, and cooks. The average age of the regiment is twenty-seven and all applicants have to be under thirty-four. But whereas officers retain their ranks on joining, all other soldiers have to revert to the rank of trooper, even if they are already wearing a sergeant's stripes in their own regiment. They will, of course, receive extra pay for parachuting—if they are not already earning that before they join. And the career structure within the regiment is quite good after a few years. But it all means that he who joins the regiment must be very clearly motivated if he is to lose his rank and status and his public identity.

He has also to be supremely fit. This is first tested during an intensive medical examination. Then if he passes, he is encouraged to start his own private exercise routine before joining one of the two four-week selection courses which are held every year, one in Scotland and the other in Wales.

The Army's official recruiting pamphlet for the SAS, which is itself a restricted document, mixes friendly encouragement with magisterial advice. Recruiting is never so buoyant that the Army can afford to deter a young hopeful before he starts. On the other hand, only one out of every five is accepted following the gruelling physical tests and searching interviews. 'Have a go, but do not be disappointed if you fail' sums up the friendly challenge that the Army throws out. 'No one need be ashamed if he has done his best' says the pamphlet, like a headmaster addressing a class before 'O'-level examinations. Not everyone makes a good tank driver or even a clerk, so it follows that not everyone is going to make a good SAS trooper.

That is something of an understatement, because the four-week selection course is exhausting and exhaustive and even the fit young man is fatigued by the end of it. Map reading, mental self-reliance and sheer physical stamina are among the qualities most searchingly explored, and in all these areas the four weeks become progressively more taxing.

The applicants start by trekking over mountain country in groups of four or five, each man carrying a 25-pound pack on his back. But the squad grows smaller, the pack grows heavier and the mountains steeper as the course progresses. On the final test each man is sent off on his own with a 55-pound pack to cover $37\frac{1}{2}$ miles of the steepest peaks of the Brecon Beacons in twenty hours.

There are tests which he has to carry out on his route. But he is never told how many more of these tests lie ahead or what standards are expected. He has to struggle on 'in the dark'—which is said to be the most exacting test of all. Officers have to undergo much the same sort of self-examination. But for them it is even worse. The officers' course lasts for five weeks not four, and the *en route* tasks are even tougher.

'If you are unable to do this you will fail' says the SAS grimly. And an Army doctor writing in the Royal Army Medical Corps *Journal* several years ago warned that most young men assuredly would fail unless they had specially prepared themselves for it beforehand.

The whole idea is that the SAS man should be able to operate on his own under self-discipline. This is what distinguishes the regiment from most other units, even the Parachute Regiment. It follows that whether or not a man passes the selection course does not depend entirely upon his ability to complete the final $37\frac{1}{2}$-mile hike in time. Several years ago a soldier failed to turn up at all. It was only after several days when the regiment was starting to organize search parties to look for him, that he finally staggered out of the mist. He had stumbled into a deep, mountain bog, but had had the good sense to lie on his pack, live on his emergency rations and wait until a farmer with a tractor came within shouting distance, by which time he was immersed up to his chest. He passed the course.

Those who do pass begin a fourteen-week period of continuation training at Hereford. Seven weeks are given over to general training, three weeks to combat survival and four weeks to special parachuting training. They have to start by learning to swim 1,000 yards fully clothed, and it is generally acknowledged that after everything that has gone before, the final four weeks of parachute jumping at RAF Brize Norton comes as light relief. A recruit can be rejected at any stage as being not up to standard and it is only at the end of the fourteen-week training that a soldier is accepted into the 22nd regiment.

Even so, the next twelve months are regarded as a probationary period, during which they have to absorb more specialized skills like jungle warfare, demolition work, medical aid and signalling. Then after the twelve months they start still more advanced tuition in ski-ing, medicine, mountaineering, radio communications, underwater swimming and languages. Most are taught languages only to colloquial level, but those with a special gift go far beyond this. Even the languages they are taught, however, are never disclosed in case this might indicate those areas of the world in which they are operating. And an SAS driver has to be able to strip a gearbox at night by the light of his headlamps.

The organization of the 22nd regiment is similar to that of an ordinary infantry battalion, but with several specialist offshoots. There are four operational squadrons, each with seventy-two men and six officers, and each squadron is in turn divided into five troops. There is an amphibious troop, an air troop, a surveillance troop, a mountain troop. Each of these consists of an officer and fifteen men. The fifth is a specialized signals troop of twenty-four men, most of them seconded by the Royal Corps of Signals. In addition to these squadrons there are a number of special sections, including a research cell, an intelligence centre, a parachuting centre and a training wing. The training wing is in turn split into a counter-revolutionary warfare cell, an initial training cell and a Northern Ireland cell—the most recent addition to the regiment.

But the regiment rarely operates as such. Even the squadrons exist for administrative convenience for most of the time. The SAS prefers to operate in small teams of four, in which their specialist individual skills are best exploited. Each man in the team is expert in one of the following: medical aid, demolition work, languages and communications. The specializations are not mutually exclusive because each man can do everything should the need arise. It is more a case of one man being particularly good at one of those skills.

No man is sent out on operations until the commanding officer is satisfied that he is ready for it. But the responsibility of keeping up his training to the required standard is very much a matter for the soldier himself. He decides whether his small arms marksmanship needs brushing up, and when and how he should attend to it. Rare visitors to Hereford have been impressed by the standards which the men set themselves. One officer described a visit to the hand-gun range, during which a trooper suddenly darted from the shadows, fired four times at a moving target on the cinema screen and drilled four neat holes through the head of his 'assailant'— before diving back behind cover.

On the other hand, the Army insists that the SAS are taught no more than the basic military skills. The difference between them and soldiers in other regiments lies in the standard to which the SAS men develop those skills. Certainly individuals who serve with the regiment can seem disappointingly normal when removed from the hush-hush atmosphere of Hereford. Few are of SG-1 intelligence standard. A survey conducted several years ago did suggest, however, that while the average trooper was only of 'bright normal intelligence' with 'an exceptionally high degree of physical fitness' he was more inclined to be more introverted than soldiers in other regiments. He also showed marked signs of at least some of the following characteristics—'shyness, suspiciousness, forthrightness, self-sufficiency and anxiety'. How long he spends in the 22nd regiment depends upon a number of people including himself. Although the basic posting to the regiment is for three years, many stay for twice or three times as long before returning to their own units. But the CO too, who himself has simply been posted from another regiment, has to decide whether a man has outlived his usefulness at Hereford. Any sign of staleness or declining standards, and the man is sent packing. The threat of being 'RTU.' (returned to unit) is said to be the most effective sanction against misbehaviour.

Scores of stories surround the SAS and the initiative tests which they are sometimes asked to carry out. On one occasion a number were required to break out of a high security Borstal. One out of three got away, but the Home Office were said to be satisfied as a result that their security was good enough. Another reputed test involved the plotting—though not the execution—of a bank robbery. But the police got to hear of it, and the experiment was not repeated. On another occasion the 22nd regiment was said to be collecting dead rats so that troopers could practise cooking them as part of a combat survival course. But none of these stories has ever been confirmed.

The SAS troopers certainly dress normally enough—each man in a sand-coloured beret carrying the cloth badge and motto, a sweater, blue canvas belt, but no badge of rank.

Torn between a desire to promote the SAS's fighting reputation and a distaste for bad publicity, the Ministry of Defence has tried, on the one hand, to refer to the regiment in whispers and, on the other, to talk reassuringly about what 'ordinary chaps' they all are. But perhaps the motto 'Who Dares Wins' should be changed to 'Who Dares to Use Them Wins'.

The Parachute Regiment. After the guardsman's bearskin the most famous headgear in the Army is the red beret of the Parachute Regiment. It caught the public imagination so successfully during the Second World War that it has since been copied by other airborne forces throughout the world. It has become a hallmark for daring and discipline, and promises to be one of the most enduring British contributions to military folklore.

Yet the British Army was not the first to have paratroopers. Nor was an Englishman the first to experiment with a parachute.

A Frenchman first tried jumping from a balloon with a canopy strapped to his back as long ago as 1797, and an American first did so from an aircraft in 1912. The Russian and the German armies were the first to see the military application, in the 1930s. In 1936 the Russians dropped as many as 1,500 men with their equipment on an exercise, which was observed for the British Army by an astonished General Wavell. But it was not until after the Germans had used airborne troops in their blitzkrieg operations at the start of the war, that the War Office woke up to the possibilities.

Fortunately the idea attracted Winston Churchill who was always sympathetic to 'offensive' warfare. On 12 June, 1940 he wrote a famous memorandum calling on the Chiefs of Staff for 'at least 5,000 parachute troops', and nine days later the Central Landing School was set up as a training camp at Ringway Airport near Manchester. No. 2 Commando started training on 8 July and the first operational raid took place on the Tragino aqueduct in Italy in February 1942, with mixed results.

Major-General Frederick 'Boy' Browning, sometimes called the 'father' of British airborne forces, was drafted in to command them from the Grenadier Guards on 29 October, 1941. The Parachute Regiment itself was not formed until 1 August, 1942, as part of the Army Air Corps. But this was more of an administrative development than anything else and the regiment today still looks back to June 1940 as the time when it all started.

More than 3,000 airborne troops were killed in the war, but more than 8,000 were listed as 'missing' which better reflects the hazardous operations they were involved in. Those who survived the war emerged with a regimental march ('The Valkyries'), a badge which shows the mythical Greek warrior Bellerophon mounted on his winged horse Pegasus, and a motto 'Utrinque Paratus' which means 'Ready for Anything'.

They had also acquired a nickname, 'The Red Devils', which had been given to them by the German Army. The soubriquet which was probably never meant as a compliment, was first applied to the 1st Parachute Brigade during the campaign in North Africa. In a signal to all parachute units in January 1943 General Browning said: 'General Alexander congratulates the Brigade on achieving this high distinction.' 'The Red Devils' is now the official title for the Army's free-fall parachuting display team.

The most famous operations involving British airborne troops during the war were those at D-Day, Arnhem and the Rhine Crossing. Since the Rhine operation in March 1945, however, there has been only one drop in anger, and that was during the

Anglo-French invasion at Suez, on Guy Fawkes' Day 1956, more than twenty years ago.

This does not mean that the paratroopers have twiddled their thumbs in camp ever since. In 1948 the 16 Independent Parachute Brigade took under its wing the Parachute Regiment with its three remaining battalions and then survived remarkably well until 1975. During that time the three battalions served throughout the dwindling world, from Palestine to Belfast, via the Far East, Germany, Suez, Cyprus, Borneo and Aden. The difference has been that apart from regular exercise jumps, the paras have served as ordinary infantry soldiers—if rather élite infantry, trained to go anywhere and do anything in a hurry.

Throughout the defence cuts of the 1950s and the 1960s the presence of a number of paratroopers in high places in the Army helped to ensure that the Parachute Brigade survived, and even prospered with a wartime job to do and with the necessary tools to do it. In 1976, however, the brigade headquarters was axed under the Government's 1974–75 Defence Review. With it went the bulk of the supporting units like artillery, signals and engineering troops which would be necessary for any major airborne operation. The Joint Airborne Task Force (Jatfor), a combined RAF–Army concept involving the 16 Brigade, also went, along with many of the 35 Hercules 'dropping' aircraft assigned to it.

Reaction to this has been somewhat ambivalent. On the one hand, the Parachute Regiment has survived with its three battalions, and with no serious threat to them imminent. On the other hand, their parachuting role has diminished and there is no sign of it being restored to its former pre-eminence.

The RAF's 38 Group would not even be able to make the best use of the aircraft it has left because with all the various demands made upon its pilots it does not have the time or the manpower left to devote enough time to close formation flying. Nor are its Hercules aircraft fitted with the Adverse Weather Air Delivery Systems (AWADS) which would be necessary for airborne operations in bad weather or at night. Under peacetime regulations it would now take ninety minutes for the twenty-one available aircraft, flying at three-minute intervals, to drop one battalion and its supporting troops and equipment. That is far too long. It would, of course, take less time in wartime because everyone would be forced to take greater risks. But that means that casualties would be higher, which is not a very comforting thought.

There is not even a permanent office at the Ministry of Defence which 38 Group could liaise with. True, there is a surviving organization called the Land Air Warfare Committee (aptly abbreviated to LAWK). But that is only an *ad hoc* committee with no office of its own. There is no one specifically tasked to oversee airborne training and operations.

Moreover, only one of the three battalions is kept fully trained for airborne duties at any one time. It is based at Aldershot as a Parachute Contingency Force with the new 6th Field Force, which would be assigned to Nato's Supreme Allied Commander (Saceur) in wartime. It has a few engineers, signallers and other supporting troops attached to it—but no artillery. So it could carry out only very limited operations. It is not even allowed to spend all its time on airborne training, but has to take its turn in Northern Ireland like everyone else.

The other two battalions are used simply for infantry work. One has recently been stationed in Berlin and the other with the 5th Field Force at Osnabrück—but they could be anywhere. They carry out training jumps from time to time to retain their expertise and to qualify for parachuting pay. The battalions will also take it in turns to be posted as the parachuting force at Aldershot. But it means that each will be serving as an airborne unit for only two years out of every six.

Joining the Red Berets. There are still more than 2,000 troops in the Parachute Regiment. Most of these are serving with the three battalions. But about 100 are based at Browning Barracks, the Aldershot depot where recruits are accepted and trained.

The regiment is worried that one of these days the soldiers themselves might perceive that their capacity for airborne warfare has been cut to shreds. Morale might then suffer as a result—and so in time might recruiting. If this did happen it would be a new experience for the regiment. So far its reputation as an élite fighting force has ensured that more than enough young extroverts have wanted to join.

As a result of this the regiment has been able to pick and choose, usually accepting only those boys with a SG-2 intelligence score and above—and only those who are classified as Commitment-A recruits. Commitment-A people not only know which part of the Army they want to join before they step into the careers office, but steadfastly refuse to join any other. If they are not allowed to enter the unit they prefer, they decide not to join the Army anyway. It is one way of ensuring that one gets what one wants.

After the Defence Review the regiment had to turn away men in their hundreds because its intake was restricted. Like other infantry units its battalion size was cut from 750 to 650. Unlike many others, however, it was over-strength anyway. The 1st Battalion had as many as 800, and all of them high-quality soldiers. Recruiting was constrained so tightly for a while that in one six-month period the regiment was allowed only seven recruits from the whole of Scotland—and at a time when recruiting for the whole Army was officially described as 'buoyant'. It meant that those seven were very high quality indeed—but it broke the hearts of many an Army careers officer as the rejects were turned away.

Those who do manage to squeeze their way in, might well spend the next few weeks wondering if their choice was wise. At least, they might if they were not Commitment-A boys, highly motivated and willing to accept all that is thrown at them.

Training lasts twenty-two weeks. It starts with nine weeks basic training, including one adventure training expedition. Then after two weeks more weapon training and three weeks at the battle school in Wales, they spend a week on the parachute selection course. The toughness is legendary, the high (or 'low') point being the so-called log race in which teams of eight race uphill carrying a telegraph pole or something much like it. About twelve per cent fail.

After a week's leave, in which to recover, the survivors go on to a four-week parachute training course at the Parachute Training School, RAF Abingdon. After two further weeks of airborne training, including two airborne exercises, they emerge as fledgling 'paras'.

The recruits do eight jumps during training, two from a balloon and the rest from an aircraft. Surprisingly few flunk it when the moment arrives—mainly because by that time the unlikely lads have been efficiently weeded out.

Those who serve in the battalion which is assigned to the 6th Field Force will continue to do about six jumps a year on airborne exercises, including a number at night. They will also carry out a number of jumps from a balloon as part of their continuation training. The other two battalions do continuation training jumps only.

The regiment's relationship with the SAS is close, so close that the SAS would find it difficult to exist on its own. Every year the regiment supplies about one in three of the SAS's intake. For the SAS it is a valuable, perhaps indispensable source of recruiting. For the Parachute Regiment though it is a drain on manpower. It means that the paras' own intake has to allow for the eventual loss to the 22nd regiment. On the other hand, it is a useful argument for the paratroopers as they put their own case for survival.

Not that all paras pass the SAS course. Paratroopers have to be tough, resourceful and intelligent, capable of dropping behind enemy lines at night and carrying out daring operations. But once on the ground they fight very much as infantry, the men obeying without question the commands of their officers and NCOs. The SAS by contrast have to operate in groups of four men and sometimes on their own, and in circumstances where blind obedience to some higher authority is neither desirable nor possible.

Not all paratroopers can fit into this different pattern of operations. One very bright, tough parachute officer who ingloriously failed the SAS selection tests—much to everyone's surprise—admitted that he had been like a fish out of water in the unaccustomed environment. 'I had been brought up to command a body of troops' he confessed later in the Aldershot mess. 'In a four-man team I was completely lost.'

The regiment's reputation for toughness, like that of the SAS, has sometimes rebounded. In 1968 some forty-two boys from the Junior Parachute Company at Aldershot walked out in protest against long hours and too much 'bull'. More seriously, it has pursued the three battalions during their tours of duty in Northern Ireland where at one time the term 'Paras' seemed in danger of becoming a dirty word. The regiment's unpopularity increased after the 'Bloody Sunday' tragedy of 30 January, 1972, where in the space of twenty minutes a company of the 1st Battalion shot dead thirteen Catholics and wounded fourteen more after a civil rights march in Londonderry.

The subsequent report by the judge, Lord Widgery, who conducted a tribunal of inquiry into the disaster, was promptly dismissed as 'whitewash' by the disaffected Catholic population. But Lord Widgery also pointed out that the soldiers' training had helped to make them aggressive and quick in their decision-making, and the affair led a number of people to question whether the paras were the right kind of troops to carry out peacekeeping operations, where restraint was called for.

Uncertain Future. The paras reacted either indignantly or philosophically according to temperament. Some pointed to the gallantry shown by members of the regiment while in Ulster, notably by Sergeant Michael Willetts of the 3rd Battalion who was awarded the George Cross in 1971 after losing his life while helping to save civilians from a time bomb at Springfield Road police station in Belfast.

But one result of 'Bloody Sunday' was a second tragedy when seven people including a Roman Catholic 'padre' were killed and nineteen others injured by a retaliatory bomb which the IRA planted in the officers' mess of the 16th Brigade at Aldershot. The

Mess itself was virtually destroyed by the blast, in February 1972, only three weeks after the Londonderry shootings. Meanwhile the 1st Battalion returned to the province in 1978 for the first time in six years.

But the regiment has recently been more concerned about its future than its past, amid growing doubts in Western armies over airborne operations. These doubts have centred partly on the vulnerability of the paratroops and their slow-flying aircraft above the modern battlefield with its airborne radar scanners and guided missiles. In 1973 the Parachute Regiment reduced the minimum dropping height from 800–1,000 feet (which had remained much the same since the war) to 650 feet. This is as low as one could possibly jump if one is to give one's reserve parachute time to open in an emergency. Moreover this was only to be a peacetime height. In war it was planned that the troops would jump as low as 300 feet, allowing for no margin of error at all. All this was designed to enable the dropping aircraft to fly to the zone as low as possible, ducking beneath the enemy's ground radar screens. This might mean a casualty rate of one in five, but it seemed to improve the viability of airborne operations in general.

However, there are also doubts about the vulnerability of para-troopers once they are on the ground. With their scanty arms and protection, would they stand much of a chance against troops in Western Europe where the emphasis is on heavy armour and firepower? Would they not suffer the same fate as those caught at Arnhem by two German Panzer divisions in 1944? The enemy would surely be able to use a sledgehammer to crack a nut every time—however brave the paras might be.

There still seem to be jobs for the paras to do. One is the seizure of reception areas for other troops in wartime. Another is the securing of lines of communication during the period of tension which might precede the outbreak of any future war in the West. Then again they could simply be used as quick reaction troops, sent to a trouble-spot if only to reassure the threatened ally by the strength of one's commitment.

But the Parachute Regiment cannot ignore the doubts which have for long surrounded airborne operations. Few seriously believe that the money will be forthcoming to rebuild the depleted brigade forces in Britain. They are beginning to think they should explore ways in which they might make the most of what is left.

One would be for the Army to give all its infantry soldiers some rudimentary parachute training so that a large parachute force could quickly be formed in wartime if necessary, with the Parachute Regiment as the nucleus. But this is most unlikely to happen. For one thing there are not enough aircraft or supporting units to accompany such a force. For another, even the Parachute Regiment itself does not think that it would be cost effective. While perhaps two out of every three men in an ordinary infantry regiment would pass their parachute selection tests successfully, the other man would fail. The Parachute Regiment carefully selects its men first, so that the failure rate is low. This it maintains is the best approach to what is after all quite a specialized form of military training.

A better solution might be to link up with other Nato airborne forces. Most already wear the maroon beret and are infected by the same camaraderie. Most of their air forces have the C-130 Hercules too. A kind of Euro-Jatfor could be built up.

Alternatively one could try to construct a Special Forces division in Britain, out of the Parachute Regiment, the Special Air Service and the Royal Marine Commandos. They all have different functions at present, but their training is not all that dissimilar and they are all looking for more or less the same kind of man.

The paras managed to win some sympathy, and support, in 1978, when French paratroopers were dropped into Zaïre to save the lives of threatened European expatriates during a guerrilla invasion. Critics of the Government's defence cuts were quick to point out that Britain no longer had the capacity to launch a similar operation to help its own nationals in countries like Rhodesia and Zambia. A group of Conservative MPs even demanded that 16 Parachute Brigade be re-formed.

But their cries will probably be in vain. It is an expanded airborne role in Europe that the paras need, if they are to survive as anything more than just another crack infantry regiment. The Red Devils are standing at a crossroads and are hoping that someone is going to show them the way.

12

Gurkhas

Origins. However tough the paratroopers and the SAS might like to think themselves their place in military legend comes some way behind that of the Gurkhas. 'Among the world's professional soldiers no body of fighting men has a higher reputation' wrote Field-Marshal Lord Slim, who as a former Gurkha officer was biased. But most people would agree with him, particularly those who have never met any.

Whether they are 'plucky little beggars' or 'cruel little blighters' seems to depend on whose side they are fighting on. Fortunately they have been on Britain's side since around the time of the Battle of Waterloo. That is one reason why the British look upon them with such affection.

Another reason is that the qualities usually attributed to them of loyalty and tenacity are those which the British still cherish, rightly or wrongly, as their own. Their motto 'Kaphar Hunnu Bhanda Marnu Ramro', an old proverb which roughly means that 'it is better to die than be a coward' is the sort of sentiment that makes British officers quite misty-eyed, however untrue it may be.

Their prowess with the kukri, their traditional flat-bladed knife, is something of a pub joke, though not always very funny. During the First World War it was something of a nuisance because they tended to throw away their rifles when going 'over the top' and rely upon their kukris, which were of limited use against machine-gun nests, except at close quarters. At one time the Army tried to discourage them from carrying it. But their right to do so has since been officially enshrined.

Technically they are mercenaries, though their officers wince at the word, pointing out that Gurkhas take an oath of allegiance to the Queen. They tend to refer to her as 'Our Queen' and without doubt serve her loyally. Thirteen have won the Victoria Cross since it was instituted in 1856, and the only VC now serving in the British Army is a Gurkha NCO, Rambahadur Limbu of the 10th Princess Mary's Own Gurkha Rifles who won it as a lance-corporal against Indonesian troops in Borneo in 1965.

The word Gurkha comes from Gorkha, an ancient principality whose warlike ruler captured much of what is now called Nepal in the eighteenth century. By 1814 the British East India Company was so fed up with the belligerent tribesmen across the border that it launched a series of punitive expeditions against them. Two years later the two armies decided that they might as well fight on the same side.

There is an agreement with the King of Nepal that they should not serve outside the Far East. But the King has granted dispensation during both world wars, and seems quite happy to allow Gurkhas to be in England now. Between 1939 and 1945 some forty battalions of them fought all over the place and the brigade of Gurkhas, including British officers, won ten Victoria Crosses.

In 1948 after the old Indian army had come to an end with the granting of independence to India, the ten Gurkha regiments were divided between the new Indian army and the British. Under a tripartite agreement between Britain, India and Nepal, Britain took the 2nd, 6th, 7th and 10th regiments, each with two battalions. India took the rest.

The idea originally was to form a Gurkha division of 16,000 men. But this was dropped after a series of defence cuts. The deepest was that of 1968 which reduced the size of the Gurkha brigade to around 6,700 by disbanding three of the eight battalions. It would have come down slightly more, but the rundown was halted in 1970 because of the Northern Ireland troubles. It was decided instead to post a Gurkha battalion to Britain to help out while the rest of the British infantry were otherwise engaged in Ulster.

After the Defence Review of 1974–75, however, the Gurkhas were told that they would have to lose 1,000 men—mainly by merging two of the remaining five battalions. After the uproar of the 1960s the announcement caused surprisingly little fuss among ex-officers. The Gurkhas themselves accepted it with their customary stoicism.

The Homelands. The British Gurkhas come from a relatively small area of Nepal in the Himalayan foothills. Most are peasants who scratch a bare subsistence out of what soil they can find between 5,000 and 8,000 feet above sea-level. That is lower than the Sherpas who live to the North, but higher than the Indians, who live in the Southern plains or Terai where it is hot, flat and full of jungle.

The Gurkhas are tough because they have had to be since birth. Some live four hours' march away from the nearest firewood and others have to scramble up and down the steep escarpments to fetch fresh water. Few can afford pack animals, and there are few roads, so men, women and children have to trek barefoot over the mountains carrying loads of up to 160 pounds—far more than their own weight. This is why Gurkhas have such strong legs, which make them look ungainly on the flat but enable them to shin up and down steep slopes like mountain goats.

Britain recruits its soldiers from two main areas and four main tribes or clans. The 7th and the 10th draw their men from Central-East Nepal where the clans are the Limbus and the Rais. The 2nd and the 6th rely upon the Central-West and on the Gurungs and the Magars. The supporting corps come from both areas. Each tribe has its own tongue or kura and the Rais are said to have up to ten kuras and seventy dialects.

The lingua franca is an off-shoot of Sanskrit, which the British call Gurkhali. This is the working language of the Gurkha regiments, and British officers have to take a six-month course in it before being posted. It is surprising how officers who have never managed to master French or German can become quite fluent in Gurkhali. The Army decided several years ago to switch to English as the working language, but the experiment has not gone very well.

Experts can tell Gurkhas apart without listening to them speak. The Rais are said to be small and quick with neat, round faces, while some though not all Limbus are taller, with larger features and slower speaking. Many Gurungs have finely cut features, though still with Mongolian overtones.

There are also differences in their social life. In the Western areas Gurkha homes are grouped together in villages while their lands are some distance away. This means that Gurkhas from the West are used to communal life, and to meeting with their friends in the evenings. In the East they live in scattered homesteads which are divided from each other by their lands, like country farms in Britain. This means that soldiers in those regiments which find their recruits in the East are less sociable, or so the theory goes.

Some come from settlements which are so remote that no one has ever bothered to give them a name. The Gurkha, asked where he comes from, will say 'Number 3 East', which is the number of the local recruiting area. One man who was recently serving as a Queen's orderly in England had to walk for ten days through the mountains, after leaving the nearest town behind him when he went home on leave.

The Nepalese government is trying to improve communications among the Himalayan foothills. More air-strips are being opened and an East-West highway is being constructed with help from

Britain, China and the Soviet Union. This should link up with roads running along the river valleys from North to South, creating a rudimentary network across the country.

In some ways this is not in the Army's interests. The Gurkha is valuable because of his toughness which itself is the product of his hard upbringing. Already some officers have been dismayed by the number of Gurkhas who retire with their savings to a more comfortable life on the Southern plains, where their children grow up in relative comfort. If civilization is introduced throughout the Himalayas the reservoir of talent upon which the Army has been drawing since 1816 could start to dry up. The occasional transistor can now be heard, scattering pop music over the foothills, which officers mutter darkly could be the beginning of the end.

Recruiting. So far Gurkhas are still embarrassingly easy to find. Every year the Army needs about 400 but is confronted by a hopeful 8,000, lured by travellers' tales of the Eldorado that awaits those who serve someone else's Queen and Country. During Confrontation with Indonesia in the 1960s the Army needed 1,000 a year, which at least made it easier for recruiting officers.

Two systems of recruiting have been tried in the past. One was the 'own steam' method under which all the applicants trekked down from the hills to one of the two depots, Dharan in the East and Paklihawa in the West. But this meant that they deserted their lands during the autumn harvests. This was particularly wasteful as so few in the end could be accepted by the Army.

The other method was that of the 'galla', which is Gurkhali for 'group'. A recruiting officer called a 'galla wallah' would go off into the hills and sign up young men whom he would then bring back to the depot on his own. But this system was open to bribery and corruption.

So the Army has worked out a compromise. The galla wallah travels into the hills between September and December and compiles a short list of about 800. Then these come down to the depots for the final selection in the New Year.

This still leaves the recruiting officers with quite a difficult job, particularly as some young boys try to join at the age of fourteen. A system of X-raying the wrists has had to be adopted so that Army doctors can find out their real age before clearing them. Medical examinations are important because a lot of potential Gurkhas suffer from tuberculosis. But at least the keen competition means that the Army can pick out the very best men.

The depots are changing. Dharan and Paklihawa were developed near the railheads in the days when Gurkhas were transported by train for hundreds of miles across India. Dharan which has a Gurkha hospital represents too large an investment to be scrapped. But Paklihawa is being closed and Western recruiting will be concentrated at Pokhra, which is smaller and cheaper and more central.

Pay and Conditions. Many Gurkhas join the Army because their fathers once belonged to it. But most join simply to make money. It is one of the very few ways in which they can. On the face of it they cannot make very much. Because of the tripartite agreement in 1948 their pay in the British Army is tied to that of their compatriots in the Indian Army. As a result their basic salary is less than a quarter of that for British soldiers.

Britain manages to get round this to some extent by paying local overseas allowances (LOAs) to those stationed outside Nepal. This brings the earnings of those in Hong Kong to about half of those for British troops. In Britain, Gurkha soldiers receive more or less the same as British troops, which is one reason why service in the United Kingdom is the most popular posting of all. A Gurkha battalion costs only about a third as much as a British unit, which is one of the reasons why the Ministry of Defence is so keen to retain them.

Nor do Gurkhas do very well in the allocation of married quarters. Because they marry young, the Army says that it could not afford to supply a quarter for all the families who would like them. Those below the rank of colour sergeant have to wait for up to nine years before they can bring their wives and children to Hong Kong. Until then they can only meet when the Gurkhas have six months home leave every two-and-a-half years or so. The Army says that the Gurkha does not mind this because it is cheaper to leave his wife behind. But the real reason is that the Ministry of Defence finds it cheaper that way, and Gurkha officers agree that the position is not very satisfactory. They are afraid to kick up a fuss, however, because they do not want to price the Gurkhas out of existence.

Training and Discipline. Gurkha recruits are trained at Sek Kong in the New Territories of Hong Kong. Training lasts for forty weeks which is much longer than for British soldiers because the Gurkhas have to be taught English. They also have to learn a number of Western ways including the complications of a modern lavatory, which is a rare luxury in the Himalayas. Some have to be introduced to the wonders, and the dangers of electricity, although the number of those without any experience at all of modern civilization is steadily declining. They have to be taught how to read a map and measure distances. Most of them have been used to measuring distances by the number of days it takes to travel along them by foot. A Gurkha will say that he lives 'five days from Dharan' which after all is a more realistic way of looking at it.

Not only is training longer but it is tougher, and discipline is more vigorously maintained. For the first three months recruits are not allowed to smoke or drink or leave the barracks. Old fashioned 'bull' is practised in Gurkha regiments to an extent which would cause resentment in Bulford or Aldershot. Exactly why is difficult to say. The British officers insist that the Gurkhas like it, but this may be because nobody has ever given them the chance of doing anything else. It seems more likely that it is the British officers who like it.

Recruits at Sek Kong live in large bare huts with seventeen beds in each, which is all reminiscent of the British Army twenty years ago. They dutifully scrub their belts, spit on their boots and lay out their kit on their bunks every day like guardsmen, without bothering to ask the reason why.

Some parts of army training come easily to them. They can scramble 1,500 feet up the local hill or khud in less than fifteen minutes without pausing for breath. They have the quick eye and instinctive fieldcraft of countrymen. Rarely do Gurkhas fail to excel at the annual Bisley shooting trials and the 10th Gurkhas won the major unit competition two years running in the mid-1970s.

On the other hand, while their legs are like tree-trunks, the muscles in their arms and the upper parts of their bodies are often underdeveloped. So they need special exercises, particularly to improve their co-ordination. Curiously they are very poor at ball games when they start, although by the end of training they are as mad about football as anyone else.

Their diet is different from that of English troops. Their basic food is bhat (which is Gurkhali for rice) consisting of rice with a form of curried meat, usually mutton, chicken or goat. In the Far East they have two meals of bhat every day plus an English breakfast with perhaps a bowl of mulligatawny soup. But when stationed in England they eat only one meal of bhat and then have an English-style lunch, which most of them seem to enjoy.

They are very well disciplined off duty, far better than English soldiers who tend to get drunk. Gurkhas seem to spend most of their evenings in barracks anyway. Officers say this is because they want to save money. But it is also true that those in Hong Kong probably cannot afford a very lavish life-style.

They even have to seek permission from their commanding officer before dating a girl, and permission to marry is usually refused. This is more sensible than it sounds and is practised at the request of the Nepalese government. Although the old custom of arranging marriages for one's children is gradually dying out, Gurkha parents still have conservative views about the kind of girl they fancy as a daughter-in-law. Moreover a girl from Southern England who finds a Gurkha attractive company during a night out in Aldershot might have a nasty shock when she arrived at his home in the Himalayas—particularly after a ten-day walk through the mountains to get there.

The Gurkhas do not seem to mind the restrictions. Their upbringing on a diet of maize and rice and little home comforts makes the life of a British soldier seem soft and easy. And the money, however sparse it may look to British eyes, represents substantial wealth to a man who has never had any. Nor do they seem to mind too much the restrictions which are placed upon some of their Hindu customs. The annual festival of Dashera involves not only young Gurkha soldiers dancing in 'drag' but the sacrifice of a number of animals, preferably water buffaloes to appease the gods. Water buffaloes cannot be sacrificed in Britain because of public sensibilities or in Hong Kong because of the cost.

In Britain the Gurkhas are not allowed to sacrifice anything that breathes, so the ceremony has to be heavily symbolic. In Hong Kong they are allowed to dispatch a selection of chickens and goats, while the water buffaloes are slaughtered by proxy in Nepal. British officers, for all their upbringing in Royal Berkshire or wherever, still nervously cross their fingers as the day of Dashera approaches in the autumn, for fear that a botched ceremony could bring twelve months bad luck to the battalion.

Promotion. Gurkhas sign on for four years, then extend this every two or three years as they wish, until after fifteen years they qualify for a pension. Corporals and below then have to go. But sergeants can stay for eighteen years, warrant officers for twenty years, lieutenants for twenty-four years and captains for twenty-eight years. The Army likes to think of its Gurkhas leaving with £2,000 saved up to buy themselves a comfortable retirement. But the problem is how to get rid of them, not one of persuading them to stay.

Gurkhas can be commissioned. In fact there are several kinds of Gurkha officer, and it all gets slightly confusing. The best known are the Queen's Gurkha Officers (QGOs) who are really sub-officers, half-way between warrant officers and full commissions. They act as platoon commanders or as deputy commanders of companies. But they have their own mess, except when stationed in Britain, where they are allowed to share the Officers' Mess.

Then there are Gurkha Commissions, awarded to men who, like QGOs, have been promoted from the ranks. These are full commissions rather like the Quartermasters Commissions in the rest of the British Army. Gurkha Commissions were started in 1948 after the Tripartite Agreement. But they were meant only as a stop-gap, and there are few of them left.

Their place is gradually being taken by the Sandhurst Commissioned Gurkhas, young men who have been to the RMAS just like British officers. Most are the sons of Gurkha NCOs and QGOs, who have been educated at the Gurkha High School in Hong Kong. Ideally they will one day reach the rank of lieutenant-colonel. But the scheme started only in the 1950s and none so far has reached these dizzy heights.

British officers are sceptical about their chances of ever doing so. They argue that RMAS Gurkhas tend always to be inferior to their British counterparts and are likely to remain second-class citizens in the Officers' Mess. On the other hand, the British officers have a vested interest in the argument. Promotion for them is difficult enough as it is without their having to compete with the Gurkhas themselves, so perhaps their judgement is biased.

British Officers. The principal commands in the Gurkha brigade are still monopolized by British officers, some of whom come from families which have served in the same regiments for generations. Altogether there are about 125 British officers and although a Gurkha posting is not as popular as it was, the Gurkha brigade has no great difficulty in finding enough. They need only two long-term officers and four or five short-service officers out of Sandhurst every year.

Apart from the family ties, the Gurkha demonstration company at Sandhurst is a helpful reminder to cadets of the attractions of serving out East. As a result the brigade has enough applications for it to be choosy about whom it accepts. In 1977–78 no cadets were accepted at all, because none came up to standard.

How long the brigade will continue to attract enough young men who are good enough, is questionable. A number of Gurkha officers have reached high office since the Second World War, notably Lord Slim who became Chief of the Imperial General Staff, and more recently General Sir Walter Walker who was appointed to command Nato's Northern flank. But the number of senior posts which are tied to Gurkha officers has declined.

At one time the Gurkha brigade in Hong Kong always had a

Gurkha brigadier in charge. But now that the number of brigades in the colony has been pruned from two to one, the commander of the 48th Field Force that remains could come from anywhere. The first commander after the reorganization in Hong Kong was in fact an officer from the Royal Green Jackets—dubbed the Black Mafia by the rest of the Army because of their success in winning the best jobs everywhere.

As it is there is only one brigadier's job kept exclusively for Gurkha officers, and that is the post commanding the depot at Dharan. A Gurkha colonel runs the brigade headquarters at Hong Kong, and after that the highest 'tied' Gurkha appointments are all for lieutenant-colonels.

The chief weakness for an ambitious young officer, is that he is destined to spend most of his career in the Far East, without the experience of mechanized infantry work that he needs to win promotion in the Army as a whole. To get round this, the Army cross-posts Gurkha officers with other battalions in BAOR or perhaps Northern Ireland. But they also receive about £1 a day extra, called Gurkha Service Money in recognition of the fact that their career prospects are not quite as bright as those of their fellow officers elsewhere. A young man emerging from Sandhurst still has to decide whether he wants a taste of adventure in the Far East, or whether he should settle for a more boring but safer route to the top by opting for a commission in some county regiment at home.

Ex-Gurkhas. Britain pays out about 16,000 pensions every year to Gurkhas who have retired since 1948. Those who retired before Indian independence are paid by the present Indian government. As with pay, pensions are tied to those paid by the Indian and Nepalese armies, under the Tripartite Agreement—although nothing was actually written down. It is very much a 'gentlemen's' agreement. By British standards pensions are small, only about £8 a month in some cases. But it is enough to make a man comparatively affluent in the Himalayan foothills.

The job of paying out the pensions presents problems of its own. There are few banks in Nepal, and Gurkhas share a countryman's distrust of banks anyway. So once a year a British officer with an escort and sacks of Nepalese rupees sets out from Dharan, Paklihawa and Pokhra to pay the pensioners *in situ*, and in hard cash. It is very much a case of Mahommet going to the mountain.

They are away for several months at a time, stopping for two or three days in each centre while the pensioners struggle down from the slopes, to collect their dues. It is all rather medieval, but so far nobody has come up with a better method.

In normal circumstances Gurkhas do not need very much money. Self-sufficient in food and drink, they need only enough to buy kerosene, cloth, salt and a few other necessities. However, ex-soldiers have come to expect a rather higher standard of life than that of most of their fellow-countrymen.

Circumstances in the Himalayas are rarely normal anyway. Blizzards, floods and landslides continually threaten those who live there. In 1968 more than forty-two inches of rain fell in seventy-two hours in one area full of ex-servicemen. More than 1,600 died or were made homeless in the floods which followed. With only one doctor for every 100,000 people, which is the second lowest ration in the world, life can often seem like a battle for survival.

In 1967 the Gurkha Welfare Appeal was launched to help ex-soldiers in trouble. The sudden cut in the number of battalions threatened to overload the welfare services which already existed. There was an uncomfortable feeling, anyway, that Britain was lagging behind India and Nepal in caring for those Gurkhas who had retired.

As a result of the appeal more than £1,500,000 has been invested, producing an annual income or rather more than £100,000. The British Government pays the administrative costs so ninety-five per cent of the money goes directly to those who need it.

Most of the money goes to help families in distress. The rest goes to widows, because pensions end when the soldier dies. The scheme is run by the brigadier at Dharan and the cash is distributed through a number of welfare centres scattered round the foothills.

The British Army also looks after money contributed by the Canadian International Development Agency (CIDA). A Canadian welfare fund was started by soldiers who had fought alongside the Gurkhas in the two world wars. Then the Canadian government stepped in and offered to pay two dollars for every one that the fund organizers could raise themselves. But unlike the British money the Canadian funds are always spent on big projects like building schools and hospitals.

Such welfare schemes create their own frictions. One village with no ex-soldiers living there might resent the attention being paid to another. Then again, one family might be helped when its house is blown down in a hurricane, while its neighbours over the road might not. But there is not much that the Army can do about this. It is after all one of the benefits of joining up, and one more reason why the recruits still come forward.

The Organization. There are still five battalions and over 6,400 men in the Gurkha brigade. But how long all these will remain is debatable.

The full titles of the four regiments are: The 2nd King Edward VII's Own Gurkha Rifles (The Simoor Rifles); The 6th Queen Elizabeth's Own Gurkha Rifles; The 7th Duke of Edinburgh's Gurkha Rifles; and the 10th Princess Mary's Own Gurkha Rifles. The rest of the Brigade includes the Gurkha Transport Regiment, the Gurkha Engineers Regiment and the Gurkha Signals Regiment.

All the infantry regiments have one battalion each, except the 2nd which has two. The other three lost their second battalions in 1968. The 2nd is the oldest and arguably the most élitist, clinging to its supposed reputation for effortless superiority.

Three of the battalions are stationed in the New Territories of Hong Kong. Their camps are called Burma Lines, Cassino Lines and Gallipoli Lines to commemorate Gurkha battle honours. A fourth is at Church Cookham, Hampshire, from where its soldiers sometimes mount the guard at Buckingham Palace. The fifth is in Brunei where it is expected to remain until 1983 under the 1978 agreement with the Sultan.

The government announced in 1975 that as part of the economies following the Defence Review, the size of the Gurkha Brigade would be cut by 1,000 men. This would be accomplished by merging the 1st and 2nd Battalions of the 2nd Regiment, but the cut was linked to the withdrawal of the battalion from Brunei. Withdrawal was postponed until 1983 after prolonged haggling with the Sultan, and two months later the government decided to cancel the amalgamation too and to leave the Gurkha Brigade as it was.

The government had little option. To have scrapped a Gurkha battalion while at the same time keeping the unit in Brunei would have meant losing either the battalion in Britain or one of those in Hong Kong. With the Army already feeling overworked, underpaid and generally fed up, the government could hardly afford to risk making matters worse. So, thanks partly to the stubborn Sultan of Brunei, 1978 was a good year for the Gurkhas. 'Whitehall 1978' was another battle honour to add to the list.

In 1978 the battalion in Britain supplied two companies for the operation in Belize, Central America, for the first time. But what Gurkha officers would really like is to have a battalion sent to BAOR for a while, or even to Northern Ireland. The chance that one of them might be sent to Northern Ireland looks very slim because successive British Governments have turned down the idea, although there are those who argue that the Gurkhas with their fieldcraft and their uncompromising attitudes would

clean up terrorism in South Armagh more quickly than one could
say 'Provisional IRA'.

The chances of going to BAOR, however, look slightly brighter
than they used to. Until recently the Gurkhas had been considered
unsuitable because they lacked the experience in mechanized
warfare training. It would be expensive and perhaps unnecessary
to start training the Gurkhas for the kind of work that was already
being done by British battalions.

However, the Gurkhas think that there could be a place for them
in the new Fifth Field Force which consists of light infantry like
the Gurkhas, travelling in trucks rather than armoured personnel
carriers. The odds are still against them getting what they want.
But at least there is a hope that they might, and the Gurkhas in
Hong Kong are clinging to it.

Officers point out that the Gurkhas were originally recruited
for India, but have ended up fighting in France, North Africa,
Italy, Greece, Burma, Malaya, and most recently Cyprus during
the troubles there in 1974. So why should they not once again
demonstrate their versatility in support of the Queen and Country
that hires them?

13

Specialists

Chaplains. The Royal Army Chaplains Department (RAChD) dates from 1796 when the first chaplain-general was appointed. He decided that something had to be done when, on organizing his clergy for an expedition to the Continent, he found that most of them had gone on leave. The RAChD was born, appropriately, on Christmas Day and the first new recruits turned up at the following Easter. In the First World War 4,500 padres served with the British Army, 172 of whom lost their lives. In the Second World War ninety-six died out of 3,600. No other officer element in any regiment or corps lost such a high percentage. Four Victoria Crosses have been won by the department, one during the Indian Mutiny and three between 1914 and 1918, although chaplains during the First World War came under fire after the Armistice for heavy drinking.

The RAChD now has an establishment of 189, although it has been raised temporarily to about 200 to cope with the commitment in Northern Ireland. The organization resembles a mishapen pyramid. At the top is the Chaplain-General who is equal in rank to a Major-General but is usually called Archdeacon. The present incumbent, The Venerable Archdeacon Peter Mallet is only the sixteenth holder of the office since 1796, but this is because a number of his predecessors overstayed their welcome. The CG is always a member of the Church of England while his deputy, equal to a Brigadier, is always nonconformist. Then there are eight assistant CGs (full colonels) including one Methodist, one from the Church of Scotland and six from the Church of England. There is also a ninth who is head of the Roman Catholic Chaplains. Roman Catholics come under the RAChD but they have a tangential structure, because the papacy upsets the normal chain of command.

Beneath the colonels come twenty-five lieutenant-colonels, otherwise known as Class 2 Chaplains, and below them come the rest of the department who are Class 3 majors or Class 4 captains. There are 105 Anglicans, twenty-five Roman Catholics, eighteen Church of England, six Methodists and two from the United

Reform Church, which includes Congregationalists, Baptists and Presbyterians.

The idea is that the strength should reflect the denominational split in the Army, which is currently:

Church of England	66·92 per cent
Church of Scotland	11·59 per cent
Roman Catholics	15·68 per cent
Methodists	4·11 per cent
United Reform Church	1·68 per cent

The other 0·2 per cent might be classed as 'others' or perhaps 'don't knows'.

In practice it does not seem to matter all that much. The Army has been unable to provide its units with a full range of padres since the end of National Service, so each regiment has to make do with what it can get. The thirty or so Roman Catholics are distributed round the globe as equitably as their senior chaplain can manage, and Church of England padres are kept for the Scottish regiments. But the other Protestants are very ecumenical and it is the luck of the draw whether a regiment will be allotted an Anglican or a Methodist or an URC. As a result Protestant Church Services tend to be something of a compromise and a High Anglican, mindful of his Mass, would be difficult to accommodate.

The ecumenical approach is dictated partly by money and partly by manpower—which is almost like saying the same thing twice. The Free Church complement is usually up to strength and so is the Roman Catholic—although only just. But the job of finding enough Anglicans willing to sacrifice the comparative comfort of a country parish for the turbulence of Army life has always been a struggle.

In recent years the Anglican padres have been slightly below strength. As a result most regiments have to share their padre with several others, much as country parishes have to make do with one vicar. One unfortunate consequence is that a number of padres have to keep shuttling between Britain or Germany and Northern Ireland, as their congregations are posted for successive tours of duty in the province.

The RAChD accepts only those who have spent at least two years as a civilian priest. So in the case of Anglicans this means that they cannot join until they are about twenty-seven. The top age is thirty-four, so most recruits tend to be in their late twenties or early-thirties, which is quite a good age for ministering to a youthful Army.

Despite its manpower problems the RAChD is surprisingly choosy. Applicants, who are usually attracted by an advertisement in the *Church Times* or *Methodist Recorder*, have to turn up with their wives at Bagshot Park, the handsome stately home in Surrey which Queen Victoria built as a wedding present for her son the Duke of Connaught. The department has been there since 1946. Officially it is still on loan from the Queen, and an ugly rumour ran around the place several years ago that she wanted it back as a home for Princess Anne. Fortunately for the chaplains this proved to be untrue. Surrounded by its parkland and festooned with chimneys it provides them with one of the most comfortable head-quarters in the Army. With its private chapel, museum, dark wood panelling and its smell of furniture polish, Bagshot Park has acquired a distinctly ecclesiastical character.

The RAChD never advertises its pay scales in case the glitter of gold attracts the wrong kind of person. Even so it must attract quite a few because the starting salary for a captain must appeal to an impoverished curate and his family. On the other hand, they say that the figures can be misleading. A chaplain does not receive a rectory with free rent and rates. Nor does he get paid for weddings or funerals or for, say, taking services at the local hospital. It is not until he has risen to be a Class 3 or Class 2 Chaplain that the Army life starts to pay off, in financial terms anyway.

The Army is also wary of 'muscular Christianity'. Chaplains during the Boer War were notoriously jingoistic, and even in more recent times the typical padre seemed to be a rugby playing extrovert with a pipe clenched between his teeth, a golden retriever at his heels and a public school accent. Peter Mallet says that the RAChD has now managed to rid itself of this image.

But even today a chaplain has to be a pretty fit and vigorous young man, prepared to jump into a Land Rover and map-read his way across country when on exercise. He also has to act as a father figure to young soldiers' families who might be overawed by the sight of a clerical collar. So the RAChD likes to think that it is always looking for someone rather special.

Few have trouble with their conscience—or in answering the predictable question about whose side do they really think God is on. They point out that they are ministering to men and their families in peace and in war, and the fact that they happen to be in the Army is quite incidental.

Chaplains like most professional people joining the Army enter on short service commissions, and convert to a regular commit-ment only after five years, by which time they and the Army have been able to take a good look at each other. Along with the other professions they take an abbreviated one-month course at Sandhurst. But Chaplains are taught only how to unload guns and never how to fire them.

Many return to the civilian clergy on retiring from the Army. Several Chaplain-Generals have become Cathedral Deans and even Bishops, although the record for filling bishoprics belongs to the RAF.

Church attendances in the Army have gone up slightly but remain much better overseas than at home. Sunday morning services seem to be part of the British way of life which soldiers want to retain when abroad. Services in the field are also well attended perhaps because they only take twenty minutes or so and have a novelty attraction.

At least Army chaplains do not have to worry about raising money for church repairs; the Department of the Environment sees to all that. This means that church collections can go to the Army charities and in 1976 £80,000 was donated in this way. The freedom from worry about death-watch beetle or a leaking roof is one compensation for a life which can be more arduous than is sometimes believed.

Teachers. The Corps of Army Schoolmasters, all warrant officers who came next to the RSM in regimental status, was formed in 1846. A Corps of Army Schoolmistresses followed two years later to help staff the Army schools that had now sprung up all over the place. The schoolmistresses survived until 1961. They were a formidable band of ladies in their early days. But the schoolmasters were swallowed up by the Army Education Corps which was founded in 1920.

The emphasis switched from general education to current affairs during the Second World War. It seemed sensible to ensure that soldiers knew what they were fighting for. But the corps also managed to squeeze in quite a lot about the social evils of the world that had been left behind in 1939 and some older Conservatives still cynically refer to the Labour election victory in 1945 as the AEC's only battle honour.

A number of famous politicians served in the corps either during the war or as National Servicemen just after it. They include George Wigg and Edward Short, now both Labour peers, and Conservative MPs, Peter Walker and Mark Carlisle. During the National Service era the RAEC was popular among graduates, who looked on it as a soft option when compared with the prospect of two years in the infantry or the other combat arms.

In those days it was 1,500 strong. NCOs, including many highly qualified young academics, did the teaching while the officers simply looked after administration. But all the non-commissioned ranks disappeared with the end of National Service in 1963 and now the RAEC has only 630 officers, including fifty from the WRAC, who do everything themselves. Most are graduates. Extra seniority is given to young officers as they emerge from Sandhurst, according to their qualifications. The brightest and best can start as captains with up to seven-and-a-half years seniority. But despite this encouragement, only one in ten has a first-class or an Upper 2nd Class Honours degree. To make up weight a number of non-graduates are accepted every year from teachers' training colleges, but only for short-service commissions.

The RAEC Centre is at Beaconsfield, where the corps runs three central schools. One is the School of Instructional Technology where they research teaching methods in cooperation with the Directorate of Army Training. Another is the Army School of Education where the corps' own officers go for special-to-arms training.

The third is the Army School of Languages (ASL) where they teach Russian, German and Arabic to intelligence officers and military attachés, and English to foreigners—mostly Gurkhas. There is also a Chinese language school in Hong Kong. Intensive courses up to colloquial standard in Arabic and Russian last ten weeks. But most attachés go up to interpreter level. This takes eighteen months for Russian speakers. At one time the 'Russians' used to go to Paris to live among the White Russian community there, but most of their hosts there have died so this has been abandoned.

Some of the corps' best work is done at Corsham, Wiltshire, where more than 500 boys are sent each year for a ten-week course at the Army School of Preliminary Education to bring their reading and writing up to standard. It is a pretty low standard with a reading age of only eleven years and nine months. But it is good enough to make the boys trainable.

When recruiting is good the Army does not really need to accept semi-illiterates in the first place. But there are a number of menial jobs to be done which the more intelligent and better educated would soon grow tired of doing. So it accepts some of those with a reading as low as seven to nine years and a spelling age of under six. Most of the boys are so conscious of their inadequacy that the motivation is high and officers with a social leaning find the work very satisfying. The Army arguably does not boast enough about the work that it does there.

RAEC people also join the staffs of junior and other training schools, teaching anything from basic electronics for REME apprentices to English grammar for the Military Police. The theory is that all soldiers need a certain amount of basic education to do anything. For similar reasons they teach NCOs who need to pass the Education Promotion Certificate examinations before becoming sergeant and then warrant officer. (About one in three fail these the first time, but they can keep on trying until their commanding officer's patience is exhausted.) The Army Examinations Board officially comes under the Director of Training, but most of the chief examiners are RAEC men.

Most of this coaching of examination candidates goes on at Army Education Centres which are dotted round the main garrison areas. Sometimes, too, the teachers go peripatetic, visiting soldiers in their barrack rooms—in Ulster, for instance, where men cannot be spared to go all the way to the AEC at Lisburn. But the AECs also act as community centres where soldiers and their families can learn anything from shorthand and typing to upholstery and needlework. This happens overseas more than in Britain, where they can go to the local College of Further Education for the same sort of thing.

Lawyers. It was decided in the late 1930s to start a uniformed legal branch in the Army. But the war came along and the Army Legal Services (ALS) was not created until 1948. There had been lawyers before then, but they were mostly ordinary officers who happened to have some legal training. Even after the ALS was formed it had to wait ten years before being given its own cap badge—which is equivalent to a baby being baptised. It was turned into a corps in 1978, and called the Army Legal Corps (ALC).

It is still among the smallest corps with only forty-six officers. A small number of other ranks who work as clerks or drivers do not belong to the ALC but are drafted in from the RAOC or the WRAC. The officers join after qualifying as civilian lawyers. About half are usually barristers and half are solicitors, which the Army regards as a healthy mix—although it seems to make little practical difference.

They join on short service commissions and many leave after five years. More get out after ten years and still more after sixteen—by which time they should have the rank, status and pension of a lieutenant-colonel. Few wait around until the compulsory retiring age of sixty, unless they have made it to the single major-general's appointment as director or to one of the two brigadier positions below that.

8*

There is no very compelling reason why they should join at all. Unlike doctors and dentists they are paid very little more than other soldiers, although this is now being reviewed. The average civilian lawyers must be better off.

On the other hand, Army lawyers lead a more interesting life than does the usual country solicitor who spends much of his time conveyancing or administering wills. Not only is there a certain amount of travel, but there is quite a lot of court work and the general legal experience is much more rounded than one might think.

The work falls into two main categories, legal aid and disciplinary. The former is basically solicitors' work and the latter is more like that of a barrister. But they switch from one branch to the other on two-year postings, whatever their legal training.

Legal aid involves advising soldiers with problems, much like a family solicitor. It also includes finding a courtroom lawyer to represent someone who has been charged with some civilian offence in, say, West Germany. A soldier who tries to hire a civilian lawyer on his own might find himself faced with a bill for £1,000, so the ALS can save him a lot of money.

The two main legal aid offices are at Bielefeld, West Germany, where seven officers deal with some 300 cases a month for the soldiers of the 1st British Corps, and Aldershot. There are also small centres at Hong Kong and Cyprus. But the office is only the base and the lawyers travel round units for monthly clinics, which are advertised well in advance. Business is usually brisk and the visiting lawyer might find himself wading through a waiting-room with twenty-five anxious soldiers in it.

The disciplinary side, however, represents the main part of the ALC work, and is the one which most of them enjoy. There are again two main offices, at Rheindahlen in Germany and at the UKLF headquarters at Wilton. Their basic function is to advise commanders. A battalion CO can now hand out up to sixty days detention if the accused man pleads guilty. But he has to seek advice from the ALS people first.

They are also closely involved in advising on court martials (CMs). As many as 1,800 are held every year, although the total is now expected to decline, as since 1 July, 1976, COs have been able to deal with most theft cases on their own unless the defendant elects to go for trial.

Most are district courts martial (DCMs), held at Field Force level. These can administer up to two years' detention which is generally enough. But there are also about 100 General Courts Martial (GCMs) held at divisional or district level, which can hand out stiffer punishment.

A DCM is presided over by a major who does not belong to the ALC, but is on a two-year posting from another regiment, doing nothing else but sitting in court. With him sit two other officers, probably captains. But a GCM has a colonel or even a brigadier as president, while the rank of the other officers depends upon that of the accused.

The prosecutor is normally the adjutant of the accused man's unit while the defending 'counsel' is another officer, chosen either by the defendant or the CO. This is generally good enough. But if the defendant insists upon hiring a civilian barrister to represent him the ALS has to supply an officer to prosecute. An ALS member may sometimes find himself appearing in what they like to call a 'Mickey Mouse' case simply because the man in the dock has insisted upon proper legal representation.

But in ninety-eight per cent of Courts Martial there are no lawyers at all. All Army officers are taught elementary law as part of their training and this is thought to be adequate. After all, major crimes like murder, manslaughter, rape and treason are tried only by civil courts when committed in Britain, though GCMs can deal with them overseas.

Sentences are always 'subject to confirmation and promulgation'. This means that they are confirmed later only after being examined by lawyers. In this case, however, it is not the ALS officers who are involved but the Judge Advocate and his staff who come under the Lord Chancellor's department. Moreover if it is a complicated case a man from the JAG's department sits in court throughout it.

The ALC considers the confirmation procedure an unnecessary complication. But it is all part of the system of checks and balances. The ALS, to their disappointment, are spending less and less time in court and the role of the JAG may be seen also as more rather than less important as the years go by.

Cooks. For centuries the British soldier went in to battle lean and hungry. This was partly intentional because the Army believed that he fought better that way, and partly accidental because there were few proper cooks and not enough wholesome food. Even in modern times a soldier's food was a bad joke, and it remained so until the end of National Service.

Until 1941 when the Army Catering Corps (ACC) was formed as an offshoot of the old Army Service Corps, regiments provided their own cooks who were given rudimentary training at Aldershot before being let loose in the cookhouse. By 1963 even the ACC was in a bad way, short of recruits and morale after years of mass catering for conscripts. It was the need to find more volunteers in the mid-1960s which forced the Army to take another look at its priorities. No regiment or corps has been transformed so astonishingly during the past fifteen years.

By the late 1960s the ACC was fully recruited. Today it can afford to be very choosy about whom it accepts. Most of its members are committed to joining it before they enter the Army Careers Office and they spend an average of 9·4 years in uniform, which is one of the highest retention rates in the Army. Many already have passed in cookery at their Certificate of Secondary Education Examination and a few have additional City and Guilds qualifications too.

Another surprising thing about the ACC is its record in military competitions. Perhaps because the cooks feel they have to prove something, they do well in shooting and endurance tests. Several years ago they won an important marksmanship contest, and then more recently walked away with the prize at the Cambrian Marches—a rough, tough endurance exercise in the Welsh Mountains.

The corps is now 5,500 strong if you include student cooks at the apprentices' college in Aldershot. There are only 167 officers, however, most of whom now join directly from Sandhurst.

Their Aldershot headquarters reflects the new image. It is overshadowed by the Army School of Catering itself—a twelve-storey tower block with fifty-two gleaming kitchens for the learner cooks. Half the instructors belong to the Corps and half are civilian chefs, some of whom have been with the Corps for a generation. Their Bible is the *Army Manual of Catering*, a bulky volume packed with recipes which is often sought by civilian mass catering firms.

Recruits take their B-2 trade test after twenty-one weeks and this carries them through to the rank of corporal, after which they will need to pass the B-1 before being promoted sergeant, or the A-1 to become staff sergeant. It is a kind of progression from cottage pie through chicken fricassee to lobster thermidor, and A-1 Army cooks would get an honourable mention in any restaurant. Officers too have to work up to a B-1 cookery test after arriving from Sandhurst, so that when they are working on administration they will at least know what Army cooking is all about. Officers also spend thirty-three weeks during their training as civilian caterers with the firm of Trust House Forte.

Judicious man management has been one of the reasons for improved morale. Army trade qualifications are recognized by the City and Guilds as being comparable to civilian qualifications, although many also take the City and Guilds own examinations while in the Army just in case future employers do not share the same view. This means that on leaving the Army they can easily find jobs. Some even open their own hotels and restaurants. A number have gone to work on oil rigs in the North Sea. Surprisingly few enter the kitchens of the big London hotels, chiefly because hotels train their own cooks, but also partly because many Army cooks like to get away from mass catering in their second career.

Another reason for the improved status has been a talent for public relations. The corps has exploited its high success rate in cookery competitions and has encouraged individual enterprise. It was an ACC cook who made Princess Anne's wedding cake. The glass cases on the ground floor of the Aldershot Tower Block contain icing sugar creations which are an art form in themselves. Among them are a model of Guildford Cathedral, and a vase of flowers with each leaf and petal delicately turned and veined.

Some of the more accomplished cooks take a special course on household cookery, before being allocated to generals' official residences in various parts of the world where they might have to cater for frequent, important parties. For instance they have to learn how to make jam and chutney, a specialist line which is not generally taught.

The rising price of food has caused some desperation in the ACC. The daily allowance for one soldier's food in 1977 varied between 65p and 70p according to what food was in season. But soldiers have already had to get used to eating small eggs instead of large ones for breakfast, in an attempt to cut down costs. At the more extravagant end of the spectrum, smoked salmon and caviare have been dropped in favour of more modest hors d'œuvre at Army banquets, and the 8″ gateau has replaced the 10″ gateau as an economy measure. Still this gives an idea of how far the Army has advanced in its thinking about food. In some ways it is the soldier himself with his wider horizons who has forced the Army to provide a more exciting diet than the old regiment of sausage and chips and rice pudding. On the other hand, the ACC in its ambition to provide the very best has sometimes advanced rather too far. Its cooks are sometimes criticized for over-decorating soldiers' food. Tommy Atkins certainly has an enviable choice as he tucks into his daily entitlement of 3,800 calories.

Most of the food served in barracks is fresh. The Army is constantly examining the case for serving more convenience foods. In Northern Ireland and at week-ends when time is short and facilities are limited, tinned meat and frozen sprouts have their value. But for most of the time they are an expensive alternative, and an unnecessary one when one has trained cooks at one's disposal.

There is also a continuing debate about the standard of soldiers' dining-rooms. The ACC shudder at the term 'cookhouse' and encourage the rest of the Army to talk about 'dining-room' or even 'restaurant', although most regiments regard this as being rather too chichi. More seriously, the cooks are unhappy about the standard of comfort in many of them. The trouble is that soldiers spend an average of only thirteen-and-a-half minutes on each meal. If they were encouraged to linger longer, the Army would have to build larger dining-rooms. About sixty per cent of the Army eats at home anyway.

In Aldershot itself the provision of food has gone through as much of a revolution as the cooking of it. Instead of each of the garrison's thirty-seven units ordering its own food from different sources, an ACC group catering establishment now supplies them all on a wholesale basis. From huge kitchens and butchers shops, nine vehicles a day tour a twenty-mile radius, delivering oven-ready meat, cakes and pastries to ninety-seven dining halls and messes. It is a £3,000,000 a year business with 26,000 pounds of bacon and ham going out to feed 4,000 soldiers every month. Smaller, less grandiose schemes have been started elsewhere. But the economic advantages depend upon the scale of operation and the Aldershot experiment itself is likely to remain unique.

Doctors. The Royal Army Medical Corps of today was not founded until 1898. It was an amalgam of three separate branches, a regimental medical system, a medical staff corps of doctors, and a hospital corps consisting largely of nurses. The Sudan Campaign in the same year provided its baptism of fire. Nowadays the RAMC has between 500 and 600 officers, though not all these are qualified doctors. There are also 3,000 other ranks, including qualified male nurses and medical assistants—who are well trained in military skills like map-reading and driving.

Doctors are among the most highly qualified professionals in the Army, and certainly among the best paid. The corps is headed, for instance, by a lieutenant-general, who also controls the Army dentists and the Queen Alexandra's Royal Army Nursing Corps. Then there are as many as six major-generals and twelve brigadiers. After twenty-three years all specialists and three out of every four general practitioners can expect to become full colonels, earning more than other Army colonels too. Other branches of the Army may well envy the doctors their promotion ladder.

Pay is linked to the average earnings of a civilian general practitioner over a career of thirty-five years. But the RAMC points out that the initial advantages of joining the Army as a captain—at a time when one's civilian colleagues are undergoing heavy expenditure, tails away over the years. Even a major-general on £12,000 a year in 1977 was said to be worse off than a civilian specialist who with merit awards and some private practice might boost his earnings to £20,000 a year.

As a result many young medics stay in the corps for the first five years, picking up a useful specialist qualification on the way— with Army encouragement—then leave to join a lucrative civil practice. As a result it is usually a struggle to fill the surgeries. There is currently a shortage of about ten per cent among the qualified Army doctors, and it used to be twenty per cent.

Many of those who stay are those who were attracted by military life in the first place. But there are also significant advantages. In the Army there is roughly one doctor for every 1,500 patients compared with one for every 2,500 or even 3,000 outside. (The RAF with one doctor for every 750 do even better.) The facilities are also quite high.

Moreover while the status of the civilian GP has if anything declined over the years, that of the Army MO has gone up. In the days of National Service a visit to the doctor was almost a punishable offence. It was certainly not an easy business and was made to deter all but the genuinely sick. Nowadays the Army has moved towards the more fashionable, more economic system of group practices with doctors travelling to take clinics in nearby regiments. Even so the corps still tries to allot one of these doctors to a specific unit, so that the regiment can identify with its own 'Doc'.

There are occasions when it may be difficult to maintain the confidence of the consulting room. Army doctors deny, however, that this places them in a very difficult position. 'The regiment is the patient' is the philosophy and they acknowledge that they might have to take the commanding officer into their confidence for the good of the unit.

The range of experience differs from that of the civilian doctor, with much more social and preventive medicine, a lot of children's doctoring, some psychiatry, psychology and, of course, pathology. Even the treatment of gunshot wounds is something of a special subject, because the wounds have to be left unstitched until all traces of the bullet have been removed along with dead tissue. All these things have to be taught.

Non-commissioned ranks are also highly qualified. The RAMC claims that some of its private recruits are better qualified than many officer cadets at Sandhurst. A high proportion of SG-1 soldiers end up in the corps.

Families still complain. Wives protest that they cannot easily find a doctor to visit their sick children, particularly when abroad. On the other hand, civilian families make similar complaints about the National Health Service—and perhaps with more justice.

The RAMC would become still more important in wartime. It forms a whole series of medical units whose role includes the evacuation and treatment of casualties, from regimental aid posts to base hospitals. It mans Field Ambulance formations, each one commanded by a lieutenant-colonel or perhaps a major, and controls fleets of ambulances, including tracked, armoured ambulances like the Samaritan or the variant of the FV-432 armoured personnel carrier. It also has the right to call on helicopters for the speedy evacuation of the seriously wounded and its men also have to be trained to evacuate casualties from the battlefield after a nuclear attack.

More than any other service it requires massive and rapid reinforcement in wartime and the TAVR is specifically organized to provide these extra men.

Dentists. It was not until 1921 that the Army recognized the need for a dental service of its own, and a warrant establishing one was signed by Winston Churchill. As many as 3,000 dentists served in it during the Second World War, and the Army Dental Corps had 'Royal' added to the title in 1946. (A private soldier from the corps was actually the first British soldier to escape from a prisoner-of-war camp.)

It remains, in peacetime, a smallish family corps in which everyone knows everyone. There are only 200 officers, of whom 180 are dentists, and 351 other soldiers. Of these 210 are surgery assistants, 108 are technicians and thirty-three are hygienists—who can administer simple treatment like scaling teeth, rinsing children's teeth with fluoride washes and advising on oral health.

There are also a small number of civilian dentists employed to help out in some places. There is a need for them in Germany, for instance, where seventy-eight Army dentists have to cope not only with the soldiers, but also with their families, including 35,000 children.

The problem in places like BAOR is made worse by the very fact that families can get free dental treatment from the Army when living outside Britain, while when at home they have to go to a civilian practice like everyone else. As a result many save up any treatment they need until they are sent abroad.

It is easy to understand why. Despite the fearsome picture of an Army dentist which once coloured people's attitudes, the standard of treatment now is very high. Army dentists, for instance, scorn the use of dental plates for fitting false teeth, and fit sophisticated crowns and bridges as a matter of routine. As a result families receive the kind of care which they would probably have to pay for privately if they tried to get it in England.

The RADC has also to act as a kind of watchdog over people who might otherwise take advantage of the government. One of its functions is to monitor claims for treatment placed by those stationed in faraway places where they might be dependant upon the local dentists. Defence attachés and their families are a good example. Some of the claims submitted for reimbursement can be quite extravagant. One officer's wife was persuaded when abroad to have all her existing fillings out although her records showed that there was nothing wrong with them, and have them replaced with gold. The bill came to £2,000 which the RADC, amid much acrimony, refused to allow.

The standard expected of recruits is also quite high. One weakness of the system is that officer cadets, who make up most of the recruits, are signed up after they have passed their 2nd Bachelor of Dental Surgery examinations (2nd BDS). In other words they are accepted on to the Army's payroll on the strength of their theoretical knowledge, before they have actually tried their hand with a drill. But the corps gets round this by accepting them only on short service commissions and re-assessing them after the first five years before deciding whether to take them on for a full career.

Cadets may be accepted if they have passed only their Licentiate of Dental Surgery (LDS) examination, which is rather lower than the BDS. But they will still be expected to take their BDS during the first five years, and he who fails has little chance of being accepted permanently.

This anyway has been the position throughout the 1970s, when the corps has been fully recruited. Dentists are said to have been attracted partly by the guaranteed income and low expenditure during their early years. Many are also frustrated refugees from the National Health Service.

Like Army doctors they are paid more than other officers in the same rank, and promotion prospects are also very good. They enter as captains in the certain knowledge that in thirteen years' time they will end up as lieutenant-colonels. Ten years later still, all those who are good enough to become specialists, and about half of those who are general duty dentists, will also become full colonels.

Some officers in the RADC feel rather guilty about these special advantages. Other Army officers, they admit, have to work hard to reach the rank of lieutenant-colonel. They also wonder if it is right that they should then receive more than the battalion commander who has more ultimate responsibility.

On the other hand, they point out that they have to have these privileges if they are to be paid comparable rates with those of their civilian colleagues. As it is there have been signs of a fall-off in recruiting since the spate of defence cuts in the mid-1970s. There are some shortages among the non-commissioned ranks, particularly among dental clerks, so that Army wives and daughters sometimes have to be employed to help out.

Vets. The role of the Royal Army Veterinary Corps (RAVC) began to decline when the tank replaced the horse. In a sense it has been succeeded by the Royal Electrical and Mechanical Engineers. Now there are only twenty-seven officers and 140 soldiers whose spiritual home is split between the directorate at Droitwich in Worcestershire and the training centre at Melton Mowbray.

The Corps' title is inadequate. Although its officers are qualified veterinary surgeons who treat the Army's depleted stocks of animals, they are also responsible for procuring the animals and to some extent for training them.

The centre at Melton Mowbray is a rather temporary looking collection of wooden huts built around a private stud farm which the Army bought for its remount services (the official name for the provision of new horses) in 1911. There are 360 acres, most of it grazing land laid out behind an impenetrable maze of housing estates. One needs a tracker dog to find it.

About half their work is concerned with horses and the other half with dogs. The commandant himself belongs to the Ministry of Defence's Animals Purchasing Commission.

Horses for the Army (the Household Cavalry, the King's Troop Royal Horse Artillery, the Royal Military Police, and the RAVC itself) are bought twice a year in Ireland. A three-man team visits two dealers, one in County Waterford, and one in Meath, who have been supplying the Army for many years. The main buy is in June–July, then there is a second 'topping up' visit in March.

The Army buys its horses when they are about four years old, but does not issue them until twelve months later. This not only gives the RAVC a good chance to examine them, but also means that the Army gets them cheaper. But with the price of a cavalry officer's charger touching £800 in 1977, a trooper's mount £650 and a RHA horse £600, it is quite big business.

Horses spend the twelve-month interval grazing on the fields at Melton. Between fifty and sixty are there at any one time, and the RAVC alternates the grazing with a number of bullocks and sheep to maintain good pasture management. The Army School of Farriery, the Army School of Equitation and an animal hospital are also at Melton, and the atmosphere at one end of the place is extremely horsey.

At the other end it is equally doggy. The Army has a total of some 1,350 dogs, about 150 of them labradors who are trained for specialist tracking and 'sniffing', while the others are mostly Alsatians used for guard duties and patrolling. Alsatians are preferred because they are good at picking up air scent, are the best dogs for frightening unwelcome visitors and are easily obtainable. Dobermann Pinschers by contrast, though excellent guard-dogs, are uncommon in Britain.

Availability is important because of cost. Although the Army sometimes pays up to £45 for a good Alsatian, most of its dogs are acquired cheaply. Many come from private owners who can no longer afford to feed them, or have lost interest in what once seemed a good idea. The RAVC only accepts dogs, however, as opposed to bitches, because bitches tend to have a disruptive influence in the kennels. The RAVC rejects more than half the dogs offered to them, but for those which are accepted, life with the Army has its advantages. They are well fed on commercial biscuits and tinned dog food. The vets themselves do not do badly either, enjoying whole Stilton cheeses bought from a nearby manufacturer, and Melton Mowbray pies.

Army horses are issued untrained to the regiments but dogs are trained in Melton itself, before being posted to units at home and overseas. All animals, however, return to Melton to die when they are finally 'cast'—the official term—the horses at the age of fifteen and the dogs at the age of eight.

Vets like lawyers are paid only marginally above the rate for the Army as a whole. They do not even get much guaranteed promotion. The basic rank among officers is that of major. Even so, the corps has little difficulty in finding recruits.

This is partly because it never needs all that many, and partly because of the horses. Civil vets find it difficult to enter what are called equine practices because these are always looking for partners with some experience. Because it is a profitable field in which to specialize, these practices can afford to pick and choose. So horsey-minded vets sometimes join the RAVC for a few years to get the experience they need.

There are others who simply cannot afford to buy their way into a practice when young, so they settle for a steady income. Some like it so much that they then make a full career of it. They grumble about the pay but as long as the corps continues to find enough recruits it has little leverage with which to win a better deal for them.

Police. The 'Red Caps' in the Royal Corps of Military Police are headed by a brigadier whose official title is the Provost-Marshal. Provost-Marshals date back at least to Norman times when they had to protect the monarch when he went to battle—as well as superintend the layout of the tents at, say, Agincourt or Crecy. From time to time they hired their own strong men who had nothing to do with the Army. It was not until the middle of the last century that they were given a proper police force to command.

At first these were only seconded cavalrymen who were posted to Aldershot and the Curragh in Dublin under the command of an NCO from the 7th Hussars with the endearing name of Sergeant-Major Trout. The first permanent force of Military Police consisted of a group of cavalrymen which was formed in 1877, although the modern corps did not come into its own until the First World War, when the internal combustion engine and the huge armies in Europe brought problems of traffic control. In the Second World War there were 50,000 of them, including a company from the Automobile Association—which still exists in the Territorial Army. After the Anzio landings in Italy some troops took the wrong turning and landed up among the enemy, because nobody had arrived to show them the way. So traffic control was rather important.

One vital crossroads in North-West Italy was so dangerous that for every MP killed there a red cap was hung on a nearby tree—which came to be known as Red Cap tree.

The number of MPs is now being gradually reduced from 2,450 to about 2,000, including 130 officers, as the need for them in Northern Ireland decreases. Recruiting is good enough for them to rely mostly on 'committed' boys who sign on specifically to join them. Most are SG-2s but a significant number are SG-1s and all have to score seventy per cent in the RO 21 intelligence test. They also have to be 5′ 8″ tall and to weigh 135 pounds—which the MPs think is too light anyway.

By the end of their sixteen weeks training at the depot in Chichester about forty per cent have failed to make the grade. Those who succeed pass out as lance-corporals. But the corps was still losing people at the rate of fifteen a month in 1976 and ten a month in 1977. Unpopular tours of duty in Northern Ireland have been blamed. Of all those who leave about one in five joins the civil police. On the other hand, about one out of every five recruits comes from the civil police in the first place, so it is a fair exchange.

After four or five years an MP can apply to join the Special Investigation Branch (SIB) which does the Army's detective work. The SIB was founded in 1939 after the British Expeditionary Force in France sent an urgent request for help in dealing with all the villains in its ranks.

There are just over 200 of them, all of whom wear plain clothes like civilian detectives. They even have their own badge which is a silver branch with nineteen twigs to represent the nineteen original members. As it usually takes several years to make him a good detective, a man will normally remain in the SIB for the rest of his military career. They have a Crime and Intelligence office at Great Scotland Yard from where they link up with other military police and civil police throughout the world. They even have their own fraud specialists.

The image of MPs has improved, though some other branches of the Army think that it still has some way to go. It was at its worst in the 1950s when a predatory MP looking for a likely victim could cause panic among young National Servicemen. Some offices even had charts showing the individual arrest rate and a Red Cap whose tally had dropped felt obliged to go out and improve it. All that has happily been changed.

Military Offenders. Crime in the Army seems to have been going down. In 1977 a total of 203 soldiers, or 8·7 out of every 1,000 in the Army, were convicted by Court Martial of one or more offences. The total number of offences, which ranged from serious assault to being absent without leave (AWOL), was 1,545. In 1974 the number of guilty men (and presumably women) was 1,706, or 11·6 out of every 1,000, and the offences totalled 2,117.

Property offences including theft and criminal damage actually rose from 455 to 536 in 1975 and 507 in 1977. But desertion and AWOL convictions went down during the four years from 759 to 432, disciplinary offences were down from 132 to sixty-eight, criminal assault from 197 to 183 (237 in 1976) and other offences including drugs, drunkenness and traffic crime were down to 355 from 574.

How these figures compare with the civilian rate of crime, the Ministry of Defence is reluctant to say. Attempts to draw parallels have always been abandoned because of the difficulty of finding comparable age groups. On the one hand the Army figures should be lower because no one with a serious criminal record is recruited in the first place and those who acquire one are quickly discharged.

Also soldiers who commit civil crimes while in Britain are dealt with by the civil courts. On the other hand, offences like AWOL or insubordination have no civilian equivalents.

Soldiers who are sentenced to detention go to the Military Corrective Training Centre (MCTC) at Colchester. This is the nearest thing that the Armed Forces now have to a prison. Until the Second World War miscreants were sent to Military Prisons and Detention Barracks (MPDB) which usually existed side by side. The most notorious was at Aldershot whose glass roof gave rise to the nickname 'glasshouse'. The Army now frowns upon the term and likes to think that it has largely died out. One can understand why. The old MPDB were designed to punish offenders and to deter them from doing it again. Discipline was strict to the point of being brutal and the close-cropped inmates raced around all day at the double without learning very much apart from the unassailable fact that things could hardly get much worse.

The last of them at Shepton Mallett was closed down between 1964 and 1966. The Forces switched entirely to the MCTCs which had been based on recommendations of the Dempsey committee of 1941. As far as the Army is concerned, Colchester is the only one left.

There are two wings at Colchester. At 'A' Wing the emphasis is on military training to prepare servicemen for their eventual return to their regiment or RAF station (the Royal Navy has a place of its own). The training is organized in three stages, each one easier than the last. Progress from one to another depends upon good conduct. 'D' Wing takes all members of the Forces who are being discharged after release, and the idea is to rehabilitate them for civilian life.

The MCTC is run by the Military Provost Staff Corps which like the Military Police comes under the Provost-Martial. It was founded in 1901 and at one time about one in every four of its 134 members was transferred from the Military Police. But fewer MPs now apply, mainly because it means spending one's entire career at Colchester.

In 1977 there were 920 servicemen in detention there. These included 692 soldiers, 109 airmen, ninety-five sailors and twenty-four marines. But 343 of the soldiers had committed no more heinous a crime than desertion or being absent without leave. The others included 202 for dishonesty, sixty-eight for violence, twenty-two for indecency, nine for drug offences, nine for drunkenness, five for insubordination and five for vehicle offences. The overall number has tended to go down. The 920 in 1977 could be compared with 1,516 in 1970. Apart from a slight rise in 1973 and

1974 there has been a steady fall since then—although 1977 was the first year in which the total had fallen below 1,000.

The success rate of 'A' Wing has been reasonably high. Of the 608 soldiers returned to their units in 1976, as many as seventy-one had been promoted or recommended for promotion within a year, and 236 were reckoned to have improved. But a further sixty-three had not improved, 130 had been discharged as being beyond hope of rehabilitation, twenty-four had bought themselves out, twenty-four had disappeared without leave once more and six had ended up back at Colchester.

The MCTC was certainly praised by a Home Office penologist and a prison governor who visited it at the Army's request in 1974. They said in their official report: 'After much experience of civil prisons, it was refreshing for us to observe young and fit soldiers instead of the usual prison population. . . . Those detainees whom we met, including men to be discharged from the services, also impressed us as being well worth all the complexities and uncertainties of rehabilitation training and treatment.'

14

Regiments of Women

Army Nursing. Women have been going to war since Queen Boadicea led the Iceni against their Roman conquerors in the early years of the first millenium. But until recently their contribution was intermittent, and rarely so dramatic. Some have at times dressed in men's clothes and flattened their curves, to win acceptance in one expeditionary force or another. In 1677 two of them arrived in Tangiers to join what was later to become the Queen's Regiment. But the deception did not last for long.

It was in the more feminine role of nurse and helpmate that women first established for themselves a place on the battlefield. But even that took them hundreds of years. If Florence Nightingale was not the first to nurse soldiers *in situ*, she was the first to offer more than marginal comfort. There were at that time no ambulances, no stretcher-bearers, no sanitation—and no plans to provide any. The image of The Lady with the Lamp may be the product of mid-Victorian journalism. But the discipline and organization, and professional dedication, which she introduced during the Crimean War, contributed most of all to the status of women at war.

In 1881 the Army Nursing Service was inaugurated and in 1902 this was transformed by royal patronage into the Queen Alexandra's Imperial Military Nursing Service—a title which got what it deserved by being colloquially interpreted as 'Queer And Impossible—Mostly Not Sane' or worse 'Queer Assortment of Individuals—Mainly Non-Sexed.' Queen Alexandra herself suggested using the Order of Dannebrog Cross from her native Denmark as the emblem, with an 'A' cypher in the middle and a motto beneath 'Sub Cruce Candida'—Under the White Cross.

In 1914 there were still only 300 regular members—although after mobilization there were more than 10,000 by 1918. In 1939 there were fewer than 700 when the Second World War started. Nurses had officer status only—a principle dating back to the start of the Army Nursing Service, when it was recommended that the widows and daughters of officers would be preferable recruits.

Soldiers' wives, it was pointed out, would be too much on the level of the soldiers themselves, although social rank should not necessarily prevent a 'good sensible woman' from being accepted. The pre-Nightingale image of Army nurses had swung from one extreme to another.

This all changed again in 1949 when the service was officially absorbed by the Army under its present title of the Queen Alexandra's Royal Army Nursing Corps. In the Second World War they had looked very much like soldiers. Khaki had been introduced, partly because it was more practical and partly because they could not buy anything else. Peaked caps replaced the old brimmed hats and slacks were substituted for skirts—first in the tropics and then more or less everywhere. When tending to stretcher cases on the ground skirts had obvious disadvantages for the nurse, if not entirely for the patient. They had also behaved like soldiers—though not for the first time. They had been bombed, imprisoned, shipwrecked and sometimes confined to slit trenches—like everyone else.

Now, however, they were not only to look and behave like soldiers, but to become soldiers themselves. In 1950 'other ranks' or servicewomen, were admitted for the first time. The Royal Army Medical Corps Director of Music composed a regimental march by arranging Purcell's 'King Arthur' and the air 'Gentle Maiden'—and called it 'Grey and Scarlet' after the Corps' traditional colour scheme. Later the Corps became recognized as an official training establishment by the General Nursing Council.

The change was not greeted with universal enthusiasm. The women relished it or, at worst, accepted it as a logical progression. Many servicemen felt, however, that their romantic vision of the ladies with the lamp had no place for a barrel-bosomed sergeant-major stomping round the wards in brown brogues.

Since their formation in 1902 the women in grey have been awarded 1,300 decorations, nine of them posthumously, for gallantry and dedication to duty. Among the first to be decorated was Sister Norah Easby who served in the Balkan Wars 1912–13, was wounded during the First World War while on front-line duty near Bethune, and was granted the OBE, the Military Medal and the Royal Red Cross Medal. Among the latest was Mrs. Sheila Fox who won the George Medal while serving on the Anzio beach-head during 1944. In the First World War 195 of the 10,000 who served, lost their lives. In the Second the figures were 220 out of 12,000.

The QAs. There are now between 1,500 and 1,600 in the Corps, whose size has diminished in parallel with that of the Army as a whole. Recruiting is usually good, but better for servicewomen than officers. In 1976 there were only 535 officers against a target figure of 585. On the other hand, there were more than 1,000 servicewomen—well over the establishment strength of 886.

The difficulty of finding officers, most of whom are qualified state registered nurses (SRNs), has lasted for years, and has much to do with the difficulty of finding qualified SRNs anywhere, within the Army or without. Nor have the QAs been helped by a changing balance of fortunes. Until recently the Army nurse was better paid than her civilian counterpart and had a better chance of travelling round the world. Now, however, civilian nursing pay and conditions have more or less caught up and in some respects have moved ahead. Moreover the chances of travel with the Army have shrunk, while the opportunities open to a trained civilian nurse to find work overseas have expanded.

But the Corps can still offer more job security, accommodation which is normally better than that in a civilian hospital, a communal life for those who like it and a tradition of duty and dedication which is free from any union restrictions and civilian pressures. Moreover parents rather like their daughters to enter the Corps because of the greater emphasis on discipline. Actually the Corps likes to be thought of as maternal rather than authoritarian. 'We don't exactly count heads when they come in late, but we do try to be responsible for them' one officer said. Parents, anxiously watching their young leave the family nest for the first time, find that comforting.

Servicewomen with four 'O' levels can join as student nurses to train for three years before qualifying as SRNs. Those without can join as pupil nurses to train for two years to become State Enrolled Nurses (SENs). Others can join as medical clerks, dental assistants or ward stewardesses—a relatively new 'trade'.

Officers are qualified SRNs who have normally completed at least one year of post-registration work in hospital before being commissioned. They join on eight-year short-service commissions consisting of two or more years in 'the colours' and the rest in the reserves—but can convert to long-term regular commissions later. Recruits who are qualified SENs have to join as servicewomen, but have the advantage of starting work as trained nurses immediately instead of having to train. Promotion should therefore come more quickly.

'Home' for the QAs is the Royal Pavilion Centre which is set among 100 acres of woodlands and shrubbery on the fringe of Aldershot. It was purpose-built on the site of the old Royal Pavilion from which Queen Victoria used to review the troops. All that remains of the old structure now is the tunnel which connected the pavilion with the kitchens—kept at a safe distance so that the Queen would not be troubled by the smell. The new building was opened by Princess Margaret the Colonel-in-Chief, in 1967. With its interesting use of flat roofs, grey bridges, split levels and steps, it reminds some nurses of a battleship. Here officers stroll on the lawn outside the mess on summer evenings, chattering over coffee about their pink camelias or their biggest rhododendron in Europe, which is assiduously nursed by the gardener.

All recruits come here for a five-week basic training period, during which they imbibe something of the military ethos before being posted to one of the Army's seventeen military hospitals. A typical intake might consist of sixty-two including twenty-nine pupil nurses, fourteen qualified SENs, fourteen ward stewardesses and six dental assistants. Student nurses in deference to their higher intelligence rating, come on their own in three intakes of twenty-five a time each year. Officers come here also, and all QAs return at intervals for promotion courses, middle management courses and so on. It is very much the Corps' Alma Mater.

The military indoctrination is minimal. But recruits learn something about the Corps, practise orienteering—a modified form of map-reading—do plenty of PT and even a certain amount of drill, which curiously they adore. 'We just can't stop them doing it—the little beasts,' one officer grumbled cheerfully. They also enjoy receiving their new wardrobe of six ward dresses, one number two dress (grey military jacket and skirt), one raincoat, one grey cape with scarlet lining, PT kit and flat shoes. They get an allowance to buy court shoes, petticoats and also tights—in regulation Woolworth's pearl grey. Officers also in due course buy their own mess dress—an elegant pale grey evening dress with chiffon sleeves, scarlet collar and inverted pleat. (Apart from the difficulty of finding handbags to match, the officers love it.)

Nine of the seventeen hospitals kept going by the Army, are in Britain. These are the Cambridge and the Louise Margaret Maternity Hospital in Aldershot, the Duchess of Kent at Catterick, the Royal Herbert at Woolwich and the Woolwich Maternity Hospital, the military hospitals on Millbank, London, at Tidworth and Colchester and the Royal Victoria at Netley which is now the Army's psychiatric centre. There are also military wings attached to a number of civilian hospitals, including the Musgrave Park Hospital in Belfast whose name has become familiar during the Irish troubles. There are five in Germany, at Hanover, Munster, Rinteln, Iserlohn and Berlin and three elsewhere—in Cyprus, Hong Kong and Nepal. The Nepal hospital which looks after the

Gurkhas, is staffed mostly by locally employed girls but has a British QA matron and four officers.

The director of the Corps is always a brigadier—and has been since military ranks were introduced in 1949. She can serve until the age of fifty-nine. A colonel commands the Aldershot centre and matrons at the hospitals are either colonels or lieutenant-colonels. A ward sister might be any rank from lieutenant to major depending on her seniority. Some girls are commissioned after considerable civilian experience, in which case they might quickly jump to captain on joining.

Wastage is the central problem for all women's services. It is higher for women than for men, and for the QAs it is particularly bad. This is partly because the relatively small number of military hospitals makes it difficult for a girl to continue working after marriage. Moreover the opportunities outside the Army for fully trained nurses enable a girl to exercise the female prerogative of changing her mind at some breakpoint in her career, and leaving to seek work in a civilian environment. Girls are asked to give seven months' notice before leaving to be married. But this is not always possible, and the Corps sees no point in being harsh on those who fail to do so. Apart from marriage the obvious break-point in a girl's military career comes after she has qualified. Although seventy-five student nurses may join every year, only about half have recently been staying in the Corps to take commissions after qualifying.

It was the high wastage rate which compelled the Corps to turn to personnel selection methods several years ago—first for student nurses and then for all recruits. Girls now spend twenty-four hours completing tests and interviews before being offered a place. As a result wastage has been cut by half during the first six months of a girl's career. In 1975–76 there were 750 applicants for about 500 places. By personnel selection methods the Corps was able to select the most strongly motivated, who were most likely to stay. Student nurses are now even queuing up to join. But given the expense of nursing training it is hoped that those who join should also stay instead of breaking away at the first opportunity.

Like all women's services the QAs are sensitive about their public persona. They are particularly touchy about the acronym 'QARANC'—which is guaranteed to freeze the smile on the face of any colonel who hears it. The predilection for acronyms is one military habit which the Corps have never learned to live with.

In general their image has not only survived the Army take-over in 1949 but actually improved. This perhaps has less to do with the Army's influence than with the professional status that the

QAs have acquired and the reputation that the Corps has won as a training organization. This reputation is still growing. In September 1970 five sisters enhanced it by their work in Jordan when, under the official classification of civilians, they accompanied the RAMC team which took 2 Field Hospital to help casualties in the civil war. In 1972 a captain on exchange duty in Australia was highly praised by the Australian Army for her work during a Queensland earthquake.

The trappings of life are military. A nurse has her rank, her uniform—and an obligation to salute the Queen's Commission when appropriate. A candidate for a commission has to satisfy a selection board that she has other qualities beyond nursing skills, though the QAs still wince at the mention of 'officer quality'. To this extent they are part of a stratified society which is more Army than civilian.

On the other hand, the atmosphere is professional for most of the time. An officer is officially addressed as 'Ma-am' but more often 'Sister' or 'Colonel' and when appropriate as 'Matron'. Moreover, one can hardly salute when in nursing uniform so the embarrassment of having to conform to that uniquely military custom is happily deferred when on professional duty.

The relationship between military hospitals and local civilians is very close. On average, between thirty and forty per cent of their patients are civilian. They serve their areas much as do hospitals in the National Health Service.

As a result it is the clean crisp image of the nurse that has impressed itself upon the public subconscious, rather than a cartoon of a sergeant-major in skirts, bearing her hypodermic syringe like a bayonet. Certainly the QAs themselves seem happy enough about the way in which the public think of them.

Women Soldiers. The direct ancestor of the Women's Royal Army Corps (WRAC) was the Women's Army Auxiliary Corps (WAAC) —later to become the Queen Mary's Army Auxiliary Corps. This was formed in 1916 to provide women for service in France. They were a disciplined, uniformed corps of women, recruited because of the manpower shortage, which by that time was acute. They worked as cooks, waitresses, drivers, storewomen, telephonists, telegraphists and clerks, releasing men from the rear supply lines of the war effort for service at the front. It is doubtful if the men involved ever felt very grateful for the privilege.

The QMAAC was disbanded in 1919. But the idea of using women in war lingered on. The discussion became more urgent in the 1930s and in 1938 the Auxiliary Territorial Corps (ATS) was formed.

More than 20,000 women between eighteen and fifty were to be enrolled for four years' service and 17,000 joined in the first year. This makes it sound more successful at first than it was. In fact the ATS had its share of teething troubles. Many of the officers who joined in that first year belonged to the leisured classes who had the time to spare, but not much else. A large proportion were titled, which at least pleased some of the other recruits. One woman wrote in to say that she did not mind what she did to help 'but please I would much rather do it under a lady.'

Other difficulties were of a different order. The question of whether or not to issue underclothes for this sudden influx of women resulted in a flurry of memoranda. Would ordnance officers object to handling ladies' under-garments? Eventually it was decided after consultation with old comrades' associations, experienced through the First World War, that a woven vest and panties should be issued—preferably with a brassiere top, compiled from cotton and wool of a strong weave. A suspender belt and knickers to match the uniform were also recommended. Dame Helen Gwynne-Vaughan, the first director of the ATS added to one long memo on the subject: 'If they like to provide crêpe de Chine undies of their own and wash them (as no doubt they would) in their off-duty time, I see no objection.'

Having crossed this obstacle the ATS went from strength to strength. The big push forward came in December 1941 when conscription for women was introduced and the size of the corps rose to 215,000 in June 1943. The number of job opportunities expanded until there were 124 different trades open to women. They were paid two-thirds the equivalent rate for men. The first ATS contingent left for France in 1940 and by 1945 they were serving in most parts of the war. In 1945 the ATS also gained its most illustrious recruit when Princess Elizabeth, the present Queen, joined as a 2nd Subaltern—the equivalent of 2nd Lieutenant. But in terms of numbers the June 1943 figure was the peak.

Women demonstrated their value so well during the war that the Government decided to keep some of them in uniform. A small ATS force remained until 1 February, 1949 when together with the Queen Alexandra's Royal Army Nursing Corps, the Women's Royal Army Corps was formed as an integral part of the British Army.

The Women's Royal Army Corps. The WRAC today has about 4,000 servicewomen and 310 officers. In overall 'womanpower' it is thus nearly three times the size of the QARANC. But the ratio of officers to servicewomen is noticeably different. Apart from the director who is a brigadier, there are only five colonels and seven lieutenant-colonels, which suggests a shortage of room at the top.

Like the QARANC again, the Corps is slightly above strength. This suggests that recruiting is no problem. In fact it has its ups and downs, which curiously seem to follow shortly behind the ups and downs in male recruiting—just as women have historically followed their menfolk. But the ups and downs have never been as pronounced as they are for men. The 1973 trough in male recruiting was succeeded by a trough for women. But the trough was never as deep and the recovery was quicker.

So recruiting fluctuates—but then so does the requirement. Women have found themselves a role in the Army but it remains a supporting role. In a bad year for Army recruiting the WRAC might be briefed to find up to 2,000 servicewomen—to fill the places in the ranks. When the flow of male recruits resumes, the WRAC might have to reduce its annual target to, say, 1,750—which was the figure in 1976. The number of officers being admitted was then running at around forty-eight.

Demand for recruits has dropped anyway because of a reduction in the wastage rate. The average length of stay for a junior officer has been extended from just under three years to just under five, which is quite an achievement. This improvement in the wastage rate is due partly to the adoption of personnel selection—which has benefitted the WRAC as much as any other branch of the Army, and partly because of the high number of girls who now continue in the Corps after marriage. Because the WRAC is more ubiquitous than the QARANC, it finds it easier to offer a girl a posting near to her new husband, whether he is in the Army or not. A significant proportion of WRAC girls do marry soldiers and the Army, in its own interests, tries to accommodate both as far as possible. It is by no means uncommon for a WRAC wife to be higher in rank than her husband—and serving on the same camp.

Despite these improvements, wastage remains a problem. An officer is asked to give seven months' notice on getting married if only to ensure that the girl who is to succeed her gets six months' notice of her new posting. They are said to be quite conscientious about this. On the other hand, whether the newly-weds give notice or not, there is still the constant upheaval. More seriously there is a continual shortage of officers at the level of captain and of servicewomen at the rank of sergeant or corporal, because the length of time it takes them to reach that rank is about the same length of time it takes them to find a husband. And by no means all girls remain in the Army after marriage.

It was to counter these shortages among NCOs, that the WRAC began to admit junior leaders to the Corps centre at Queen Elizabeth's Barracks, Guildford, in 1975. Junior leaders, who enter at the age of sixteen-and-a-half, are just as likely to be married some day as anyone else. But at least the Corps should get more service out of them first. The scheme has been expensive, however, and the WRAC have been watching it anxiously in the hope that it might pay dividends.

Like the rest of the Army the WRAC are over-subscribed on some trades and short on others. They can always find plenty of girls who want to be drivers but, surprisingly, can never find enough cooks. The personnel selection centre at Queen Elizabeth's Barracks operates a guaranteed vacancy scheme through which a girl can book a vacancy in the trade of her choice. It is nearly always possible for a potential cook to enter on the spot, but a driver might have to wait four or five months for a place. For the SG-1s and SG-2s there are jobs as intelligence analysts, experimental assistants in gunnery or perhaps military policewomen. The less bright might become stewardesses, and other opportunities range from communications operators and clerks to bandswomen and hairdressers.

The range of jobs open to women in the Army has widened over the years, but only slowly. This is partly because women continue to be non-combatant, partly because there are some jobs for which they would just not be strong enough and partly because the supply of suitably qualified girls is often not enough to meet the demand. Girls tend to be less well endowed with technical skills than are male recruits. On the other hand, while there are many potential computer programmers, there are also plenty of civilian jobs for them, so that few end up with the Army. One recent innovation has been the appointment of young WRAC officers to posts as assistant adjutants in a number of regiments, notably the Royal Artillery. The motive of regiments like the Gunners has been self-interest. They simply cannot find enough young men to do the job. But it provides a good opportunity for the WRAC to extend the experience of a number of young lieutenants, and the addition of a dewy-eyed blonde has certainly done much to brighten up a number of adjutants' offices in Britain and in Germany.

About a quarter of the WRAC are now based in Germany, although women are usually confined to units well behind the front line. A large number are also now engaged in Northern Ireland, where most of them have relished the experience of being involved in active service. The trend in general has been to integrate the WRAC more and more closely with the rest of the Army. The whole subject has recently been subjected to a study by the

Committee on the Future Employment of Women in the Army. This committee, established by the Director of Manning (Army) has been examining such perennial subjects as the admission of WRAC officer cadets to Sandhurst, the disciplinary procedures for women and, perhaps most important, the question of weapon training.

At present women get no weapon training at all. Not only are they left in ignorance on how to fire a rifle, but they are not even shown what one looks like. Girls who have been filling these new posts as assistant adjutants have complained that they arrived on the scene without knowing the difference between, say, a self-propelled gun and a Chieftain tank. Other Nato women's services are non-combatant—as indeed are servicewomen almost everywhere, including Israel. But other Nato countries provide weapon training for their women, and the United States in particular are widening the scope for their servicewomen with almost excessive zeal. The WRAC together with the other women's services in Britain have never sought progress on quite that scale. But perhaps there is now a good case for teaching the WRAC how to use small arms if only in self-defence, and some basic knowledge about other fighting equipment.

Integration with the men's Army has already gone quite far. After six weeks' basic training at Queen Elizabeth's Barracks, girls leave to learn their trade alongside men in the established Army training centres. There are in fact only three WRAC units as such—one in Aldershot, one at Mill Hill, North London, and one at Rheindahlen in West Germany. Elsewhere they join men's units which, not surprisingly, is what most of them prefer. Few girls view with enthusiasm the idea of a two- or three-year posting in, say, the Guildford centre where the company and the atmosphere are predominantly feminine.

WRAC recruits give a variety of reasons for joining the Army. Some say they like the opportunity to travel—although senior officers point out that a surprising number find convenient excuses when a posting to Hong Kong or somewhere actually does materialize. Others say that they like the communal life and some officers relish the opportunity for assuming executive responsibility at such an early age. Many are, no doubt, attracted by the material benefits. Basic pay is now equal to that for men, although women receive an X-factor of only five per cent against ten per cent for men. This is because women are non-combatant and do not suffer quite the same social turbulence.

The primary reason why most women join the Army, however, is probably the one which they are least likely to mention—the

9

chance of catching a husband in a predominantly masculine world. Integration has been welcomed by all.

There are certainly plenty of opportunities for socializing. For instance, officer cadets attend the WRAC College at Camberley—for an eight-month course or an eight-week course depending on 'maturity'. This provides them with a unique opportunity for establishing contact with Sandhurst, two miles down the road. The two colleges share a number of lectures. An enterprising girl could even find herself a spouse before her passing-out parade.

One advantage of this annual rush to the altar is that it helps to counter the un-feminine, 'butch' image which persists despite constant attempts to get rid of it. It is not surprising that it should, given the popular concept of soldiering, but it remains a source of irritation and distress. WRAC officers frequently complain that the public have a preconceived idea of what a woman soldier should be like, and are reluctant to let go whatever happens. The image was not helped by the well-publicized affair in 1967 when six girls were discharged after an investigation into homosexual practices at Inglis Barracks, Mill Hill. Such an incident may be unusual. But the public sees it as confirmation of what it has always believed.

The Feminine Image. Women detest the acronym 'WRAC'—pronounced 'RACK'—even more than the QAs dislike being referred to as the QARANC. Brigadier Eileen Nolan who retired as director of the Corps in 1977 argues that the Women's Royal Naval Service are blessed with a more pleasing persona because the acronym 'WREN' suggests something dainty and feminine. 'WRAC' on the other hand is said to sound flat and ugly. They prefer to be known by the initials, 'W.R.A.C.' and only a brave and insensitive man would be unaware of the looks in an Officers' mess if he transgressed this cardinal rule.

At Queen Elizabeth's Barracks, a large, bright complex of modern red brick—full of hockey pitches and open spaces—the Corps goes to some trouble to emphasize what Frenchmen call 'la différence'. Girls are not only allowed to use make-up at all times, but are actually encouraged to do so by visits from beauticians who instruct them on skin care. They can wear their hair in whatever style they please and at whatever length—as long as it is kept above the collar when in uniform. The bun is popular among girls who can then let their hair down when off duty. Officers insist that the standards of smartness they demand are no more than the head of a typing pool might require in a civilian office. 'Bull' is a word detested almost as much as 'WRAC' and is never ever used—

although sometimes an over-enthusiastic NCO or even an equally enthusiastic recruit, has to be restrained from excessive spit and polish.

Great care is taken over tailoring the off-the-peg uniform to fit—although this is a necessity because, as one officer explained 'We get some very funny shapes.' Perhaps as a result, the uniform is very popular. Girls are given two service uniforms, each consisting of a lovat green tunic and skirt, a peaked hat, a beret, a cardigan, a raincoat, a greatcoat, a pair of gloves, a pair of flat shoes, a sling bag which can be worn with a short or long strap, shirts, summer blouses and a tie.

Some girls find difficulty in wearing a beret, and most have trouble knotting a tie to the satisfaction of their betters. But the tie is fast giving way to the tab collar—a permissible alternative. The most popular item of clothing is the double-breasted overcoat, which girls find very flattering. Many it is said, would wear it in midsummer if allowed to do so. Also popular with officers is the Mess Dress—a square-necked gown in gold brocade with green silk epaulettes to denote rank and a green sash with gold braid which is thrown over the shoulder. Sergeants and warrant officers wear a similar dress with a round, rather than square neck, and made of beige crimplene. They wear their badge of rank in the form of a brooch. Tropical dresses are issued to girls who are going abroad, to be worn with beige or white sandals, and PT instructors enjoy the distinction of wearing a scarlet skirt.

Like the QAs they draw an allowance to pay for court shoes and underclothes. The shoes have to be black with heels no higher than about two inches. But apart from those stipulations girls can choose which styles they prefer. Tights are a regulation colour —last reported to be Morley's Sun Beige—but the colour changes because manufacturers keep switching their commercial shades. Uniform skirts have to be worn with the hem at mid-knee level, which most acknowledge to be a happy compromise between the fluctuating extremes of fashion.

The Corps is often exasperated by the frequency with which the media portray girls drilling on the barrack square. The six-week basic training at Guildford is divided into 290 study periods, only thirty-three of which consist of drill. The idea is that girls should be taught how to salute and how to march in unison—if only because they might one day have to march behind a band on Remembrance Day. Drill occupies a similarly low position on the curriculum for officer cadets at Camberley. Yet Press and Television cameramen cannot resist photographic squads of marching girls. A Nationwide film of Guildford which appeared on BBC

Television in 1976 was particularly galling for the WRACs. Every-thing filmed by the cameramen was edited out by the time it was shown—except the usual 'square-bashing'—and the whole film was accompanied by the sound of marching feet.

Homesickness is a problem which confronts the services in general and the women's services in particular. Girls tend to be more attached than men to the comforts of the family hearth and many who join the WRAC have never been away from home before. Officers are astonished by the extent to which many of their recruits have been dependent on their mothers. The realization that they henceforth have to look after themselves comes as a cold shower on an early morning. The telephone is a useful crutch for young girls anxious to hear the familiar family sounds once more. On the other hand, the ambient noise of the family hearth drifting over the telephone wires can often make a girl more homesick than ever. Discipline can also be a problem, particularly in an integrated regiment, where a man can be nonplussed by the sight of a sobbing girl. This is one reason why WRAC officers believe there is a good case for keeping disciplinary procedures in their own hands. 'We can see through the tears' one said grimly.

Perhaps the most surprising section of the Corps is its full-strength, forty-one-strong staff band. They play at concerts and tattoos all over the world, and lead contingents of the WRAC themselves—to the strains of the regimental quick march, a com-bination of 'Sweet Lass of Richmond Hill' and 'Early One Morning', or the slow march 'Greensleeves'. The band who practice in a purpose-built bandroom at Guildford, say that girl instrumentalists are surprisingly easy to find because of the number of schools which now have their own bands. But girls often have to be trans-ferred from other instruments to play, say, the big bass, horn or the big drum. A clarinettist was last reported to be playing the big drum—complete with bearskin. 'We look to the bigger girls to take over these parts' says the director of music Captain Lynette Hopkin.

15

Reserves

Birth of the TAVR. If Britain went to war not much more than half of the Army would consist of regular soldiers. The others would be reserves, summoned from their factories and offices to plump out the Army to its operational size.

There are about 170,000 reserves, 110,000 of whom are former regulars, men and women who now belong to the Regular Reserve, the Regular Army Reserve of Officers, the Long-Term Reserve or to a group known rather endearingly as the Army Pensioners. Army Pensioners are simply those who have completed the full twenty-two years in the Army, and are not quite the greybeards that their title suggests. They are in theory liable to be called up until they reach the age of sixty. But in practice it is likely that only a few chosen specialists under the age of fifty-five would ever be used. Soldiers who leave the Army after less than twenty-two years join the Regular Reserve, before being passed on to the Long-Term Reserve where they remain on the books until they are forty-five.

The other 60,000 are part-time soldiers in the Territorial and Army Volunteer Reserve (TAVR). The TAVR was formed in 1967, but its origins really belong to 1907 when the Territorial Force was created by Lord Haldane, Secretary of State for War. It was re-christened the Territorial Army (TA) after the First World War.

The TA in 1965 amounted to a complete army of ten divisions and four independent brigades. If war broke out, the regular Army would hold the front line while the TA was mobilized—and this is what happened during the opening phase of the Second World War.

The trouble was that in the 1960s it looked as if the next war would be a short sharp exchange, which would hardly give the TA time to put their boots on. Moreover, the machinery of the TA was creaking badly. Although its establishment stood at over 210,000, most of these were National Servicemen who were drafted to the TA for three-and-a-half years after completing their two years'

conscription. There was, in fact, a recruiting ceiling of 130,000.
But recruiting was going badly anyway in an age when most young
men had to take their turn at soldiering whether they wanted to
or not. It was hard to persuade them to stay in the TAVR for longer
than they had to.

The typical TA regiment was a collection of country gentlemen
and 'old sweats', who looked on their local Drill Hall as a kind of
social club which they were actually paid to attend. Units had not
been re-equipped since the Second World War and the cost of doing
so was prohibitive.

In 1965 the Labour Government was looking for ways of pegging
the annual Defence Budget at £2,000 million by 1969/70. The
Army, charged with the task of reviewing its own expenditure,
decided that the TA should bear the brunt. It needed overhauling
anyway. The two senior officers who redrew Haldane's sixty-year-
old concept were Major-General Michael Carver, Director of Army
Staff Duties (DASD), later to become Field-Marshal Lord Carver,
and General Sir John Hackett, Deputy Chief of the General Staff,
who was made Principal of King's College, London, after his
retirement. The names of Carver and Hackett seemed appropriate
to the aggrieved TA, and the working party which was appointed
to see through the Army's reforms designed its own exclusive tie
decorated with a crossed carving-knife and hatchet to symbolize the
slaughter.

The old TA was killed off. In its place was born the new TAVR,
an amalgam of the TA and the Army Emergency Reserve (AER),
with an establishment of 64,000 and a changed military role. Instead
of being an Army in its own right, the new TAVR would simply
provide reinforcements for the regular Army in wartime. The
Army wanted to call it simply the Army Volunteer Reserve, but the
TA howled and kicked to such effect that the 'Territorial' was
added to ensure that something of the past would live on, in name
if not in deed.

Most of the units would be supporting arms and services because
they seemed to be what the Army would need most if it suddenly
had to cope with the exigencies of war. What upset the old TA
die-hards most of all was the disappearance of many of the old
yeomanry units, because so many of the die-hards belonged to
them. In the event the government agreed to keep on many of these
'axed' combat units in a special Category Three of the TAVR,
with a face-saving responsibility for home defence.

But then came the defence cuts of 1968-69 which saw these
Category Three units reduced to the size of eight men cadres. Also
a casualty of the cuts was the TAVR Category Two, the 'Ever

Readies', a body of reserves which had a special commitment to install call-up when it was not thought worthwhile mobilizing the whole of the TAVR.

The Conservative Party returned to power in June 1970, dedicated to the task of doing something for the TAVR, many of whose members were still suffering from shellshock after the traumas of the past few years. The TA had been one of the sacred cows of the Tory establishment and the government felt obliged to do something for its offspring. One of its first acts was to expand the TAVR by 10,000 men with twenty new major units of 500 men formed from most of the cadres left over from 1968–69. Some of these new units were yeomanry units, but they were to serve in an infantry role—a decision which would have shocked their members ten years before, but which was now regarded as a kiss of life.

This gave the TAVR an establishment of 74,000, and recruiting to meet the new target started well enough amid a blaze of publicity. In 1973 it began to fall back and during 1973–75 the strength slumped by 5,000. Then it steadied, paused for breath and shot forward again, recovering its losses and providing the TAVR by 1977 with about 60,000 men and women, the same total as in 1972. Its establishment stood at 72,500 which meant that the volunteers were 82·3 per cent recruited. But at least the TAVR emerged unscathed from the next big Defence Review, carried out by the Labour Government during 1974–75.

Organization. Of the regular Army reserves only the Regular Reserve itself has any training obligation. In theory its members are supposed to train for two weeks every year—although in practice they do not.

In wartime some of these former regulars would join the British Army of the Rhine, to raise the size of a typical infantry battalion from 650 to a fighting strength of about 800. Others would join units of the TAVR. One of a number of criticisms made by the Defence and External Affairs Sub-committee of the House of Commons Expenditure Committee in 1977, was that these men would be called up without any refresher training since leaving the regular Army—despite the fact that they would have lost most of their professional skills within six years of returning to civilian life.

Part-timers in the TAVR have a training obligation, although how long this is depends upon which part of the TAVR they belong to. There are two main parts as well as a few smaller sections and about 2,000 individual members.

The smaller of the two main sections, including thirteen per cent of the soldiers, involves what are known as sponsored units. These are all specialists whose military role corresponds to their civilian jobs. TAVR postal workers, telephone operators or engine drivers might belong to these units, which are 'sponsored' or organized by the appropriate corps of the Army. This part of the TAVR is descended from the old Army Emergency Reserve.

But eighty-two per cent of the TAVR consists of the better known independent units, bequeathed by the old Territorial Army. There are about 100 major units, including thirty-eight infantry battalions, two armoured reconnaissance regiments, two medium and three light air defence regiments of the Royal Artillery, seven regiments of Royal Engineers, two of the Special Air Service and the Honourable Artillery Company—which is a law unto itself. A little over two-fifths are combat 'teeth' arms, one fifth is made up of engineers and signallers and the other two-fifths are logistics units.

If war broke out the TAVR would be used to reinforce BAOR and other forces committed to Nato, and to help defend the British homeland. There are different call-up liabilities, but most belong to Group A, which has a general liability. Only bands, the universities' Officer Training Corps and a few other units intended for service in Britain have the more limited Group B obligation.

Independent units have to attend two weeks camp every year, and a minimum of twelve more days' training. But in practice the keener volunteers attend one training night a week at their local TAVR Centre (the old Drill Hall) and one weekend every month. Sponsored units have to do only four days' out of camp training a year.

They get paid for all this, but not very much. In 1977 all volunteers received an annual bounty of £60 and an extra training bounty rising from £35 during the first two years to £55 after four years. They are also paid almost the same rates as those for regular soldiers for every full day's training they complete.

In 1977 it was estimated that the average private earned no more than £200 a year, and a major about £500—some of which might be lost on mess bills. And only the training bounty was tax free. So while a TAVR part-timer can reflect that he has a paid hobby to occupy his spare time, he can hardly look upon his military training as a lucrative second career.

Ministry of Defence policy in recent years has been to link the TAVR more closely with the regular Army. The 1974–75 Defence Review brought it more closely under the Army's administrative organization, with units grouped together with regular units in the

military districts and field forces in Britain. This was carried a
stage further in 1978 when the Ministry announced that the deputy
C-in-C at United Kingdom Land Forces headquarters would be
given a second 'hat' as Inspector General of the TAVR. By acting
as the focal point for the TAVR at UKLF, he would encourage the
'One Army' ideal which the government was pursuing.

To an outsider, however, all this has made the administration
of the TAVR seem more complex than ever. For instance, recruiting and property management for the independent units remains
under the control of the local TAVR associations, which were
formed by Lord Haldane in 1907 and are still doggedly hanging
on. Not even the names have been brought into line because the
TAVR in the associations' title stands not for Territorial and Army
Volunteer Reserve but for Territorial Auxiliary and Volunteer
Reserve.

The associations set up by Haldane had not only to recruit and
house the volunteers but to feed and clothe them too. The Lord
Lieutenant of each county, traditionally responsible for raising
soldiers for the Queen (or King) were appointed presidents and the
organization has rumbled on ever since—though with modifications.

There are now fourteen associations whose boundaries corres-
pond loosely to the Army districts—with a local Lord Lieutenant
still serving as president. (The others can serve as vice-presidents
if they want to.) They look after the 494 TAVR Centres which
remain, for the most part, solid barrack-like buildings, which have
stood the test of time. The Army shrinks from the old term 'Drill
Hall' because 'drill' is now a dirty word—and because it smacks
too much of the old TA. Each association is virtually autonomous
because the TAVR Council at the Duke of York's Headquarters
in London is more of an advisory body with little power to dictate
policy.

Some professional soldiers regard the associations as a squire-
archical anachronism and argue in favour of a complete takeover
of the TAVR by the regular Army. Total integration, however,
would be expensive in terms of money and manpower because
paid civil servants would have to take on much of the work that is
now performed by voluntary labour.

Moreover the associations provide an important link between
the TAVR and society. However clumsy the system looks in theory,
in practice it works—and no irrefutable case has yet been presented
for changing it.

In 1973 the Army introduced a scheme under which TAVR
officers could serve up to eighteen months with regular units, and
in 1975 the scheme was extended to ordinary soldiers. This was

9*

meant to improve the standard of training and to strengthen the ties between the regulars and the part-timers.

It has worked quite well for officers with up to fifty taking advantage of it at any one time. For soldiers, however, it has been something of a flop. While the Army had expected four times the number of officers to come forward, in fact by 1977 fewer than fifty at any one time were doing so. The Army has blamed this on the economic recession which has made part-time soldiers reluctant to interrupt their civilian careers. But TAVR men also seem genuinely reluctant to become more than part-time soldiers. They prefer to keep their uniforms in their wardrobes for six days of the week.

Still the Army is worried about the adequacy of some units to perform the roles they have been assigned in wartime. However keen a volunteer unit may be, its training time is limited—and some units are widely scattered around the country. It is partly because of these limitations that the TAVR has no tanks.

Curiously it is not the armoured reconnaissance units or the artillery regiments which have caused most concern, but the infantry. Infantry work is now so specialized and so diverse that it is difficult to know on which aspects the part-timers should concentrate. Moreover, if war did break out suddenly the TAVR would have to move quickly into action instead of being able to rely as in the past upon three months in which to bring units up to scratch. A fundamental re-appraisal of the role of some units was proposed to the Ministry of Defence's Advisory Committee on the TAVR in 1978 by an eight-man committee led by Major-General Peter Shapland, former Director of Volunteers, Territorials and Cadets.

Manpower Problems. Recruiting is uneven, but it could be worse. It went through a bad patch in 1973–75 when the membership fell by 5,000. But it has recovered during the last few years and is now back to the level of 1972.

Infantry units have been well over eighty per cent full, the armoured reconnaissance regiments ninety per cent, the Royal Artillery 100 per cent and the Parachute Regiment 110 per cent. (Jumping out of aircraft is the sort of thing that appeals to the enthusiastic amateur.) Even the RAMC, down to sixty per cent of its strength several years ago, has recently improved, and two field ambulance units are now at full strength.

The pattern of recruiting is different from that for the regular Army. Regulars tend to enlist when civilian job security is poor. But TAVR volunteers are reluctant to join at such a time because they do not want to incur their employers' displeasure by taking time off for training. They are more likely to do so when jobs are plentiful.

For most of the time, however, the TAVR has to struggle to maintain its strength, let alone increase it. This is not because it is hard to find recruits but because it is difficult to keep them. Men tend to sign on for two years at a time. But the average length of service is only three years, which means that there is an annual turnover of manpower of about thirty per cent.

This is higher than the Army would like. Some coming and going is desirable, to create room at the top and to retain the right blend of youth and experience. But the Army would like to reduce the annual change-round to between fifteen and twenty per cent.

If a man decides to leave there is not much that the Army can do about it. Anyway, it might be because he has moved to a new job in an area where there is no TAVR unit nearby. Transfers to other units can be arranged without much difficulty, but the soldier has to be prepared to lose ground in the race for promotion. Most say that they have joined the TAVR because they had friends already serving. When they move away they leave those friends behind, and the Army has to encourage them to re-join.

Like the regular Army, the TAVR is helped and hindered by tribal loyalties. On the one hand a man's loyalty to his local regiment is good for morale—his own and that of the regiment. On the other it can make him reluctant to serve in any other unit if he moves to some other part of the country.

This makes it difficult for the Army to tidy up the present distribution of units, which can often sound absurd. Only the Honourable Artillery Company has its men together in one place. Some are better off than others. For instance, the 101st medium regiment RA has all its batteries within a twenty-mile span of Tyneside. The 5/8th King's Regiment is spread over Liverpool, Manchester and Warrington and the 4th Royal Green Jackets whose headquarters are in Davies Street, near Bond Street underground station in London, has its companies strung across London, from West Ham to Fulham—and three more centres at Bletchley, Aylesbury and Oxford.

But they are the lucky ones. One light air defence regiment has its headquarters at Newtonards, outside Belfast, a battery at Coleraine fifty-five miles away, another in Glasgow with one of its troops in Edinburgh and another battery in Arbroath with a troop in Dundee. The 51st Highland Volunteers have headquarters at Perth and companies in London and Liverpool. And the 5th battalion Light Infantry has its headquarters in Shrewsbury, with its companies scattered between Shropshire, Hereford, Cornwall, Yorkshire, and Durham.

Such units come together only on their annual fortnight's camp. Yet to reorganize them on more rational lines would upset local loyalties and would risk doing more harm than good to recruiting. However, it is another reason why the Shapland Committee was concerned about the efficiency of such units in wartime.

One big advance in the TAVR has been the practice of paying the soldiers by cheque. In the old days they were paid in cash—which they promptly spent at the Drill Hall bar. Now the money goes straight into the bank, which pleases the wives if not the TAVR Centre's bar committee.

Anything that pleases the wives is worth thinking about. Girl friends, attracted by the sight of their young men marching along the High Street behind the regimental band, quickly become wives and mothers who resent seeing their husbands disappear for one weekend in four, or spend a fortnight every year in camp. So the Army is always looking for ways in which the wives might be made to feel wanted—and quite a few have now been persuaded to join themselves, forming husband and wife teams in the unit.

Still more difficult is the job of placating the soldiers' employers. The Army calculates that the average man now gets four weeks holiday a year, although many have less. While it expects that he would want to spend three of those four weeks with his family, it thinks that he should be able to use the remaining week for his annual camp without undue hardship. The other week of camp they ask the employer to 'donate' in the form of unpaid, additional leave. Successive governments make periodic appeals to employers to ask for their help.

The response is mixed. The Post Office is the most understanding of all, and the civil service generally is helpful. But the response of nationalized industries varies, and so does that of private employers. Some go so far as to give the part-timer an extra fortnight's paid leave. Others grumble that if an employee wants to spend a fortnight running around playing soldiers, he should be prepared to do so in his own time and at his own expense.

During the last few years when jobs have been hard to find, a number of soldiers have been refused employment because of their time-consuming hobby—and others have been forced to take their annual fortnight out of their summer holiday, or lose their pay. Employers as a result of the Employment Protection Act have been wary of taking on more workers than they need, so they cannot spare the men. Some TAVR soldiers claim to have lost up to £150 by attending annual camp.

All this has helped to contribute to the TAVR's manpower wastage—which was the central problem addressed by the Shapland Committee. Among the proposals made in 1978 was one to revert to the old title of Territorial Army. The new name of TAVR has never really caught on and many senior officers confess that they can never remember what the initials stand for. The title of the old TA, with its record in two world wars, would have a better chance of catching the imagination of both soldier and employer.

The committee also suggested better cash incentives, with increments timed so as to encourage men to sign on for at least three years—and then for another three. One recommendation was for the liability bounty to be scrapped, and replaced by a larger training bounty—which is tax-free anyway.

Another was to create more training posts for majors and warrant officers in the TAVR, to encourage promotion. The highest rank to which a TAVR soldier can aspire is that of colonel. The present Dean of Charing Cross Hospital is a brigadier in the RAMC—but he is an exception. It is difficult enough to become a colonel—or even a lieutenant-colonel.

The average TAVR unit is commanded by a regular officer. A part-timer can rise to command his own unit, but it is very much a question of supply and demand. TAVR officers in their late thirties or early forties tend to be in responsible jobs from which they cannot get away for long enough to carry out the work of a battalion CO. The training major, adjutant and quartermaster are also regulars, and so are the regimental sergeant-major and a sprinkling of other warrant officers and NCOs. There are usually about thirteen regular officers and NCOs in a TAVR battalion.

Whether the Shapland committee proposals will go far enough remains to be seen. A number of TAVR officers fear that they will not. They point to a shortage of training equipment for some units whose wartime vehicles are stored in West Germany. Some transport units have only a few trucks—which have to be shared.

They also complain about the TAVR Centres, most of which were built in the 1930s or before, when the Army was not as mechanized as it is today. One suggestion put forward unofficially was for the Army to invest in purpose-built, modern cow-sheds, which would house modern equipment more efficiently.

These disenchanted young men point to units in which the average lieutenant is aged thirty-two instead of twenty-two—because there are not enough captains' jobs to move on to. Unless there is enough equipment, enough promotion and enough incentive, then boredom could set in—followed by dwindling figures and inefficiency.

So the TAVR has its problems. It has emerged in better shape than might have been expected ten years ago. But if war did break out the Army would depend upon its reserves to move into the front line more quickly than ever before. The timetable for mobiliz ing them has been improved in response to a Nato demand— though the details are secret. It suggests, however, that the TAVR might need to be given a higher place in the order of priorities if it is to be an important contribution to defence in the 1980s and not just an extrovert club.

The Honourable Artillery Company. The record for survival among British regiments, part-time or full-time, belongs to the Honourable Artillery Company (HAC), whose charter was granted in 1537 by Henry VIII. Because it was grafted on to an existing organiza- tion, the Guild of St. George, some argue that it is even older than that. It quickly developed into a breeding-ground for officers to lead the London-trained bands, and its members commanded the bowmen and pikemen called out to resist the Spanish Armada at Tilbury in 1588. Some years ago the HAC tried to have the Armada recognized as a battle honour. The application was politely but firmly turned down.

Its role as a production line for the officer class has continued. About 4,000 HAC men were commissioned into other regiments in the First World War, as were 3,800 more in the Second. Now- adays the regiment is trained for a special reconnaissance role in Germany, which its members insist is too secret to talk about. Cynics suggest that these mysterious 'special duties' are just a good excuse devised by the Ministry of Defence for the HAC to pursue its own sweet way independent of the rabble. Because it was formed before the regular Army the HAC has no allegiance to any other regiment or Corps.

It is certainly different. Its Captain-General is the present Queen, and its members include the Duke of Edinburgh, the Duke of Kent, and Prince Michael—although they do not exactly turn up for drill nights. Charles II belonged to it, even though the HAC changed sides several times during the Civil War and wisely ended up fighting for Cromwell. More typical of its middle class member- ship is Edward Heath, and a number of Judges, professional men, and business people, who pay the £18 a year subscription to use the regiment's extensive facilities.

These middle-aged, often elderly members do not belong to the HAC's TAVR fighting strength, although in theory they could be called to arms if the occasion demanded. They belong to the Veteran Company which was founded as an indirect result of Haldane's reorganization in 1907. Until then the HAC had no official establishment. It was just a case of how many turned up. When Haldane laid down its official strength, the HAC found to its embarrassment that it had far too many. To avoid getting rid of any, it ingeniously formed the Veteran Company to absorb all the old and infirm. After the First World War the actual membership was 3,000, but its official strength was supposed to be only 1,000. So the Veteran Company swelled to 2,000, and it is about the same size today.

There are also about 400 young men in the fighting section of the HAC. They tend to be well-to-do young accountants, lawyers and stockbrokers, with jobs in the City of London. They fulfil their military obligations just like anyone else in the TAVR. But even the lowliest trooper belongs to the officer class and the atmosphere is more like that in a public school cadet force than a modern reconnaissance regiment. Intelligence ratings are extremely high, which partly explains the regiment's high success rate in TAVR competitions. While Royal Artillery gunners are carefully feeding data into their computers the HAC's languid young stockbrokers, who spend all day enmeshed by figures, are doing the same sums in their head. They even won a tough route march in Wales several years ago, much to everyone's else disgust, when they entered for the first time and left crack teams from the paratroopers, the Special Air Service and Welsh Infantry Regiments gasping in the gutter.

After a five-year apprenticeship in this corps d'élite they can if they wish leave the TAVR as such and join the Veterans' Company, which means that they can henceforth use the HAC like a London club. This leaves room in the ranks for some other fresh-faced young man to fill, providing that he passes the scrutiny of the Court of Assistants, the HAC's board of directors.

It is all very British—even down to the terminology. The HAC was traditionally half artillery and half infantry. At the time of the last TAVR reorganization all its members became a mixture of both with their new reconnaissance role. The HAC was faced with a terrible decision of whether to talk about gunners and batteries, which would offend the infantry men among them, or whether to refer to privates and companies, which would upset the gunners. So in the best tradition of British compromise, they adopted cavalry nomenclature, with troopers and squadrons and thus upset everyone. They now spend much time playing with signals equipment and become quite expert in morse. But they still have to know their artillery drill if only to fire the saluting guns at the Tower of London on the Queen's birthday.

The Armoury, their elegant headquarters in City Road, was built in 1735. Here members can lunch in the panelled dining-room or dine in candlelight and considerable style at innumerable dinners held throughout the year for one or other of the HAC's many internal societies. It has its own squash courts, tennis courts, sports teams, masonic lodge and special constabulary.

But the most familiar part of the HAC for most Londoners is the Company of Pikemen and Musketeers who dress up in Civil War regalia to take part in the pageantry of the City of London. There are sixty-three of them, who still use the 1635 drill book of William Barriff. 'Assume a lazy posture', thus becomes their command for 'stand easy' and 'have a care' is the pikemen's equivalent for 'shun'. They tend to be drawn from the older Veterans, portly men whose spectacles and clipped moustaches never look quite right with the red breeches and curved helmets which accompany their bizarre hobby. There is an attempt to recruit younger men to this historic company. But they might be called on to accompany the Lord Mayor of London on official visits overseas, and only the most senior members can usually find the time. Curiously, only the Army has the right to call them up and the Lord Mayor should officially ask permission—but nobody bothers about this.

The HAC has its own band and corps of drums. The drummers by unwritten tradition tend to be Old Harrovians, which sets them apart from their contemporaries in other regiments. The HAC claims to have the only Old Harrovian bass drummer in the British Isles. One well connected member several years ago became quite fascinated by his duties as drum major and travelled widely, practising the art. When the band was performing at a military tattoo in Berlin, he stayed with the general who happened to be his uncle, but astonished the staff by leaving the official residence each morning at the crack of dawn to practise marching and counter-marching with the band.

Student Soldiers. About 200 TAVR officers and between fifty and sixty regular officers are spawned each year by the universities' Officers' Training Corps (OTC). The OTCs are paid for out of the TAVR budget and are closely linked to the reserves in every way—although the cadets are not liable to call-up. Northern Ireland would be destitute of TAVR officers if it were not for the OTC at Queen's University, Belfast.

Their origins go back to the last century and the Cambridge Corps actually has a battle honour because the Cambridge University Rifle Volunteers fought in the Boer War. So did many volunteers from London University, but they did so as individuals and not as an OTC unit. There are now seventeen of them since the formation of the latest at Cardiff in 1975-76. But as each OTC now serves a number of local polytechnics too, about fifty-eight colleges of some kind are covered by the system.

The OTCs have been going through a bad time, buffeted by the wave of anti-militarism which has swept through British universities. At the end of 1976 there were 2,300 OTC members including training officers, against an establishment of 3,200. But recruiting went up by eleven per cent in 1975-76 and the Army, conscious of changing attitudes in the country at large, is hoping for better times ahead.

To join, students have to pass a security screen and also a check on their nationality. This has upset student organizations but the Army argues that the OTCs are there to benefit Britain not anyone else and that foreign nationals are welcome if their own countries will contribute cash to train them.

Oxford and Cambridge always have regular officers to command them and so, at present, have Sheffield, Birmingham and Belfast. All OTCs have a sprinkling of regular soldiers anyway. But to appoint a regular officer as CO amounts in most cases to a confession of failure to find a local TAVR man to do the job. The officer cadets do similar training to the TAVR and are paid about the same rates as a private soldier. They sit for the Certificate of Military Education, after which they can apply for a TAVR commission—perhaps in their final academic year. If they join the regular Army, they go to Sandhurst with six months seniority and do a shorter course.

Schoolboy Cadets. Another organization which has had its problems is the Combined Cadet Force (CCF) which has Army corps in 288 British schools and a current membership of 28,000. Until the end of the 1960s CCF training was compulsory in most public schools. Now it is compulsory in only fifteen of them after a change of Army policy. Even at Wellington, once full of Army sons, CCF training is compulsory for only two years. The Army encourages most schools to make it either voluntary or at most an optional subject—with some other form of extra-mural activity as an alternative. The Army likes to think of the CCF as an exercise in public relations rather than recruiting, and the old image of compulsory drill and cold showers did not do much good either way. Nowadays at least those boys who join are those who want to.

Eton CCF always has a regular adjutant from the Guards. But most rely upon some enthusiastic young master who runs the

Corps as a TAVR commitment, or upon a permanent instructor part of whose wages may be paid with the help of an Army grant.

The Army stills suffers from the after-effects of what it likes to call the 'schoolboy revolution'. While anti-militarism has tended to fade among the schoolboys themselves, it lingers on among the 1960s generation who are now re-emerging as junior masters— even more influential then they were before. Two courses at Sand- hurst for potential CCF masters almost had to be abandoned through lack of support several years ago. However, the Army is taking heart from the fact that a number of grammar schools are trying to continue with their CCFs after going comprehensive. One sixth form college is even trying to create one.

If sons of the top people join the CCF, some of the not-so-top join the Army Cadet Force (ACF). This, too, is regarded as more of a public relations operation, although the links between the ACF and the regular Army are quite distinct. In 1975–76 nearly one in three juniors joining the Army and one in six adults had already served in the ACF.

The history of the ACF goes back to 1860 when some of the Volunteer battalions raised their own cadet companies unofficially. Later in the century some independent cadet battalions were formed, combining military training with social work for boys. In 1977 there were about 44,000 teenage members and some 1,600 detach- ments. Membership rose in 1976 and 1977 after standing at around 38,000 for several years. The organization has been successful enough for the Army to call a halt to any further expansion. The cadets themselves do not cost much, but their huts have to be maintained and the annual ACF budget of between £5 million and £6 million is about all that the Army can afford.

Each ACF unit is supposed to be between twenty-five and thirty strong, and when a detachment has fewer than fourteen members it goes on to a 'black list'. There were about 178 on the black list in 1976. On the other hand, it is not quite as simple when it comes to deciding which, if any, of these units should be closed down. A cadet force in the North of Scotland might have only a dozen or so boys. But this might still represent a high proportion of the local teenage populace and the detachment might be providing a useful service to the community. One ACF platoon has been opened in an approved school. Another in the East End of London has as many as seventy-four boys.

They are 'armed' with elderly ·303 Le Enfield rifles, doctored so effectively that not even the IRA could make them work. They also use the BSA Meteor air rifle which is a cheap way of improving their markmanship. In 1971 the Army announced the end of the cadets' familiar khaki battledress. The boys are now dressed in similar fashion to the modern Army, with lightweight green trousers, a heavy woollen jersey and combat shirts.

Ideally each unit is run by two TAVR officers and an adult instructor. But as often as not the Army has to be content with just the adult instructor, whose military background may extend no further than the boy scouts. The instructors are kept up to scratch by peripatetic Army training teams and by courses at the Cadet Training Centre at Frimley, Surrey. The centre also runs courses for all ranks in 'citizenship training' and the Duke of Edinburgh award scheme. Cadets, who join the ACF for up to four years from the age of twelve-and-a-half, meanwhile work their way through their four grades of the Army Proficiency Certificate. But neither the CCF nor the ACF belongs to the Army Reserves.

PART FOUR

MILITARY SOCIETY

16

Welfare

The social welfare of soldiers and their families has been under spasmodic scrutiny since the Second World War. It is a complicated subject for a number of reasons. One is that they are already sheltered by the regimental system with its paternalistic overtones. Another is that a number of voluntary organizations have been helping out for so long that they have become almost an integral part of the central establishment. Given the back-up of the welfare state, the system with its band of civilian helpers should be able to cope with most troubles, at least when a unit is stationed at home.

Not everyone thinks so. In 1976 the Army Welfare Inquiry Committee reported that the regimental system for all its cosiness, was no longer adequate for an Army in which women and children outnumbered the men. This seemed particularly true abroad where problems arising from the turbulence of Army life and the frequent separation of families seemed more acute. Although the committee's brief was to look at the needs of the Army in Britain, its members were alarmed by what they saw on short exploratory visits to BAOR. They said: 'We found there a combination of vulnerable young families living in a strange land, many of them in high-rise flats at some distance from their unit locations and often without the head of the family, and too few social workers operating without the back-up services available from the local authorities in the United Kingdom. This particularly struck as a recipe for social distress.'

The committee wanted the Army to have a new welfare organization of its own, like that already operating in the Royal Navy. This would provide the specialized, professional support which was needed today, said the report. But the Ministry of Defence disagreed. It opted instead to improve the existing hotch-potch of welfare services while at the same time reducing where possible the hardships which can make military life sometimes seem intolerable.

SSAFA. Outside the regiment and the welfare state the most familiar social welfare service for the Army is that run by the Soldiers, Sailors and Airmen's Families Association, usually known as Ssafa. It was Ssafa which started it all anyway, and its mixed bag of professional and voluntary workers can regard the welfare state as something of an *ingénue*. As the Army Welfare Inquiry Committee under its chairman, Professor J. C. Spencer, recognized in its 1976 report, Ssafa's relationship with the Army is unique.

The association was founded in 1885 by Major (later Colonel Sir James) Gildea of the Warwickshire Regiment. Gildea who has a claim to be regarded as one of the eminent Victorian philanthropists saw the need to care for the families of soldiers who went overseas with the Second Egyptian Expeditionary Force. (That is why Soldiers comes before Sailors in the title.) But it quickly grew into a worldwide organization and Queen Alexandra, while still Princess of Wales became its first president. The Ssafa badge still consists of two intertwined 'A's, which was her personal monogram. The Ssafa Officers' Widows Branch also run a block of rent-free flats for officers' widows and unmarried daughters in Wimbledon, which is called Queen Alexandra Court.

By the end of the last war Ssafa had 29,000 voluntary workers and was administering over £1 million a year. Since then it has shrunk like the armed forces themselves.

Its professional workers include twenty-two social workers and ninety-four health visitors, all of whose salaries are paid by the Ministry of Defence. Except for one administrator at the London headquarters in Queen Anne's Gate near St. James's Park, all the health visitors are abroad—one for every 1,257 families. The majority, eighty-one of them, are in West Germany, five are in Cyprus, five are in Hong Kong and two are in Gibraltar. All are highly qualified state registered nurses and midwives and they provide pregnant wives and young mothers with much the same service that civilian families have from the National Health Service in Britain—except that Ssafa insists that its own standards are higher. The Jarrett committee which examined the medical services for the forces in 1973 recommended that the Ssafa health visitors should be left undisturbed to get on with their job.

Of the social workers, fourteen are in West Germany, two are in Hong Kong, one is in Cyprus, four are in England and one is in Northern Ireland. The five in Britain were appointed on a temporary basis in 1973 to help out in the big garrison areas because the local authorities said that they could not cope. (Ssafa says that the real reason was that the civilian social workers 'hadn't a clue' how to deal with service problems.)

These professionals, in their grey uniforms and black tricorn hats, are supported by 1,200 Ssafa branches throughout the country, staffed by a mixture of full-time and part-time voluntary workers. They do quite a lot of visiting on their own, advising service families where to turn for financial aid, looking after families while their husbands are away and keeping a motherly—or fatherly—eye on those in hospital. Most of them have ex-service connexions of their own and seventy-five per cent of their work is with ex-service people. But they also raise money for the central Ssafa organization as well as for themselves, and campaign for better conditions for troops. They have been active over conditions in Northern Ireland.

The annual general meeting at Church House, Westminster, consists of flowery hats and rapturous applause on the one hand, and tough talking on the other. Ssafa can be quite hard when it wants to, as it showed in a prolonged pay dispute with the Ministry of Defence on behalf of its social workers in 1977–78. If there were to be any serious move to displace it in favour of any new organization, Ssafa would certainly not go quietly.

WRVS. One organization which has gone quietly is the Women's Royal Voluntary Service, the old wartime WVS who were awarded a 'Royal' in 1966. Since 1944 its uniformed women workers have done for the single soldier what Ssafa has done for the families, though the emphasis has been rather more on running social clubs. This partly ended at Christmas 1977 when most of the forty-two workers overseas were withdrawn.

The trouble was that they ran out of money. Until 1975 their work was funded by the Naafi under its rebate scheme for service welfare funds. But Naafi switched its priorities in 1975, arguing that the need for WRVS helpers in Germany had largely gone. The Army tried to keep the clubs going for a while, but for similar reasons found that it could not continue to do so, and the WRVS had to order an evacuation.

They remain in Berlin, and there are also seventeen in Britain, five of them serving with the troops in Northern Ireland and the others working with junior regiments on the British mainland. These are paid by the Ministry of Defence. Their work with boys' regiments started in 1955 after the Miller Committee pointed to the beneficial 'influence of a mature woman' upon young men, many of whom were away from home for the first time. So far the Army seems to have agreed.

The Naafi. The most famous acronym in the Army is Naafi. Along with Ensa, Itma and Vera Lynn it entered the folklore of Dad's Army in the Second World War and has remained there ever since. If the Battle of Waterloo was fought on the playing fields of Eton, then perhaps the ésprit which led to El Alamein was nurtured beside the tea-urns and indigestible buns of the Naafi canteen.

It has become so familiar that many have forgotten what it stands for or why it began. Naafi image-makers sometimes wish they would remember, because its dissatisfied customers do not always realize how dreadful things were before Naafi started.

Even in the early years of this century troops were served breakfast at 7.30 a.m., lunch at 12.30 p.m., and nothing more until the next day. Inefficiency and corruption meant that the food was bad, and the regimental canteens where soldiers had to supplement their diet were not much better.

Naafi's ancestor was the Canteen and Mess Co-operative Society which three enlightened officers founded in 1894, with the idea of providing an honest and efficient service. This led to the Navy and Army Canteen Board which was formed to cope with the increased demand during the First World War. Then in 1921, following an investigation of future needs, the Navy, Army and Air Force Institutes (Naafi) began work as a permanent body.

The Second World War was Naafi's finest hour. It grew into a colossal trading organization with a £200 million business, 120,000 staff and 10,000 establishments in over forty countries serving 5,000,000 customers. Tea was a penny a cup, coffee three-halfpence and apple pie two pence a slice. It sold piping hot 'char' on Arctic convoys, ice-cold beer from tents in the desert and whisky to troops in Italy which was ferried across in the torpedo tubes of sympathetic submarines. More than 500 of its staff were lost on active service, which was proportionately one of the highest casualty rates in the war. The exploits of Naafi managers were often heroic—including one officer who swam ashore after being shipwrecked off Ceylon, clutching his canteen records, in a waterproof bag.

Today the Naafi is still big business with 350 family shops, over 400 clubs and canteens, nearly 300 service shops, which are usually attached to clubs selling anything from cigarettes to razor blades, about sixty ships canteens and 200 other establishments like petrol stations, sub-post offices, and mobile shops. Although Germany and other overseas stations account for little more than a third of these trading outlets, they provide more than half the total turnover.

Naafi likes to think of itself as the 'Forces Co-op', which is more or less what it is—with a policy-making council consisting of senior officers and a board of management which is mostly civilian. Five per cent of the monthly turnover at its clubs is paid into the welfare funds of local units. Customers at its shops get five per cent back in cash dividends or trading stamps—which Naafi says are worth much more than commercial trading stamps. Then some of the final profit at the end of the year is paid into central welfare funds.

Naafi has had its lean years, particularly during the 1950s when it had to live off its reserves. The reserves are now almost exhausted, but a run of good years recently has kept it out of trouble. In 1977 it announced a turnover of over £22·4 million and a gross surplus of £15·5 million. Of this £6·5 million was paid back to customers in discounts and dividends, £1·5 million went into unit welfare kitties and £750,000 was given to central welfare funds. About forty per cent of its profits came from family shops, thirty-two per cent from clubs and service shops and the rest from wholesale transactions with messes and other business.

The organization has come a long way from the 'cuppa and a bun' days of the last war. It now sells cars, boats and insurance, books entertainers for its clubs and runs a flourishing mail order business. It has about 1,300 vehicles of its own, a tea and coffee factory, bakeries, mineral water plants, computers and cold stores. It is the largest automatic vending machine operation in Europe with a £2 million annual business and was among the first organizations to open self-service stores. The first started in Cairo in 1953.

Naafi is not universally admired. It has a love-hate relationship with most soldiers and their families, who grumble about its services while knowing that they cannot do without them. Naafi managers like mothers-in-law and tax inspectors are always on the defensive about their public image.

They argue that Naafi prices are highly competitive. While a housewife can buy some brands more cheaply outside, these are balanced by Naafi's own 'Wise Buys' bargain offers so that a basketful of goods in Naafi compares favourably with any other grocery chain. Naafi certainly makes apparent efforts to be competitive with constant price testing among other High Street stores. A recent survey of shelf-prices at thirty-five other self-service chain stores in six British towns showed sixteen were cheaper than Naafi, nineteen were dearer and all thirty-five were significantly more expensive when Naafi dividends had been taken into account.

Prices might be lower but for the difficulty of balancing profitability with the need to provide a service. While visitors see mostly the large show place supermarkets in places like Detmold, Rhein-dahlen and Tidworth where the tills are always ringing, the average Naafi shop is a relatively small establishment in an underpopulated camp where profits are hard to come by.

Another difficulty is that service families expect to see familiar English brands on the shelves wherever they are. So distribution costs are often high. Naafi had to pioneer frozen crumpets in BAOR and even tried planting lettuces at Gan, the isolated RAF station in the Indian Ocean. But this was not a horticultural success.

Naafi marketing chiefs pour out statistics, some of which throw an interesting light on the habits of service families. For instance, seventy-three per cent use tea-bags compared with less than fifty per cent in civilian life, and more than fifty per cent have freezers against thirty per cent outside. More than eighty per cent of troops in Germany own cars, twenty-two per cent of which are less than a year old, and forty per cent of the wives use the family car during the day. Perhaps because of this, while ninety-four per cent of BAOR families live nearer to local German shops eighty-five per cent do most of their weekly shopping on one visit to the Naafi. The organization is closely involved in Britain's wartime plans and supplies for ninety days are kept in special wartime stocks, from which they are constantly rotated through Naafi shops. If a Third World War did break out Naafi managers would shut up shop, don their uniforms and tin hats and trundle off to the front in their mobile canteens to refortify the Dunkirk spirit. It is indicative of the importance attached to their work that details of Naafi's mobilization plans are highly classified by the Ministry of Defence.

Church Canteens. A number of religious organizations have been serving tea and sympathy to servicemen for well over 100 years, before Naafi was even dreamed of. Naafi anyway tends to serve only the tea.

They began in the tradition of Victorian philanthropy, providing material comforts on the one hand, and spiritual guidance on the other. But the missionary zeal has always been restrained, which is perhaps one reason why they have survived for so long. Another reason may be that soldiers are not as tough as they sometimes like to appear, and the folksy homely atmosphere which the churches have tried to create in their non-alcoholic clubs and canteens has been a welcome relief after the discipline of the barrack square.

The tradition grew haphazardly but quickly. Some organizations served the troops in the Boer War, and during the First World

War they were all over the place. When Naafi started it was decided that there was room for both kinds of service, and the two have complemented each other ever since.

When the Second World War started so many churches rushed forward to help that they were advised to form a joint council through which they could liaise with the forces. This became the Council of War Work, under whose central direction a total of 147,000 workers ran 4,384 clubs and 1,553 mobile canteens during the war. Naafi which had plenty to do anyway, welcomed the additional help.

After 1945 the organizations were once more asked to soldier on under their council—whose name was changed to the Council of Voluntary Welfare Work (CVWW). The retired colonel who runs the council from a small office at the Duke of York's Headquarters in Chelsea, complains that the title is so misleading that he gets frequent calls to help unmarried mothers and delinquent youths.

The council is now made up of ten organizations. These are:

The Church Army
The Church of England Soldiers', Sailors' and Airmen's Clubs
  (Cessac)
The Methodist Church
The Mission to Military Garrisons
The Royal Sailors' Rests
The Salvation Army
Sandes' Homes
Toc H
The Young Men's Christian Association (YMCA)
The Young Women's Christian Association (YWCA)

In 1978 the total number of clubs and canteens which they ran for the services in various parts of the world were as follows:

Country	Clubs	Staff	Mobile canteens
United Kingdom	30	170	13
Gibraltar	1	9	0
Cyprus	8	55	0
Hong Kong	2	22	2
BAOR and Berlin	59	544	35

Many of the clubs are struggling for survival and have been for some time. Those in BAOR are only now making good the losses they suffered in the 1960s when they were caught by the rising Deutschmark. In the UK nearly all of them are doing badly, and many have had to shut down. The Church of Scotland has pulled out completely, and other members of the council have tried to fill the gaps that this has left.

There are a number of reasons, none of them very surprising. Some of the clubs have proved too large and uneconomic to maintain as the forces have shrunk in size. Others in small garrisons have suffered when the unit has been drafted to Northern Ireland for four months. Several in BAOR have been left stranded in the wrong locations because of the Army's reorganization. Many have found it difficult to recruit staff at the wages which they can afford to pay. The days when volunteers were ready to work for little more than their keep have gone—and are unlikely to return in peacetime.

But the chief reason is that the organizations have found it difficult to compete for business in an age of television, the motor-car and, most significantly, the married soldier. Young wives on an evening out want something more exciting than the YMCA with a cup of tea to drink and the *Daily Mirror* to read.

The clubs have been limited by the requirement that they should complement rather than compete with Naafi. The relationship has worked pretty well, and indeed they rely upon Naafi for some of their supplies. Unlike Naafi they sell newspapers and magazines and, of course, they still try to add the human touch. A young soldier buying a birthday card for his mother in a Naafi shop might have to choose one on his own. In a church canteen a lady not unlike his mother might help to choose one for him. That anyway is the different image which the canteens like to foster. On the other hand, if the soldier wanted to buy a present for his mother, he would probably have to visit the Naafi anyway.

The Army is sympathetic to the CVWW's problems. Although the council's organizations are supposed to pay three per cent of their turnover to unit welfare funds, as Naafi does, most commanding officers appreciate that they are struggling to provide a service to their soldiers, and turn a blind eye to the regulations. But they still have to pay rent, rates, heating and lighting bills for their premises—and for the CVWW office in Chelsea.

The Spencer Committee in 1976 recommended that the CVWW's charter should be reviewed, with a view to removing the rebate requirement and widening the scope of the shops. The ministry agreed to do so. But meanwhile the churches need a little tea and sympathy themselves.

Radio and Television. Special broadcasting for forces abroad began in the Second World War. The Russians, Germans, and Americans started it while Britain characteristically entered the

field late with a lot of catching-up to do. It was not until July
1942 that the Army was given its own broadcasting section and
not until New Year's Day 1944 that the first British Forces
Experimental Station opened in Algiers. From there it spread
throughout the world.

The stations were semi-autonomous and had independent names
like the British Forces Broadcasting Service (BFBS) in the Middle
East and the British Forces Network (BFN) in Germany. It was
not until 1963 that they were united under one system called BFBS
with a central headquarters in London.

At one time in the war there were fifty stations. Today there are
only five, in Germany, Cyprus, Gibraltar, Hong Kong and Malta,
and when British forces leave Malta in 1979, there will only be
four. There are 200 on the staff but only 110 are UK-based civilians.
The rest are locally recruited. It is financed by the Army on behalf
of all three services and in 1976–77 it cost about £2,400,000 to run.
That included £500,000 which was spent on the new television
service so BFBS argues that it is not a very heavy burden on the
English economy.

Stations are on the air for seventeen hours or more a day. But
only thirty or forty per cent of the material is locally produced.
Between twenty and thirty per cent is compiled at headquarters
in Dean Stanley Street, just off Millbank in London, while forty
per cent, including the news is relayed from the BBC.

Like Naafi managers BFBS radio broadcasters must sometimes
feel that nobody loves them. Criticism has increased since 1977
when the director Ian Woolf replanned programme schedules
on the lines of a commercial station, with serious programmes
restricted to the evenings. In the daytime, BFBS radio means
middle-of-the-road pop music, introduced by a variety of disc
jockeys and interspersed with news and 'Promos'—announce-
ments promoting local events of interest to servicemen and their
families. Most of the complaints have come from officers and
their wives, particularly the wives who want something more
articulate. The disc jockeys have also astonished their audiences
by misreading Army abbreviations like L/Cpl or Lt.-Col.

Ian Woolf argues in reply that seventy per cent of his audience
are under thirty and that most of those tuned in during the day
are the wives of ordinary soldiers, who listen to the same kind of
programmes when at home. He was forced to give way, however,
over 'Woman's Hour'. BFBS stopped relaying the BBC programme,
pointing out that it attracted a listening audience of only thirty
per cent. A howl of protest went up from the officers' wives, and
the programme was eventually restored. 'I even had generals

begging me to put it back after pressure at home' says Woolf, who remains unrepentant.

A more serious criticism is that BFBS lacks editorial freedom. Not only is it financed by the Defence budget but local stations are very much under the thumb of the local commanders and their staffs. Broadcasters are not allowed to disseminate views which are contrary to government policy. Nor can they dabble in local controversial issues.

This has led to curious lapses in their coverage. BFBS in Cyprus never interviewed Archbishop Makarios in thirty years, and the discontent over Army pay and conditions in 1977 was never even hinted at on BFBS. The services were left to read all about their own troubles in the newspapers when these arrived from London. This is a fact of life which the BFBS has learned to live with, but it pleases no one very much.

The new television service in BAOR has been by contrast an almost unqualified success. The only regret seems to be that an idea which was first discussed in 1959 did not materialize until 1975. Programmes are distilled in London from the three British television channels and are then flown or shipped to Germany according to their topicality. Fears that the 'best of British TV' would turn out to be a stream of ITV programmes aimed at a mass audience, have not materialized. Soldiers instead have been given an intelligent mixture including documentaries like 'Panorama' and 'World in Action' or 'Tomorrow's World', children's programmes like 'Blue Peter' or special interest talks like 'The Sky at Night'.

There are no old films, a concession to the Services Kinema Corporation which says it could not cope with the competition. Nor is there yet a TV news bulletin. But several home-produced programmes have been surprisingly successful including a language teach-in called 'Instant German'. The plan is to work up gradually to a five per cent input of home-produced material. The use of BFBS's girl announcers too has helped to give the single channel an identity of its own and the reward has been a peak-time audience of eighty per cent, which is more than the BBC or ITV usually expect in Britain.

BFBS had to fight through a great deal of bureaucracy to establish the TV service. That is one reason for the sixteen-year delay. Another has been the difficulty of siting transmitters where they do not offend German environmentalists. The transmitters themselves have had to be low-powered and highly directional to deter more than a fraction of the German population in the BAOR area from watching British programmes free.

Since these difficulties were overcome, BFBS has found a heartening amount of good will. Apart from voluntary donations to the British trade unions concerned, the BBC and ITV programmes are being used free of charge. BFBS is just acting for most of the time as a relay station.

BFBS also runs Combined Services Entertainment, which provides about forty-five live variety shows a year for troops in faraway places, in the manner of ENSA during the war. Most of the shows are taken in fact to Northern Ireland, but they also go to Belize and elsewhere.

The future shape of BFBS is uncertain. An independent committee under the Army's Director of Personal Services began to review it in 1977. One possibility is that the size of the radio network will be further diminished now that television has taken over most of the television audience in Germany. One possible result might be a combined service, with radio catering for eighty per cent of the audience during the day and only fifteen per cent at night.

But there have also been suggestions that the whole system of forces broadcasting could be taken away from an independent service like BFBS and put out on contract. London Weekend television company already provides the operating staff—so why should it not take over the whole project? Or so the argument runs. This is partly the Establishment's reply to BFBS's constant appeal for more freedom from civil service control. If bureaucratic control is so distasteful, then the whole system should be handed to private enterprise. But it would be cruelly ironic if BFBS having fought for television and for editorial and administrative freedom were to lose everything in consequence.

Cinemas. Soldiers have had their own cinemas since the Second World War when a night at 'the pictures' was often the only escape for bored and lonely troops. Free shows were first provided by the Army Kinema Services (AKS) a branch of the RAOC. A number of prosperous-looking film executives still knot their regimental ties once a year and stalk off to the AKS Old Comrades' Association annual dinner.

In 1946 it was civilianized and renamed the Army Kinema Corporation (AKC) which started life with £300,000 from the Army Central Fund. Old AKS hands were allowed early demobilization to join the new outfit. The 'K' was retained in the spelling of cinema to avoid confusion with the initials of the Army Catering Corps.

A generation of National Servicemen whiled away their evenings in AKC cinemas all over the world, and many still refer to the organization by its old name. In fact it became the Services Kinema Corporation (SKC) in 1969 through an amalgamation with the RAFKC which had done a similar job for airmen. The SKC also looks after Royal Navy shore establishments in Britain, but the Navy handles the rest on its own.

The SKC is a registered charity which is run by a council. This includes senior serving officers, and a board of management whose chairman is Sir Louis Gluckstein, QC. The managing director is always a retired modern major-general and the present one is Major-General J. M. Sawer who used to be Signals Officer-in-Chief. His deputy is always a retired air vice-marshal.

Its headquarters is at Chalfont Grove, one of those country houses that Queen Elizabeth I slept in, on the outskirts of Chalfont St. Peter, Buckinghamshire. Although it has 1,100 staff world-wide, only 500 are British-based and the others are locally employed.

If the SKC's business consisted solely of running cinemas then it would be in some trouble. Just after the war the AKC had over 100 in Britain alone and a similar number in BAOR. But in 1978 the total had come down to seventy-four and this is expected to fall steadily over the next few years. In Britain the total was down to nine following the closure of seven in 1976. But the biggest fall in the next few years is expected to be in BAOR where at least one in four of the present forty-eight cinemas should disappear as their audiences start watching the new television service instead. Business has been halved at those Army cinemas so far affected by the TV network.

This does not necessarily mean that soldiers abroad or in remote parts of Britain will miss the main films of the day. The SKC policy is to switch from 35mm films, which need big equipment, purpose-built cinemas and full-time staff, to 16mm, which can be shown on small, mobile projectors by part-time operators in improvised, darkened rooms.

On the one hand, the SKC would like to switch completely to 16mm films in the 1980s because of the savings on overheads if it closed all its cinemas. (The quality of 16mm film is not as high, but is perfectly adequate.) On the other hand, it cannot hire 16mm films on their own. It has to take a package. To show 'Jaws', the highly profitable film about the man-eating shark, the SKC hired three 35mm and twelve 16mm prints. So it will have to keep some fulltime theatres in being unless it can work out a new deal.

Like all service organizations it has to strike a balance between making money and performing a public duty. The remote garrisons where it loses most are the very places where it is needed. Similarly while it might save money by changing the programmes less frequently, most of those who want to see a particular film in some small garrison have done so after two nights, after which they might want to see something else. But the SKC is gradually moving towards a four-day week now—partly because there are simply not enough new films being produced to keep pace with the rapid turnover.

Soldiers still get quite a good deal. They see films through the SKC as soon as civilian audiences, and more cheaply. Admission prices in British SKC cinemas went up from 50p to 55p in 1978, and should have gone up earlier but for a decision to hold down the costs to servicemen during the period of discontent over pay and conditions. In Germany the price was a standard DM3·40. Both these prices compared favourably with civilian cinemas. Soldiers in Northern Ireland see films free, a concession which cost the SKC up to £40,000 a year until the Ministry of Defence agreed to foot the bill.

General Sawer and his staff refuse to act as arbiters on service morals. This means a running battle with the service authorities who do not always agree. The X-film 'Emmanuelle' attracted box office sales second only to 'A Bridge Too Far'—the film about the Battle of Arnhem—but it upset some senior officers and particularly their wives. The 'Exorcist' horror movie also brought Army chaplains to their feet in protest. The SKC argues that any film which is good enough for the British Board of Film Censors is good enough for soldiers—who could see it in civilian cinemas while on leave. But they do draw the line at the 'Naughty Knickers' kind of 'rubbish' which appeal to the dirty mackintosh brigade in British cities. And they did agree for different reasons not to put on 'A Raid on Entebbe' for a while in Germany following bomb attacks by Arab terrorists on German civilian cinemas that were showing it.

Despite their efforts to cut costs the 35mm cinema account made dismal reading in the annual report for 1976–77, with a £16,000 deficit in Britain and a £158,000 loss in Europe, although the 16mm account showed a profit in Europe of £13,700. On the other hand, the corporation as a whole had an overall surplus of £500,000, including a trading surplus of £230,000. This followed several years in which it had just managed to break even.

This is because the SKC's cinemas represent a diminishing part of its overall business. Sixty per cent of its work consists of producing training films for the Ministry of Defence—which pays the costs. This is a responsibility which goes back to the early days of the AKS, but as the forces become more and more obsessed with visual teaching aids, trade is booming.

It also lends its expertise to maintain audio-visual equipment in the services and to advise on acoustics in building programmes. One of its successes was the Alanbrooke Hall at the Staff College in Camberley which has been cited as a perfect example of cooperation between architects and acoustics engineers.

The profits come from the burgeoning business of selling and renting television sets and similar electronic equipment at SKC shops. These are usually attached to cinemas and are run by the cinema managers, and it is these shops which lay behind the smiles on the faces of executives at Chalfont St. Peter when the 1977 accounts were published.

How long they will continue to smile is a matter for conjecture. Sir Louis Gluckstein has warned the corporation that it cannot expect this record business to continue after everyone in Germany has a television set. General Sawer, mindful of the uncertain future has already proposed an eventual merger between the SKC and BFBS, and close links with Naafi. The idea has so far been coolly received, particularly by the BFBS. But in a few years they might all be forced to look at it again.

17

Ex-Soldiers

Whether old soldiers die or simply fade away, they have to be looked after. Otherwise many would do so in pain or poverty, and most of them in relative obscurity, far away from the tunes of glory which might have once lured them to the battlefield.

Today there are an estimated five million of them, nearly one in ten of the British population. About a million are survivors of the two world wars and many more have fought overseas since 1945 in such places as Korea, Kenya, Malaya and the Middle East—or for that matter in Northern Ireland. About 400,000 of them are partly disabled.

Britain's record for caring for ex-servicemen has not always been distinguished. There are those who would argue that it still falls far short of the ideal. But it is better than it was, and the man who is really down on his luck should be able to find help somewhere.

A number of corps and regiments founded their own charitable funds in the early nineteenth century, and civilian charities began to proliferate. The result is an untidy mixture of societies and funds, each one designed for some specific purpose. What the ex-serviceman most needs is advice on which one he should turn to.

Most need no more help than that already provided by the Welfare State. But many want some assistance, if only to find a new job or to buy a home of their own after a lifetime of coming and going.

It is in everyone's long-term interests that they should get this assistance, and should be seen to receive it. Otherwise young men seeing old soldiers flung on the scrap-heap, would be reluctant to follow them into the Army. So it is not just a question of sentiment. If it were so, the ex-serviceman would indeed be in a bad way because his service for Queen and country, glorious or not, is usually forgotten quite quickly.

Preparing to Leave. Returning to civilian life can be traumatic.

For one thing most soldiers have never had to look for a job before, so they do not know how to set about it. They have also become accustomed to living like Bedouins, moving constantly from camp to camp—but always with the Army to organize things for them. Suddenly they have to settle down in one place and fend for themselves.

Resettlement, as it is called, begins eighteen months before the soldier leaves, with an interview with one of the six lieutenant-colonels and thirty-six majors who are the Army's resettlement officers. There is another twelve months later, and all ordinary soldiers have to attend. For officers it is voluntary, but three out of four now take the opportunity against only two out of four several years ago.

They are probably wise to do so, because resettlement officers are still sometimes surprised by the ingenuous optimism of many of their Army colleagues. They often find that the best advice they can give at this stage is negative—to discourage an eager young officer who wants to be an accountant but has no qualifications and is no good at mathematics, or a sergeant who fancies himself as an insurance salesman but lacks the 'gift of the gab'. Others want to do a job which means living in one part of the country, while their wives want to live in another—usually near to their mothers.

There are two-day 'Second Career Advice' courses for senior NCOs and upwards, and one-day sessions on how to buy a house and how best to spend their gratuities. A senior warrant officer might suddenly find himself with £10,000 to invest, so the Pay Corps calls in specialists to counsel caution. Courses are voluntary but the number attending them has risen from 500 to 8,000 in the last few years.

The Army tackles the process of resettlement with relentless method, as if it were a beachhead landing. After the advice, comes the training, long-term and short-term. Every soldier who has served for six years can attend a twenty-eight-day course at one of two resettlement centres at Aldershot and Catterick, just before they leave. There is a choice of over thirty-five subjects and about 5,500 attend them every year.

Some are simply re-orientation courses, for a REME craftsman, for instance who, after servicing three-ton trucks wants to learn how to look after family saloons as a garage mechanic. Others are no more than introductions to quite skilled civilian industries. Most senior officers who do not feel quite the same pressure to start a second career, take the handyman's course which shows them how to look after their house in their old age. Resettlement

officers are always aggrieved because visiting Press and TV cameramen are never interested in anything but a shot of a general painting
a ceiling or building a wall under the supervision of a burly
bricklayer.

An increasing number of Army trade tests are now being recognized by civilian industries. So a growing number of soldiers are
leaving with useful qualifications already in their pocket. An
officer who has done nothing more than attend staff college is
immediately exempt from part one of the Chartered Institute of
Secretaries examination.

Soldiers are also encouraged to join a trade union before they
leave. Some unions are reluctant to accept people who are unemployed, so the Army advises soldiers to join while they have the
chance. Bandsmen usually join the Musicians' Union because
they can then take outside engagements in their spare time without
upsetting anyone. But most of the others, who cannot use the
unions to bargain over their pay and conditions, see no particular
advantage in paying out union subscriptions for nothing—so they
leave it until the last minute before they do so.

Finding a Job. There are three organizations which try to find
jobs for soldiers when they leave. This is just as well perhaps,
because the Army is unimpressed by the efforts of the national
employment agencies. It points out that these handle only one in
ten of the 10,000,000 to 11,000,000 jobs which change hands in
Britain every year.

The Army itself moved into the job market in 1976, it had to
alter the manpower cuts of 1975 which at one time seemed likely
to throw many more redundant servicemen on to the street. But
it says that it would have done so anyway at some stage, and the
sudden cuts acted only as the spur. The other services had had
their own employment officers for some time, and there had already
been complaints that the Army was lagging behind.

The Army's employment cell, is still run on a shoestring from
Empress State House, a skyscraper in West Brompton, London.
But it claims to have 650 on its books at any one time and to have
scored a sixty per cent success rate since it started. Many employers
like taking on soldiers, who tend to be loyal and conscientious,
and not as dim-witted as television comedy shows sometimes make
them appear.

For sergeants and above it runs a job matching service, collecting details from the soldiers on the one hand, and suitable vacancies
on the other—and bringing them together like a marriage bureau.
Those below the rank of sergeant have so far had to make do with

a circular which is sent round units listing likely job vacancies which are coming on to the market. The rest is up to them. But they all go on to the books six months before they leave, and can stay on them until three months after their release, in case they still need help.

If they are still jobless after three months they have to rely upon the two more established organizations, the Regular Forces Employment Association for non-commissioned ranks, and the Officers Association. The RFEA in Bloomsbury Square has been around for more than ninety years, and the Officers Association, which has other responsibilities besides resettlement, was started in 1920. So both are very experienced. Since the 'golden bowler' days of 1957 when many soldiers were leaving the Army, they have been part of the official resettlement organization, and they receive grants from the government, as well as from forces' benevolent associations.

About one serviceman in three registers with the RFEA, although the rate for soldiers is slightly below that for the other services. In recent years about two out of every three who do register, have been found a job by them, although the success rate for soldiers is again slightly below the average. The success rate used to be higher, but has been affected by unemployment in Britain during the 1970s.

The variety of jobs which they go to is surprisingly wide. Out of 6,758 servicemen who passed through the RFEA's books in 1976, 196 became policemen, sixty-four traffic wardens, and car-park attendants and seventy-four were turned into firemen. Government departments took 265, and 297 became postmen. But most, as many as 4,306, vanished into private industry, the largest single number of them, 829, to become skilled manual workers.

A sergeant-major from the Royal Armoured Corps aged forty-one, became a sales manager for £4,150 a year. Another sergeant-major, in the WRAC, started work as an assistant families officer for an annual £2,300 and a REME sergeant, aged forty, found a £6,000 job as an overseas administrative officer. Out of 14,000 men and women who left the services in six months only 571 were still unemployed at the end of that time. This could have been better. But it could have been very much worse at a time when jobs were not easy to find. In general, ex-servicemen seem to have been competing on at least level terms with civilians during recent years.

The Officers Association has a smart address in Belgrave Square, thanks to a eighty-two-year lease with which it was presented in 1965. But behind its massive porch and stout oak door, it has difficulty in making both ends meet and recently had to cut its staff from twenty-seven to nineteen, thereby creating resettlement problems of a different kind.

It conducts exhaustive interviews with officers who ask it to find them a job—there is usually a three-week waiting list—and circulates details of their clients around 1,500 firms, some of whom have been snapping up retired officers for many years. It usually takes six weeks, but some have been fixed up with a job in as little as twelve days.

About 1,300 officers register with the association every year, which is less than half of those who could. Again the RAF use it most, followed by the Navy, but Army officers are turning to it increasingly as the years go by.

Of these who do register, fewer than one in three are found jobs by the Association itself. But others find jobs on their own while the rest form a residue which is carried through to the next year. About 900 are on its books at any one time in an average year. But this varies a great deal according to the job market in Britain. In 1962 the difficulty of finding work was so acute that the number rose to 1,040. In 1974 it was down to 560, since when it has steadily climbed alongside the rising unemployment figures.

Officers, including ex-National Servicemen or those in the TAVR, can stay on its books for as long as they like. Some return years after they have left, to look for a second or third job. Others return within a year because their firm has closed or because they have been made redundant. The service is free, but many make a donation after being fixed up.

All ranks can apply, but the most senior rarely need to. The over-fifties are too old to start a proper second career, so they tend to join large charities or public bodies, which are comfortable rather than richly remunerative. The largest single group tend to be majors aged between thirty-eight and forty-five who are still young enough to move successfully to industry, and who have useful experience in man-management to offer. Then come the young men in their twenties, leaving with a short-service commission, and able still to start at the bottom rung of some other promotion ladder.

The jobs vary, although not perhaps as widely as one might think. So many officers seem to enter administration and personnel management. Recent examples include a major-general who at the age of fifty-four started work as a sales representative at £7,500 a year, which for a modern major-general is something of a come-down, a lieutenant-colonel who became an appeals director for £4,000 a year, a major who earned £3,000 as a savings administrator

10*

and another major who started at £3,800 as an office manager.
One characteristic seems to be that officers do not necessarily earn
higher civilian salaries than other ranks—particularly skilled
craftsmen or senior NCOs. Resettlement can sometimes be a great
leveller.

Army Benevolent Fund. The Army's own central charity is the
Army Benevolent Fund. It was founded in 1944 to prepare for the
return of soldiers to civilian life after the Second World War.
Although the old, established regiments had funds of their own,
these looked like being hopelessly inadequate after a war which
had seen some 4,000,000 men and women serving in the Army.
The memory of what had happened to many soldiers after 1918 was
still painful.

Moreover while some of the regimental associations were
relatively rich, others were not, and some of the new arms like the
Royal Electrical and Mechanical Engineers had virtually nothing.
It was the need to help these new young corps that was seen to be
the ABF's main purpose, and it received rebates from Naafi and
other service canteens to help it on its way.

In one sense it was far-sighted. In another it was quite the reverse.
For some reason it was felt that the ABF would be needed for
only about twenty years, so it was given no machinery to raise
money. It was only in the 1950s that it was appreciated, after
a lengthy study, that the ABF should become permanent—and
only in 1960 that an appeal committee was formed to start raking in
new funds.

Some of this cash now comes from the public, either as donations
or legacies or through sponsored events like military displays
and an annual variety show at the Palladium theatre in London.
The rest comes from the Army itself, particularly through the
Day's Pay Scheme which was started in 1965. Every soldier is
encouraged to surrender a day's pay annually to his regimental
association which then passes on a hefty contribution to the
ABF.

The contributions vary hugely. Some regiments expect only
about sixty per cent of its soldiers to join the scheme. Others insist
on 100 per cent. Some of the corps and regiments are very large,
while others are tiny by comparison. Many regiments with only
one battalion can manage only a few hundred pounds, and the
smaller specialist corps obviously contribute much less. In 1976–77
the Foot Guards regiments with admirable uniformity each contributed £1,000. But the largest sums came from the big corps
and regiments—£21,000 from the Royal Artillery, £23,000 from

the Royal Corps of Signals and as much as £27,000 from the REME.

In general terms the ABF now earns a total of around £1¼ million every year, and spends roughly the same amount in grants and loans to those who need help. Some of its money goes to national charities like Ssafa and the Forces Help Association. The rest goes to individuals—but not directly. What usually happens is that an ex-soldier might approach his regimental association for assistance. The association provides some of the cash itself, but asks the ABF to provide the rest.

It sounds a curious system because the ABF receives money from the regiments with one hand, and gives it back to them with the other. But by providing a central pool it enables the richer regiments to help the poorer ones. The retired major-general and his staff who run the ABF from the Duke of York's Headquarters in Chelsea do not exactly see themselves as Robin Hood and his Merry Men—and their methods are certainly different. But the effect is much the same. The Northern Ireland Special Relief Fund also comes under them, and so do one or two other smaller charities.

More than £500,000 annually goes out in the form of loans, mainly resettlement loans to soldiers who are on the point of leaving. They can apply for one during their last year in the Army, so that they can put down a deposit on a house, then repay it at about £20 a month when their final gratuity comes through.

The people who benefit through the compassionate grants made by the ABF and the local associations, vary widely. In 1976–77 there were 18,000 of them, ranging from the young widow of a lance-corporal killed in Northern Ireland, who received a £3,000 grant to help pay the mortgage and other commitments while lawyers argued for two years over the compensation due to her, to an eighty-year-old disabled First World War veteran and his blind wife who had a small weekly allowance to help combat the effects of inflation.

Then there are free holidays for widows and children, regular donations to schools and homes catering for the children of servicemen, and training grants for the disabled. It is by now part of the unofficial establishment which the Army could not do without.

Meanwhile those who want a little extra insurance for their families can join the Soldiers' Widows Fund or the Single Soldier's Dependants Fund. Widows in need can then claim up to £1,100 and dependants up to £750. The contributions are very low and many soldiers take advantage of them. One of the most valuable functions performed by Ssafa and similar bodies is to advise widows and often the old soldiers themselves upon the help available to them.

Royal British Legion. The credit for keeping down the number of ex-service charities to manageable proportions should go to Earl Haig, who was arguably a better general after the First World War than during it. They mushroomed after 1918 when disillusioned soldiers returning from the trenches were rewarded with inadequate pensions, sub-standard housing and unemployment. It was Haig, always a believer in strength in numbers, who insisted that they should merge in the interests of cost-effectiveness. Five of them did so on 1 July, 1921 to form the British Legion which remains one of the largest and best-known charities in Britain.

By the end of 1922 it had 116,000 members who had already helped to provide cash grants for nearly a quarter of a million destitute ex-servicemen. 'Most dreadful is it', said *The Times* sombrely, 'to think what the case would be but for the British Legion.'

Jobs and pensions, particularly for the widows and disabled, were from the start its main priorities, and housing became so after the end of the Second World War. Some of its victories have been quite spectacular. The most significant was in 1943. Until then ex-servicemen had had to prove that their illness was the result of their time in uniform before qualifying for a disability pension. But Parliament finally agreed under pressure, that the burden of proof should be transferred to the state. As a result seventy per cent of those who applied for disability pensions after the Second World War, were successful, against only thirty per cent after 1918.

But the Legion still deals with up to 17,000 pension cases a year. Some still arise as a result of the First World War, as old men suffering from chronic bronchitis blame it on gas attacks which they suffered in the trenches. It recently won £5,000, after a two-and-a-half-year battle, for one elderly man who developed tuberculosis many years after he had been discharged from the Army. Another late victory was on behalf of one old man who finally received compensation for the loss of a thumb in 1908. It even won a pension for the actor-comedian Spike Milligan on the grounds that he had suffered from nerves as a result of his wartime service.

The Legion is also Britain's most important private employer of disabled people, with over 1,500 men and women in its special workshops. In one or two factories it has had to admit disabled sons of ex-servicemen, or even disabled civilians with no service connexions because it has run out of numbers.

The three best-known workshops are the British Legion Village near Maidstone in Kent, the Cambrian Tweed Factory at Llanwrtyd Wells in Wales and the poppy factory at Richmond, Surrey. Workers at the Village print much of the Legion's own literature on their presses, and make a variety of goods including garden sheds, clothes airers and road signs for local authorities. Originally there was a tuberculosis hospital there too but that was taken over by the National Health Service after the last war.

The tweed factory runs at a big loss, partly because as the Legion admits, it is in the wrong place, far away from any large towns. The poppy factory, too, where badly disabled people make 36 million poppies and 70,000 poppy wreaths every year for the Poppy Day Appeal in November, is inefficient by commercial standards. The Legion says that it could make the poppies in a quarter of the time and could cut the costs below the present £500,000 a year if modern technology and fit workers were employed. But like the tweed factory it provides jobs for people who would otherwise be unable to find any—so the commercial sacrifice is well worthwhile.

By no means all the Legion's enterprises rely upon disabled people, and not all of them make a loss. One in every three London cab drivers is trained at the Legion's taxi school which has been running in Kennington since 1928. More than 5,000 have been trained there since it opened.

The Royal British Legion Attendants Company is the country's second largest car-parking organization with 1,000 attendants, many disabled, looking after over 350 car parks, including those at the House of Commons and the Tower of London. The Legion's own housing association is also thriving with more than 5,500 houses and flats, mainly for widows and elderly couples.

The Legion itself reached a peak after the Second World War when it had around 1,250,000 members scattered throughout 4,800 different branches. Since then it has declined to its present membership of 800,000. Of those only about 650,000 are ex-servicemen and their wives. The others are associate members without service connexions who join simply to use the local club facilities. No club is allowed to have more than forty per cent associate members and the Legion would prefer not to have any at all. But they help to bring in money and the Legion cannot afford to do without them.

The number of branches has fallen to 3,800, which includes about thirty still in the Irish Republic, but not Scotland where they have their own organization. This number is still falling as smaller branches, particularly in the country, are forced to merge.

Like all charities the Legion has been badly hit by inflation, and its chairman in 1977 referred to deep concern about its financial position following a disappointing Poppy Day Appeal. Members' subscriptions of 60p a time pay for the running costs—including the £3,000 it costs to mount the annual Festival of Remembrance at the Albert Hall. But its charitable work relies almost entirely upon the annual Poppy Day collection. The appeal has recently brought in around £3 million or just over. But the Legion would like to have about £5 million. The search for collectors every year has become in itself a difficult chore.

The Legion is to a large extent a victim of its own image, which is dated and downbeat. Many of its own members feel that it places too much emphasis on remembering the past, instead of publicizing the good work that it does—for young soldiers wounded in Northern Ireland as much as for war veterans. In the entrance hall of the Legion's headquarters in Pall Mall, London, hangs an original manuscript of Laurence Binyon's verse: 'They shall grow not old as we that are left grow old . . .' and it is indeed true that the Legion itself has grown old and grey in the public mind.

Officers can join it, but very few do. They have their own Officers Association which they automatically belong to, and it is to the Association that they would turn if they wanted help. The Association is half-in and half-out of the Legion anyway, and receives part of the Poppy Day money for its own good works. Some of the Legion members feel that it somehow manages to get the best of both worlds.

But many ordinary ex-servicemen are also reluctant to join the Legion because of its reputation at local level of being a collection of drinking clubs. The Legion is aware of its reputation, and regrets it. Much of its most valuable social work is done at branch level. They will even help people in debt, paying the old soldier in food and clothing vouchers to ensure that he does not spend their charity at the nearest pub. But because all the cases are strictly confidential, the public never hears of them. So the impression of beery nostalgia remains.

The Legion will probably have to find some way of correcting this impression if it is to continue to be as effective in the future as it has been in the past. Its officers insist that the need for its good works will continue 'for as long as there are armed forces', and point to the expansion programme now going on at the Village in Kent, as proof of their faith in the Legion's destiny. But it will have to persuade a great many people to believe in its future or it will be forgotten as easily as the people it serves.

Chelsea Pensioners. The most famous, though not the most typical accommodation for old soldiers is at the Royal Hospital, Chelsea. It was founded by King Charles II in 1682 and was opened ten years later in the reign of William and Mary. The idea of providing a hostel for veterans of Britain's new standing army probably came from Louis XIV's Hotel des Invalides in Paris. There seems to be no evidence to support the popular legend that Nell Gwyn persuaded her royal lover to go ahead with it.

It was designed by Sir Christopher Wren and it remains one of the most beautiful, though not necessarily the most comfortable, places in London to live in. The government takes care of its upkeep —and that of the pensioners, whose food, clothing, heating, lighting and medical care is paid for under the Defence budget. (In 1977 it cost £1,380,000.)

In fact the pensioner gets a very good deal. He forfeits his Army pension on entering, but he keeps his old-age pension and any other private funds that he may have. There is no means test and, far from being destitute as many people imagine, some of them are quite affluent—especially as they are lavishly entertained wherever they go. One man recently flew to Australia to visit his daughter.

Not all old soldiers are eligible. They have to be over sixty-five and to have served long enough to receive an Army pension, or to be over fifty-five and in receipt of a disability pension. This opens the door to a number of ex-conscripts who might have served for only a few months in either of the two world wars. They also have to produce references and a doctor's report and to convince the Hospital of their probity. The Hospital admits that it sometimes gets 'conned'.

A more important restriction still is that they should be single. This limits the field to widowers, bachelors and divorcees. The Hospital authorities recoil from the thought that some aggrieved woman may turn up one day in search of her escaped spouse.

There is room for about 450 Pensioners, but the Hospital has not been as full as it might have been in recent years. By the mid-seventies the number had slumped to 350, which caused some concern. After a publicity campaign the total had risen to quite a healthy 420, with, in 1977, a short waiting list. But it is hardly a case of turning people away by the dozen. This might have something to do with the Welfare State which enables old soldiers to be more independent than they used to be. But it is not the kind of lifestyle which would appeal to everyone.

It is after all very institutionalized, and certainly someone who had not been in the Army would find it rather strange. They have to wear uniform when in and around the Hospital—a single-breasted blue suit for most of the time. They also have a smarter, double-breasted blue outfit for walking out, and, of course, the famous scarlet rig-out for ceremonials. They are indeed noticeably proud of their uniforms, so much so that rather than risk entrusting them to be cleaned free by the Quartermaster, many of them pay to have them done by a dry cleaner's shop in King's Road. They can wear civilian clothes when away from the Hospital, but most of them prefer to stay in uniform, if only because they like the fuss that people make of them.

They are divided into six Companies of Invalids, as they are called, each one commanded by a Captain of Invalids, who is a retired officer on the Hospital staff. Those who misbehave can be hauled before the Adjutant, another retired officer, and they are expected to turn up for church parade every Sunday in the Hospital Chapel. The Hospital finds that being old soldiers they are embarrassingly adept at finding reasons why they should be excused on any particular Sunday.

Their accommodation might seem rather functional for a widower who has become accustomed to the comforts of his own home. They live in what are called the Long Wards, 200-foot long corridors divided into tiny wainscoted cubicles nine foot long by six foot wide. These used to be only six foot square, but they were enlarged in the mid-fifties because some pensioners had to squeeze past the furniture. This consists of a bed, table, chair, wardrobe, chest-of-drawers, bedside light and wireless headphones, which seems to be all that most of them want. But an increasing number have bought portable television sets, and most of them hang pictures or something on the wall to provide some personal identity. They are expected to clean their own bedspaces. But the Hospital also employs maids, because many of the old men are too feeble and dim of eye to make a thorough job of it.

The military overtones are very gentle. The pensioners are officially addressed as 'Mr.' and they can come and go much as they please. The Hospital encourages most of them though to earn a little extra pocket money by doing odd jobs around the place, which stops them from growing too degenerate. Two of them work as batmen for the Governor, currently General Sir Antony Reid, who thinks that he has the finest job available to a retired officer in Britain. He is probably right.

Army habits die hard. The pensioners even in their old age tend to live by the sun, rising and going to bed early. But they might also spend the evening in their own club. They have three meals a day—a large breakfast, a large lunch with several choices and a high tea, another Army tradition, in the early evening. 'They lead,' says General Reid 'the life of Riley.'

The 110-bed infirmary is kept pretty busy. It was re-opened by the Queen in 1966 after the old building had been bombed in the war. Its busiest time though is said to be just after Christmas because so many of the old men catch colds when staying with relatives for Christmas in unheated houses.

The last Boer War veteran died in the mid-seventies. But there is still one man aged ninety-four and the average age is as high as seventy-nine. On the other hand, a number of Korean War Medals are now said to be appearing, which is a sign of the passing years.

Between sixty and seventy die every year, so there is a constant turnover of residents. But the old men accept it all quite philosophically and the atmosphere is never depressing. 'I hear old 'arry's died,' one will say, and the others will nod their heads sadly.

18

Civil-Military Relations

One disadvantage of an all-professional Army is that it feels cut off from the rest of society. When soldiers and civilians come face to face they stare at each other curiously like visitors from another planet. Apart from those who served in the war or on National Service, few civilians know much about the Army and fewer still want to learn.

After all the Army is a world of its own. It has its own clubs, its own churches, doctors, welfare workers and social castes. Although one hears a lot about the turbulence of Army life, in one sense it is more settled than life outside. A soldier's world is enclosed like a womb, and most people rarely see him.

So far Britain has managed to avoid having a military caste in the more sinister sense. Officers avoid strutting around the West End of London in gold braids and epaulettes, except when on special duty. As soon as they finish work for the day they change into civilian clothes, and staff officers at the Ministry of Defence wear lounge suits for most of the time. An increasing number of families now live among the civilian community when stationed in Britain, and their children go to civilian schools. Unlike soldiers in many countries, they are never looked upon as a privileged class. Indeed soldiers feel that the reverse is often true.

The Army also makes a deliberate effort to strengthen its links with civilian society. It has to do so, or civilians would know nothing of the Army outside those glossy recruiting advertisements which few people seriously believe. If it did not bother to cultivate these contacts, it would be forgotten until the next war broke out. Soldiers gloomily reflect that it is forgotten for most of the time as it is—but it could be much worse.

Public Relations. The man in charge of spreading the word about the Army is its Director of Public Relations (DPR), a brigadier at the Ministry of Defence. A picture hangs in his office of Sir Roger L'Estrange who is said to have been the Army's first DPR in 1662. But the lineage sounds rather dubious and one wonders how he spent his time.

The Army certainly attaches great importance to the job now. Since the early 1960s it has always been filled by some rising star—which has not always been the case in the other two services. The Army's DPR is almost certain to become a major-general unless he falls flat on his face, and many of them go even higher.

It is also looked upon as one of the most difficult jobs for ambitious young brigadiers. For one thing, since the early 1950s he has had to command a mixed bag of soldiers and civilians. The PR staff used to be all military, but civilians were introduced gradually in the 1960s, first in Britain and then in BAOR and elsewhere overseas. As a result the hierarchy is most peculiar. In some places, like the Ministry of Defence, there is an officer in charge with civilian assistants. In other parts of Britain and overseas, you find a civilian at the top and military people helping.

The Ministry of Defence public relations staff was cut by twenty-five per cent in the mid-seventies. But the Army's DPR still has ninety-nine people working for him worldwide, although sixteen of these are officially tri-service, working for the other two services as well. Of the other eighty-three, there are thirty-five military and forty-eight civilians. But a number of the civilians are very much old soldiers who retired when their jobs were civilianized in the 1950s and 1960s, and returned to their same desk next day in lounge suits instead of khaki.

The DPR himself is now commanded by a civil servant, the Chief Public Relations Officer at the Ministry of Defence. Until 1977 he came under the Adjutant-General on the Army Board, so was able to represent official Army thinking. But the system was changed as part of the ministry's policy of centralized power. The Army was not very pleased about it, but has concluded that it makes little practical difference in the end.

The DPR's main difficulty though is that he has to deal with journalists who, unlike soldiers, do not always do what they are told, or even asked. Relations between the brigadier and the Press are usually very good. But he often finds himself having to explain to wrathful senior officers at the ministry why the Press are hounding the Army for something or other, and why he is quite unable to stop them.

It also means that he has to work long and eccentric hours. While the Army expects him to be at his desk first thing in the morning, the Press expect him to be there late in the evening, and even available by telephone at midnight should the need arise.

The average DPR finds that about forty per cent of his time is taken up by public relations within the Army—informing the soldiers themselves about what is going on. But that is not really his job. The important part is the other sixty per cent, which is split between superintending the dissemination of news about the Army to the media, and making decisions about what the Army should say when quizzed about some awkward story. The former is called 'positive' PR, and the latter is 'defensive'—which are terms with a nice military ring about them. Much of the time of PR people at district level is taken up by compiling 'local boy stories' about individual soldiers or regiments for their local newspapers. It is unglamorous, but important if the Army is to keep itself in the public eye.

The Northern Ireland troubles of the 1970s proved something of a turning point in the history of the job. The need to supply the world's Press with instant facts and figures elevated the PR department to a position of high importance. Every unit was told to appoint a PR officer, and a significant decision was taken to allow soldiers to give instant interviews on television or radio. It was a wise decision because the ordinary soldier turned out to be extremely articulate, and his honesty and professionalism did more for the Army's image than a truckload of hand-outs and advertising posters. By contrast an attempt by the Ministry of Defence to introduce a propaganda policy in Ireland was a failure.

The DPR's chief military assistants at the ministry, a lieutenant-colonel and a major, keep a careful tally of the stories which appear in the media. During 1977 the Army boasted a total of twenty-four hours of television time, including thirty-six programmes in which it was featured for more than ten minutes, and sixty-two hours on radio including forty-five programmes of more than ten minutes duration. Over 120 main articles appeared in the national newspapers, an average of over two a week. Not all these stories were complimentary. But it was all useful publicity, and not a bad count when one considers that the Army is only one of three services, and that Britain is supposed to be largely uninterested in its forces in peacetime.

On the other hand, the PR staff has to work hard for some of this reward, if only by arranging facilities for reporters and photographers to visit the soldiers *in situ*. In 1977 there were eighteen overseas facilities for radio reporters, nineteen for television and 101 for newspapers. There were also thirty-four major Press visits in Britain, and a great many smaller facilities for individuals in search of news, good or bad. However, the Army, mindful of the importance of the job, considers the effort worthwhile.

'Soldier' and 'Soldier News'. In-service communications lies partly in the hands of *Soldier*, a glossy monthly magazine which has been a familiar sight in messes and clubs since the Second World War. The idea was conceived in the Western Desert. But it did not materialize until March 1945. The first edition was never issued, and copies which are still lying around are now quite valuable.

In the dying stages of the war *Soldier* had a lot of competition because every command seemed to have its own newspaper or magazine. But these vanished after the war ended and *Soldier* started to do very well, with a circulation of 125,000 and a readership which was many times higher.

It began its life in Brussels, mainly as a magazine for Britain's Liberation Army in Europe. Its offices moved first to Hamburg, and then to London in the 1950s. Since 1971 it has been centred on Aldershot with a staff of twenty, including a part-time cleaner.

Circulation is now about 39,000. But the magazine has had to struggle against rising costs in an age of inflation. It is expected to pay its own running costs and just about does so, but it would have desperate problems if its printing contract were not handled by Her Majesty's Stationery Office.

Its readership varies between 150,000 and 200,000 and if everyone bought his own copy there would be no problem. But many units buy only half a dozen copies altogether, then place them in the Officers' Mess or Junior Ranks' Club for general consumption.

It was unfortunate in being caught by the freeze in the mid-seventies, just when it was about to raise its price from 10p to 15p. It did go up to 15p eventually, but by that time it should have been 20p. In 1978 it was selling for 20p when it should have been 25p. So it is always 5p behind its economic cost and the staff are fearful of putting on too much at once in case circulation plunges.

What the staff would like most of all is more editorial freedom. They argue that if they were able to discuss the issues that soldiers are really interested in, like pay and conditions, many more people would buy it. As it is they have to ignore such controversial issues and keep to nice, chatty articles about units, which while attractively produced and photographed, interest only those who are serving in them.

In 1977 it began to include a section called 'Soldier News' which tried to project news rather than features. Thanks to an outspoken columnist called Anne Armstrong, wife of a lieutenant-colonel who was then on the DPR's staff in London, *Soldier* began to attract national attention for the first time in many years. An interview with the Adjutant-General on the subject of forces' pay ruffled feathers at the ministry. But it was reported in national newspapers, which is the sort of publicity that *Soldier* needs.

Soldier News was so successful that in 1978 the Army expanded it into a separate newspaper, first on a monthly basis and then, from 1979, as a fortnightly.

Civil Aid. The Army also has a peacetime role, which entails giving Military Aid to the Civil Authorities (MACA). This means backing up the government, central or local, in anything from internal security to building a children's playground. In many Third World countries where the Army is the only available pool of loyal, skilled manpower this is the most important contribution it can make.

In Britain, civil aid is divided into three main sections. One is Military Aid to the Civil Power (MACP), another is Military Aid to the Civil Ministry (MACM), and the third is Military Aid to the Civil Community (MACC). Not all, however, provide the kind of publicity that the Ministry of Defence likes to make use of.

The most sensitive is MACP which covers internal security. The most obvious example of MACP in practice is in Northern Ireland where the Army operates officially in support of the police —the civil power. All MACP has in fact been brought under the control of DS-10, a department which was set up in the early 1970s to coordinate all the Ministry of Defence's involvement in Ulster.

But MACP also includes other anti-terrorist operations at home. The most obvious examples are the anti-hijacking exercises which have been conducted periodically at British airports since police and troops in armoured cars first converged on Heathrow, London's main airport, in January 1974. The 1974 operation caused a stir at the time, but subsequent exercises are now largely forgotten, except by those unlucky enough to be catching a flight on the day when one is taking place. Most passengers have become so scared of finding themselves in a hijacked aircraft that they accept the need for troops as well as police to be prepared to deal with terrorists. In 1975 SAS troops actually had to put their training into practice at Stansted Airport.

The use of armed force to keep law and order at home remains a delicate subject in Britain. In 1974 after the Conservative government had been locked in bitter, fruitless conflict with the miners, some journalists began to speculate, though without much real conviction about the danger of a military take-over in Britain. It is doubtful if the Army would be powerful enough to wrest the reins of government from the democratically elected rulers of the day, even if it wanted to. But the speculation served to remind the civil servants in DS-10 that they were handling a very hot potato.

The Army is an authoritarian organization whose members are taught to do what they are told. Their instinctive loyalty is to the Queen, her government of the day, and to the concept of law and order. Many find it hard to sympathize with civilians who step out of line. Serving soldiers usually have to keep their opinions to themselves during periods of social or industrial unrest. But there have been occasional lapses whose effect has been quite disproportionate to what was actually said.

The year 1972 was a bad one for those concerned for the image of MACP. Two things happened in May. In the first place an article in the *Sunday Times* drew attention to certain passages in *Low Intensity Operations*, a book on counter-insurgency by Brigadier Frank Kitson, newly-appointed Commandant of the School of Infantry, which had been published quietly six months before. In the second place *The Times* carried an interview with senior officers at the headquarters of United Kingdom Land Forces as part of a series on 'The Mood of Britain'.

Kitson, now a major-general and Commandant of the Army Staff College, speculated on the possibility of the Army being called upon to support the police in the breakdown of law and order in Britain. The officers at Wilton gave vent to their feelings about left-wing extremists and dismissed graduate trainees at the BBC as being two-thirds Marxist.

None of those involved said anything more than would have been heard at lunch in any officers' mess, where soldiers often betray their impatience with the apparent unwillingness of trade unions to perceive what is in the national interest. Kitson's book, however, also carried a foreword by the Chief of the General Staff, Sir Michael Carver (now Lord Carver) which seemed to bestow official blessing on all its sentiments. In conjunction with the Wilton interview it seemed to reawaken fears that one day the hard-won liberty of Englishmen would be eroded by the armed forces under the euphemistic banner of 'Law and Order'.

It all reinforced the need for the civil servants in DS-10 to advise the Army upon what is and is not acceptable if the government is to continue to use the Army from time to time. DS-10 advises soldiers, for instance, upon the terms of the Yellow Card, the instructions issued to soldiers in Ulster on when and when not to open fire, upon the use of CS Gas (or 'smoke' as they prefer to call it) and on the use of armoured cars. One of their regrets is that the declining numbers of wheeled armoured vehicles forces the Army to use tracked vehicles, like the Scorpion with its 76mm gun, for the simplest operations—thereby giving rise to the awesome cry of 'Tanks!'

The subject of MACM is almost as delicate because it entails the use of troops to carry out essential services in the case of a damaging strike. One of the most controversial passages in the Kitson book was one which advised on the need for the Army to retain a number of specialists, knowledgeable about the running of ports, power stations and sewage works and even mines and industrial plant, in case the workers might one day be unable or unwilling to carry on.

Civil servants in DS-6 which handles MACM insist that troops are used sparingly, and only when invited to help by the authorities. They are limited, anyway, by their sparse numbers and their other Nato commitments. In 1974 during the general strike called by Ulster Unionists against power-sharing in Northern Ireland, soldiers manned petrol pumps and stood by for other tasks. However, it quickly became apparent that their ability to keep even a skeleton service going in the face of a total breakdown of normal facilities was very limited.

But they have been used at intervals during the 1970s, and the public have had cause to be grateful to them. In 1970 they toiled away as dustmen in Tower Hamlets, part of East London. In 1973 they were fighting fires in Glasgow and in 1975 they were dustmen again in the same city. The most famous example of MACM at work was the firemen's strike in Britain in 1977–78. More than 20,000 troops were used at any one time including 10,000 soldiers. In nine weeks they tackled about 40,000 incidents and suffered 312 casualties including two deaths when one of their antiquated Green Goddess fire-fighting vehicles crashed. They worked long hours and lived in primitive conditions, and apart from the firemen themselves, who were bitter about the use of troops, the public were grateful to them.

In February 1978 plans were drawn up for soldiers to man petrol tankers during a strike of tanker drivers. But the strike ended before the plans, codenamed Operation Raglan, neeeded to be put into effect. This was a relief to everyone, including those in DS-6 because the use of troops again, so soon after the firemen's dispute, would have been extremely embarrassing.

DS-6 looks after MACC too. But unlike MACM it is a subject which the civil servants quite enjoy talking about. It is all good clean stuff with the Army using its skills and often its spare time for the general good of everyone, although even here the attitudes of trade unions have sometimes to be examined first.

There are three kinds of MACC. One involves helping out, free of charge, after some national disaster either in Britain or abroad. Post-war examples include the East coast floods in Britain in 1953, the 1963 earthquake at Skopje, Yugoslavia, the collapse of the colliery tip at Aberfan in 1966, the Torrey Canyon oil spillage 1967 and the 1978 blizzards in Scotland and the West of England. In West Germany, BAOR troops have often helped to fight forest fires.

In another part of MACC the Army lends individuals to help advise youth organizations or even the government. They have helped to advise on the restoration of canals in Britain and several years ago were even consulted on the reorganization of a Borstal institution.

The third kind of MACC involves helping anyone in a good cause. Sappers, who are most in demand, have built bridges in the Scottish Highlands and in Kenya. Soldiers have helped to maintain mountain paths in Snowdonia, North Wales, and an adventure playground for children in Sussex. About sixty such jobs are carried out every year in Britain, and a dozen or so abroad. They used to do more abroad, but this has declined as the Army has lost its overseas bases.

The Army asks for the costs of materials to be reimbursed, but otherwise regards it as a useful way of improving public relations—especially in countries where the Foreign and Commonwealth Office has a strong interest. Soldiers usually enjoy the change, and it is often good training. 'Ah, now let's turn to MACC,' say the people in DS-6, their faces brightening with relief.

Bands. Some of the best public relations work for the Army is performed by its bands, and the Army knows it. There have been military bands of one sort or another since the early eighteenth century and long before that troops were led into battle by fifes, drums and trumpets. The first bands had only eight players, including two oboes, two bassoons, two clarinets and two horns. They were led by Masters of Bands, who were civilians, often foreign, who were paid privately by the regiments.

But the modern military band with its high standards owes most to the Duke of Cambridge who as Commander-in-Chief founded the Royal Military School of Music at Kneller Hall, Twickenham, in 1856. He perceived the need after a military review during the Crimean War, when the massed bands proved incapable of playing even 'God Save the Queen' in tune.

Today there are still seventy-eight bands in the Army and 3,500 soldier musicians, which says much for their powers of survival.

There are twenty-three staff bands, which are the biggest, and fifty-five regimental bands. The staff bands are divided into major and minor bands and their size varies accordingly.

The Household Cavalry bands have forty-four musicians, the Foot Guards' bands have sixty-six and the Royal Artillery staff band, the biggest of all, has eighty-five. Most other staff bands have fifty-five, and all regimental bands have thirty-one—although only twenty-six of these are needed at any one time. Most of the larger bands have string sections as well and the Royal Artillery has virtually a symphony orchestra at its disposal.

Regimental bands are led by a bandmaster who is a Warrant Officer Class One. But these move from regiment to regiment on promotion, with the hope of ending up as the Director of Music for one of the big staff bands, as a captain or major. It is very likely that the director of music in one of the Foot Guards started his career as a private, playing the clarinet perhaps in a much less notable regiment.

Recruiting is never a problem, except for some instruments like the bassoon. The Grenadier Guards accept only one out of every fifteen applicants and the WRAC has a long waiting list. All have to be able to play well before joining the Army and about sixty per cent can play more than one instrument. Ideally a band looks for those who can play a string instrument as well as brass or woodwind, and with so much music now taught in schools it can usually afford to pick and choose.

Kneller Hall exists to improve the standards, not to teach first-time players. Soldier musicians go there for pupils' courses and perhaps in time a bandmaster's course when they are taught to have a working knowledge of every instrument in the military repertoire. Some of Britain's leading musicians teach there and the standards are very high.

One of the attractions for young recruits is the training and experience. Another is the pay. Although basic rates are the same as in other parts of the Army, they can earn extra by outside engagements. But for this opportunity many of the better Army musicians would probably take their talents elsewhere.

A band's engagements are officially divided into four categories, and most earn them no extra money at all. Category One covers big national or international events, at home or abroad, sponsored by the government, like the opening of a British Trade Week in Tokyo. Category Two includes service commemoration parades or charity performances. For both categories the bands receive only their out-of-pocket expenses. Category Three jobs are those performed for one's own regiment or perhaps for a neighbouring unit. The soldiers are paid extra money if they are playing late at a dance in the mess, but that is all.

The extra money comes mainly for Category Four jobs which are outside engagements. These include anything from BBC concerts to an afternoon's thumping away at a local fête. The fees are negotiated by the bandmaster or director of music, then distributed among the men. But the band can only accept outside engagements when not required for official Army duties.

The bands can also accept recording jobs. Fees are negotiated with the recording company, and the contract is signed by the commanding officer. But the fees have to be adjusted to the Musicians' Union rates. The most famous recording success yet was that made by the Royal Scots Dragoon Guards of the hymn tune 'Amazing Grace' which became Top of the Pops and at one time in the early 1970s was being sold at the rate of 10,000 copies a day. But soldiers can also take on individual engagements provided that they belong to the union—which most of them join. In 1976 it was estimated that bandsmen could earn up to £40 a month from these outside jobs—and bandmasters and directors of music made much more.

All Army musicians have a second job which they would turn to in wartime. Most are trained as medical orderlies. It does not sound very glamorous but it helps the Army to justify hanging on to so many of them.

In 1969 the Army lost sixteen of its bands, although some of these belonged to regiments which disappeared. In the Defence Review of 1974–75 the staff bands lost ten per cent of their manpower. But the regimental bands protested that they could not survive with fewer than thirty-one members and they got away with it.

In 1976 the cost of all bands in the three services was put at £15,200,000. This might seem a lot. But it is not a very high proportion of the Defence Budget. Even the Treasury seems to concede that the 'Oompah' of our military bands is worth the price.

Sport. Sport is another area in which soldiers and civilians can meet on equal terms. Soldiers have been keen on sport since knights went jousting and have done quite a lot to export British games throughout the world. The Army likes to think that it introduced rugby to Fiji, and even claims that cricket was first popularized in Australia by a group of young officers in Sydney in 1803. In 1872 the Royal Engineers even won the FA Cup although they seem unlikely to do so again.

Army sport was not very well organized until the First World War. But morale was helped so much by playing football behind the front line in France that in 1918 the Army Sport Control Board was formed to put things on a proper basis. It started with a grant of £5,000 from the Army Canteen Fund and set about building pitches and playing fields, which in many garrisons are still of an enviable standard.

Since 1956 the Board has been financed partly by the Army's own Central Fund and partly with public money. The division is about fifty-fifty. In 1978 it received £100,000 of which £48,000 came from public funds. This money goes to finance the thirty-two sports which the Army officially recognizes. But large items like a new yacht for the Sailing Association which now has about 10,000 members, or a new glider, have to be paid for by special awards from the Central Fund. A new £18,000 yacht was one recent big item. Another was a £650 horse for the Saddle Clubs Association. The state maintains the sports grounds and provides transport, so in general the Army does not do badly. But the Treasury agreed to pay for a new athletics track at Aldershot recently, only on condition that civilians could use it too.

The Army characteristically divides its sport into major and minor, according to how many soldiers take part in them. It spends its money accordingly. The aim after all is to provide recreation for soldiers, not to breed international athletes. The main winter sports are football, rugby, cross-country running and hockey—in which the standard is very high. The main summer sports are cricket, swimming and athletics.

But other officially recognized sports include tennis, squash, badminton, boxing, judo, gymnastics, fencing, basket-ball, ski-ing, canoeing, mountaineering, gliding, golf, sailing, riding, modern pentathlon, biathlon, free-fall parachuting, cycling, sub-aqua diving, and since quite recently fishing and archery.

The standards are quite high, though there is no major sport in which the Army as established a marked ascendency—as the RAF has done in athletics over the last twenty years. In National Service days when so many young professionals were playing for the Army, the standard was astonishingly high and the Army even once beat England in a friendly football match. It is unlikely to repeat that performance. But the Army was beaten only 2–1 by Chelsea not so long ago. The Army cricket team plays the 2nd XIs of the main counties as well as the universities, and the rugby team has fixtures against leading English clubs like Harlequins and London Irish.

The influence of the officer class is not as great as it used to be. Polo thrives but only because its small following happens to be very enthusiastic. In a recent match between the Army and the

Royal Navy the Prince of Wales was playing for the Navy and the Duke of Edinburgh and Lord Mountbatten were among the spectators. But that is not typical. In 1977–78 only two officers could find a place in the rugby team and the cricket XI is now composed almost entirely of non-commissioned ranks.

The highest standards are usually reached in those sports which have military undertones. The Army biathlon (a combination of ski-ing and shooting) team won the Norwegian Army Championships a few years ago, which is rather like the Norwegians beating England at cricket. And the British modern pentathlon team (running, riding, swimming, shooting and fencing) which won the gold medal at the 1976 Olympic Games had a soldier, Lieutenant Jim Fox as one of its members.

But it is no longer possible for a soldier to spend his Army career on the sports field without damaging his chances of promotion. Although the Army will encourage a promising young athlete to reach his peak, he still has to make a choice between the two. One young soldier who was offered a Welsh rugby trial at fly-half recently had to abandon his playing career because it was threatening his chances of being promoted to sergeant. Before the last war the more easy-going Army of the day might well have made him a sergeant as a reward for winning international recognition on the rugby field.

Adventurous Training. Copywriters, whether for advertising or PR try to wring as much glamour as they can from the Army's use of Adventurous Training (AT). For most soldiers AT started in 1971, although junior regiments had been hard at it for some time.

The idea is to provide a substitute for all those hair-raising operations East of Suez which were part of day-to-day life in the age of Empire. It is supposed to foster those manly virtues like courage, initiative and self-reliance. But it also helps recruiting by helping the Army to move away from the old mental picture of troops lined up on a barrack square, or polishing their boots in a Nissen hut.

Soldiers are encouraged to attend one or more of nearly 400 courses which are held every year at AT centres in Britain and overseas. Many of the AT activities are also classed as Army sports, like canoeing, mountaineering and free-fall parachuting. But they all have a whiff of danger hanging over them, whether illusory or real.

So far it has been very successful. In 1971 about 2,500 went on AT courses, and 5,500 strode off into the sunset on 'expeditions'— a word which still sounds desperately Victorian. In 1976 as many as 9,000 were on AT courses and 40,000 were roaming the world on expeditions, which are always led by those who have qualified as instructors at AT centres. One mountain training centre in Norway takes 350 soldiers from Britain and 650 more from BAOR on instructors' courses every year.

One reason that the Ministry of Defence likes the idea of AT is that it is cheap. In 1976 the AT budget was only £400,000. Those who go on expeditions are allowed only a few pounds from Army funds, and have to find the rest themselves. Actually their regiments usually dip into their regimental funds to help them, and they can often borrow equipment from special centres. But while it may not cost them all that much, it costs the Ministry of Defence even less.

Some of the bigger expeditions provide the kind of image-building publicity that copywriters dream about. The most notable recently has been the successful climbing of Everest by a joint Anglo-Nepalese team in 1976. This cost more than £100,000 altogether, but the Ministry of Defence did not pay all of it, and must have regarded its share as being a good investment considering the publicity which resulted. The only embarrassing feature was that the two NCOs who reached the summit belonged to the SAS—and the ministry were in a dither over whether or not to admit it.

Other expeditions too have caught the public imagination. Not all have been organized by the Army. A civilian society which is contemplating making an assault upon some forsaken part of the world might receive financial help from the ministry by inviting soldiers to come along and applying to Whitehall for help. If the Army thinks that it could be classified as Adventurous Training, it usually cooperates.

Lieutenant-Colonel John Blashford-Snell, who has recently commanded the Royal Engineers Junior Leaders Regiment at Dover, made a name for himself in the 1970s by leading a number of expeditions, two of which were particularly notable. One was the first crossing of the Darrien Gap, the hostile terrain between South and Central America. The other was an exploration of the Zaïre river in rubber dinghies. With his military moustache and pith helmet, which he even wears in his back garden on hot summer days, Colonel Blashford-Snell has lent to some of the bigger Army expeditions that extra splash of colour and gentle eccentricity. Other expeditions in recent years have included a North–South circumnavigation of the globe, and a crossing of the Sahara Desert.

These voyages into the unknown inevitably sound rather anachronistic, as if the Army is searching round for something exciting to do. But they provide good experience for the men involved. Most of the expeditions anyway are rather modest affairs, like hiking over Salisbury Plain or rock-climbing in North Wales. And all help the Army to remind people that it does not spend all its time on the rifle ranges or, still worse, the drill square.

Museums. The Army has always had a keen sense of history, especially its own. Soldiers tend to be romantics who respect the past and prop up the reputations of fallen heroes. This does not necessarily make them good historians, but it makes them admirable conservationists.

Their storehouses are the 135 regimental and corps museums, which not only contribute to the *ésprit* of a modern battalion but often preserve the links between the battalion and the local population. Some are quite large, like those of the Royal Corps of Signals at Blandford, Dorset, the Royal Artillery at Woolwich, the Royal Engineers at Chatham and the Royal Armoured Corps at Bovington, also in Dorset, whose display of tanks makes it a tourist attraction in the summer.

The most significant, however, is the National Army Museum in Royal Hospital Road, Chelsea. The museum began in 1960 in a disused chapel and riding school at Sandhurst, but moved to its present, purpose-built block in 1971 after a £1 million appeal. The appeal's success was largely due to the energy and determination of Field-Marshal Sir Gerald Templer, who is the museum's founding father and chairman of its executive committee. When it was opened by the Queen, on Armistice Day, it was the first new London museum to be built since the last century.

The lease on the site, next to the Royal Hospital, home of the Chelsea Pensioners, had to be bought from the government for £160,000. But the government pays for the museum's upkeep, and the Ministry of Defence provides money to buy exhibits. The chairman of the council is always the Parliamentary Under-Secretary for the Army, and other ex-officio members include the Adjutant-General and Quartermaster-General.

At present the museum covers the history of the Army from the raising of the Yeomen of the Guard, in 1485, to 1914. The last exhibit shows a soldier marching off to the First World War. But only Phase-1 of the building programme has so far been completed. The museum will bring the story of the Army up to date when Phase-2 is opened in the near future.

Exhibits include the prayer-book used at the burial of Sir John Moore, the cloak which was wrapped round the dying General Wolfe and Florence Nightingale's lamp. But the museum also has a fine collection of weapons, uniforms and paintings, and its director, Mr. William Reid, regards its display of medals and insignia as the finest in the world. These include seven Field-Marshals' batons, more than thirty Victoria Crosses and all the orders and decorations of the late Duke of Windsor.

It has a close relationship with the regimental museums, like that of a friendly big brother. Curators from the regimental museums, usually retired officers, are encouraged to attend professional museum courses at Chelsea, and they happily lend exhibits to each other.

A recent survey indicated that about one in every three visitors to the National Army Museum comes from overseas, many from the United States. So it is very much a shop window for the Army —an antique shop perhaps but one which plays a part in maintaining good civil-military relations.

19

Clubland

Attrition in Clubland. Army officers have always been natural clubmen. The regiment after all is a kind of club, and life in the mess with its rituals and its decorum is not all that far removed from that in some of the masculine establishments in Pall Mall and St. James's.

But service clubs themselves were relative late-comers to the West End. They began to appear in the early nineteenth century when officers on leave from the Napoleonic Wars found that they had nowhere to go. They had neither the time nor the money to join the socio-political establishments like Brook's, White's or Boodles'. A few service clubs did exist, like Flanders and the Peninsular, but they had no permanent premises of their own and the members used to meet in coffee houses. For the rest of their time officers drank and gambled in less reputable houses where they quickly lost their money and their character. Service clubs started with the rather puritanical purpose of luring them away to more respectable surroundings.

The Guards Club opened in 1813, but that was very much a family affair. The first general club was the United Services, often referred to as the Senior because it accepted only majors and above. The Junior United Services followed, but both the Senior and the Junior soon became so over-subscribed that a group of officers who had just retired from the Indian Army grew tired of waiting for a place and founded a third, the Army and Navy Club in 1837. It was originally to have been called the Army Club but the Duke of Wellington refused to join unless the Royal Navy were allowed in too.

In 1862 another group of officers formed the Naval and Military for similar reasons. Then followed the Cavalry in 1890, and the Junior Army and Navy in 1911. This made a total of seven, five of which were surviving—if only just—in the middle 1970s.

Today there are only three. One is the Cavalry and Guards at the Western end of Piccadilly overlooking Green Park and the Hyde Park Underpass. Another is the Naval and Military, slightly further to the East in Piccadilly, and the third is the Army and Navy whose address is 36 Pall Mall but whose entrance is in St. James's Square in the heart of clubland.

The Army and Navy is usually referred to by its members as 'The Rag' because Captain 'Billy' Duff, one of its members in the middle of the last century, was so disgusted by the bill of fare late one night that he described it as no better than 'rag and famish'. The Army loves nicknames, and the club, while it might have been offended at the time, is now quite proud of the tradition.

The Naval and Military is still more widely known as the 'In and Out' which derives from the stern instructions on the entrance and exit to the club's small forecourt. The first people to call it that were hansom cab drivers before the First World War who found the real, rather unimaginative names of service clubs confusing. More people now know it as the In and Out than as anything else. The Cavalry and Guards as befits its dignity is known simply as the Cavalry and Guards.

The two which most recently succumbed to rising costs and falling popularity, were the two oldest of them all, the United Service and the Guards. Most of the United Service Club's 2,000 members, prised out of the heavily protected Nash building on the corner of Pall Mall and Waterloo Place, moved into the In and Out. The Guards abandoned their eighteenth-century building in Charles Street in the following year and the club merged with the Cavalry, whose new name reflects the amalgamation.

The marriage between the Cavalry and the Guards seems to have been a happy one, probably because both clubs were similar family affairs and because their members all come from the same strata of society. But the absorption of the Senior by the In and Out was rather more bitter. The members of the United Service settled down well enough, slumping into armchairs which were not all that different from those they had just vacated. They were soon snoozing away as if they had been there all their lives. But the In and Out management has never fully forgiven the Senior for selling all their effects at a famous auction in 1976, particularly for letting the silver go for a paltry £41,000. The In and Out feels that it should have been given first choice.

All three surviving clubs are rather smug about their fallen comrades. Far from reflecting that 'there but for the grace of God go the rest of us' they accuse the Guards and the Senior of digging their own graves by refusing to change with the times. The Senior in particular has won little sympathy, because of its élitist policies. In its heyday the club not only closed its doors to junior officers but was rather snooty about accepting applicants from unfashionable regiments, particularly those from the supporting corps. Even qualified doctors from the RAMC were regarded as second-class citizens. So, reflect the survivors, they paid the penalty.

The Cavalry and Guards, Army and Navy, Naval and Military. The existing clubs can also sound rather sniffy about each other. The Army and Navy seems to think that the Naval and Military prostituted itself by its decision several years ago to allow civilians to join, thus forfeiting its claim to be regarded as a service club at all. The Naval and Military in fact regards this as the most progressive move it has ever made, comparable to its pioneering decision in the 1930s to allow women into the all-male sanctum of a 'gentlemen's' establishment. Anyway it points out that the Rag sold its birthright in 1964 when it knocked down its grand old building with its cavernous halls and lofty ceilings and replaced it with the present twentieth-century imitation. The Rag protests in turn that this was the most enlightened decision that *it* has ever taken. The conversion of the old premises which had a basement, two main floors and an attic, to the present club which has an underground garage, sub-basement, and eight more floors with low ceilings and smaller, cosier rooms, has been its salvation. The Cavalry and Guards club says little about anyone.

Ostensibly all three are healthier than they have been for some time. All have record or near-record memberships which they like to attribute to their go-ahead policies and good business sense. Sceptics argue that this state of well-being is the direct consequence of club closures elsewhere. All three in fact admit to concern about the long-term future. With the possible exception of the In and Out which has become largely a civilian club with a service atmosphere, they are catering for a closed and depleted section of the clubland community. Moreover they have too many elderly members and not enough young ones.

They have managed to preserve their separate identities very well. Arguably they are more different now than they have ever been, because of the differing strategies which they have pursued in the fight for survival.

The Cavalry and the Guards is the smallest, the most exclusive, the most luxurious, and the most expensive for most, though by no means all of its members. Its president is the Duke of Kent who like his brother Prince Michael is a member in his own right as a cavalry officer. Prince Charles and Princess Anne are honorary members and the Queen Mother is patron of the ladies section. The smoke room is known as the Field-Marshals' Room because of the cavalry field-marshals whose gilt-framed portraits in oils stare gently down upon the dozing inhabitants. The latest addition is Field-Marshal Lord Carver whose painting has had to be sited high on the wall to protect it from the vandalism of some of the more boisterous members.

It is not exactly restricted to the Cavalry and the Guards. Others who can join include officers and ex-officers of the Royal Horse Artillery and those of the Royal Artillery who have served for at least six months with a cavalry regiment, the Royal Tank Regiment, the Royal Green Jackets, TAVR officers from Yeomanry regiments and the Honourable Artillery Company. It is also open to corps officers who have been attached to Cavalry and Guards regiments—but only at the discretion of the committee—and to 'gentlemen' over twenty-one who are sons of members. Wives, daughters and sisters can join the ladies' section.

For serving officers it is not all that expensive. In 1978 it cost up to £35 to join, then one day's pay a year for subalterns and two days' pay for other officers up to the rank of colonel. Senior officers like all those who have retired have to pay the full rate, which leaped alarmingly from £60 to £110 a year for all those living in Britain on 1 January, 1978.

When the Guards Club closed, 800 of its members moved over to raise the membership to a record total of 3,300. This fell back to 3,000 in 1978 after the rise in subscriptions. Only 995 of the 3,000 in 1978 were serving officers. About 185 more were lady members and the rest were retired officers from one regiment or another.

The food is very good, good enough for members and their wives to dine out there in the evenings. The menu is not particularly cheap though and while the club points out that it is much more reasonable than the hotels around the corner in Park Lane, this is not a very convincing comparison. Still it is a very comfortable sanctum in the West End with its atmosphere of heavy drapes and thick carpets and one can understand why members sometimes grow anxious over the long-term future.

Where the Cavalry and Guards looks exclusive and rich, even if it is not, the Army and Navy looks prosperous and middle-class. It is the most modern and most functional of the three, the liveliest and in the eyes of its members, the most businesslike.

The example of its business acumen which is most often cited is the 1964 rebuilding. Not only did it sell the ladies' annexe to pay the bill, but it sold the annexe to the same group which built the present club, so relatively little cash changed hands. By any standards it seems to have been a commercial success.

Its critics complain that it lost some of its character in the process. Of all the three surviving clubs it now most resembles an officers' mess, with its light panelling and chintz. One expects to come across the colonel's lady in an ante-room arranging flowers. It claims to be the only general service club left in London, and one has to have held the Queen's Commission if only for a day. One wonders how an officer wanting to get away from it all could do so at the Rag. But when an officer refers to his club it is probably the Rag that he means.

Its growth in membership in recent years has been quite spectacular. Down to 2,800 at the time of the rebuilding, by 1978 it had 6,000 in addition to 1,500 lady members. About one in five was from the Royal Navy, only about one in three was serving and at the latest count some 500 were aged between thirty and forty.

Its success, it insists, is mainly due to its policy of making the place a family club to which officers are encouraged to bring not only their wives but also their children if they are over eight years old. But these impedimenta have to be kept out of the main dining-room which is all-male at lunchtime.

In 1978 most full members living within fifty miles of London had to pay a £51 subscription whether serving or not. But those under twenty-nine pay only a third of that, the under-twenty-ones pay nothing at all and there is no entrance fee. The club also prides itself on having kept a careful balance between the subscriptions and the club prices in the dining-rooms and bars, which is apparently the way to ensure that you have plenty of members and that they use the services that the club provides.

If the Cavalry is the most exclusive and the Army and Navy the most modern, the Naval and Military is the grandest and most cosmopolitan. It cheerfully describes its ambience as 'scruffy gentility' which apparently is what the members crave.

Its official title is something of an anachronism now because so few members are actually serving in the Navy or the Military. On the other hand, most of its older members have held commissions at one time or another. And those who have not have still to be proposed and seconded by those who have. This is not a very exacting requirement, but it does help to preserve the club's links with its service background.

Moreover its service membership has recently gone up as the result of a conscious policy. In 1977 it decided that all serving officers could join for an annual subscription of £10 a year until they reach the rank of lieutenant-colonel, when they have to pay between £20 and £25. Those not serving at the time have to pay the full £80. The theory is that serving officers can have their membership subsidized by the expense accounts of their better-off businessmen colleagues. About 300 serving officers took advantage of the new offer in the first twelve months.

The club has been through some hard times. In the late 1960s it became known as the Down and Out which reflected its depressed circumstances. But the decision to admit civilians, whether they have held commissions or not, and extensive redecoration, together with the absorption of the United Service members has put it on its feet—for the time being anyway.

All three clubs have bedrooms which are well used on week nights. The Cavalry and Guards has thirty-nine, the In and Out has fifty and the Rag has as many as eighty. Prices for double rooms with private bathrooms ranged in 1978 from £17 at the In and Out through £15 at the Cavalry to a mere £11 at the Rag, though the Rag's price did not include Value Added Tax (VAT). Not only do the rooms make money on their own but they help to fill the place in the evenings. The diminution of evening trade has been one of the most marked trends in clubland in post-war London, where most people now go home to their families and an evening in front of television. But the Army and Navy claims to be reasonably busy because of its residents.

In the old days, which are not really all that long ago, an officer's choice of club was dictated by his commanding officer or by regimental tradition. Nowadays he is more free to shop around for a 'best buy'. The most judicious should perhaps switch from club to club in the manner of a housewife moving between Tesco and Sainsbury supermarkets. He could, for instance, join the Army and Navy for nothing until the age of twenty-one when, if he is eligible, he might move to the Cavalry and Guards for a while to take advantage of the relatively low subscription for junior officers. Then he should belong to the In and Out for most of his service career, changing back to the Rag on retirement.

But most young officers nowadays, with a mortgage to pay and children to educate, decide not to join a club at all. Anyway they might well resent taking their wives to a club which, like the In and Out, insists that women have to go in by a side entrance round the corner in Half Moon Street, and have to eat at one end of the dining-room. All three clubs still like to think of themselves as gentlemen's establishments to which ladies are welcomed—but only on certain conditions. To many young officers, reared in an age of female emancipation this sounds like the nonsense that it is. But if the clubs want to insure against an uncertain future, they have to attract these young officers somehow.

Major William Ellery Anderson, secretary of the Naval and

Military, says that three service clubs are still too many—particularly as RAF officers automatically have to join the RAF Club, next door to the Cavalry and Guards. RAF officers have their subscription deducted at source and the Cavalry would like to do the same if only the Army would allow it—which it will not.

The ultimate solution would be for all three to combine to form one united services club—in other words revert to the position of 1815. But then Major Anderson would like them all to join the In and Out whose premises—where Lord Palmerston once lived—are by far the biggest. And not surprisingly his rivals do not exactly agree.

In principle many think that the evil day of further amalgamations will come. In practice they remain reluctant to do anything about it yet; things will have to get worse, much worse, before they surrender.

The Union Jack and the Victory. Ordinary soldiers have their London clubs too. They are less exclusive than the establishments in Pall Mall and Piccadilly. But they are perhaps less of an anachronism, and they offer soldiers quite a good bargain.

There were three of them until 1976, when the Chevrons Club for NCOs became a victim of inflation. Its Queen Anne premises in Dorset Square where the club had lived since 1918 were sold to Arab buyers for £225,000. So it is not only officers' clubs which have found the 1970s heavy going.

Of the two remaining, the most familiar is the Union Jack whose modern escarpments rear up twenty-six storeys high opposite a side entrance to Waterloo Station, just off the unfashionable Waterloo Road. The other is the Victory Services Club in Seymour Street, a stone's throw from Marble Arch. Both are registered charities and both curiously enough were founded at the same time.

The Union Jack was opened by King Edward VII in 1907 as a memorial to those who were killed during the Boer War. More than 12,500,000 servicemen and their families have stayed there since. More than 1,000,000 stayed there during the First World War and over 1,800,000 during the Second, when it was so full that they sometimes had to sleep in the corridors. It was also used extensively by National Servicemen, stranded in London for the night or up for a weekend in town. It was clean, warm and cheap, and that was all they asked.

The present club is not the one which they remember. The old building was pulled down in 1972 because it was uncomfortable to live in and expensive to maintain. Younger soldiers found its tiny cabins and echoing corridors less congenial than the modern barracks in which they spent most of their time.

The new building was financed partly by a £350,000 appeal and partly by a thoughtful deal with Finance for Industry Ltd. who wanted a site next door. It consists of two tower blocks, one twenty-six storeys high for servicemen on their own, and the other ten floors high for servicewomen and families.

It is smaller than the old place, but much more chic, with low ceilings, modern lighting, fitted carpets and furniture from John Lewis. Some traces remain, like the oak panelling which was donated in memory of Jewish soldiers who died in the Boer War. That survives in the library. The inscribed panels listing holders of the Victoria Cross have been incorporated, and so have a number of plaques, including one 'In gratitude for a scrap of comfort'. It commemorates an anonymous donor who for many years sent donations to the Union Jack after the First World War, each one identified only by that brief explanation. But the picture windows and splashing fountains have little in common with the place which Edward VII opened.

Nor is the atmosphere reminiscent of officers' clubs in the West End. All the facilities are there, a members' dining-room and bar, a families' dining-room and bar, billiards room, writing room, smoking room, conference area and even a sauna bath. The staff are also encouraged to behave more like 'club servants' than hotel workers and to expect no tips. The comptroller after all is Colonel C. A. la T. Leatham whose own club is the Cavalry and Guards. But the pop music in the hall and the procession of young fathers with collapsible push-chairs and wives in plastic raincoats, could never let him confuse the two.

It is after all more like a hotel than a club, with most of its revenue coming from the 417 single rooms and fifty-five doubles. As such it is a remarkably good bargain with single rooms in 1978 prices at £4·25 and double rooms at £7·90 with provision for children of all ages. The policy has always been to keep the charges for a single room below one day's pay of the humblest private.

Not surprisingly it is full at weekends. Soldiers who had grown accustomed to the old Union Jack building where one could be sure of a bed at any time, are learning the hard way that they should now book in advance. But the club already regrets that it did not build more rooms for married couples.

All serving 'other ranks' of the armed forces are automatically members and pay no subscription. Ex-regulars can also join for £2 a year, and some do use the Union Jack as a club, dropping in for a drink before catching the commuter train home from Waterloo.

Then there are temporary honorary members like National Service-men and foreign nationals in Britain, who have to pay more for a room and cannot usually stay there at weekends.

The Ministry of Defence sometimes arranges for parties of foreign servicemen to stay there, sailors from a visiting warship on the Thames maybe, or more frequently German soldiers on a visit to London from the tank training areas at Castlemartin in Pembroke-shire. But British servicemen always have priority. The prospect of turning away one's own troops because the place is full of Germans, does not appeal.

Financially the club has been through a worrying time. The Ministry of Defence donates £8,000 a year to compensate for the loss of subscriptions from servicemen. But apart from the con-cessions on tax and rates that come through its charitable status, it has to keep going on its own. It ran up a £190,000 deficit while it was rebuilding, and even when it was re-opened, the servicemen did not at first flock forward.

However, with the occupancy rate now running at seventy per cent, the club hopes that the worst of its worries are over. The Union Jack over the entrance still flutters bravely enough.

The Victory is not strictly speaking an other ranks' club because officers can join it too. It claims to be the only club in the world which is open to all ranks of all the armed forces, serving or retired. But it is more comparable with the Union Jack than, say, the Army and Navy, and the two co-exist in very friendly competition.

It opened in 1907 as the Veterans' Club for ex-servicemen. Major Rider-Haggard, brother of the author, was one of the co-founders. After the First World War it changed to the Allenby Club, when Field-Marshal Viscount Allenby became its president, then later it became the Victory.

At the end of the Second World War it was quite a small affair with only 2,000 members and premises in Holborn. But in 1948 with the help of an appeal supported by the Lord Mayor of London, it took over the old Connaught Club in Seymour Street, which had been used as a club for American servicemen during the war. It has been there ever since, on a long lease from the Church Commissioners.

It has also expanded with phenomenal success, from a member-ship of 2,000 to a peak of 35,000 in 1967–68. It fell back to 30,000 in the early 1970s but had recovered to 33,000 by 1978, only 7,000 short of the maximum permitted.

Until 1970 it was only for ex-servicemen. (One of its regulars served for only three days in the Army.) Then it opened its doors to serving men and women and thus won recognition as a registered charity—with all the perquisites entailed like tax and rates reductions.

It still has a strong ex-service bias and only 3,000 of the 33,000 are serving. But every one in three of these is an officer which helps the club's image, and recent recruiting has been almost on a fifty-fifty basis between officers and other ranks, as officers flee from the rising costs in Pall Mall and elsewhere.

The Victory is certainly very cheap at only £3 a year plus VAT. Accommodation is cheap too with single rooms in 1978 ranging from £2·30 for a night and only £1·20 if one shares it, as some of the club's First World War veterans prefer to do on a trip up to town. Of the 300 rooms, fifty-nine are for married couples who pay £3 a head. For a room only five minutes' walk from Selfridges, that is astonishingly cheap.

The Victory rooms are clean, warm and rather soul-less. They have washbasins and bedside lights, but no private bathrooms, telephones or television sets. Those seeking luxury or perhaps even a cosy touch of home would have to go elsewhere, and pay for it.

It has the air of a large, cheap, institutional hotel which has seen better days. Even in winter the heating is turned off in the bedrooms during the daytime to save money. And there are strong service undertones. All the male staff have served in the forces at some time or another and Old Comrades Associations hold annual dinners in the club's big hall.

Relations with the police are very close. This is partly because of the club's detailed records of more than a million people who have belonged there since it opened. But the police also make use of the big hall whenever there is a noisy demonstration taking place in Central London. They bring in their own caterers and set up base camp there, with the result that a line of police vans is often drawn up outside the front door.

The club enjoys this special relationship with the forces of law and order. The police even asked if they could join the club recently. But their application was regretfully turned down under the terms of the club's charitable status.

Nato servicemen stationed in Britain can join, however, and so can members of the Royal Observer Corps. The club has also a strong RAF bias. Nearly half of its members have RAF connexions against forty-four per cent who are soldiers or ex-soldiers and very few sailors.

About 9,000 of the 33,000 are women, 6,000 of them members' wives who can join for an additional £3. The rest are servicewomen. Men and women can bring three guests at a time so the Grill Room or the noisy cafeteria are often full of women on shopping trips in the West End, taking the weight off their legs before making another assault on Oxford Street.

A number of ex-servicemen stay there during the week while on business in London. Although the maximum unbroken stay is ten days one can leave for the eleventh and return for another ten. Unlike the Union Jack it is busier during the week than the weekends, perhaps because of its greater ex-service tradition. There is even a room called the Desert Rats' Lounge where members, no doubt some of them old Desert Rats, doze away the winter afternoons.

The club went through a worrying time when the Union Jack re-opened. But business seems as brisk as ever. The rooms are full eighty-five per cent of the time, and members still have to book three weeks in advance if they want a single room.

In 1977 it made a surplus of £18,000 and was still able to serve steak for £1·50 in the Grill Room. The Union Jack and the Victory may be to Pall Mall what a Corner House restaurant is to the Savoy Grill. But in the fight for survival which characterizes clubland, it is arguable which will live the longest.

The Royal United Services Institute. Officers who prefer work to play at lunchtime can join the Royal United Services Institute which has regular midday meetings. They can for that matter apply to join several other institutes for the study of defence and foreign affairs, like the Royal Institute of International Affairs or the International Institute for Strategic Studies—which are intellectually the most elegant. But servicemen find these academic and abstruse and generally prefer the RUSI's more practical, approach. It studies tactics which the others do not, and its director is always a retired senior officer.

It was founded in 1831 as the United Service Museum with the Duke of Wellington as its first vice-patron. But the museum itself was dispersed in 1962. The original minutes made it clear that it was to be not a club but a learned society in which 'neither politics, gambling, eating and drinking enter its design, from which the two former attributes are absolutely excluded on principle.' It claims to be the oldest institution of its kind in the world.

Its headquarters is in Whitehall, opposite the statue of Field-Marshal Earl Haig on horseback. Actually one should say that Haig is opposite the RUSI—which arrived there first. A cool, stone building, it was built between 1892 and 1896 after Queen Victoria had been persuaded to release the site next door to Inigo

Jones's famous Banqueting House, which is virtually the only surviving remnant of the old Whitehall Palace.

The RUSI produces a quarterly journal as well as other books and pamphlets by individual authors, and sponsors the annual Trench Gascoigne essay competition. Its midday speakers could hardly be more distinguished. The Secretary of State for Defence himself periodically defends his policies to an audience which is not always sympathetic. But the atmosphere is restrained and rarely very heated.

A recent survey indicated that thirty-seven per cent of the 5,230 members are serving officers and forty-two per cent are retired, while the rest have no service connexions at all. There are even a few other ranks, from the Intelligence Corps, for example. Until recently the rules of admission seemed specifically to exclude non-commissioned ranks. Now the anomaly has been corrected, but few seem to be interested.

The RUSI has complained for some time that not enough serving officers join it. Officers reply that with the number of courses which they have to attend they no longer have the time. But the Institute still regrets that more do not seem able to find the odd hour to use its facilities, which include a superb library of military literature.

More members would certainly help the RUSI which relies upon annual subscriptions to make up nearly half its income. But it says that recruiting is now reasonably good, particularly among junior and middle rank officers. Certainly the average audience at a RUSI meeting looks rather younger than those gathered round most lunch tables in clubland. Perhaps that is another sign of the times.

20

Conclusions

Military Conservatism. The most remarkable thing about the Army is not perhaps that it has changed so much, but that it has changed so little. A National Serviceman of twenty-five years ago returning to his old camp, would no doubt be surprised and impressed by what he saw. Soldiers are better dressed, better equipped, better fed, for the most part better housed and better paid—though many would dispute this. Relationships between officers and other ranks are easier than they were, in most regiments anyway, and are characterized by a mutual respect which seems genuine enough.

But these are largely the distinctions between a conscript Army and one composed entirely of volunteers, who need to be encouraged. Moreover they reflect changes in British society as a whole and are arguably less pronounced in the Army than elsewhere.

Historically the Army has resisted change until its trenches have been overrun, after which it has retreated in orderly fashion, regrouping and defending its new positions. It opposed the innovations introduced by Cardwell and Haldane, but has ever since fought stoutly to retain them. By training and by inclination soldiers tend to be conservative with a small 'c'—and usually with a capital 'C' as well.

The present shape of the Army has been moulded by a series of compromises, which explains why there are little bits sticking out here and there. Since the start of the Second World War the cavalry regiments have been grouped under the Royal Armoured Corps with centralized recruit selection and training. For the last ten years or so the infantry has been divided among a number of administrative divisions—a compromise between the old pattern and the final solution of a Corps of Infantry, which remains a heretical concept.

But for all the modifications which have been introduced, the Army has by and large managed to preserve the regimental system; in the case of the Royal Artillery this has actually been strengthened as the years have gone by. Old regiments have gone, new conglomerates have swallowed them up—like giant industrial combines.

But even the large, amalgamated regiments have managed to preserve a sense of identity. And the Army, once the dust has settled, has gone on much as it did before.

An *avant-garde*, even within the Army, has argued that the regimental system has overstayed its welcome. Young officers have complained, in private if not in public, that it is wasteful in terms of training and administrative costs—although the divisional system has partly answered this—and that it is not flexible enough in wartime. It also encourages soldiers to be parochial in their outlook.

The system has certainly served Britain well in the past. It has given soldiers a sense of belonging, and has stiffened morale on and off the battlefield. It has also helped recruiting, though it may have complicated it at times. The regiment is like a family and the greatest honour that an officer can realistically covet is to be given command of it for two years of his life.

It is fiercely paternal, though less so than it used to be. Regular soldiers tend to be better educated, more sophisticated than they were, and less ready to be patronized. But an officer will still refer to 'my chaps' in the manner of a father reflecting upon his son and heir.

The system encourages a complex caste structure, not unlike that in Britain as a whole, but more entrenched and more explicit. All armies have some form of élitism, but in most cases this is based upon professional prowess—like that enjoyed by paratroopers, commandoes and special forces. In the British Army there is social élitism too. So there are "posh" regiments like the Cavalry and the Guards and the Royal Green Jackets—the so-called 'Black Mafia', who in terms of winning top jobs must be the most successful of all. These tend to look down upon the line regiments in the infantry, who look down upon the non-combative supporting corps, upon whom they all ultimately depend.

Officers never admit this—and certainly they do not seem to mind. They are after all accustomed to living in a disciplined society in which everyone knows his place. But wives sometimes feel uncomfortable when the caste system spills over into the married quarters of a garrison.

On the other hand, all sections of the Army are also very professional. Their political dedication to duty in Northern Ireland has been universally admired, and with justice. The regimental system has worked well in fortifying soldiers under constant strain, and there is no overwhelming argument for changing it again.

The Conscription Argument. Nor is there any imminent threat to the Army's professional status. But a threat could arise if recruiting began to fall seriously behind. So far the Army has managed to make both ends meet, even in hard times. But the falling birth-rate in the 1960s could make the mid-1980s a difficult period for recruiting officers. The American Army which went all-professional in 1972 is already starting to have post-natal nerves over the prospect ahead, and even the Soviet Army which relies upon conscripts for much of its strength could find itself with problems.

Some people argue that conscription should be brought back anyway. It would involve all young men in the defence of the country and would help to mature them. It would provide a flow of recruits who would need to be paid only minimal wages during their short service with the colours. Ex-soldiers particularly, regard National Service as a form of corrective training for modern youths who grow their hair too long, vandalize telephone boxes and have little respect for their betters. But it would cost a lot to run a large training establishment of the kind that would be needed for National Servicemen. Moreover this would be wasteful because by the time that a conscript could become useful to the Army, it would be time for him to leave, and the knowledge which he had been so expensively taught would quickly become outdated.

If general conscription was introduced the drain on the country's industrial manpower would be enormous. If only some youths were accepted and others rejected, it would be unfair, as was the unpopular American draft during the Vietnam War.

Many soldiers admit that they think a spell in the ranks would be therapeutic for recalcitrant young men. But they also agree that a reluctant conscript is not much good to anyone else. The Army would soon lose its professional efficiency if it came to be regarded as a punitive organization, specializing in the treatment of petty criminals.

This is particularly so at a time when military technology is becoming more complex. National Service would provide the Army with a number of highly intelligent boys to train. But it takes time to train a man to fire an anti-tank guided missile so well that he could hit a tank in battlefield conditions. It also demands a high level of motivation.

The introduction of National Service would probably be politically unacceptable, whichever party was in power. So it is unlikely to come about. But it is a possibility that has to be kept in focus.

The Size of the Army. The Army has been uncomfortably stretched by the need to send troops to Northern Ireland. On the other hand, but for the exigencies of the Ulster campaign, it would probably be smaller still.

Before the last war it was 220,000 strong. But 55,000 of these were in India (about the same number as in BAOR today), 19,000 in Egypt and Palestine, 8,000 in Gibraltar, 16,000 scattered elsewhere round the Pax Britannia, and 122,000 in Britain itself. Sir Basil Liddell-Hart writing in 1957 argued that as most of these commitments had gone, 140,000 would be enough in future. If one accepts that estimate, the Army is 30,000 to the good.

Even if the Army is considered large enough in peacetime, it could turn out to be far too small if war broke out. Some of its critics have concentrated on the need for more reserves. The Defence and External Affair sub-committee of the House of Commons Expenditure Committee complained in 1977 that there were no plans to bring in any more reserves for the Army in Germany after only a short period of fighting. The existing reserves would be needed to plump out the Army to its wartime size. All training establishments would be run down so that those stationed there could be drafted to the front—and that would be that. If the British Army is to make much of an impact upon any war in Europe the war had better be a short one.

Charles Douglas-Home in *Britain's Reserve Forces*, which was published by the Royal United Services Institute in 1969, argued that Britain's military training establishments should also be opened to civilian apprentices. They could then be taught a trade by the Army in return for undertaking a period of call-up liability in the reserves. This would not only help to strengthen the reserves, but would improve the contact between the Army and civilian society. Perhaps even its critics would acknowledge that the Army was doing a useful job.

But the Army has never been enthusiastic. For one thing, it looks on its technical training as a good way of attracting recruits. If boys were able to learn a trade there without actually having to join the Army it would lose some of its most valuable young men.

Moreover regular soldiers have had other things on their minds. They have been concerned about the supply of reinforcements reaching them quickly enough, and in sufficient numbers. But they have been still more worried by their own workload, the rising cost of their equipment and their own pay and conditions. Given that the Ministry of Defence cannot afford to do everything, then it should concentrate its resources upon building up the skills of its small but highly professional Army, and on ensuring that it is 'ready to give the Russians a bloody nose' should D-Day dawn. That is how many of them see it anyway.

Military Bureaucracy. A serving officer writing in *The Times* in March 1977, complained anonymously that the Staff College was turning out an Army of bureaucrats. They were trained for committee work and decision-making by concensus. There seemed to be no room any more for the man of initiative who could do great things on the battlefield. In the past there had always been time on the outbreak of war to change gear. The earnest young officers who were best at staff work and administration could be found jobs which suited them, leaving space at the front for the dashing, often maverick, leaders who by divine Providence usually seemed to emerge in the country's hour of need.

In the next war, however, there would be little time for the Army to get the right men into the right places. It would have to move into its battle positions with what it had, and hope for the best. General Redvers Buller who passed out top of his year at Staff College failed dismally as a commander during the Boer War and had to be replaced. Yet, according to the anxious officer in *The Times*, he was the sort of man one could well expect to be in charge, come Armageddon.

This is carrying the argument too far, and *The Times* article drew a sharp riposte from Major-General John Stanier who was Commandant of Staff College at the time. But it reflects the impatience that some young officers feel with the bureaucratic life that an Army has to lead in peacetime. Many a young officer who comes into the Army seeking something different, finds himself spending much of his time sitting behind a desk, shuffling paper in and out of his In-tray, while his secretary brews the coffee. It was partly a shortage of men to do all the hum-drum administrative jobs on camp, which led to complaints from BAOR in 1977–78 that some of its regiments were being overworked. In peacetime there are families to be looked after, mess accounts to be drawn up and soldiers' problems to be sorted out, as well as military training. It is a case of imitating the action of a tiger in war, but behaving like a paper tiger for the rest of the time.

In the past the Army always seemed to be involved in some colonial imbroglio which provided experience of action for its young men. Northern Ireland has to some extent done so too, although the political overtones have hardly allowed the fledgling fighter to throw his weight about.

Historically the British have been slow starters in wartime.

They have tended to lose a few battles before they started winning, mainly because they have never been ready in time. But it is a fault they must try to overcome, because the weight of firepower and the emphasis on mobility suggest that the next war could be short and sharp, and sudden.

The Soldiers. Cartoonists present a distorted view of soldiers as they do of anyone else. Privates are short and lumpy in uniforms that do not fit, Guards officers are all dandified fops, sergeant-majors have barrel chests and voices to match, while all generals are irascible old men with bristling moustaches. In fact most soldiers now tend to be ordinary people with mortgages and family cars and working wives.

Officers no longer have batmen as an automatic right. Commanders, usually generals, are allowed to have 'orderlies' or the odd civilian 'domestic assistant' if their job entails a lot of entertaining, but that is all. Few have staff cars exclusively reserved for them, although when in command there is usually one available—probably nowadays a 1·5 litre Ford Cortina for brigadiers and below, or a 2·3 litre Ford Granada for those above. Most officers now enjoy fewer perquisites than their equivalent ranks in civil industry.

For all the similarities between civilians and soldiers, and much of the work that they do, there are also differences—some of them indefinable.

For one thing soldiers are instinctively loyal to the Army, or to any organization which employs them. This was among the points noted by a major from the Parachute Regiment and an executive of Bulmer's Cider Company, who exchanged jobs for four months as an experiment in 1977–78. Businessmen are often cynical about their firms, and so are many professional men. But soldiers rarely are. Perhaps this is because loyalty is a quality which a recruit is taught to respect from the moment he swears allegiance to the Queen. But it probably has more to do with the sort of person who is attracted to a military career in the first place.

Few soldiers are iconoclastic by nature. They tend to be intelligent, rather than intellectual, and extroverted rather than introverted, with a taste for sport and the outdoor life. This is what one would expect. They wear their hair longer than they used to, but still more tidily groomed than has recently been the custom elsewhere. Officers tend to dress more smartly than their civilian counterparts, and with a greater care for what is appropriate for the occasion. All ranks pay more attention to manners than is usual in the last quarter of the twentieth century. They are gracious hosts, slightly old-fashioned in their observance of etiquette, and sometimes polite to the point of being patronizing.

These are sweeping generalizations. But one can perhaps generalize about the Army more than one can about most sections of society. Colonel Blimp may have retired and gone to live in Tunbridge Wells, but a military stereotype does live on, as the Army itself will acknowledge. The Army is an institution, like cricket and the Church of England, whose image is etched upon the country's subconscious. It has managed to blur the edges of that image, as it has become more technical, better educated and more professional. But the basic shape remains and there are no plans on the drawing board which will quickly change it.

Select Bibliography

Although most of this book was researched through personal interview, I have made use of facts and figures in the following:

All Bull: The National Servicemen, edited by B. S. Johnson (Quartet 1973)
All the Queen's Men, Russell Braddon (Hamish Hamilton 1977)
Arms and Strategy, Laurence Martin (Weidenfeld and Nicolson 1973)
'Artillery in the 1980s' *RUSI Journal*, Dec. 1974, Lt.-Col. Brian Blunt
Britain and Her Army, Corelli Barnett (Allen Lane 1970)
The British Army in Ulster, Vols. I and II, David Barzilay (Century Services Ltd. 1973 and 1975)
Discovering Military Traditions, Arthur Taylor (Shire Publications 1972)
A History of the Royal Army Dental Corps, Leslie J. Godden (RADO 1971)
History of the United Service Club, Major-General Sir Louis Jackson (United Service Club)
Nepal and the Gurkhas (HMSO 1965)
Queen Alexandra's Royal Army Nursing Corps, Juliet Piggott (Leo Cooper 1975)
The Red Devils, G. G. Norton (Leo Cooper 1971)
The Report of the Army Welfare Inquiry Committee (HMSO 1976)
The Regiments Depart, Gregory Blaxland (William Kimber 1971)
Sandhurst, Brigadier Sir John Smyth (Weidenfeld and Nicolson 1961)
Service to the Services: The Story of Naafi, Harry Miller (Newman Neame 1971)
Service with the Army, Dame Helen Gwynne-Vaughan (Hutchinson 1945)
A Short History of Queen Mary's Army Auxiliary Corps, Col. J. M. Cowper (pamphlet)
The Soldier in Modern Society, Lt.-Col. J. M. C. Baynes (Eyre Methuen 1972)
'A Soldier's Tank' *RUSI Journal*, Sept. 1975, Major Robin Rhoderick-Jones
The Special Air Service, Philip Warner (William Kimber 1971)
The Story of Sandhurst, Hugh Thomas (Hutchinson 1961)

APPENDICES

Deployment of the British Army in 1946 and 1979

1946 figures: 9,646
1979 figures: 9,646

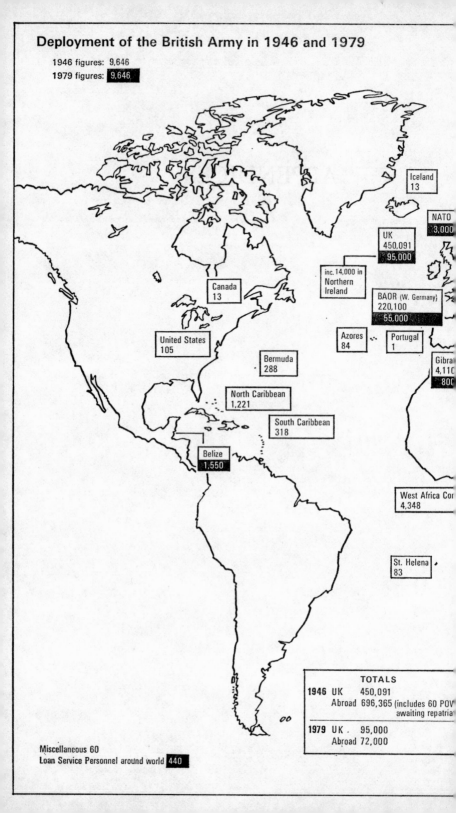

Iceland
13

NATO
3,000

UK
450,091
95,000

inc. 14,000 in
Northern
Ireland

BAOR (W. Germany)
220,100
55,000

Canada
13

Azores
84

Portugal
1

Gibra
4,110
800

United States
105

Bermuda
288

North Caribbean
1,221

South Caribbean
318

Belize
1,550

West Africa Con
4,348

St. Helena
83

	TOTALS	
1946	UK	450,091
	Abroad	696,365 (includes 60 POW awaiting repatria
1979	UK	95,000
	Abroad	72,000

Miscellaneous 60
Loan Service Personnel around world 440

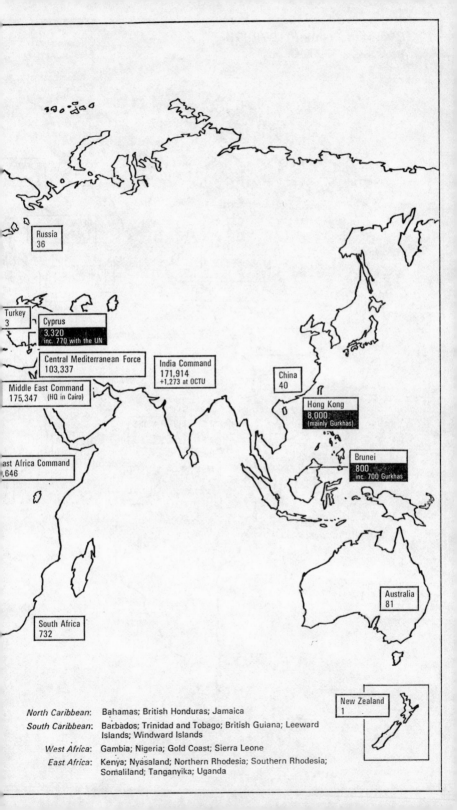

Russia
36

Turkey
3

Cyprus
3,320
inc. 770 with the UN

Central Mediterranean Force
103,337

India Command
171,914
+1,273 at OCTU

China
40

Middle East Command
175,347 (HQ in Cairo)

Hong Kong
8,000
(mainly Gurkhas)

Brunei
800
inc. 700 Gurkhas

East Africa Command
,646

Australia
81

South Africa
732

New Zealand
1

North Caribbean: Bahamas; British Honduras; Jamaica

South Caribbean: Barbados; Trinidad and Tobago; British Guiana; Leeward
    Islands; Windward Islands

West Africa: Gambia; Nigeria; Gold Coast; Sierra Leone

East Africa: Kenya; Nyasaland; Northern Rhodesia; Southern Rhodesia;
    Somaliland; Tanganyika; Uganda

Overseas Training 1978/79
Regular and Reserve Armies

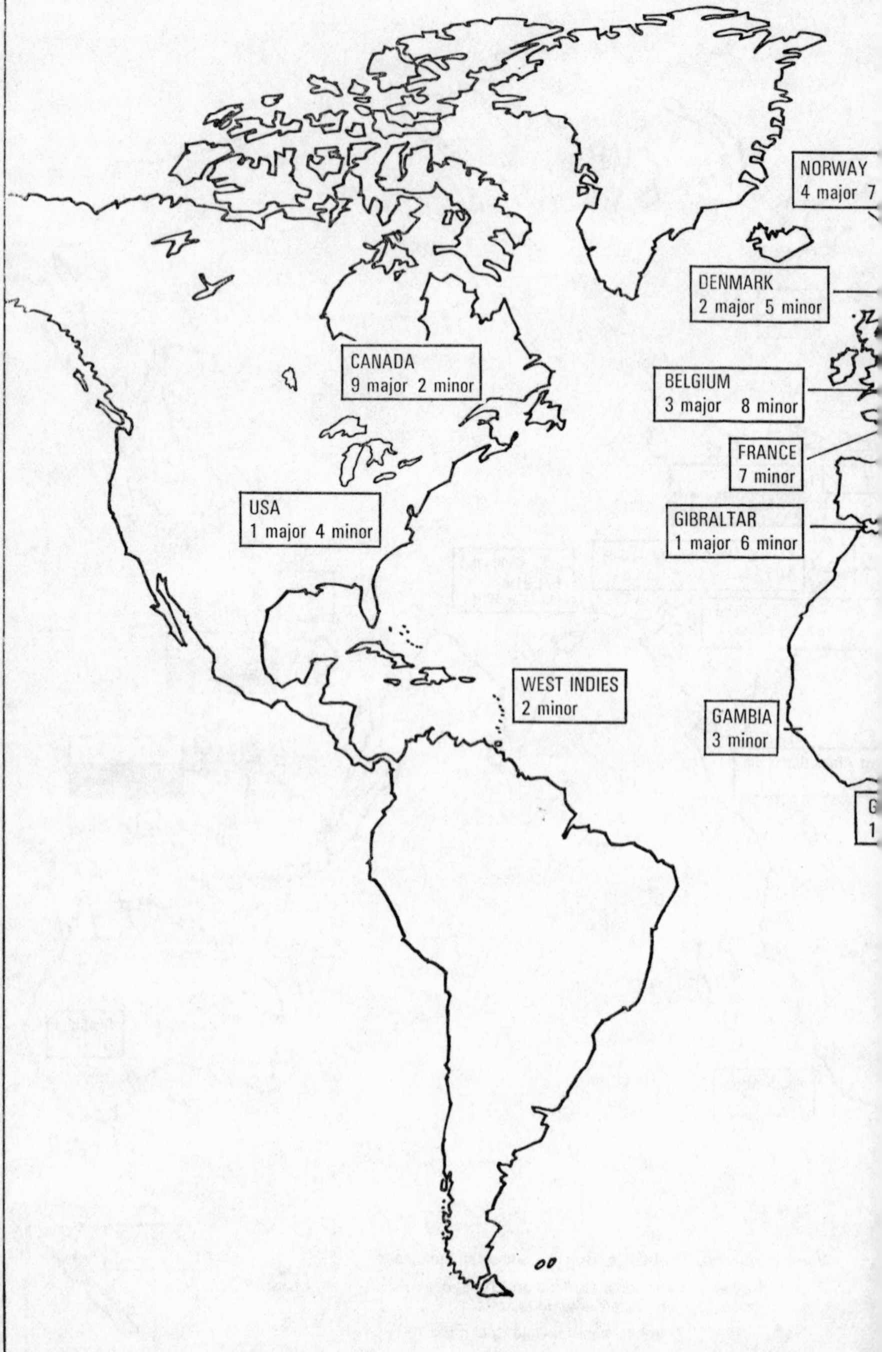

NORWAY
4 major 7

DENMARK
2 major 5 minor

CANADA
9 major 2 minor

BELGIUM
3 major 8 minor

FRANCE
7 minor

USA
1 major 4 minor

GIBRALTAR
1 major 6 minor

WEST INDIES
2 minor

GAMBIA
3 minor

G
1

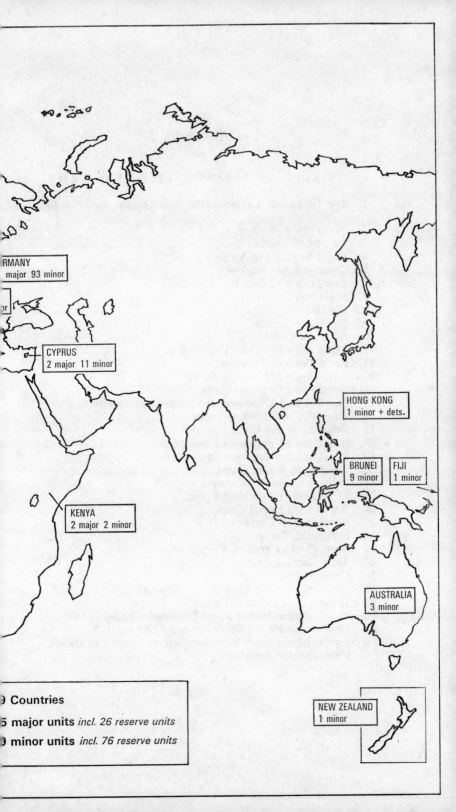

RMANY
major 93 minor

or

CYPRUS
2 major 11 minor

HONG KONG
1 minor + dets.

BRUNEI
9 minor

FIJI
1 minor

KENYA
2 major 2 minor

AUSTRALIA
3 minor

NEW ZEALAND
1 minor

9 Countries

5 major units incl. 26 reserve units

9 minor units incl. 76 reserve units

Appendix 3

ORDER OF PRECEDENCE IN THE ARMY

1. The Household Cavalry. (The Life Guards and The Blues and Royals.)
2. Royal Horse Artillery.
3. Royal Armoured Corps.
4. Royal Regiment of Artillery.
5. Corps of Royal Engineers.
6. Royal Corps of Signals.
7. Regiments of Foot Guards.
8. The Infantry.
9. Special Air Service.
10. Army Air Corps.
11. Royal Army Chaplains Department.
12. Royal Corps of Transport.
13. Royal Army Medical Corps.
14. Royal Army Ordnance Corps.
15. Corps of Royal Electrical and Mechanical Engineers.
16. Corps of Royal Military Police.
17. Royal Army Pay Corps.
18. Royal Army Veterinary Corps.
19. Royal Military Academy Band Corps.
20. Small Arms School Corps.
21. Military Provost Staff Corps.
22. Royal Army Educational Corps.
23. Royal Army Dental Corps.
24. Royal Pioneer Corps.
25. Intelligence Corps.
26. Army Physical Training Corps.
27. Army Catering Corps.
28. General Service Corps.
29. Queen Alexandra's Royal Army Nursing Corps.
30. Women's Royal Army Corps.
31. Royal Monmouthshire Royal Engineers (Militia) (TAVR).
32. The Honourable Artillery Company (TAVR).
33. Territorial and Army Volunteer Reserve (other than above).
34. Ulster Defence Regiment.

Appendix 4

THE REGIMENTS IN 1979
(including post-1945 amalgamations)

THE HOUSEHOLD CAVALRY

The Life Guards.
The Blues and Royals.
  (Formed in 1969 by an amalgamation of the Royal Horse Guards and
  the Royal Dragoons.)

THE ROYAL ARMOURED CORPS

1st The Queen's Dragoon Guards.
  (Formed in 1959 from the 1st King's Dragoon Guards and the Queen's
  Bays.)
The Royal Scots Dragoon Guards.
  (Formed in 1971 from the Royal Scots Greys and the 3rd Carabiniers.)
The 4th/7th Royal Dragoon Guards.
The 5th Royal Inniskilling Dragoon Guards.
The Queen's Own Hussars.
  (Formed in 1958 from the 3rd The King's Own Hussars and the 7th
  Queen's Own Hussars.)
The Queen's Royal Irish Hussars.
  (Formed in 1958 from the 4th Queen's Own Hussars and the 8th King's
  Royal Irish Hussars.)
The 9th/12th Royal Lancers (Prince of Wales's.)
  (Formed in 1960 from the 9th Queen's Royal Lancers and the 12th
  Royal Lancers (Prince of Wales's).)
The Royal Hussars (Prince of Wales's Own).
  (Formed in 1969 from the 10th Royal Hussars (Prince of Wales's Own)
  and the 11th Hussars (Prince Albert's Own).)
The 13th/18th Royal Hussars (Queen Mary's Own).
The 14th/20th King's Hussars.
15th/19th The King's Royal Hussars.
16th/5th The Queen's Royal Lancers.
The 17th/21st Lancers.
The Royal Tank Regiment (consists of four regiments, the 1st, 2nd, 3rd
  and 4th).

The INFANTRY (all regiments have one battalion unless stated)

The Guards Division:
  Grenadier Guards. Two battalions.
  Coldstream Guards. Two battalions.
  Scots Guards. Two battalions.
  Irish Guards.
  Welsh Guards.

The Scottish Division:

  The Royal Scots (The Royal Regiment).
  The Royal Highland Fusiliers (Princess Margaret's Own Glasgow and
    Ayrshire Regiment).
    (Formed in 1959 from an amalgamation of the Royal Scots Fusiliers
    and the Highland Light Infantry).
  The King's Own Scottish Borderers.
  The Black Watch (Royal Highland Regiment).
  The Queen's Own Highlanders (Seaforth and Camerons).
    (Formed in 1961 from the Seaforth Highlanders and the Queen's
    Own Cameron Highlanders).
  The Gordon Highlanders.
  The Argyll and Sutherland Highlanders (Princess Louise's).

The Queen's Division:

  The Queen's Regiment. Three battalions.
    (Formed in 1966 from an amalgamation of four Home Counties
    regiments, the Queen's Royal Surreys, the Queen's Own Buffs,
    The Royal Sussex and the Middlesex).
  The Royal Regiment of Fusiliers. Three battalions.
    (Formed in 1968 from four Fusilier regiments, The Royal North-
    umberland Fusiliers, the Royal Warwickshire Fusiliers, The
    Royal Fusiliers and The Lancashire Fusiliers).
  The Royal Anglian Regiment. Three battalions.
    (Formed in 1964 from The Royal Leicestershires and three East
    Anglian Regiments, the 1st East Anglians (Royal Norfolk and
    Suffolk), the 2nd East Anglians (Duchess of Gloucester's Own
    Royal Lincolnshire and Northamptonshire) and the 3rd East
    Anglians (16th/44th Foot)).

The King's Division:

  The King's Own Royal Border Regiment.
    (Formed in 1959 from The King's Own Royal Regiment and The
    Border Regiment).
  The King's Regiment.
    (Formed in 1958 from The King's Regiment (Liverpool) and The
    Manchester Regiment).

The Prince of Wales's Own Regiment of Yorkshire.
  (Formed in 1958 from the West Yorkshire Regiment (Prince of
    Wales's Own) and the East Yorkshire Regiment (Duke of York's
    Own)).
The Green Howards (Alexandra Princess of Wales's Own Yorkshire
  Regiment).
The Royal Irish Rangers (27th (Inniskilling) 83rd and 87th). Two
  battalions.
  (Formed in 1968 from three regiments, the Royal Inniskilling
    Fusiliers, the Royal Ulster Rifles and the Royal Irish Fusiliers).
The Queen's Lancashire Regiment.
  (Formed in 1970 from the Lancashire Regiment (Prince of Wales's
    Volunteers) and the Loyal Regiment (North Lancashire)).
The Duke of Wellington's Regiment.

The Prince of Wales's Division:

The Devonshire and Dorset Regiment.
  (Formed in 1958 from the Devonshire and Dorset Regiments).
The Cheshire Regiment.
The Royal Welch Fusiliers.
The Royal Regiment of Wales.
  (Formed in 1959 from the South Wales Borderers and the Welch
    Regiment).
The Gloucestershire Regiment.
The Worcestershire and Sherwood Foresters Regiment.
  (Formed in 1970 from the Worcestershires and the Sherwood
    Foresters (Nottinghamshire and Derbyshire) Regiments).
The Royal Hampshire Regiment.
The Staffordshire Regiment.
  (Formed in 1959 from the North Staffordshire and South Stafford-
    shire Regiments).
The Duke of Edinburgh's Royal Regiment (Berkshire and Wiltshire).
  (Formed in 1959 from the Royal Berkshire Regiment (Princess
    Charlotte of Wales's) and the Wiltshire Regiment (Duke of
    Edinburgh's)).

The Light Division:

The Light Infantry. Three battalions.
  (Formed in 1968 from four regiments, the Somerset and Cornwall
    Light Infantry, the King's Shropshire Light Infantry, the King's
    Own Yorkshire Light Infantry and the Durham Light Infantry).
The Royal Green Jackets. Three battalions.
  (Formed in 1966 from three separate Green Jacket Regiments
    originally known as the King's Royal Rifle Corps, the Rifle
    Brigade and the Oxfordshire and Buckinghamshire Light Infantry).

Others:

> The Parachute Regiment. Three battalions.
> The 22nd Regiment Special Air Service.

The Gurkha Brigade:

> The 2nd King Edward VII's Own Gurkha Rifles (The Sirmoor Rifles).
>   Two battalions.
> The 6th Queen Elizabeth's Own Gurkha Rifles.
> The 7th Duke of Edinburgh's Own Gurkha Rifles.
> The 10th Princess Mary's Own Gurkha Rifles.

ROYAL ARTILLERY

King's Troop Royal Horse Artillery.
1st Royal Horse Artillery.
7th Royal Horse Artillery.
5th Heavy Regiment RA.
12th Air Defence Regiment RA.
16th Air Defence Regiment RA.
22nd Air Defence Regiment RA.
29th Commando Light Regiment RA.
32nd Guided Weapons Regiment RA.
50th Missile Regiment RA.
94th Locating Regiment RA.
2nd Field Regiment RA.
4th Field Regiment RA.
19th Field Regiment RA.
25th Field Regiment RA.
26th Field Regiment RA.
27th Field Regiment RA.
39th Field Regiment RA.
40th Field Regiment RA.
45th Field Regiment RA.
47th Field Regiment RA.
49th Field Regiment RA.
Depot Regiment RA Woolwich.

Appendix 5

OFFICERS:

Rank		Annual Salary in £s
Field-Marshal		27,936
General		25,474
Lieutenant-General		20,314
Major-General		16,714
Brigadier		15,251
Colonel	after 8 years	14,175
	6	13,838
	4	13,502
	2	13,165
	on appointment	12,828
Lieutenant-Colonel	after 8 years	12,078
	6	11,789
	4	11,500
	2	11,211
	on appointment	10,921
Major	after 8 years	10,054
	7	9,853
	6	9,651
	5	9,450
	4	9,249
	3	9,048
	2	8,846
	1	8,645
	on appointment	8,444
Captain	after 6 years	7,799
	5	7,616
	4	7,433
	3	7,250
	2	7,067
	1	6,884
	on appointment	6,701

Rank		Annual Salary in £s
Lieutenant	after 4 years	5,962
	3	5,819
	2	5,677
	1	5,534
	on appointment	5,391
Second-Lieutenant		4,352

WARRANT OFFICERS AND SENIOR NCOS:

	Annual Salary in £s			
Rank	Band 4	Band 5	Band 6	Band 7
Warrant Officer 1	6,357	6,771	7,247	7,788
Warrant Officer 2	6,050	6,464	6,939	7,481
Staff Sergeant	5,757	6,171	6,647	7,188
Sergeant	5,475	5,889	6,365	—

CORPORALS AND BELOW:

	Annual Salary in £s		
Rank	Band 1	Band 2	Band 3
Corporal I	5,109	5,497	5,937
Corporal II	4,798	5,186	—
Lance-Corporal I	4,505	4,893	5,333
Lance-Corporal II	4,231	4,619	—
Lance-Corporal III	3,971	4,359	—
Private I	3,971	4,359	4,798
Private II	3,730	4,118	—
Private III	3,503	3,891	—
Private IV	3,287	—	—

Notes:

1. A number of specialist corps, notably doctors and dentists, are paid at higher rates than these. Servicewomen receive slightly less.

2. The rates quoted here for all NCOs and privates are Scale B rates paid to men who are committed to between 6 and 9 years' service. Scale A men committed to less than 6 years receive about £109 a year less. Scale C men, committed to more than 9 years, earn about £163 a year more.

3. Service pay was raised twice during 1979, first by the Labour Government following the usual review in April, then again by the new Conservative Government in May. This was in accordance with the Conservatives' promise to restore full comparability with civilian pay as soon as possible after coming into office, instead of making the Services wait for this until April 1980.

The Northern Ireland bonus was also raised from £1 a day to £1·10 a day in April 1979. Accommodation charges remained the same, but food charges were raised to £1·20 a day or £8·40 a week.

Appendix 6

OVERSEAS EMPLOYMENT OF THE BRITISH ARMY SINCE 1945

Serial	Date	Location	Event	Casualties
1	1945*	JAVA and SUMATRA	Post-war operations	50 killed
2	1945–1948	INDIA and PAKISTAN	Independence operations	
3	1945–1947	GREECE	Post-war operations	
4	1945–1954	TRIESTE	Post-war operations	
5	1945–1948*	PALESTINE	Independence operations	223 killed
6	1946–1954	EGYPT	Canal security operations	54 killed
7	1947	ADEN	Disturbances	
8	1947–1948	NORTHERN IRELAND	Disturbances—Belfast and Londonderry	
9	1948	GOLD COAST	Riots	
10	1948	BRITISH HONDURAS	Threat of invasion by GUATEMALA	
11	1948–1960*	MALAYA	Operations against communist/ insurgents/terrorists	509 killed; 2,560 wounded
12	1948–1951	ERITREA	Shifta terrorists	
13	1949–1952	ERITREA	UN Plebiscite	
14	1949–1951	SOMALILAND	Aid to civil power	
15	1949	AQABA	Garrison to secure harbour	
16	1950–1953*	KOREA	War	1,263 killed; 6,005 wounded
17	1950	SINGAPORE	Hartog riots	
18	1951	JAMAICA	Hurricane	

Serial	Date	Location	Event	Casualties
19	1951	AQABA	Moussadeq Oil Nationalization	
20	1952–1956	NORTHERN IRELAND	IRA Campaign	
21	1952–1956*	KENYA	Operations against Mau Mau	537 killed; 498 wounded
22	1953	IONIAN ISLANDS	Earthquake, aid to civil power	
23	1953	CYPRUS	Earthquake, aid to civil power	
24	1953	BRITISH GUIANA	Constitutional Crisis	
25	1953–1955	PERSIAN GULF	Buraimi Dispute	
26	1954–1959*	CYPRUS	Eoka terrorists	105 killed; 603 wounded
27	1955–1958*	ADEN	Internal security operations	1 killed
28	1955–1956	SINGAPORE	Riots (two periods)	
29	1956	HONG KONG	Double 10th Disturbances	
30	1956–1957	BAHREIN	Assistance to Government	
31	1956*	SUEZ	Operations	16 killed; 99 wounded
32	1957–1959*	MUSCAT and OMAN	Operations	7 killed; 6 wounded
33	1957	BELIZE	Threat of civil unrest	
34	1957	TOGOLAND	Aid to civil power	
35	1958	NASSAU	Strike. Aid to civil power	
36	1958	ADEN	Assistance in arrest of Jifri brothers gang	
37	1958	JORDAN and LEBANON	Assistance to Governments	
38	1958	BAHAMAS	Aid to civil power	
39	1959	GAN	Riots	
40	1960	CAMEROONS	Aid to civil power	1 killed
41	1960	HONG KONG	Typhoon Mary aid to civil power	
42	1960	JAMAICA	Rastafarian uprising	2 killed
43	1961	KENYA	Floods	

Serial	Date	Location	Event	Casualties
44	1961	KUWAIT	Support to Amir against threatened Iraqi invasion	
45	1961	BAHAMAS	Threat of Invasion	
46	1961	ZANZIBAR	Elections aid to civil power	
47	1961	BELIZE	Hurricane HATTIE aid to civil power	
48	1962	BELIZE	Belize Freedom Fighters—Guatemalan incursions	
49	1962	BRITISH GUIANA	Riots in Georgetown	
50	1962	HONG KONG	Refugees from China	
51	1962–1966*	BORNEO	INDONESIAN Confrontation	114 killed; 182 wounded
52	1963–1966*	MALAYSIA	Brunei disturbances	
53	1963	SKOPJE	Earthquake—Yugoslavia civil assistance	
54	1963–1966	SWAZILAND	Reinforcement—strikes	
55	1963	ZANZIBAR	Elections. Aid to civil power	
56	1963–to date*	CYPRUS	Greek–Turkish Communal Strife and UN operations	
57	1963	BRITISH GUIANA	Communal riots and State of Emergency (can count as two ops)	
58	1964	ZANZIBAR	Revolution	
59	1964	TANGANYIKA		
60	1964	UGANDA	Army Mutinies (can count as one op)	
61	1964	KENYA		
62	1964–1967*	ADEN	Radfan ops and Aden Terrorists	181 killed; 1,321 wounded
63	1965	MAURITIUS	Riots	
64	1965	EL SALVADOR	Earthquake aid to civil power	

Serial	Date	Location	Event	Casualties
65	1965	BECHUANALAND	BBC Radio transmitter guard—Rhodesia crisis	
67	1965	MALAYA	Flood relief	
68	1965–1977	OMAN	Assistance to Sultan in suppressing externally supported rebellion	
69	1966	HONG KONG	Disturbances	
70	1966	SEYCHELLES	Unrest. Aid to civil power	
71	1966	BRITISH HONDURAS	Border operations	
72	1966	HONG KONG	Floods	
73	1966	VIENTIANE	Floods—Laos	
74	1966	BASUTOLAND	Famine Relief	
75	1966–1967	LIBYA	Evacuation of British Nationals and rundown of bases in Benghazi, El Adem and Tobruk	
76	1967	HONG KONG	'Red Guard' Riots	
77	1968	SICILY	Earthquake. Aid to civil power	
78	1968	BERMUDA	State of Emergency	
79	1968	MAURITIUS	State of Emergency	
80	1969–to date*	NORTHERN IRELAND	IRA campaign	271 killed; 3,025 wounded (to date)
81	1969–1971	ANGUILLA	Political unrest	
82	1969	BERMUDA	Black Power Conference	
83	1969–1976*	DHOFAR/OMAN	Assistance to Sultan in suppressing externally supported rebellion	
84	1970	TUNISIA	Floods. Aid to civil power	
85	1970	JORDAN	Medical relief	

Serial	Date	Location	Event	Casualties
86	1970	PAKISTAN	East Bengal Floods. Aid to civil power	
87	1971–1972	MALTA	Withdrawal and return	
88	1972	*QE2*	Bombscare—Para drop	
89	1972	BRITISH HONDURAS	Reinforcement	
90	1973	*QE2*	Guard against Arab threat	
91	1974*	CYPRUS	Evacuation British etc. nationals, Turkish invasion	
92	1976–1977	BRITISH HONDURAS (BELIZE)		

* Award of campaign and/or UN medals.

Appendix 7

PRINCIPAL WEAPON SYSTEMS AND APPROXIMATE NUMBERS IN SERVICE IN 1979

Main Battle Tanks:
Chieftain	900

Tracked Reconnaissance Vehicles:
Scorpion light tanks (with 76mm gun)	250
Scimitar (with 30mm cannon)	250
Striker (with Swingfire anti-tank missiles)	50 plus

Armoured Fighting Vehicles:
FV432 (armoured personnel carrier)	2,000 plus
FV438 (with Swingfire anti-tank missiles)	100 plus

Armoured Scout Car:
Fox (with 30mm cannon)	250 plus

Infantry Weapons:
Milan anti-tank missiles	One platoon per battalion
General Purpose Machine Gun	Section weapon
Sterling Sub-Machine Gun	Individual weapon
Self-Loading Rifle (SLR)	Individual weapon
(Light Anti-tank Weapon (LAW) on order)	

Helicopters:
Scout (to be phased out)	100
Lynx (replacing Scout)	100
Gazelle	125
(TOW anti-tank missiles on order for Lynx)	

Artillery:
Lance nuclear missiles	12 (one regiment)
175mm Self-Propelled Gun M107	30 (one regiment)
155mm Self-Propelled Gun M109	36
8-inch Howitzer	24
Abbot 105mm Self-Propelled Gun	150
105mm Light Gun	75

Rapier Anti-Aircraft Missiles	100 plus
Blowpipe Anti-Aircraft Missiles	125
Cymbeline Radar Sets	25

Engineering Equipment:

Armoured Vehicle Launched Bridge	30
Medium Girder Bridge	50
Airportable Bridge	5
Bar Minelayer	75

Key to Abbreviations

AG	Adjutant General
ABF	Army Benevolent Fund
ACC	Army Catering Corps
ACF	Army Cadet Force
ACGS(OR)	Assistant to the Chief of General Staff (Operational Requirements)
ACIO	Army Careers and Information Office
AFCENT	Armed Forces Central Europe
AFPRB	Armed Forces Pay Review Body
AKC	Army Kinema Corporation
AKS	Army Kinema Services
ALC	Army Legal Corps
ALS	Army Legal Services
AMETS	Artillery Meteorological System
AMF	Allied Command Europe Mobile Force
APC	Armoured Personnel Carrier
ASL	Army School of Languages
ASM	Academy Sergeant-Major
AT	Adventurous Training
AT	Ammunition Technician
ATGW	Anti-tank Guided Weapons
ATO	Ammunition Technical Officer
ATS	Auxiliary Territorial Service
AWADS	Adverse Weather Air Delivery Systems
AWOL	Absent Without Leave
BAOR	British Army of the Rhine
BATES	Battlefield Artillery Target Engagement System
BFBS	British Forces Broadcasting Service
BFN	British Forces Network
CAROT	Committee on Army Regular Officer Training
CBF	Commander British Forces (Hong Kong)
CCF	Combined Cadet Force
CDS	Chief of Defence Staff
CGS	Chief of General Staff
C-in-C UKLF	Commander-in-Chief United Kingdom Land Forces

CIDA	Canadian International Development Agency
CM	Court Martial
CMS	Common Military Syllabus
CVR(T)	Combat Vehicles Reconnaissance (Tracked)
CVWW	Council of Voluntary War Work
DASD	Director of Army Staff Duties
DCD	Director of Combat Development
DCM	District Court Martial
DCT	Directorate of Clothing and Textiles
DPR	Director of Public Relations
DHSS	Department of Health and Social Security
DM(A)	Director of Manning (Army)
DMO	Director of Military Operations
DPR(A)	Director of Public Relations (Army)
EOD	Explosives Ordnance Disposal
EPC	Education Promotion Certificate
FACE	Field Artillery Computer Equipment
FCZ	Forward Combat Zone
FMBT	Future Main Battle Tank
FRIS	Families Ration Issue Scheme
GCM	General Court Martial
GNP	Gross National Product
GOC	General Officer Commanding
GSR	General Staff Requirement
GST	General Staff Target
HAC	Honourable Artillery Company
IFF	Identification Friend or Foe
IRA	Irish Republican Army
JATFOR	Joint Airborne Task Force
JSSC	Joint Services Staff College
LAD	Light Aid Detachment
LAWC	Land Air Warfare Committee
LMD	Light Mobile Digger
LOAs	Local Overseas Allowances
LSL	Long Service List
LSP	Loan Service Personnel
MACA	Military Aid to the Civil Authorities
MACC	Military Aid to the Civil Community
MACM	Military Aid to the Civil Ministry
MACP	Military Aid to the Civil Power
MBT	Main Battle Tank
MBT-80	Main Battle Tank-80
MCTC	Military Corrective Training Centre
MGO	Master-General of the Ordnance

MICV	Mechanized Infantry Combat Vehicle
MMBF	Mean Miles Between Failure
MVEE	Military Vehicles and Engineering Establishment
NASP	Nuclear Ammunition Supply Point
NCO	Non-commissioned Officer
NDC	National Defence College
OIR	Officer's Intelligence Rating
ORC	Operational Requirements Committee
OTC	Officers' Training Corps
PADS	Position and Azimuth Determining System
PGN	Precision—Guided Munitions
PIRA	Provisional Irish Republican Army
PQS	Progressive Qualification Scheme
PUS	Pre-University Studies
PUSA	Permanent Under-Secretary for Administration
PVR	Premature Voluntary Release
PWO	Prince of Wales Own Regiment
QGO	Queen's Gurkha Officer
QMAAC	Queen Mary's Army Auxiliary Corps
QMG	Quartermaster-General
RA	Royal Artillery
RAC	Royal Armoured Corps
RAChD	Royal Army Chaplains' Department
RAF	Royal Air Force
RAOC	Royal Army Ordnance Corps
RAMC	Royal Army Medical Corps
RAPC	Royal Army Pay Corps
RARDE	Royal Armaments Research and Development Establishment
RAVC	Royal Army Veterinary Corps
RCB	Regular Commission Board
RCC	Regular Commission Course
RCDS	Royal College of Defence Studies
RCT	Royal Corps of Transport
RCZ	Rear Combat Zone
RE	Royal Engineers
REME	Royal Electrical and Mechanical Engineers
RFEA	Regular Forces Employment Association
RHA	Royal Horse Artillery
RMAS	Royal Military Academy Sandhurst
RMP	Royal Military Police
ROFs	Royal Ordnance Factories
RSC	Recruit Selection Centre
RSRE	Royal Signals and Radar Establishment

RUC	Royal Ulster Constabulary
RUSI	Royal United Services Institute
SACEUR	Supreme Allied Commander in Europe
SAM	Surface to Air Missile
SAS	Special Air Service
SBA	Sovereign Base Area
SCAMF	Standing Committee on Army Manpower Forecasts
SG	Selection Grade
SIB	Special Investigation Branch
SKC	Services Kinema Corporation
SLOs	Schools Liaison Officers
SLR	Self-loading Rifle
SMC	Standard Military Course
SSAFA	Soldiers', Sailors' and Airmen's Families Association
SSC	Short Service Commission
SSG	Sum Selection Grading
SSLC	Short Service Limited Commission
TA	Territorial Army
TAVR	Territorial and Army Volunteer Reserve
TSG	Total Selection Grading
UDR	Ulster Defence Regiment
UKLF	United Kingdom Land Forces
UNFICYP	United Nations Force in Cyprus
VCGS	Vice-Chief of the General Staff
WEPC	Weapons and Equipment Policy Committee
WAAC	Women's Army Auxiliary Corps
WOSB	War Office Selection Board
WRAC	Women's Royal Army Corps

Index

Committee on the Structure of the Army (1964), 76

Common Military Syllabus, 76

Commonwealth Division, 14

Communist: coup in Czechoslovakia (1948), 15; rebels in Dhofar, 163, 188; uprising in Greece (1946), 14

Companies, 119; cadet at Sandhurst, 66

Companies of Invalids, 292

Company of Pikemen and Musketeers, 260

Compensation, 147–50

Computers, use in Artillery regiments, 3, 89, 259

Connaught Club, 317

Conscription, 3, 11, 15–17, 322–3; end of, 17–20, 36

Contractions, 5, 20–2, 44

Cooks, 53, 223–6

Cormorant Club, 75

Corps of Army Schoolmasters, 219

Corps of Army Schoolmistresses, 219

Council of Voluntary Welfare Work, 273–4; organizations forming, 273

Council of War Work, 273

Court martials, 125, 222, 233

Craftsmen, 29; see also Trades

Crime in the Army, 125, 233–5; types of, 233

Crime and Intelligence Office, 233

CS gas, 137, 299

Cymbeline, mortar locating radar, 89

Cyprus, 4, 14, 16, 17, 31, 32, 48, 49, 141, 160–2, 167, 198, 222, 275; evacuation 1974, 160; Sovereign Base Areas, 160–2; troops in, 161; welfare organizations in, 268

Dalyell, Tam, MP, 146

Day's Pay Scheme, 286

D-Day, 197

Defence budget, 23, 81, 83, 250, 291, 303

Defence Costs Agreement (1975), 151, 152

Defence Equipment Policy Committee, 83

Defence and External Affairs Subcommittee of the House of Commons Expenditure Committee, 251, 324

Defence Ministers, 19–22

Defence Operations Analysis Establishment, 82

Defence and Overseas Committee of the Cabinet, 25

Defence and Overseas Policy Committee, 26

Defence Review, 22, 27, 81, 101, 108, 114, 117, 122, 154, 198, 199, 205, 214, 251, 252, 303

Defence Secretary, 21, 26, 27, 28

Defence spending, 20, 22, 25, 47; savings in, 81

Defence staff, 19

Defence White Paper (1967), 21; (1975), 22

Dempsey Committee, 234

Dentists, army, 228–30

Department of the Environment, 104, 106, 219

Department of Health and Social Security, 148

Deployment, 99–163, 332–3

Deputy Chief of Defence Staff (OR), 82

Deputy Chief of the General Staff, 250

Deputy Chief Scientist (Army), 27

Deputy Under-Secretary (Army), 27

Desert Rats, 114, 319

Detention Barracks, 234

Detmold, 121, 124, 170, 272

Devon Regiment, 19

Director of Army Recruiting, 44, 46, 47, 50, 52, 57

Director of Army Staff Duties, 23, 31, 33, 46, 73, 82, 250

Director of Combat Development, 82, 83